ENGAGING THE EVIL EMPIRE

ENGAGING THE EVIL EMPIRE

WASHINGTON, MOSCOW, AND THE BEGINNING OF THE END OF THE COLD WAR

SIMON MILES

CORNELL UNIVERSITY PRESS
Ithaca and London

Copyright © 2020 by Cornell University

All rights reserved. Except for brief quotations in a review, this book, or parts thereof, must not be reproduced in any form without permission in writing from the publisher. For information, address Cornell University Press, Sage House, 512 East State Street, Ithaca, New York 14850. Visit our website at cornellpress.cornell.edu.

First published 2020 by Cornell University Press

Library of Congress Cataloging-in-Publication Data

Names: Miles, Simon, 1988– author.
Title: Engaging the evil empire : Washington, Moscow, and the beginning of the end of the Cold War / Simon Miles.
Description: Ithaca, New York : Cornell University Press, 2020. | Includes bibliographical references and index.
Identifiers: LCCN 2020016628 (print) | LCCN 2020016629 (ebook) | ISBN 9781501751691 (cloth) | ISBN 9781501751707 (pdf) | ISBN 9781501751714 (epub)
Subjects: LCSH: Cold War. | World politics—1975–1985. | United States—Foreign relations—Soviet Union. | Soviet Union—Foreign relations—United States.
Classification: LCC D849 .M5412 2020 (print) | LCC D849 (ebook) | DDC 909.82/5—dc23
LC record available at https://lccn.loc.gov/2020016628
LC ebook record available at https://lccn.loc.gov/2020016629

For my parents

I'm a believer in quiet diplomacy and so far we've had several quite triumphant experiences by using that method. The problem is, you can't talk about it afterward or then you can't do it again.

—Ronald Reagan to John Koehler, July 9, 1981

We have more contact with the Soviets than anyone is aware of and whether to have a meeting or not is on the agenda at both ends of the line.

—Ronald Reagan to Paul Trousdale, May 23, 1983

Contents

Acknowledgments   ix

Abbreviations   xiii

Note on Transliteration and Translation   xv

Introduction: Grand Strategy and the
End of the Cold War   1

1. Red Star Rising: The World
   according to Washington and Moscow   11

2. Arm to Parley: Reagan Rebuilds and
   Reaches Out   33

3. Talking about Talking: Continuities
   and Crises   57

4. Trial Balloons: Reaching Out and
   Laying Groundwork   84

5. New Departures: The Beginning
   of the End of the Cold War   106

   Conclusion: Winners and Losers   130

Notes   141

Bibliography   201

Index   223

ACKNOWLEDGMENTS

In completing this project, I have accumulated a host of debts. Any attempt to acknowledge them must begin, as it did, in the archives: the archivists and declassification specialists in the Australian, British, Canadian, Czech, French, German, Russian, Ukrainian, and US archives facilitated my research there and made it extremely fruitful. Without their professionalism—and patience—this book would not have been possible.

Several institutions supported my research. A three-year fellowship from the Social Sciences and Humanities Research Council of Canada gave me the freedom to conduct much of the international archival research on which this book is based. Without this support from the government of Canada, the end product would undoubtedly have suffered. Two successive World Politics and Statecraft Fellowships from the Smith Richardson Foundation also gave me the freedom to make the story I tell as international as possible. I also received valuable financial support from the American Grand Strategy Program and the Josiah Charles Trent Memorial Foundation Endowment Fund at Duke University; the Eisenhower Institute at Gettysburg College; the Gerald R. Ford and George H. W. Bush presidential libraries; and the Center for Russian, East European and Eurasian Studies, the Robert Strauss Center for International Security and Law, the William P. Clements Jr. Center for National Security, and the Department of History at the University of Texas at Austin.

The research for this book began at the University of Texas at Austin. While there, I benefited from the guidance and insights of a group of outstanding historians in the History Department and the Lyndon B. Johnson School of Public Affairs: Frank Gavin, Will Inboden, Mark Lawrence, Charters Wynn, and Jeremi Suri, my adviser, who each made this a better work of history and me a better historian. For that, I am in their debt. I had the good fortune to spend three years as a visiting fellow at the Bill Graham Centre for Contemporary International History at the University of Toronto's Munk School of Global Affairs. I am very grateful to John English and Jack Cunningham for giving me an intellectual home there. Toronto is where my journey as x **ACKNOWLEDGMENTS**

a historian began as an undergraduate thanks above all to Bob Bothwell and Lynne Viola, scholars who remain role models and whose influence shaped this project throughout. And I still draw on what I learned during my year at the London School of Economics and Political Science, especially working with Arne Hofmann.

I had the great personal and professional good fortune to finish this project at the Sanford School of Public Policy at Duke University. An interdisciplinary community of colleagues and students, especially those in my grand strategy and Cold War seminars, made me reexamine important issues. I am particularly grateful to Roman Glitminov, Max Labaton, Masha Stoertz, and Elise van den Hoek for their research assistance, Linda Simpson for her kindness and patience, and to Jack Matlock for his generosity and insight. Peter Feaver and Bruce Jentleson have been wonderful mentors and friends; a new faculty member could not ask for better, and I am indebted to them both. I am also grateful to the school's leadership, Kelly Brownell, Judith Kelly, and Billy Pizer, for their support throughout my time in Durham, and especially for making it possible to host an invaluable workshop on the book manuscript.

I presented portions of this research at meetings of the American Historical Association, the Canadian Historical Association, the International Studies Association, the Society for Historians of American Foreign Relations, and the Society for Military History, as well as at conferences and workshops at the Center for Strategic and International Studies, Columbia University, George Washington University, the Institut de Hautes Études Internationales et du Développement, the Institut d'Études Politiques de Paris, the London School of Economics and Political Science, the Massachusetts Institute of Technology, Stanford University, the Triangle Institute for Security Studies, the University of Texas at Austin, the University of Toronto, and Yale University. The feedback I received at these presentations improved the work and encouraged me to pursue new avenues of research; I am grateful to all the organizers and participants. Elizabeth Charles, Jeff Engel, Kristin Goss, Jim Hershberg, David Holloway, Mark Kramer, Jon Lindsay, Chester Pach, Gunther Peck, Mike Poznansky, Don Raleigh, Tim Sayle, Doug Selvage, Josh Shifrinson, Mary Sarotte, Bill Taubman, Joseph Torigian, Jane Vaynman, James Wilson, and Gail Yoshitani all generously read portions of the manuscript in various forms and gave valuable feedback. Jim Goldgeier, Mel Leffler, Nancy Mitchell, Mike Morgan, and Arne Westad were all generous enough to make the trip to Durham to participate in a workshop on the book, hosted by Peter Feaver and Bruce Jentleson. Having these seven distinguished scholars take the time to read my entire manuscript was an honor, and their suggestions have improved the final product immeasurably. I am grateful to the Massachusetts Institute of

ACKNOWLEDGMENTS   xi

Technology Press for permission to reproduce portions of my article "The War Scare That Wasn't: Able Archer 83 and the Myths of the Second Cold War," published in the *Journal of Cold War Studies*. At Cornell University Press, I am grateful to the two anonymous reviewers for their helpful suggestions, to Mary Gendron for shepherding the book through the production process, and especially to Michael McGandy, whose editorial guidance and friendly support made completing this project such a pleasure. Any remaining shortcomings are mine alone.

Friends and family like Violet Syrotiuk and Charlie Colbourn, Karen Colbourn, Sarah Colbourn, Elaine and Marvin Givertz, Katie and Derek Joslin, Maralyn and Michael Novack, Charles Pierson, and Catherine White made writing this book a pleasure. I owe an enormous debt of gratitude to Caryl and Dennis McManus for their support and generosity. And I could not imagine having completed this project without my wife, Susie Colbourn, who has shaped it from beginning to end. As a partner, her love and encouragement helped me see it through to completion. As a scholar, her expertise and input throughout made it immeasurably better.

I lack the words to adequately thank my parents, Murray and Silvia Miles, for everything they have done for me. They have always supported me and, equally important, have always pushed me to better myself and held me to the highest standards. I hope this book is a fitting testament to that; I dedicate it to them with my profound gratitude.

Abbreviations

AA	Auswärtiges Amt
BKA	Bundeskanzleramt
CIA	Central Intelligence Agency
DEA	Department of External Affairs
DFA	Department of Foreign Affairs
DOS	Department of State
G7	Group of Seven
GDP	gross domestic product
ICAO	International Civil Aviation Organization
ICBM	intercontinental ballistic missile
IFPAB	Interim Foreign Policy Advisory Board
INF	Intermediate-range nuclear forces
ISKRAN	Institut SShA i Kanady Rossiĭskoĭ Akademii Nauk
KGB	Komitet Gosudarstvennoĭ Bezopasnosti
KPSS	Kommunisticheskaia Partiia Sovetskogo Soiuza
KPU	Kommunisticheskaia Partiia Ukrainy
MAÉ	Ministère des Affaires Étrangères
MfAA	Ministerium für Auswärtige Angelegenheiten
MfNV	Ministerium für Nationale Verteidigung
MfS	Ministerium für Staatssicherheit
MID	Ministerstvo Inostrannykh Del
MNO	Ministerstvo Národní Obrany
MX	Missile-Experimental
MZV	Ministerstvo Zahraničních Věcí
NATO	North Atlantic Treaty Organization
NIC	National Intelligence Council
NIE	National Intelligence Estimate
NSC	National Security Council
NSDD	National Security Decision Directive
NSSD	National Security Study Directive
NVA	Nationale Volksarmee

xiv **ABBREVIATIONS**

PD	Presidential Directive
PFIAB	President's Foreign Intelligence Advisory Board
PRC	People's Republic of China
PZPR	Polska Zjednoczona Partia Robotnicza
RNC	Republican National Committee
SALT	Strategic Arms Limitation Talks
SDI	Strategic Defense Initiative
SED	Sozialistische Einheitspartei Deutschlands
SNIE	Special National Intelligence Estimate
START	Strategic Arms Reduction Talks
TEL	Transporter-erector-launcher
UN	United Nations
US	United States
USICA	United States International Communications Agency
USSR	Union of Soviet Socialist Republics

NOTE ON TRANSLITERATION AND TRANSLATION

In romanization from Russian and Ukrainian Cyrillic script, I have used the American Language Association–Library of Congress standard throughout, albeit without two-letter tie symbols. I have deviated from this only when doing so would cause confusion in the case of names and terms that have another commonly accepted spelling in English, such as "politburo" (as opposed to "politbiuro") and "Yeltsin" (as opposed to "El'tsin"). All translations are my own unless otherwise indicated.

Introduction
Grand Strategy and the End of the Cold War

A Soviet worker is to be given the honor of carrying General Secretary Konstantin Chernenko's portrait in the 1984 May Day parade. "Don't ask me to do that," he demurs. "I carried Lenin's portrait and he died. I carried Stalin's portrait and he died. I carried Khrushchev's portrait and he disappeared. I carried Brezhnev's portrait and he died. Not long ago I carried Andropov's portrait and he died too." His boss insists, "You have golden hands! You must carry Comrade Chernenko's portrait." A fellow worker then chimes in, "Let him carry the red flag [of the Soviet Union]!"[1]

Jokes (*anekdoty* in Russian) like this abounded in the Soviet Union during the early 1980s, and with good reason. A string of politburo members died in rapid succession: one every six months, on average, between 1980 and 1985.[2] In the United States, leaders also made light of the seemingly constant flow of obituaries out of the Kremlin. Vice President George H. W. Bush, as the White House chief of staff James Baker joked, should have adopted "you die, I fly" as his unofficial motto on account of his regular attendance at funerals in Moscow.[3] It seemed that there was no one Ronald Reagan could do business with in the Kremlin. And even if there were, there was little evidence to suggest that the president was willing to do so in the first place. Reagan appeared to miss no opportunity to attack the Soviet Union. In his view, its leaders could not be trusted.[4] Its ideology was a "bizarre chapter in human history" and certain to fail.[5] "The march of freedom and democracy," Reagan

2   INTRODUCTION

insisted, "will leave Marxism-Leninism on the ash heap of history."[6] The Soviet Union was "the focus of evil in the modern world" and, most famously of all, an "evil empire."[7] The Soviets gave as good as they got. According to General Secretary Iuriĭ Andropov, Reagan had nothing to say but "profanities alternated with hypocritical preaching."[8] An article in *Pravda* summed up his administration's foreign policy as little more than "nuclear insanity."[9] The Soviet press even went so far as to liken the fortieth president to Adolf Hitler.[10]

The end of the Cold War presents a puzzle to this day. "Wars, hot or cold, do not normally end with the abrupt but peaceful collapse of a major antagonist," the historian John Lewis Gaddis observed a decade after the conflict's end. "Such an event had to have deep roots, and yet neither our histories nor our theories came anywhere close to detecting these. . . . The Cold War went on for a very long time, and then all of a sudden it went away."[11] So profound a transformation of the international system had theretofore only been brought about by great-power war.[12] The end of the Cold War, by comparison, was remarkably—albeit not completely—peaceful.[13]

In the years since the Cold War's improbable and unpredictable end, the conventional scholarly and policy wisdom has coalesced around four explanations. To some, the Cold War ended because Ronald Reagan rejected the failed foreign policy doctrines of containment and détente and crafted a new grand strategy that ended it.[14] Rejecting this triumphalism, others credit Mikhail Gorbachev, whose new thinking transformed the Soviet Union and transcended the East-West confrontation.[15] Alternative explanations look beyond the superpowers entirely, focusing on the power of people: human rights activists, anti-nuclear campaigners, concerned scientists, and citizens who reshaped their world.[16] And for all these explanations centered on the agency of individuals, there are those who point instead to structural forces, the broader trends and systemic weaknesses that shaped their choices.[17]

None of these explanations accounts fully for the remarkable pace of the transformation—especially given what came before. After all, the Cold War's denouement between 1985 and 1991 is regularly cited as a textbook case of long-standing adversaries setting aside prior disagreements and beginning to cooperate.[18] And the conventional wisdom maintains that this transformation was sudden, emerging out of the deep freeze of the so-called Second Cold War from 1979 to 1985.[19] Détente, many argue, was dead—and with it, any meaningful dialogue between the superpowers during the first half of the decade. Then, suddenly, everything seemed to change for the better.

This rapid rate of change, too, presents a puzzle. One school of thought posits an abrupt "reversal" in Reagan's approach. Nearing the end of his first term, the president shifted his strategy from one of confrontation to one of cooperation, motivated in large part by fears that the Cold War might turn hot.[20] Another rejects the idea of Reagan as grand strategist; rapid change should come as no surprise when there was no consistency in US policy. Reagan's approach to the Soviet Union instead struggled to reconcile two irreconcilable impulses: seeking peace for a world that included the Soviet Union (which required working with the Kremlin) and eradicating communism worldwide (which necessitated ousting its occupants).[21] Alternatively, many seize on the fact that Gorbachev's accession to power and the beginning of Cold War's apparent shift from confrontation to cooperation both occurred in 1985. The new general secretary was the missing piece, the indispensable factor who remade not only his country but also the world.[22] And some challenge the notion that there was a rapid change at all, arguing that policy makers in Europe kept détente alive and the lines of communication open throughout the early 1980s.[23]

In seeking to understand both why the Cold War ended as it did and the deep roots of that transformation, archival evidence from both sides of the Iron Curtain led me to three conclusions. First and foremost, the key to understanding the puzzle of the Cold War's rapid and unexpected denouement at the end of the 1980s lies in the beginning of the decade. In the span of just five years, between 1980 and 1985, the Cold War transformed in two fundamental ways: from a balance of power perceived to favor the Soviet Union to the more realistic perception of one tilted in favor of the United States, and, as a result, from a war of words coupled with back-channel discussions to overt superpower dialogue and summitry. Those twin shifts constituted the beginning of the end of the Cold War.

Second, US grand strategy shaped both of these processes. From 1981 on, Reagan implemented a grand strategy with parallel and complementary tracks. The first, what the president referred to as "quiet diplomacy," was the proverbial carrot. Reagan had long seen dialogue with the Soviet Union as important not only to keep Cold War tensions under control, but also—and arguably more importantly—to cement US advantage through diplomatic agreements which would constrain the rival superpower.[24] The second, dubbed "peace through strength," was the corresponding stick. Reagan was convinced that the United States needed to rebuild its military strength in order to secure these advantageous agreements.[25] A more secure United States would create a more secure world, he believed, deterring Soviet adventurism. Reagan's grand strategy was, in the words of his second secretary of state, George P. Shultz, the "parallel pursuit of strength and negotiation."[26]

Third, successive Soviet leaders had grand strategies of their own. Gorbachev did not inherit a blank slate on coming to power in March 1985, even

INTRODUCTION

if he himself dismissed the preceding years as nothing but "an era of stagnation" (*zastoĭ* in Russian).[27] Many agree with the final general secretary, dismissing his geriatric predecessors out of hand. The end of Leonid Brezhnev's rule, along with Iuriĭ Andropov's and Konstantin Chernenko's short tenures, was no more than an "interregnum." History was waiting for Gorbachev.[28] In fact, Soviet grand strategy under all four sought, in varying ways, to reduce Cold War tensions in the hopes of creating breathing space to address the myriad economic, social, and political problems multiplying at home. For policy makers in the Kremlin, this never entailed abandoning the Cold War rivalry. They tried to strike a balance between cooperation and confrontation in order to redress the power imbalance between the two superpowers and compete more effectively.

These three interventions—situating the roots of the Cold War's end in the early 1980s, identifying the Reagan administration's dual-track grand strategy, and mapping the evolution of the Soviet grand strategy—are only possible thanks to international archival evidence. These sources illuminate how and why policy makers crafted strategy, but also how others perceived those choices and the global context in which they unfolded. Here, documents from Czechoslovakia, East Germany, and Ukraine combine with extensive research in Russian archives to produce a more complete Eastern perspective; and US materials join with Australian, British, Canadian, French, and West German records to do the same for the Western side of the story. This "pericentric" approach sheds new light not only on both superpowers, but also on the roles of their allies as actors in their own right.[29]

Such an outlook also addresses the challenges inherent in contemporary history, not least those of access and classification. Tapping into alliance networks—triangulation—can overcome these obstacles. Take, for example, the Soviet Union. Moscow sought to shape its allies' foreign policies, but exerting such control was not automatic; it required meetings, briefings, and the flow of information—all of which left a paper trail, accessible in repositories across Eastern Europe where states have made transitions to democratic governments that prioritize transparency and access to information pertaining to their communist pasts.[30] But what Stephen Kotkin terms "speaking Bolshevik" presents historians working with such intra-bloc documents with an added challenge: they must separate pro forma pablum from meaningful commentary on the activities of the Eastern Bloc or perceptions of the West.[31]

Iosef Stalin once famously dismissed historians as mere "archive rats," so focused on hunting down individual documents that they miss the big picture— unable to see the forest for the trees or, rather, the products thereof.[32] But

INTRODUCTION 5

those documents can illuminate aspects of a past unknown even to participants and eyewitnesses. In this case, new evidence from both the superpowers and their allies, in both the Eastern and Western blocs, brings to light the pivotal importance of the first half of the 1980s and the grand strategies employed by Washington and Moscow to begin to end the Cold War.

At its core, the Cold War was a struggle of global proportions between two competing systems, rival definitions of legitimacy and modernity driven either by the market or the state. Since its outbreak in the aftermath of World War II, the conflict had been defined by a mix of cooperation and competition between the superpowers. Indeed, the former was often a key means of doing the latter. Like their predecessors, leaders in Washington and Moscow during the early 1980s debated how best to engage their Cold War rival in order to come out on top.

The storied dialogue between Reagan and Gorbachev of the late 1980s did not appear out of the blue; the preceding half decade of East-West engagement, much of which has remained in the shadows, made it possible. Engagement here does not mean cooperation. Knowing the intentions with which both US and Soviet negotiators came to the bargaining table, it is hard to sustain the argument that they wanted only to cooperate with their Cold War adversary; rather, both superpowers saw engagement as a means of furthering their own, primarily competitive goals.[33] Engagement describes diplomacy in a value- and intention-neutral way: a contest, constrained in time and scope, that is a step toward the attainment of a greater objective.[34] For both superpowers, what that objective was changed during the years between 1980 and 1985, but it remained competitive in nature.

How US and Soviet policy makers approached engagement depended as much on perception as reality. Indeed, so much of the story of the Cold War is one of perception, reality, and the varying (and often vast) distance between the two. The first half of the 1980s was no different. On the campaign trail in 1980, Reagan and his advisers lamented the United States' weak position and feared the consequences thereof. Washington would have to wait if it was to engage the Soviet Union on terms favorable to the United States. Upon taking office, the Reagan administration's priority was rebuilding. Over the next five years, its outlook brightened considerably. The US economy recovered, while the Soviet economy continued its decline. Reagan's defense buildup underwrote a new confidence in US foreign-policy making. So, too, did major structural trends emerging around the world. Markets and politics were becoming freer, something that could scarcely benefit a superpower built on quasi-autarky and single-party rule like the Soviet Union. All these developments

6 **INTRODUCTION**

redounded to Washington's benefit, emboldening the Reagan administration to overtly engage the Soviet leadership. The transition was the opposite in Moscow. In 1980, Soviet policy makers believed themselves to be in a better position than the United States. Such optimism was short lived. Soviet economic and military power steadily declined, plagued by problems from Kabul to Warsaw—many of them of the Kremlin's own making. Whereas the Reagan administration took license from rising US power to begin overtly engaging the Soviet Union, the Kremlin concluded that Soviet decline, which showed no signs of abating, necessitated a return to the bargaining table.

In Washington and Moscow alike, policy makers often misjudged their own position in the world, especially vis-à-vis that of the other superpower. In reality, the balance of power between the two shifted far less between 1980 and 1985 than did their perceptions thereof. But throughout, both superpowers sought to engage from a position of strength, and both focused disproportionately on the other's pursuit of strength—mostly militarily—as compared to their professed desire to negotiate. These military measures seemed to those behind them to be defensive in nature, redressing an unfavorable imbalance; but to the other superpower, these ostensibly defensive measures appeared both offensive and threatening.[35] That same perception runs through observers' accounts, be they allies or the general public, or those of historians writing after the fact.

The central role of perception in the events and evolutions of the first half of the 1980s is an important reminder: those years may have constituted the beginning of the end of the Cold War, but that process remained highly contingent. Leaders in both Washington and Moscow responded to one another and to the changing world in which they operated, but the choices they made were far from preordained.[36] Time and again, they could have made different ones that would have set the Cold War on a more confrontational course and made the world a less safe place. A declining Soviet Union could have reacted by lashing out. A rising United States could have pressed its advantage too far. Instead, both superpowers successfully managed the potentially dangerous power shift that played out between 1980 and 1985.[37]

"Gorbachev is hard to understand," the last general secretary told his biographer William Taubman, referring, as he often does, to himself in the third person.[38] By contrast, he maintained that it was easy to make sense of what had come before him: stagnation, and nothing more. But the process of reevaluating this period of Soviet history has already begun, in part catalyzed by the ongoing opening of the Russian archives and those of former members of the Warsaw Pact. New studies of Brezhnev's tenure as general secretary move past the stagnation-centric narrative in foreign and domestic policy alike.[39]

INTRODUCTION 7

Andropov, too, has enjoyed a resurgence in historical prominence, in part because of an effort in contemporary Russia to boost the prestige of the security services, of which both he and current president Vladimir Putin served as chief.[40] Chernenko's historiographical day has yet to come. Understanding the evolution of superpower relations over the course of the first half of the 1980s requires a deeper understanding of each of these Soviet leaders. Struggles within the Kremlin over succession in all three instances—contrary to conspiracy theories that the four final general secretaries had made a secret pact to establish the order of succession in late 1978—are especially instructive for the light they shed on internal policy disputes.[41]

In Brezhnev's case, the Soviet leader from 1964 to 1982 concluded that the Soviet Union needed "peace and a reduction in tensions . . . [to] create better conditions for internal development and buy [the Soviet Union] time to win the struggle against imperialism."[42] Unwilling to do anything that might jeopardize the tenuous economic situation at home, Brezhnev looked abroad.[43] Reducing tensions internationally was the only way he could see to enable the Soviet Union to compete with the United States more effectively. He was not wrong: during Brezhnev's tenure, the Soviet Union eliminated the US superiority in strategic weapons, and Moscow came to be seen worldwide as Washington's equal. Andropov inherited many of the same problems, especially in the domestic economy, but he was less risk-averse, hoping to fix them through a crackdown on inefficiency using the tool he knew best: the KGB. An economically healthier Soviet Union, he believed, would be better able to compete with the United States; however, the unhealthy general secretary had little time to see his grand strategy through. His successor, Chernenko—a Brezhnev protégé—looked to his mentor for inspiration. Under his tenure, corruption skyrocketed and the economic situation worsened, and Chernenko's poor health meant he could not indulge in what he found most attractive about Brezhnev's approach: high-profile summitry with his Western counterparts—above all, Reagan.

By 1985, with Gorbachev at the helm, the politburo understood that it would have to engage with the West and accept less advantageous agreements than it might have pressed for even in the recent past. Gorbachev inherited a shambolic economy, whose collapse, according to one prominent Soviet economist, was inevitable—"it was just a question of when and how."[44] He inherited a military and, through the Warsaw Pact, an alliance undoubtedly and self-consciously weaker than those it faced in the United States and NATO. Though not entirely on his own terms, Gorbachev made different choices than those of his predecessors in important areas of foreign and domestic policy. To be sure, Brezhnev, Andropov, and Chernenko all appreciated that the Soviet

8   INTRODUCTION

Union's position relative to the United States was in decline. Gorbachev saw no choice but to take their efforts further, as the situation grew increasingly dire at home. The last general secretary changed the nature of the Cold War competition, but he did not "abandon it."[45]

As a historical figure, Reagan poses a host of challenges. To some, his Hollywood background served him all too well after he entered politics. When Reagan said something unexpectedly welcome, Allan Gotlieb, Canada's ambassador to Washington, instinctively doubted the president's sincerity: "This is Reagan speaking? Or is this Reagan, the actor, reading his lines?"[46] Gorbachev himself later responded fiercely to such assertions: the president was a "man of real insight, sound political judgment, and courage."[47] To others, Reagan was a simpleton, on whom the nuances of statecraft were lost.[48] And historians have not just Reagan the man to contend with but also Reagan the myth. The fortieth president has become the avatar of American exceptionalism to many, for better or for worse.[49]

Often credited with changing the Cold War game, Reagan's Soviet counterparts were skeptical that he had in fact ushered in so significant a foreign-policy departure. Few in the administration would care to admit it, but Reagan's policies bore a striking similarity to those of his predecessor, Jimmy Carter. The Carter administration had increased defense spending and Carter's willingness to speak out on human rights in the Soviet Union vexed the Kremlin. These continuities were so clear that even in 1985, analysts in Moscow concluded that US policy toward the Soviet Union would have been the same in the case of a second Carter term as it had been during Reagan's first.[50]

Reagan could articulate a deceptively simple vision for the Cold War's outcome: "We win, they lose."[51] But an end to the Cold War was a long way off. Certainly the United States should work toward "the peaceful, eventual devolution of the Soviet Empire into free states," but that process, Reagan's advisers estimated at the beginning of the 1980s, would take at least sixty years.[52] In the mean time, Reagan wanted to reduce East-West tensions—albeit on the West's terms. Identifying a singular US foreign policy during this period nevertheless poses a serious challenge. Reagan's White House staff consisted of advisers regularly at odds with one another, and not infrequently with the president himself.[53] Reagan's strong personal aversion to discord in the policy-making process, which dated back to his time as the governor of California, meant that this factionalism all too often produced policies that did not fully reflect the president's own views.[54] He was also, in his wife's words, "a loner," who did not share his private thoughts willingly.[55] From the Oval Office, the president "kept his eye on the 'big picture,'" namely US-

Soviet relations, "and tended to scant issues he believed were of little importance."[56] The challenge for the historian of Reagan's foreign policy is precisely that his grand strategy was not spelled out in the grand-strategic venues to which historians often turn, such as at meetings of the National Security Council, at which Reagan regularly said little of substance and which often ended with everyone feeling that they had won the president over to their—diametrically opposed—positions.

People, not just process, make policy. In the case of Reagan, that meant a president with a keen emotional intelligence and an ability to engender trust. Not only did Reagan have the self-confidence to see the value in personally engaging the Soviet leadership, but he was able to do so with empathy.[57] These personal relationships proved key to ending the Cold War.[58] However, Reagan's style, particularly his willingness to speak openly about his distaste for the Soviet system, also aroused far more negative emotions. Worldwide, policy makers and publics feared the president's bombast and what it might represent.[59] Hundreds of thousands took to the streets expressing their fear that the superpowers might lose control and plunge the world into nuclear war. It was this same fear of annihilation, the prominent evangelical minister Billy Graham argued in a sermon at Duke University, that brought Reagan and Gorbachev together for the Geneva Summit in November 1985.[60]

The wide range of outcomes resulting from the Reagan administration's policies at home and abroad make an assessment of his presidency all the more difficult. At home, many were critical of the "Bacchanalia of the haves"—and abandonment of the have-nots—which resulted from his economic policies.[61] Abroad, US (as well as Soviet and Cuban) intervention in Latin America's civil wars led to staggering death tolls: 200,000 in Guatemala, 70,000 in El Salvador, and 30,000 in Nicaragua. This last, lowest figure still represents a greater loss, in proportional terms, than all US casualties during the Civil War, World War I, World War II, the Korean War, and the Vietnam War combined.[62] And as support for the administration's policies in Latin America waned, they turned to solutions of dubious legality. The Iran-Contra scandal revealed US arms sales to the regime of Ayatollah Ruhollah Khomeini in Iran, the profits of which wound their way to the right-wing Contra movement working to unseat the government of Nicaragua. In thinking holistically about Reagan's foreign policy, moving past the partisan rhetoric on both sides, these failings cannot be ignored, no matter the successes in his dealings with the Soviet Union.[63]

This account of the Cold War's transformation between 1980 and 1985—the impact of power and personalities, as well as perception and misperception—plays out over five chronological chapters. Chapter 1 sets the stage, exploring

10   **INTRODUCTION**

how the world looked from Washington and Moscow at the dawn of the 1980s. Chapter 2 then examines the last two years of Brezhnev's life, shedding light on often ignored back channels between the superpowers. Chapter 3 addresses Andropov's tenure in the Kremlin, his efforts to reform both foreign and domestic policy, and the crises of late 1983. Chapter 4 is devoted to Chernenko's time in office. It takes stock of his efforts to shift superpower relations back to a détente-like footing, while examining attempts on the part of various Western leaders to carve out a role for themselves as the superpowers' chosen intermediary. Chapter 5 covers Reagan's first meeting with Gorbachev in Geneva in November 1985, exploring the internal and external roots of the nascent new thinking in Soviet foreign policy and its impact on East-West relations. Superpower relations over these five years were messy and, at times, contradictory. Moscow and Washington exchanged harsh words but also engaged in far more dialogue than is commonly thought. Within this brief window of time, both sides' outlooks changed dramatically. As US policy makers regained confidence in their place in the world, their Soviet counterparts took increasingly drastic measures to deal with a deteriorating situation, and the process of ending the Cold War had begun.

The story does not end in 1985 with this book, nor on Christmas Day of 1991 when the Soviet flag was lowered one last time over the Kremlin. Foreign-policy makers still operate in a world shaped by the end of the Cold War—one in which understanding that complex process from beginning to end, and the grievances it engendered, is essential. Examined from 1985 to 1991, as is so often the case, it is easy to see the story is one of an obviously crumbling Soviet Union and a United States inexorably headed for its "unipolar moment."[64] Why, then, should Washington not have done as it pleased in the world, expanding NATO eastward, dismissing Moscow's protestations? Expanding the temporal scope of the end of the Cold War makes for a very different story. Taking just five earlier years into account changes the picture: the Soviet Union trying desperately to stop its decline and remain a coequal superpower to the United States, and the United States keen to speed Moscow's decay. This dramatic and precipitous reversal of fortunes left an indelible mark on the minds of Kremlin policy makers today, who remember this collapse and the turmoil it caused all too well.

CHAPTER 1

Red Star Rising
The World according to Washington and Moscow

Ronald Reagan availed himself of only one intelligence briefing during the 1980 presidential election, conducted on October 4, 1980, by Central Intelligence Agency Director Adm. Stansfield Turner and three aides. Reagan and his running mate, George H. W. Bush, brought with them the putative transition director Ed Meese, the campaign manager William Casey, and the top national-security aide Richard Allen. Crammed into the living room of a Virginia country estate, the briefing was "a circus," according to participants. Lasting an hour and focusing on the situation in the Middle East, the CIA contingent concluded that they were only invited to brief the candidate because they had offered to do so in the first place—an offer made, according to Turner, "because [CIA leadership] didn't want him saying something he would regret if he became president." That meeting reinforced the Reagan team's preexisting belief that the United States was in grave trouble, both at home and abroad. As Bush put it afterward, "I feel better informed about the world, [but] I can't tell you I feel more optimistic about it."[1] "They came to their task with their minds made up," Turner bemoaned, "and no facts were going to change their conclusions."[2] Knowing how the remainder of the decade unfolded, the Reagan team's pessimism at the dawn of the 1980s is striking. Why were policy makers in the United States convinced that they had fallen behind the Kremlin at a time when, as it later became clear, the Soviet Union was already beginning to come apart at the seams? Why were Soviet

12   **CHAPTER 1**

leaders so confident in their own position despite the acute problems plaguing their country? The leaders of the superpowers—the incoming Reagan in Washington and the long-in-the-tooth Brezhnev in Moscow—saw the world and their country's position therein very differently. But both viewed the perceived balance of power as one tipped in the Kremlin's favor.

Throughout the 1980 campaign, Reagan stressed that the United States was losing the Cold War. He pointed to the Iranian hostage crisis, the ever-growing Soviet nuclear arsenal, and Moscow's international troublemaking, overt in Afghanistan and covert in Latin America, while Americans could barely fill up their cars with gasoline. He was a pessimist on the campaign trail, even if history remembers him as the ultimate optimist. When Turner tried to persuade the president in a January 20, 1981, briefing that his beliefs regarding Soviet superiority in various domains were basically wrong, Reagan ignored him.[3] Meanwhile, in Moscow, the aging Brezhnev found reason to be confident about the Soviet Union's place in the world, despite real problems at home and abroad. Whatever challenges the East faced, the West's situation seemed even more dire, with *Time* magazine asking in one cover story, "Can Capitalism Survive?"[4] And the capitalist world—above all, the North Atlantic Treaty Organization—seemed similarly in trouble, riven by discord.[5] Unlike Reagan, Brezhnev was optimistic.

Ronald Reagan's speech at the 1980 Republican Party Convention accepting his party's nomination for the presidency ran through a laundry list of solemn challenges facing the United States: skyrocketing Soviet expenditures on nuclear and conventional arms, revolution in Iran, economic malaise at home, Soviet occupation of Afghanistan and the accompanying threat to the Persian Gulf, a Third World seemingly gravitating toward Moscow, and allies looking to Washington for leadership and finding none. "Why?" Reagan asked his Detroit audience. "Because the Carter administration lives in the world of make-believe. . . . The rest of us, however, live in the real world. It is here that disasters are overtaking our nation without any real response from the White House."[6] When Reagan looked at US foreign policy, he did so from a position cultivated through years of thinking about US decline—and found an abundance of evidence to support his worldview.

Détente may have been a golden age of US-Soviet arms control agreements, but by the beginning of the 1980s, Reagan and many others believed that those agreements had failed to make the United States and its allies any more secure.[7] Soviet defense spending had nearly doubled in real terms since Brezhnev came to power in 1964, as had the size of the Soviet military research-and-development establishment. The Soviet intercontinental ballistic missile force increased sixfold, while short-range ballistic missile stocks tripled. The Soviet civil defense apparatus also underwent a major overhaul, hardening Soviet cities against nuclear attack.[8] Over the late 1970s, the Soviet Union had deployed new SS-20 intermediate-range nuclear weapons to the European theater. Faster to launch and more accurate, the new systems counterbalanced the British and French independent nuclear forces (which later came to be the bête noire of superpower arms control negotiations) as well as US forward-based systems, such as attack aircraft and nuclear-armed submarines assigned to NATO.[9] It seemed that the United States was losing the Cold War arms race, undercutting the credibility of NATO nuclear forces as a counterweight to numerically superior Warsaw Pact conventional forces in Europe. The US intelligence community could only conclude that the Soviet Union sought superiority in order to fight and win a nuclear war.[10] It was right.[11]

The January 16, 1979, overthrow of US ally Reza Shah Pahlavi in Iran dealt a triple blow to the United States. First, Washington lost a key partner in the Middle East. Then, after a group of militants loyal to his usurper, Ayatollah Ruhollah Khomeini, seized the US embassy in Tehran, taking fifty-two embassy workers hostage, nothing seemed to encapsulate US weakness better than a group of university-aged revolutionaries seizing its territory and citizens—and its military unable to dislodge them after a rescue attempt by special operations forces had to be abandoned.[12] (The Carter administration's ensuing negotiations, brokered by Algeria, remained secret.)[13] Moscow was gleeful at these setbacks, whatever the human cost.[14] At the same time as things were unraveling in Iran, the Carter administration believed that it was getting stagflation under control at home, as economic growth and employment were enjoying an uptick. However, the Iranian Revolution ensured that this was brief. As militants began occupying oil refineries and taking them offline, demand rose due to uncertainty, exemplified by motorists keeping their tanks as full as possible and oil companies hoarding product in vast storage depots. Sellers, namely the Organization of the Petroleum Exporting Countries, gouged consumers. Crude oil prices skyrocketed, and with them, inflation.[15] The hostage and oil crises compounded to make the United States look not just weak but beleaguered.

In neighboring Afghanistan, the Kremlin's attempt to secure a reliable client state mired the Soviet Army in a brutal counterinsurgency almost immediately after it invaded in December 1979.[16] To Western observers, however, it seemed that Moscow was becoming increasingly aggressive and that Afghanistan might be the first step in a Soviet move on the Persian Gulf. These assessments were wrong, but the Carter administration retaliated nonetheless, reducing trade (including in grain, on which the Soviets depended), halting

14   **CHAPTER 1**

diplomatic and cultural contacts, withdrawing the SALT 2 arms control treaty from Senate consideration for ratification, and boycotting the 1980 Olympics to be held in the Soviet Union—the first time the games would be held in a communist country. Washington's allies proved less enthusiastic. None relished imposing trade sanctions on the Soviet Union at considerable cost to themselves and their diplomatic agendas.[17]

Afghanistan was but one Third World trouble spot in the eyes of US policy makers. The Caribbean, Reagan concluded, "was becoming a 'Red' lake."[18] In Latin America, brutal civil wars in Guatemala and El Salvador pitted guerrillas against authoritarian regimes. In Nicaragua, the left-wing Sandinista regime had come to power in 1979, bringing with it a right-wing insurrection. Communist agitation in El Salvador and Nicaragua, according to Reagan, was "only a down payment. Honduras, Guatemala, and Costa Rica were next, and then would come Mexico."[19] For the region, the 1980s had "an apocalyptic quality," made worse by the involvement of the United States, the Soviet Union, and Cuba.[20] Fears of a Soviet Union on the march in the Third World gave rise to notable efforts to counter Moscow's influence, such as Britain's Operation Commonsense, the patronizing name—even by Whitehall's standards—given to a push to educate African and other Third World leaders about Moscow's pernicious designs.[21] "In a rating of threat and troublemaking," as one Reagan staffer summed up, the Soviet Union was "a true [ten out of ten], while all others are [five] or less."[22]

"While Reagan may not have the qualities necessary for the presidency," the Carter campaign acknowledged, "his arsenal as a presidential candidate is formidable."[23] Reagan and his campaign advisers laid the blame squarely on Carter. Reagan's focus on the incumbent's perceived soft attitude played well with an electorate suffering from what Carter himself had termed a "crisis in confidence," though that had much more to do with the United States' domestic situation than with events abroad, as economic difficulties dominated the public's concerns.[24] The 1950s and 1960s had been an era of growth in the US economy, but the 1970s were a different story. The decade was a wake-up call; the world was becoming increasingly globalized, and the US economy's transition to that new reality was a painful one.[25] The winner in such a world was not the Soviet Union, whose quasi-autarkic system would struggle even more to adjust, but US ally Japan and its apparently superior capitalist system. Japan had once been a defeated enemy occupied by US troops, but by 1981, the *New York Times* was publishing tongue-in-cheek op-eds with titles like "Please, Japan, Return the Favor: Occupy Us."[26] At a debate between himself and Carter just a week before election day, Reagan asked the audience, "Are you better off than you were four years ago?" He knew the voters' answer: an emphatic no.[27]

Western European public opinion reflected Reagan's thinking: 68 percent of West German and 51 percent of French respondents to one US government-sponsored poll believed that the Soviet bloc had "a military edge" over the West and that Soviet influence worldwide was growing at the expense of the West's. Though one US official optimistically wrote "Looks like a lot of room for leadership" in the margin of a document reporting on these figures, Reagan would have his work cut out for him.[28] This outlook was equally prevalent among foreign-policy elites: in Bonn, London, and Paris, analysts painted a grim picture of NATO's military capabilities compared with those of the Warsaw Pact.[29] But Western Europeans had been reluctant to follow the Carter administration's lead in rectifying that perceived imbalance. "NATO," the British prime minister Margaret Thatcher concluded, "is not doing well. It has lost its dynamism. Its members no longer get 'value for money.'"[30] In the United States, foreign-policy analysts openly predicted that Western Europe's "movement towards neutralism" could lead to the complete collapse of the alliance, or at least the abandonment of NATO's 1979 Dual-Track Decision.[31] That plan to both negotiate with the Soviet Union on mutual reductions while deploying 108 Pershing 2 ballistic missiles and 464 Gryphon ground-launched cruise missiles to US bases in Europe was unpopular and contentious.[32]

The 1980 election was a disastrous one for Carter. His campaign knew early on that he would be susceptible to attacks on the foreign-policy front from Reagan. The campaign "failed tragically," one staffer bemoaned, in communicating Carter's foreign-policy achievements and goals. The Reagan campaign cast the Democratic incumbent as "a failed leader" and a "man without direction"—and it stuck, in large part because that was what most voters already believed.[33] Even internal polls of the most loyal Democratic supporters found that only a minority of respondents supported the president, and one-third opposed his reelection outright. Carter's overall campaign strategy pulled few punches in describing the hard work ahead for the incumbent: "The public is anxious, confused, hostile, and sour. . . . More to the point the American people do not want Jimmy Carter as their president. . . . The 'lesser of evils' success to date should not obscure a fundamental truth—by and large the American people do not like Jimmy Carter."[34]

In retrospect, Carter believed that three factors had caused his defeat: the hostage taking at the US embassy in Tehran, the state of the economy, and the divisions within his own party.[35] In the election of 1980, voters rejected Carter—his foreign and domestic policies alike—because they agreed with

16   **CHAPTER 1**

Reagan's conclusion that the thirty-ninth president had made the country weaker.[36] Voters delivered Reagan an overwhelming majority of the Electoral College and 51 percent of the popular vote on November 4, 1980. The Democrats lost the White House, twelve seats in the Senate, and thirty-four seats in the House of Representatives. "This was a party defeat . . . [and] a disaster," one Democratic operative summed up.[37] To Reagan and those in Washington with whom he surrounded himself, the world looked bleak as the election year of 1980 gave way to 1981, and their taking office. The idea of "esprit de corps" (and a sense of shared hardship) crops up frequently in the reminiscences of the first Reagan administration staff, who broadly saw the world and their role in it the same way: to reassert US "pride" and "primacy" after the considerable setbacks of the 1970s. To a great extent, the Reagan camp was bound together by the common mission of being everything Carter had not been in the White House.[38] Internal campaign materials went so far as to invoke the Munich analogy, with Carter playing the role of a capitulating Neville Chamberlain to Brezhnev's Adolf Hitler.[39]

In such dire circumstances, what was to be done? Just as his Soviet counterparts believed (or at least professed to believe) in the inevitable victory of international communism, Reagan believed in the inevitability of its defeat. "Communism," he had declared in 1975, "is a form of insanity—a temporary aberration which will one day disappear from the earth because it is contrary to human nature."[40] During his time as president of the Screen Actors Guild (from 1947 to 1952 and again from 1959 to 1960), perceived communist incursions into the union movement had left him convinced of the irreconcilability of communism and capitalism.[41]

Reagan's rise to national political prominence had begun with a speech supporting the presidential campaign of Republican Barry Goldwater in October 1964. In it, Reagan declared the election "a time for choosing" between individual liberties and the type of coercive government under the Democratic President Lyndon B. Johnson that could lead only "to the ant heap of totalitarianism."[42] Speculation about his running for president began almost immediately thereafter, but instead, the Illinois native ran for the governorship of his adopted home of California, which he won in 1966. Anticommunism became Reagan's hallmark as he campaigned against fellow Republicans identified closely with US-Soviet détente. Gerald Ford tried to bring him into his administration, but Reagan turned down offers of an ambassadorship to the United Kingdom and cabinet seats as secretary of transportation or commerce. He preferred to operate outside the mainstream Republican Party.[43]

In 1976, Reagan challenged the incumbent Ford for the Republican nomination, foregrounding his plan to rebuild the US military and stand up to the

Soviet Union.[44] "The evidence mounts," Reagan asserted, "that we are number two in a world where it is dangerous, if not fatal, to be second best. Ask the people of Latvia, Estonia, Lithuania, Czechoslovakia, Poland, Hungary, all the others: East Germany, Bulgaria, Romania, ask them what it's like to live in a world where the Soviet Union is number one."[45] Reagan's rhetoric struck a chord with the public, and the Ford administration recognized détente's growing unpopularity. Around the time Reagan began his attacks, Ford stopped using the term entirely, replacing it with a phrase Reagan later used extensively: "peace through strength."[46]

There was more to Reagan's approach to the Soviet Union than hostility and strident rhetoric. The Reagan who took office at the beginning of 1981 appreciated that the United States needed a "long-range diplomatic strategy, . . . a grand strategy, . . . a plan for the dangerous decade ahead."[47] In October 1980, he had outlined his "strategy for peace for the '80s." As president, he would show the Kremlin that the United States sought neither confrontation nor conflict but would protect its interests. Reagan declared himself ready to sit down with the Soviets to negotiate on nuclear weapons in particular and to "tell them that we prefer to halt this competition and reduce the nuclear arsenals by patient negotiation."[48]

For the most part, Reagan wanted to reduce East-West tensions (on the West's terms) in order to reduce the danger of nuclear weapons. In the aftermath of World War II (as a Democrat), he had endorsed the Baruch Plan for the internationalization of atomic weapons and planned a rally in Hollywood to support it.[49] Reagan believed that the path to peace with the Soviet Union lay in verifiable reduction agreements.[50] He genuinely feared that failing to control these weapons could lead to Armageddon.[51] This could not be unilateral; for Reagan, the only way to eliminate nuclear weapons and end the madness of mutually assured destruction was to be ready to overwhelm the Soviet Union and then reduce both sides' arsenals.[52] "A Soviet leadership devoted to improving its people's lives rather than expanding its armed conquests," he insisted, "will find a sympathetic partner in [the Reagan administration]."[53]

Reagan's plan was for the United States to communicate not only with the Kremlin but also with the Soviet public as a whole in order to put pressure on the Soviet system. In his view, Washington needed to exploit the waning support for socialism throughout the Soviet Union and the fact that "'American' has become an adjective of admiration in Eastern Europe, not least because *Pravda* treats it like a pejorative." While this greatly oversimplified Soviet popular attitudes, it reflected a focus on public diplomacy and an appeal to the "hearts and minds" of the Soviet people that was central to Reagan's thinking. The United States' key weapons would be "the Xerox . . . and the 'transistor

18   **CHAPTER 1**

revolution.'"[54] His advisers even recommended that he pledge to go to Moscow early in his first term to demonstrate his commitment to engaging the Soviet Union. However, the lengths to which his campaign had gone in excoriating Carter and Ford for negotiating with the Soviets ensured that this part of the candidate's message was lost on most voters.[55]

When Reagan thought about the declining United States he would lead into the 1980s, foreign policy issues would not be his top priority after inauguration. The new president saw restoring US economic health as a necessary first step and believed that increasing military expenditures would not only enhance the United States' ability to prosecute the Cold War but also benefit the economy as a whole.[56] The Reagan team recognized "that jobs are increasingly directly related to [the US] defense posture" and saw increased defense spending as a means of securing prosperity at home. This was classic Keynesian economics from the unlikeliest of sources.[57]

Not only was economic policy a higher priority than foreign policy, but when it came to the latter, Reagan's advisers counseled prudence and the wisdom of a light touch early on. "The ills of the world that you will inherit [from the Carter administration]," they cautioned, "place extraordinary demands on the design and execution of your foreign policy." In their opinion, Reagan should not plunge headlong into foreign policy departures.[58] Certainly the United States should work toward "the peaceful, eventual devolution of the Soviet Empire into free states," but that process, they estimated, would take at least sixty years. "The goal in foreign policy is not to 'hit the ground running' but to hit it right."[59] In a time of perceived US weakness and Soviet strength, foreign-policy adviser Paul Nitze counseled, the Reagan administration needed to "proceed with prudence," carefully managing superpower relations with an eye toward a future in which the United States enjoyed greater leverage: "Outwardly, our posture should be serious, businesslike, undramatic—with emphasis on exploration of ideas, careful negotiation pursuant to principle, and careful coordination. . . . Inwardly the aim should be to buy time. Both the Soviet Union and we are faced with internal problems pressing for priority attention. In all probability, the Soviet problems over time will become greater than ours. Let us not permit things to get out of hand in the meantime."[60] Reagan could define his administration's foreign-policy program succinctly long before his inauguration, in a way that outpaced many of his advisers and that continues to elude many looking back on the early 1980s: "Along with a willingness to negotiate, America can best protect the peace by maintaining a realistic and credible ability to defend itself."[61]

This did not mean that the administration's initial policies always followed a logical or straightforward path. Bush, Reagan's vice president, would be a strong (and, during the early days, the only) supporter of Reagan's vision for improved East-West relations. Bush had represented the United States both at the United Nations and in Beijing and served as director of central intelligence; thus, he brought some foreign-policy expertise to the White House.[62] But beyond that, battles raged almost constantly within the administration, though often the issues at hand had more to do with personal and interagency power struggles than with foreign policy.[63]

Reagan delegated much of the task of personnel selection, including cabinet secretaries, to "the Troika": his chief of staff, James Baker; his deputy, Michael Deaver; and the counselor to the president, Edwin Meese.[64] Leading the Department of State would be Alexander Haig, who had previously served as deputy national security adviser to Nixon, White House chief of staff under Nixon and Ford, and Supreme Allied Commander Europe during the Ford and Carter administrations. Haig's sharp elbows and tendency to ignore White House instructions did not endear him to anyone in the administration.[65] He was at loggerheads with Reagan's first national security adviser, Richard Allen, from the outset. During the campaign, Allen had advised Reagan to downgrade the position of national security adviser from a cabinet-level post coequal with the secretaries of state and defense to a lower-level White House staff member. Allen was rewarded for his innovative thinking by being appointed to the newly diminished position.[66] Haig's feuds with Allen paled in comparison to his ongoing turf wars with Secretary of Defense Caspar Weinberger, a longtime associate of the president who spearheaded the defense buildup. Weinberger struggled to find common ground with a man who "seemed to be constitutionally unable to present an argument without an enormous amount of passion and intensity, heavily overlaid with a deep suspicion of the competence and motives of anyone who did not share his opinions."[67]

Soviet policy within the White House became the purview of Richard Pipes, whose work as a historian of the Soviet Union had earned him a negative reputation in the East—and a 1966 book titled *Mr. Pipes Falsifies History*.[68] Pipes bore the moniker of hard-line "Cold Warrior" as a badge of honor, taking pride in the fact that his strong views alienated him from other historians and Sovietologists.[69] He did not enjoy his time in the Reagan administration, jealously guarding his position and access (and parking spot) against perceived threats and regularly complaining that his sweeping recommendations "languish[ed] in limbo."[70]

Reagan had lived through World War I, the Great Depression, and World War II. He had seen firsthand how global instability led to violence and suffering. "[He] felt for some time that his destiny was," as Deaver later recalled, "to change the relationship with the Soviet Union."[71] At the dawn of the 1980s,

20   CHAPTER 1

Reagan saw yet more instability on the horizon, and over the course of the 1980 presidential campaign, he came to see a dual-track approach to the Soviet Union—cooperation and confrontation, negotiation and rearmament—as the best way not only to advance US interests but to keep the Cold War from getting any hotter. F. Scott Fitzgerald famously characterized the first-rate intellect as one able to hold two opposing ideas and still function; Reagan's Cold War grand strategy contained these polar opposites in spades.[72]

At his inauguration, Ronald Reagan was the oldest man to have ever been sworn in as president. But for all his sixty-nine years, Reagan was the picture of health compared to his Soviet counterpart, Leonid Brezhnev. The general secretary's well-being was a constant topic of conversation in foreign-policy circles. "[Brezhnev] is a sick man, slow to act, difficult to understand," one French diplomat concluded in 1979. "Without a doubt, the health of the general secretary has never seemed this precarious."[73] That same year, British Kremlin-watchers predicted that the ailing Brezhnev might "last one more winter, but not two."[74] Even Soviet allies no longer disputed that, as Bulgarian foreign minister Pet'r Mladenov allowed, "the years were wearing him down."[75] His health continued to deteriorate. Meeting the ailing Brezhnev in late 1981, Bundeskanzler Helmut Kohl later recalled, had been a "spooky" experience because of how close the general secretary seemed to death.[76]

Behind closed doors, the situation was even more dire. In his diaries, the Soviet leader wrote frequently and affectionately about "the little yellow things"—the sleeping pills on which he had been dependent since 1973.[77] His source for the narcotics was KGB chair Iuriĭ Andropov, along with Andropov's deputy, Semen Tsvigun (though Brezhnev's bodyguard claims that Andropov was giving the general secretary placebos).[78] Brezhnev's diary is littered with references to the drugs.[79] He talked freely about retiring, but his subordinates would have none of it: Brezhnev's departure would unsettle the political order in the Soviet Union, which they could not risk.[80] In many ways, Karen Brutents of the Central Committee's International Department concluded, Brezhnev in his final years was a victim of the system he had helped create.[81]

The situation at the top was the Soviet Union's greatest weakness at the time. Speculation as to Brezhnev's successor had long begun. Some looked to prior successions for insight into the future.[82] Others relied on less sound empirics, such as a count of published reviews and excerpts of recent books (ostensibly) written by politburo members, to predict who would succeed Brezhnev.[83] In Paris, a multitude of theories circulated: that the next regime would shift sharply to the left or to the right, or turn inward or perhaps outward. French analysts agreed on one thing: the injection of "new blood" into the Kremlin would somehow transform the Soviet system.[84]

Two members of the politburo came to dominate most Sovietologists' predictions: Iuriĭ Andropov (the aforementioned KGB chair and Brezhnev's alleged narcotics supplier) and Konstantin Chernenko, who oversaw the party apparatus. Initial assessments expected Chernenko to prevail.[85] He was a Soviet success story, having benefited enormously from the upward mobility that had made the communist project so compelling in its early years. As the CIA put it, Chernenko's rise "from a relatively obscure apparatchik to Politburo full member and a possible candidate to succeed Brezhnev [was] one of the most remarkable ascents of any Soviet official in many years."[86] Born in rural eastern Siberia in 1911, Chernenko rose rapidly through the ranks of the Komsomol, the party's youth organization, and then through its regional organs as a propagandist. An assignment to oversee party propaganda efforts in Moldova put Chernenko on Brezhnev's radar, who at the time was first secretary in Chișinău. When Brezhnev returned to Moscow, he brought Chernenko with him, securing his new protégé a position in the Central Committee's propaganda department. As Brezhnev's star rose, so too did Chernenko's.[87]

Chernenko's key asset was Brezhnev's patronage, and he would do whatever it took to keep it.[88] He had already organized the team of ghostwriters who produced Brezhnev's memoir of his military service.[89] When flattery no longer seemed to have the desired effect, Chernenko tried his utmost to isolate Brezhnev in order to prevent him from confirming what many suspected: that the general secretary believed the Soviet Union could do better when it came to his successor.[90] If Brezhnev and others deserted him, Chernenko's chances at higher office would disappear.

Andropov had lengthy experience in foreign policy. Born in 1914 in the northern Caucasus, he had also risen through the ranks of the Komsomol and, in 1951, gone to Moscow for party work.[91] Between 1954 and 1957, he served as the Soviet ambassador to Budapest, playing a key role in crushing the 1956 Hungarian Revolution.[92] Most observers associated Andropov with his long tenure as chair of the KGB, where he distinguished himself by either suppressing or placating dissidents and non-Russian minorities within the Soviet Union.[93] His willingness to use both carrot and stick made him, in the estimation of Western analysts, an effective pragmatist in the service of the Soviet cause. Andropov also benefited from the support of defense minister Dmitriĭ Ustinov, widely considered a "kingmaker" in the Kremlin.[94] The KGB, the military, and the military-industrial complex combined to form an almost unstoppable force behind Andropov's candidacy.

22   **CHAPTER 1**

The tide of elite opinion had turned against Brezhnev, primarily out of frustration over his failure to address the Soviet Union's mounting economic problems and to extricate the Soviet Army from Afghanistan.[95] Some CIA analysts even suggested that Brezhnev might be forced into retirement, the same method he had used to oust Nikita Khrushchev in October 1964.[96] Soviet television footage no longer hid Brezhnev's frailty, and citizens openly complained that they had "no leader."[97] The Leningrad literary journal *Avrora* encouraged Brezhnev to stop putting off the inevitable and die. *Tak Pobedim*, a play staged in Moscow, included a scathing portrayal of Lenin's feebleness at the end of his life, which Soviet audiences had no difficulty recognizing as a commentary on their current leader.[98] Andropov's supporters contributed to Brezhnev's waning influence, spreading rumors that implicated the general secretary's family in corruption and criminality. Andropov himself was not above the fray. He used the KGB's voluminous dossiers on politburo members to milk every drop of public embarrassment out of a convoluted scandal involving Brezhnev's daughter, Galina; a cache of stolen diamonds; and a circus performer known as Boris the Gypsy.[99]

Whoever succeeded Brezhnev would inherit the aging general secretary's foreign-policy apparatus. Andreï Gromyko, the Soviet foreign minister, had a reputation first and foremost for devoted service to the Soviet Union and staunch defense of Soviet interests. "If Gromyko were asked to sit on a block of ice with his pants down," Khrushchev had allegedly boasted, "he would do so unquestioningly until ordered to leave it."[100] To his Western interlocutors, Gromyko was simply "Mr. Nyet." But by 1981, his penchant for anti-American polemics was less in evidence. He seemed genuinely interested in a superpower dialogue—and particularly in understanding what motivated the new Reagan administration's foreign policy.[101] Defense minister, and champion of the Soviet military-industrial complex, Ustinov also played a key role in Soviet foreign policy making. With a background in the rocket forces, he was an unabashed proponent of arms racing, and utterly convinced that arms control was an acute threat to Soviet national security.[102]

The Soviet foreign-policy community in fact welcomed Reagan's victory in the 1980 US election. There had been no love lost between Carter and Brezhnev: the former was unpredictable; inexplicably preoccupied with human rights; and responsible for reinvigorating the arms race, which undermined détente and weakened the US-Soviet relationship.[103] At the May 1980 meeting of the Warsaw Pact leadership, the assembled policy makers pilloried Carter's "dangerous [and] adventurist" foreign policy. "The ghosts of the Cold War are not haunting the gorges of Afghanistan or the plains of Iran," they proclaimed, "but the halls of the White House."[104] Visiting Ukraine in late 1980, Congressman Stephen Solarz was lectured at length on US misdeeds: "Responsibility for the deterioration of the international situation was borne by the leaders of NATO and, above all, by the United States, who were committed to upsetting the existing military balance in their favor, escalating the arms race, provocations against socialist and other independent countries, economic 'sanctions,' curtailing scientific and technical and cultural ties, [and] on an anti-Soviet basis, are converging with the Chinese leadership."[105]

In Moscow, foreign-policy makers lamented the anti-détente course Carter had taken. He "thought only of reelection," Anatoliĭ Adamishin of the Ministerstvo Inostrannykh Del concluded, "and plays along with Americans' moods: boorish, chauvinistic, and unjust."[106] Carter refused to accept the Soviet Union's status as a great power with global interests, reserving that prerogative (hypocritically) for the United States alone. Having met little US resistance to their increased activism in the Third World over the course of the 1970s, Soviet policy makers had expected the same passivity in Afghanistan, a country on their own border, making the hostile US response all the more unwelcome.[107]

The introduction of Presidential Directive 59, which defined how the United States would use its nuclear weapons, further fueled perceptions of the Carter administration's belligerence. The document directed that nuclear war strategy not be focused solely on Soviet missiles themselves but also on "the political control system"—that is, the Soviet leadership.[108] When the memorandum was leaked mere weeks after its approval in the summer of 1980, the international outcry was swift at Washington's stated intention to strike cities, not silos.[109] The Kremlin immediately sought to capitalize on this change in US nuclear targeting policy. The Carter administration's new strategy, *Izvestiia* declared, "constitutes acceptance of [the] Maoist doctrine of [the] inevitability of nuclear war."[110]

Meanwhile, Brezhnev and other senior Soviet policy makers made numerous overtures professing their commitment to détente. To West German foreign minister Hans-Dietrich Genscher, then visiting Moscow, Gromyko proposed a meeting of world leaders to deal with major international issues. It would be "a new beat of life for détente."[111] And acting on Soviet instructions, the Polish ambassador to the United States offered to host a conference on military détente in Warsaw.[112] Even as Moscow and its allies made such overtures, they insisted that the blame for the deteriorated state of superpower relations, and the commensurate increase in international tensions, rested solely on the United States—and Carter personally.[113]

Throughout the 1980 election, the Soviet press attacked the US electoral system, but official outlets avoided criticizing Reagan directly. (Although, as

24 CHAPTER 1

one French diplomat noted trenchantly, they certainly did not intend their repeated references to Reagan as a "former Hollywood actor" to be complimentary.)[114] Observers reported that Reagan wanted to pursue a "non-partisan" foreign policy, steady and without any major fluctuations.[115] "Reagan in the White House," as one Czechoslovak diplomat put it, "will be different from Reagan on the campaign trail."[116] Brezhnev's first comments on Reagan's election pointed to a sense of uncertainty and, perhaps, opportunity. He told his audience that he would wait to see what Reagan said once in office and that any constructive gesture on Reagan's part would find a receptive partner in Moscow.[117] Soviet policy makers minimized Reagan's aggressive, anti-Soviet campaign statements in their own public rhetoric, focusing instead on his "realism."[118] The Kremlin believed that human rights issues would be far less of a factor in US foreign policy, noting approvingly that Reagan had never made them a priority during the campaign.[119] On the whole, longtime Soviet ambassador to the United States Anatoliĭ Dobrynin concluded, Reagan would be much more interested in negotiation and compromise with the Soviet Union.[120] Brezhnev clearly preferred cooperation to confrontation, especially in light of his failing health.[121]

The reason for this was simple: the Soviet leadership shared the Reagan camp's dim outlook on the United States' position in the world. Through early outreach to the Reagan administration, Moscow hoped to shape US-Soviet relations "from a position of undisputed strength."[122] Some in Moscow initially doubted the new president's sincerity, wondering if this pessimism was a cynical line of attack to win the election. They came to realize that Reagan shared their assessment of the global balance of power, would most likely want to focus his attention at home, and, in order to create space for domestic initiatives, would be willing to make deals that favored the Soviet Union. Brezhnev and his advisers hoped to extract gains from the new administration that would cement Eastern strategic superiority and, in the long run, prevent the West from ever negotiating from a position of strength.[123]

Warsaw Pact policy makers, especially those in the Soviet Union, accurately perceived that foreign policy would not be at the forefront of Reagan's priorities once in office, yet they incorrectly surmised that he could be brought to the negotiating table early on. East German intelligence, in its initial analysis of the outcome of the 1980 election, explained that Reagan had won because of the sorry state of the domestic economy and that he would govern with that in mind.[124] Czechoslovak analysts in the Ministerstvo Zahraničních Věcí also predicted that he would focus on the consequences of the US economic downturn, the declining standard of living, and widespread public discontent.[125] Andropov concurred. In conversation with his East German counterpart, Ministerium für Staatssicherheit (or Stasi) chief Erich Mielke, he suggested that Reagan would scarcely elicit public approbation if he diverted billions of dollars away from social programs toward defense, and that he would not do so out of concern for his reelection prospects in 1984. Reagan's touted defense buildup, Andropov noted perceptively, served as much to deal with the stagnant US economy as to address the national security concerns of the United States.[126]

Viewed from Moscow, Reagan's election was far from alarming. In fact, Soviet policy makers hoped it would be what kept détente with the United States alive.[127] "Reagan, who knows nothing about foreign policy," Soviet foreign affairs specialist Georgiĭ Arbatov told a West German colleague, "might evolve into a statesman." Of course, Arbatov's definition of statesman was someone who would make deals advantageous to the Soviet Union.[128] Others noted with relish the significant distance between US and European approaches to East-West relations, and hoped the latter would stymie any of Reagan's more aggressive impulses.[129] Even if they were wrong, generally more pessimistic Czechoslovak analysts suggested that at least hard-line, right-wing policies would be predictable, unlike those of "the inscrutable, zig-zagging Carter."[130]

These generally optimistic conclusions were not mere fantasy on the part of Eastern observers, rose tinted though they may have been. On November 7, 1980, for example, Richard Nixon made a special trip to Washington to attend a party at the Soviet embassy in honor of the anniversary of the Bolshevik Revolution. Asking Dobrynin to transmit his message to Brezhnev, the former president stressed that Reagan was committed to negotiation and, despite his anti-communist views, was above all a "pragmatic-minded politician." Though it would likely take several years, Nixon expressed his confidence that the United States and the Soviet Union would eventually reestablish détente-like relations under President Reagan. In the meantime, the Kremlin should not read too much into any polemical speeches he may have to make for domestic political purposes; it should, Nixon encouraged, remain focused on the two superpowers' shared objective of improved relations. Nixon, Dobrynin concedes in his memoirs, exactly predicted the dynamics of US-Soviet relations in the 1980s.[131]

"The Soviet effort to woo Reagan," Canadian diplomat Robert Ford remarked, "has come sooner and more effusively than would normally be expected."[132] Moscow's overtures stemmed from a sense of urgency in the Kremlin. Emboldened by the perceived crisis of capitalism throughout the West, Soviet foreign-policy makers appreciated that these economic difficulties strengthened their hand, but they were not blind to their own domestic issues. Though

26 **CHAPTER 1**

they looked at the world at the beginning of the 1980s and concluded that they enjoyed a position of relative strength vis-à-vis the United States, Soviet policy makers were under no illusions that this was a permanent state of affairs. The trends on the horizon and the realities they confronted on a daily basis suggested that this advantage was far from secure. The time to act was now, when Soviet strength might enable the Kremlin to secure advantageous agreements with the incoming Reagan administration.

Soon after it was launched, the Afghanistan operation began to cause serious problems for Moscow. Marshal Nikolaĭ Ogarkov, chief of the General Staff, warned against the "reckless" intervention even as he signed the documents ordering tens of thousands of Soviet troops into Afghanistan.[133] Gen. Valentin Varennikov, who planned the invasion, was also an outspoken critic of the "unjustifiable" campaign.[134] To Adamishin, the invasion was an act of "weakness [and] despair" and a squandering of Moscow's moral authority in the world, those who made the decision were "assholes" unfit to govern.[135] The most famous opponent of the war was the dissident physicist and Nobel Peace Prize winner Andreĭ Sakharov. For his outspoken critique, Sakharov was exiled to Gor'kiĭ, a city closed to foreigners.[136] Public opposition was not restricted to those with direct access to power or the media; it was so widespread, in fact, that the politburo determined that casualties' gravestones not bear any indication of their having died in Afghanistan.[137]

Soviet leaders, including Brezhnev, bemoaned the high price they had to pay for the invasion in terms of their relations with the West and the Third World.[138] Not even a year later, Yugoslav officials conveyed the Kremlin's readiness to negotiate a face-saving exit with Washington.[139] Serious study of a potential exit strategy had already begun.[140] In public, however, they still defended the invasion as necessary to maintain stability on Soviet borders. As Vadim Zagladin, head of the Central Committee's International Department, put it to Graham Allison, the dean of Harvard University's John F. Kennedy School of Government during the latter's visit to Moscow, "you wouldn't let a hostile government come to power in Quebec or Mexico. . . . You shouldn't!"[141]

The Soviet Union was on the defensive closer to home. Summertime labor strikes at the Gdańsk shipyards in Poland grew into a national political crisis thanks to the influence of the Solidarność trade union and its charismatic leader Lech Wałęsa.[142] When those strikes shut down the Lublin rail yard—a key link between the Soviet Union and its garrisons in East Germany—the ruling Polska Zjednoczona Partia Robotnicza began to see the situation as more threatening than simple labor unrest.[143] In the short run, the Soviet Union observed the situation closely and worked to isolate Poland from the rest of the

Warsaw Pact in order to prevent the movement from spreading.[144] Western leaders, for their part, feared that events in Poland might result in a Soviet-led Warsaw Pact invasion akin to that of Czechoslovakia in 1968.[145] Indeed, Moscow had begun sketching out plans for such an operation.[146] Brezhnev was no less concerned, fearing that the West would seize the opportunity to stage its own intervention in Poland and oust its communist rulers.[147]

It was not only the Poles who had grown restive. After the signing of the Helsinki Final Act in the summer of 1975, in which the Soviet Union and its Eastern bloc allies had committed themselves to guaranteeing freedom of expression and consciousness, Eastern European and Soviet citizens increasingly held their governments to account. In Czechoslovakia, for example, the Charta 77 movement grew out of the commitments made at Helsinki, aggravated by the arrest of members of the psychedelic rock band Plastic People of the Universe. Its 1,065 signatories demanded the free enjoyment of the civil liberties of which they had had a brief glimpse in the fateful spring and summer of 1968.[148]

Other Warsaw Pact member states grew increasingly—and, from Moscow's perspective, unwelcomely—independent. The Romanian regime of Nicolae Ceaușescu continued to chart its own course in foreign policy, forging economic links with Western countries and the European Community, as it had since Nikita Khrushchev denounced Stalinism—an unforgivable trespass for an avowed Stalinist like Ceaușescu. Bucharest consistently resisted Brezhnev's efforts to rein it in.[149] Many in the Kremlin suspected that other Eastern European leaders were more envious than disapproving of the Romanians' independence.[150] East Germany under Erich Honecker similarly expanded its engagement with the rest of the world, including state visits to Austria and Japan to drum up bilateral trade.[151] The most engagement Moscow's Warsaw Pact allies had with the West came in the form of loans from Western banks. Eastern European leaders had attempted to solve their problems in economic growth through massive capital investment, focusing on the heavy industry sector, which was of dubious economic viability by the 1970s. Over the course of the decade, an increasing amount of capital was required to produce the same amount of growth, and capital was something the Eastern Europeans had only in very limited quantities. As their coffers ran dry, Moscow's allies turned to the West, borrowing some $50 billion.[152]

Brezhnev enumerated these problems to Honecker at one of their regular meetings at the general secretary's Crimean vacation home: inability to produce and incorporate advanced technology, inability to make market incentives for workers and producers work, poor management, and chronic waste

28   **CHAPTER 1**

of precious, exportable raw materials.[153] Brezhnev spared Honecker an explanation of East Berlin's own culpability, along with that of other Eastern European leaders. The cost to Moscow of assisting the Warsaw Pact countries had increased from $1.7 billion in 1971 to $23 billion by 1980, hard currency that the Soviet Union desperately needed in order to address its own problems.[154] The closest Honecker and his associates could come to a solution to this shortfall was the kidnapping of West Germans on an industrial scale for ransom.[155]

Even those events that looked to the West like Soviet victories were not unequivocally so when viewed from the Kremlin. Margaret Thatcher was not wrong when she quipped that "for the Soviet Union, [nuclear] armaments were a virility symbol."[156] That metaphor certainly held true regarding the single-minded decision-making process that led to the Kremlin's decision to deploy the SS-20s to Europe beginning in 1976, with no consideration of the Western response.[157] The Soviet military-industrial complex had a momentum all its own, and once weapons like the SS-20 were produced, it was virtually impossible to stop them from being fielded.[158] As Mikhail Gorbachev recounted in his memoirs, "it was an unforgivable misadventure . . . [and] supremely naïve."[159] Serious mistakes had been made in foreign policy in the Soviet Union, no matter what the US perspective on the balance of power might have been. Georgiï Kornienko, the deputy foreign minister, later summed up the mood in Soviet foreign-policy circles at the beginning of the 1980s succinctly: "Everybody was unhappy."[160]

Not that those who worked on domestic policy were in much better spirits. But there was a glimmer of hope: in Moscow, policy makers concluded that capitalism was in crisis—if not in its death throes—based on all the same indicators assessed by the incoming Reagan administration.[161] Nevertheless, there was scant cause for optimism regarding the Soviet economy. The quality of domestic industrial goods was so poor that Soviet citizens often chose to go without. Food production was simply inadequate, despite a nearly $8 billion state subsidy in 1980. Dogged by a string of grain-harvest failures, food output did not grow. The Kremlin did not dare raise food prices to incentivize production, so long lines for basic sustenance became a fixture of everyday life. In some provincial cities, the beginning of the 1980s heralded the reintroduction of food rationing.[162] Industrialization during the 1930s and the ravages of World War II had led to a full-blown ecological crisis and almost entirely depleted the western part of the country of raw materials, which had to be transported from the less-developed eastern regions. Compared to the United States, the figures were especially concerning: the Soviet Union produced eight times as much iron ore but only twice as much steel, took a decade to build a factory that in the United States took only two years, and produced sixteen times more grain harvesters yet still had to import US grain.[163]

This shockingly low—and still declining—productivity stemmed from wholesale mismanagement throughout the economy and, crucially, the lack of any real incentives for improving the situation within the Soviet system.[164] The massive top-down state apparatus had worked for turning the agrarian economy of Tsarist Russia into the industrialized Soviet Union, but Soviet economists were now beginning to acknowledge that the system held back progress, stymied innovation, was wasteful, and produced workers who were lazy and prone to corruption.[165] To make matters worse, the workforce was shrinking apace.[166] These domestic trends had foreign-policy implications. The military saw a clear link between the economic health of the Soviet Union and its military effectiveness. A robust and dynamic economy was imperative to counter the United States and NATO.[167] Within the Kremlin, leaders feared that the West would exploit rising economic challenges to undermine the party's control.[168]

The bright spot in the Soviet economy had long been its oil exports. The oil-price hikes of the 1970s, which contributed much to the sense of pessimism in the United States, were a boon for the Kremlin. OPEC did Moscow no small favor by driving up the price of oil some 1000 percent over the course of the decade. Soviet exports generated yet higher revenues, which made it possible to import more food and technology from the West. However, this did not translate to economic growth, which had slowed to roughly 1.5 percent a year on average—a far cry from the official figure, quoted at the beginning of the 1980s, of 5 percent.[169] According to the CIA's economists, the situation would only get worse as Soviet oil production peaked by the beginning of the 1980s. Even the vast Soviet oil fields west of the Urals would no longer meet demand, nor the 640-million-ton target of the Tenth Five-Year Plan, meaning that Moscow would have to turn to regions to the east, which were vastly more difficult and costly to access and drill. As it turned out, those new fields would not come on line fast enough. The results for the Soviet Union would be painful, with an economy dependent on oil exports for 40 percent of total hard-currency earnings, as they would be for Eastern European countries who depended on Moscow for the provision of the vast majority of their oil requirements at a significant discount.[170]

The Kremlin faced a host of real problems, even if they were only partially acknowledged. But at the beginning of 1981, Soviet policy makers were more focused on sources of strength as they prepared for the Twenty-Sixth Party

Congress in February. A quinquennial gathering of select party members in the Soviet Union as well as delegations from foreign communist parties, the congress was a forum for touting Soviet achievements and laying out Moscow's policy course for the coming half decade. Soviet experts in Washington expected little. They saw Brezhnev's age and infirmity as well as the ossified, change-resistant Soviet bureaucratic system and concluded that nothing new would come of it.[171] Indeed, Soviet foreign-policy makers knew that they were stuck between a rock and a hard place, with little room and scant means to innovate. As one of them put it, it was a country with "their tail stuck in Afghanistan, their nose [stuck] in Poland, and in the middle, an economic mess."[172]

Looking outward, the Kremlin's approach to the congress nevertheless reflected the general Soviet perception of strategic superiority over the United States at the time of Reagan's election.[173] The Reagan administration would simply have to "accept the new realities of the world"—that the West had fallen behind.[174] Andropov echoed this sentiment to Brezhnev, insisting that a new peace offensive would stabilize the international situation and improve the Soviet Union's image at the expense of the United States.[175] They would, as one Canadian diplomat put it, "play the waiting game," hoping to bring a relatively weak United States to the bargaining table.[176]

Pravda's front page editorial on the eve of the congress reaffirmed the Soviet desire for "normalization [and] improvement" in superpower relations.[177] Brezhnev's speech to the congress followed suit: "The current state of relations between the Soviet Union and the United States and the severity of the international problems to be solved dictate, in our view, the need to conduct dialogue at all levels, and indeed an active dialogue. . . . Experience shows that the decisive moment here are meetings at the highest level."[178] This call for a summit so soon after Reagan's inauguration was, to US observers, unexpectedly conciliatory—and proactive.[179] The general secretary relished the prestige summitry conferred on him and the Soviet Union, but he also genuinely sought to make a more peaceful world, albeit on terms favorable to his own country.[180]

"The struggle for détente remains the cornerstone of Soviet foreign policy," Zagladin declared in summation.[181] Soviet officials regularly referred to Brezhnev's speech as being the gist of Moscow's foreign policy for the 1980s.[182] As one Soviet diplomat put it, the speech could be summarized as "everything is negotiable."[183] Friendly organizations around the world received instructions to pressure their governments to push Reagan to meet with Brezhnev.[184] The optimistic Kremlin even instructed its allies to prepare for an imminent US-Soviet summit.[185] Looking ahead, Soviet policy makers hoped to negotiate with their Cold War adversary from a position of strength, and the sooner the better, as that gap was likely to close.[186]

Reagan's first inaugural address was not the paean to the United States that such speeches usually are. He acknowledged the "economic affliction of great proportions . . . [which] threatens to shatter the lives of millions" and pledged to begin taking action on that day to improve it and to make a "new beginning." He offered Washington's support to "those neighbors and allies who share our freedom. . . . Enemies of freedom," however, would find the United States committed to peace, though "reluctance for conflict should not be misjudged as a failure of will."[187]

Once in the White House, and with the entire machinery and sources of intelligence of the US government at its disposal, the Reagan administration's perceptions of US weakness only intensified. At the first meeting of the administration's National Security Council, policy makers discussed the dangers of expanding Soviet influence throughout the world, from Poland to the Caribbean.[188] The Reagan administration believed that in the eyes of the Kremlin, "We no doubt looked to be staggering towards the final decline and fall they had been predicting."[189]

Was Reagan propagating a myth of US weakness as a result of the Carter administration's poor leadership? After all, Reagan would not have been the first presidential candidate to cynically capitalize on an image of US weakness (accurate or otherwise) to undermine an opponent. John F. Kennedy, for example, deployed such attacks against Vice President Richard Nixon during the 1960 campaign. Most famously, he accused the Dwight D. Eisenhower administration of allowing a dangerous "missile gap" with the Soviet Union to develop, though on entering the White House, he acknowledged that it had been no more than a "myth."[190] Indeed, US policy makers understood the Soviet Union's grave difficulties; during the 1980–1981 transition period, the CIA had summed up the Soviet economic situation for Reagan trenchantly: "These guys are in a lot of trouble."[191] But Reagan saw the US economy in strikingly similar terms when he took office. For many in the United States, he believed that "life was as bleak as it was for Americans caught up in the economic upheavals of the Great Depression." US economic and military power would need to be rebuilt in order to fight the Cold War. Until its capabilities were reestablished, the fortieth president believed, the United States was vulnerable.[192]

Reagan's sense of pessimism did not preclude engaging the Soviet Union from the outset. Dialogue was not incompatible with an overall more competitive policy on East-West and US-Soviet relations.[193] Brezhnev made known

32   **CHAPTER 1**

his openness to talks with the new Reagan administration and his hopes for a positive response.[194] In Bonn, West German diplomats warned against making the mistake of conflating the advanced age of the Kremlin leadership under Brezhnev with an inability to lead the country and make change, especially in foreign policy.[195] Many in the White House labored under just such a misapprehension, but Reagan himself needed no such admonition. Once in office, along with taking steps to rebuild US strength, the president began steering policy, albeit quietly at first, toward engagement with the Soviet Union.

Chapter 2

Arm to Parley
Reagan Rebuilds and Reaches Out

Ronald Reagan walked into the Washington Hilton without relish on March 30, 1981. The members of the Building and Construction Trades Department of the AFL-CIO mega-union were not exactly a natural constituency for him. The president's message that he too knew the meaning of hard work and the importance of trade unions fell on skeptical ears, coming as it did from someone with a background in, as Reagan himself acknowledged, "grease paint and make-believe." Some 660,000 construction workers were out of work in the United States at the time Reagan took office, victims of the economic turmoil of the 1970s. They—and their representatives, whom Reagan would be addressing—wanted federal funding for large-scale infrastructure projects, which would create jobs. Reagan instead preached the importance of "initiative" and "the freedom and dignity of the worker" as well as the need to cut $46.2 billion from the federal budget.[1] The speech "was not riotously received."[2]

As he exited the hotel, only sixty-nine days after his inauguration, John Hinckley Jr. attempted to assassinate the president in a bizarre bid for the affections of actress Jodie Foster. Hinckley failed (on both counts). One of his bullets struck the White House press secretary James Brady in the head, a wound that he miraculously survived; two others struck a Secret Service agent and a Washington, D.C., police officer; and one struck the armored presidential limousine and ricocheted into the president, striking him just below the

34   **CHAPTER 2**

left armpit. "Honey, I forgot to duck," he quipped through his oxygen mask to his wife, Nancy, later that day from his bed at George Washington University Hospital.[3]

This brush with mortality for the sixty-nine-year-old—and the time spent alone with his thoughts convalescing in the hospital—spurred Reagan into acting on his long-standing belief that he had to engage the Soviet leadership in order to reduce Cold War tensions.[4] From his hospital bed, Reagan penned a personal letter to Leonid Brezhnev. He opened by recounting their first meeting in June 1973. Reagan was then governor of California, and Brezhnev was President Richard Nixon's houseguest. Invoking the superpower summits of the past, Reagan asked, "Is it possible that we have permitted ideology, political and economic philosophies, and governmental politics to keep us from considering the very real, everyday problems of our peoples?" In that spirit, Reagan announced his decision to cancel the grain embargo on the Soviet Union, imposed in the aftermath of the invasion of Afghanistan, in hopes of "creating the circumstances which will lead to . . . meaningful and constructive dialogue."[5]

The attempt on his life did not transform Reagan or his views on US-Soviet competition, but it did give him a sense of urgency about putting both aspects of his grand strategy toward the Soviet Union into action. "Perhaps having come so close to death made me feel I should do whatever I could in the years God had given me to reduce the threat of nuclear war," Reagan reflected. "Perhaps there was a reason I had been spared."[6]

The president hoped this outreach would inaugurate a new phase of East-West dialogue, and he took steps to make it so. But the Reagan administration's fundamental sense of US weakness persisted, making it difficult for the president to reach out to the Soviet Union—especially in public. Because of this, Paul Nitze opined, "the relationship between the [United States] and the Soviet Union [was] more dangerous than at any prior time"—strong words from a man who had been involved in US foreign policy since the outbreak of the Cold War.[7] Much of the administration's initial engagement with the Soviet Union, however, remained quiet, leaving observers to speculate (and worry) that the superpowers were not talking. Reagan's massive investments in rebuilding US military might did little to assuage these concerns. And the negotiations that did take place between Moscow and Washington, to many, seemed to be more a public relations exercise than good faith efforts.[8] Both competitive and cooperative impulses shaped US grand strategy during the early Reagan years. "Much was made by the administration [of] the unclear or conflicting signals given to Moscow by the Carter administration," Sir Nicholas Henderson, the British ambassador to Washington, opined, "but I cannot believe that the Soviet authorities can have any very clear idea of what the Reaganauts are up to."[9] Understanding that grand strategy requires untangling these seemingly contradictory threads.

In the summer of 1981, Tyrus Cobb of the National Security Council explained to Vadim Zagladin that nearly a year since Reagan's inauguration, no comprehensive US foreign policy had been formulated. The key players could not reach agreement. The president himself remained aloof, neither resolving the open fighting within his White House nor giving his advisers meaningful insight into his own thinking. For the time being, Reagan preferred to focus his efforts and political capital on domestic and economic issues.[10] Eastern policy makers had given the incoming president's foreign policy the benefit of the doubt, expecting that US economic woes would be a significant constraint.[11] But they quickly came to realize that for the Reagan White House, implementing concrete measures to improve the US military's position vis-à-vis the Soviet Union was a prerequisite for improving East-West relations.[12] This had a further, ideological dimension: Reagan would be just as susceptible as his predecessors to the influence of the military-industrial complex, with its constant pressure for more military spending and its habitual inflation of the Soviet threat for the purposes of securing more resources.[13]

As soon as the Reagan administration's defense-policy plans became public, the condemnation flowed freely from the East.[14] Clearly, one Czechoslovak diplomat wrote, "the primitive thesis of the imminent demise of communism" determined US foreign policy.[15] Washington, Brezhnev remarked dryly, now wished to impose its own "code of conduct on the whole world."[16] Gromyko, who missed no opportunity to condemn US militarism, denounced US foreign policy—and Reagan's desire to change the balance of power in the world in Washington's favor—as the root of all global problems and the source of the greatest danger: nuclear war.[17] To Eastern policy makers, Reagan was only continuing a pattern of aggressive behavior.[18] He did not start a new arms race but rather sustained the preexisting one.[19] And naturally, Gromyko maintained, anything the Soviet Union did in that field was purely in response to US aggression. The predictions of Kremlin officials that Reagan would be inclined toward a policy of détente looked to be little more than wishful thinking.[20]

John Vessey, chair of the Joint Chiefs of Staff from 1982 to 1985, summed up the Reagan administration's plan for defense expenditures succinctly and colorfully to an audience of US troops stationed in Hawaii: "I hear a lot of talk in the newspapers which says we don't have a strategy. Well, I want to tell you that's a load of baloney. We do have a strategy. It's a very sensible strategy.

36 **CHAPTER 2**

Our strategy is one of preventing war by making it self-evident to our enemies that they're going to get their clocks cleaned if they start one."[21] In the early 1980s, the White House did not see that it was "self-evident" that the United States could deliver on this threat. National Security Decision Directive 32, for example—the administration's first internal statement of national security strategy—took as a given the "loss of US strategic superiority" to the Soviet Union and warned of "the overwhelming growth of Soviet conventional force capabilities." The document had plenty of tough talk about diminishing Soviet influence, discouraging Soviet adventurism, and limiting Soviet military capabilities, yet these remained aspirations, as US policy makers acutely felt their weaknesses.[22] They also communicated their view of the East-West military balance to the public. *Soviet Military Power*, a 1981 Department of Defense publication, told a bleak story—for the United States—of overwhelming Soviet nuclear and conventional power on land, at sea, and in the air. Its purpose? "Assisting the projection of Soviet power abroad and the spreading and solidifying of the Soviet Union's political, economic, and military influence around the world. This is the challenge we face."[23]

It fell to Caspar Weinberger as secretary of defense to remedy this and put Reagan's concept of peace through strength into action. The Pentagon had a head start thanks to the Carter administration: whatever the Reagan administration claimed, defense spending had already increased by 10 percent in real terms, funding a major military modernization program, with particular focus on the nuclear triad.[24] Trident D-5–armed submarines underwent sea trials in preparation for the wider deployment of these hard target–penetrating weapons. The development of a new US ground-based intercontinental ballistic missile—the smaller, more accurate MX—progressed. Newly deployed air-launched cruise missiles, to be launched from B-52 strategic bombers, could reliably penetrate Soviet air defenses.[25] Still, the incoming Reagan administration judged Carter's requested defense budget to be inadequate and asked Congress for an additional $32.6 billion. These funds would help modernize the US nuclear arsenal, improve military pay and benefits to deal with the outflow of experienced leaders, and launch new procurement programs. Congress gave Reagan virtually everything he asked for. During his first five years in office, they granted 90 percent of the administration's defense spending requests.[26]

These requests did not come at a time of plenty. Barely a month after his inauguration, Reagan took to television to give the public "a report on the state of our nation's economy." It was far from uplifting. "I regret to say that we're in the worst economic mess since the Great Depression," he told viewers. The root of the problem remained inflation, which, "like radioactivity, was cumulative and . . . out of control."[27] In coming up with a solution to the problem, Reagan found a partner in Paul Volcker, the chair of the Federal Reserve. "I don't kiss men, but I was tempted," Volcker recalled of his first meeting with Reagan.[28] A great many were less enamored as the so-called Reagan Recession took hold and the government's prescription seemed to be more economic pain. Not long after his first television address, Reagan announced his four-part economic plan. Massive tax cuts would reduce inflation by increasing production of goods and services and, with it, salaries. Deregulation would unshackle the US economy. Slowing the growth of the money supply—technically Volcker's domain, not the president's—would curb inflation as well. And $49.1 billion in cuts to federal government spending would restore US financial health. The Pentagon was the outlier; it needed an injection of cash to catch up with and overtake the Soviet Union. "To allow this imbalance to continue," Reagan insisted, "is a threat to our national security."[29]

The defense buildup focused primarily on enhancing US nuclear forces, which Reagan had insisted were dangerously vulnerable to a Soviet first strike.[30] The United States needed new, more advanced systems. Reagan's Pentagon embraced wholeheartedly the then-in-development MX ICBM (later dubbed the Peacekeeper), as opposed to the Minuteman missiles, the silos of which dotted the heartland. By the time of Reagan's inauguration, the Minuteman had become extremely unpopular. Those living near Minuteman bases believed—not without reason—that the missiles "practically invited a Soviet attack" on their homes.[31] MX missiles, on the other hand, could be based in a "racetrack" configuration: a strategic shell game involving the moving of ICBMs between hardened bunkers on a purpose-built road network. (Such a vast, expensive basing system made little sense as long as preexisting arms control agreements compelled the United States to make the location of all shelters known.) Reagan and his team entertained an array of ideas: placing MX missiles on airborne cargo aircraft, in silos so close to one another that incoming Soviet ICBMs would do more damage to one another than to their targets, at the bottom of pools of colored water through which Soviet reconnaissance satellites could not see, and "on old ships that could be moved around."[32]

These ideas were fanciful to say the least. Yet the overall program of modernizing the US nuclear arsenal caused grave concern throughout the Warsaw Pact.[33] In the pages of the Soviet military's top-secret internal publication, *Voennaia mysl'*, readers were warned of the increased lethality of—and pernicious intentions behind—the technologically more sophisticated US nuclear arsenal of the future. Modernization was a threat to Moscow and to the world.[34] Everything one needed to know about Washington's approach to nuclear weapons, the Kremlin maintained, could be seen in images of Hiroshima

38   CHAPTER 2

and Nagasaki devastated by US atomic bombs and Washington's ensuing "atomic blackmail" of the Soviet Union.[35]

The arms buildup also benefited US allies, even if it occasionally entailed embarrassing public admonishments by Washington to increase their defense expenditures. The United Kingdom, for example, certainly had no complaints when the Reagan administration offered extensive financial assistance to enable London to purchase new Trident D-5 missiles for the Royal Navy's nuclear submarines.[36] And when Margaret Thatcher took Britain to war over the Falkland Islands, claimed also by Argentina, Reagan backed the military expedition to the southern Atlantic in word and deed, though that support was less forthcoming and fulsome than some in Whitehall might have liked.[37] The White House characterized the expanded US military aid to its NATO allies as enabling the West to fend off a future Soviet attack in Europe or elsewhere, but French analysts suspected the Reagan administration of simply making the strategy fit the enormous defense budget Republicans clearly relished.[38]

Moscow did not see threats coming only from the West. Since the late 1950s, it looked warily to the east and the PRC, which was increasingly unwilling to accept the role of junior partner in the Sino-Soviet alliance. Though Mao Zedong couched his growing independence in the vague language of ideology and revolution, the Sino-Soviet split was above all a product of Beijing's rejection of a perpetual subordination to Moscow—and Mao's "increasing megalomania."[39] By the time Reagan took office, this was still a concern for Soviet foreign-policy makers.[40] While many predicted that Reagan would undo past progress in the US relationship with Beijing, just the opposite proved true.[41] During the campaign, Reagan sent George H. W. Bush to Beijing to cultivate ties with Chinese leaders. Reagan publicly pledged to "develop and strengthen" relations with the PRC.[42] The Kremlin made its displeasure known.[43] To them, aggressive hostility toward Moscow would likely transcend the very real ideological differences between Washington and Beijing.[44] The White House recognized that this fear could be used as leverage—but could also backfire if Moscow felt itself backed into a corner and compelled to lash out.[45] The "complex and contradictory" evolution of relations between Washington and Beijing preoccupied the Kremlin throughout Reagan's presidency.[46] The "partnership between [US] imperialism and Pekingese hegemonism," the Soviet military summed up, was a threat to all. Somehow, the two parties could overcome the contradictions between US capitalism and "Chinese social-chauvinism."[47] For all his sincere anti-communism, Reagan's willingness to improve relations with Beijing demonstrated a degree of ideological flexibility. He did stress to others, however, that as far as communism was concerned, he considered the Soviet leadership to be true believers, whereas Beijing paid lip service to the ideology.[48]

When the Warsaw Pact defense ministers met in Moscow in December 1981—their first gathering since Reagan's inauguration—pessimism prevailed.[49] "The imperialist states, led by the United States," the meeting concluded, "refuse to accept the realities of the contemporary world—the strengthening of socialism."[50] Preparations would have to be made to confront and counterbalance an even stronger and more aggressive NATO by the mid-1980s, with more advanced nuclear weapons stationed in Europe and strengthened conventional forces.[51] The fact that such massive outlays were taking place during a time of economic difficulty in the West further troubled Warsaw Pact observers.[52] (Policy makers in East Germany managed to find a glimmer of hope: "boundless increases" in military budgets left little for social programs, which, they predicted, would result in more support for socialist parties throughout the West.)[53] Reagan's defense buildup imperiled the basic Soviet strategy of bringing the United States to the bargaining table as quickly as possible while enjoying a preponderance of power.[54] Instead of negotiation, they feared, the United States sought to "create the preconditions for the solution of international problems by force."[55] Gromyko, for his part, made no secret in Warsaw Pact circles that he hoped the second year of the Reagan administration would be "calmer" than the first and that US-Soviet and East-West relations could be improved.[56]

Ideological warfare also occupied a newly important place under Reagan, who attacked the Soviet Union and its allies with apparent relish in public.[57] Initially, observers dismissed this as a continuation of Carter's anti-Soviet policies.[58] With time, however, they determined that Reagan's "vulgar speeches" signified something new.[59] In his first press conference as president, Reagan declared that the Soviet leaders "reserve unto themselves the right to commit any crime, to lie, to cheat," insisting that the two superpowers "operate on a different set of standards" morally.[60] Addressing the British parliament on June 8, 1982, after stressing the importance of talks between East and West, Reagan zeroed in on "the decay of the Soviet experiment. . . . Today on the NATO line, our military forces face east to prevent a possible invasion. On the other side of the line, the Soviet forces also face east to prevent their people from leaving." Meanwhile, he pledged, the United States would continue to lead "the march of freedom and democracy which will leave Marxism-Leninism on the ash-heap of history."[61]

Some US allies lauded Reagan's strong statement; it had been, in Thatcher's words, a "triumph," which led to "a new feeling here that we could not afford to take freedom for granted."[62] To Washington, this approach was inseparable from diplomatic engagement with the Soviet Union. The NSC suggested capitalizing on the extent to which the June 8 speech had rattled the

CHAPTER 2

politburo with a follow-up, which would make it clear how the Soviet leadership could elicit a more sympathetic tone from Washington.[63] Thatcher agreed with Reagan that "there could be no objections to dialogue conducted from a position of strength."[64]

After just a year with Reagan in office, US policy makers were congratulating themselves for finally putting the Soviet Union on the defensive, both militarily and ideologically.[65] To Reagan, "sharp, shrill" rhetoric regarding the Soviet Union was a necessary precursor to negotiation: the US public needed a "realistic understanding" of those with whom their president would be dealing in the years to come.[66] For the time being, the British ambassador to Moscow, Sir Curtis Keeble, joked with Gromyko that East-West relations deserved a grade of "one, the lowest given to Soviet schoolboys."[67]

Ending the grain embargo, the first signal to the Soviet Union of the White House's desire to negotiate, cost little.[68] At the beginning of the twentieth century, the Russian Empire had been the world's largest exporter of grain; eighty years later, the Soviet Union was the world's largest importer, accounting for 15 percent of global market demand.[69] In the United States, support for the embargo had been low from the outset. The public focused on its negative impact on farmers at home, rather than on the Soviet Union. US allies refused to participate and, indeed, made up some of the shortfall. Food shortages resulting from the grain embargo or, as was more often than not the case, poor domestic management and infrastructure in the Soviet Union galvanized the Soviet population against the United States. The Carter administration did not plan to continue it for a second year.[70] To the incoming Reagan administration, it had been a complete failure. "As such," NSC staffer Douglas Feith quipped, "it symbolized the previous administration's approach to dealing with the Kremlin."[71] But Reagan was not yet ready to take his quiet diplomacy public. When Haig informed Peter Carrington, his British counterpart, of the decision, for example, he couched it in purely economic terms. The embargo placed an unfair burden on US farmers and undermined the White House's main effort: to strengthen the economy.[72]

Western policy makers grew increasingly worried that Reagan's preoccupation with building US strength meant he would not talk to the Kremlin.[73] To maintain public support for NATO, US allies needed their voters to see the president as "more like a friendly uncle than a nuclear cowboy."[74] They also feared what the consequences for the rest of the world might be if the United States and the Soviet Union kept talking past, rather than to, each other. All could take some solace in the meeting between Haig and Dobrynin on July 2, 1981, which inaugurated overt US-Soviet dialogue. For Haig and Reagan, it was a "benchmark in determining whether there was to be any future to the US-Soviet relationship."[75] Dobrynin deemed it the most important meeting since his arrival in Washington some twenty years earlier.[76] Haig downplayed the meeting in his memoirs as "a useful exchange."[77] Indeed, for US diplomatic strategy, Dobrynin was a stepping-stone. The summer meeting first and foremost laid the groundwork for the secretary of state to meet his Soviet counterpart, Gromyko, while the latter attended the UN General Assembly in New York that fall.[78]

Neither Haig nor Reagan expected immediate major breakthroughs. "The process of serious dialogue," Haig wrote to Reagan on the eve of his meeting with the Soviet foreign minister, "can produce an altogether more solid and durable basis for conducting business and living together than the two superpowers have ever had before."[79] Reagan stressed in a letter to Brezhnev that he hoped to improve the US-Soviet relationship and renew engagement between the two countries.[80] But face to face, the two foreign policy chiefs mostly talked past each other. In their first conversation, on September 23, both agreed on the need for change but continued to insist that the other party was responsible for the downturn in relations. Promisingly, Gromyko committed to developing relations "on a realistic basis, that is, good-neighborly, normal, and businesslike," taking into account each other's security interests. Haig agreed that "[their] relationship had to be a superpower relationship," which recognized that both states had interests and influence that extended beyond their borders.[81]

Five days later, on September 28, Gromyko focused on Moscow's frustration with Reagan's insistence on superiority—frustration compounded, no doubt, by Moscow's inability to bring him to the negotiating table first. Reagan's willingness to negotiate, Gromyko charged, was predicated on the Kremlin effectively renouncing its right to have a foreign policy. Washington claimed such a breadth of interests that all Soviet engagement overseas constituted a threat. The two could agree on one thing: how pleased they were that their first meeting had caught the world's attention.[82]

After his first meeting with Gromyko, Haig dined with three of his NATO counterparts: Carrington, Claude Cheysson of France, and Hans-Dietrich Genscher of West Germany. Haig played it coy. His conversation with Gromyko had been "frank and businesslike." Clearly, a Soviet leadership facing problems in Afghanistan, Poland, and at home would have much to gain by reducing tensions with the United States. But the main theme of the four foreign ministers' conversation was uncertainty about the Soviet Union's intentions as well as its capabilities. The secretary of state emphasized at length that US-Soviet policy was not determined by the president alone, expounding characteristically on his own importance to the process. When Carrington suggested that the United States had caught Gromyko "on the wrong foot" with Reagan's conciliatory

42   CHAPTER 2

letter to Brezhnev, Haig was unimpressed by the suggestion that anything but his personal diplomatic skill was responsible for Gromyko's congeniality.[83]

In Washington, policy makers viewed the talks with cautious optimism, hoping that they would lead to a "quiet, businesslike, and . . . respectful dialogue" between the superpowers.[84] The Kremlin concurred; diplomat Sergeĭ Tarasenko told his French counterparts that although Gromyko did not enter the talks with high hopes, Moscow found the meetings encouraging and looked forward to more.[85] The British, who had feared that the Reagan administration would lose the initiative in dealing with the Soviet Union, now proposed to seize it themselves by hosting Gromyko in London for similar talks—which they anticipated would attract similar international attention. Overt diplomacy had its benefits.[86]

The Reagan White House rebuffed Moscow's calls for a summit from the outset; the United States simply had not accrued sufficient strength to be sure of a positive outcome.[87] Private engagement, however, was another matter entirely. In a 1989 interview, Reagan's second secretary of state, George Shultz, admitted that "there were some private channels" of high-level communication between the superpowers in the early 1980s.[88] French diplomats complained that their US interlocutors would tell them only that the two superpowers had talked, but never where or when.[89] Even Dobrynin—himself so often a conduit in the past—claims to have been unaware of any back channels.[90]

When Carter's last ambassador to the Soviet Union took his leave of Gromyko, the Soviet foreign minister stressed the Kremlin's continued desire for "peaceful coexistence."[91] When his Reagan-appointed replacement, Arthur Hartman, arrived in Moscow, he told a gathering of Western diplomats how struck he had been by the desire on the part of the Soviets to talk. "Behind the official language, harsh regarding the United States, in private he noticed a different type of language."[92] Hartman made it clear to his Soviet interlocutors that the Reagan administration wanted constructive relations and expanded contacts with the Soviet Union. After all, he "came to Moscow to develop relations, not to freeze them."[93] When Richard Nixon visited Czechoslovakia, the former president impressed those he met in Prague with his insistences that despite Reagan's anti-communist rhetoric, the president wanted to be a "peace-maker, not a peace-breaker."[94] But the greatest progress was made through less obvious channels; the continued sense in the White House that US military and economic strength needed to recover made these low-visibility avenues much more attractive.[95]

Arthur Burns, Reagan's first ambassador to West Germany, kept open an important back channel to the Kremlin throughout his time in Bonn.[96] An economist by training, Burns's prior government service had been exclusively in that realm: chair of the Council of Economic Advisers from 1953 to 1956 and chair of the Federal Reserve from 1970 to 1978. In terms of foreign policy, he made no secret of his belief that the United States needed to engage the Soviet Union.[97] In his first letter to Reagan from Bonn, he advised that Washington needed to seize the initiative and cautioned against belligerent, anti-Soviet statements.[98] According to Burns, "The logic of the [international] situation clearly requires that [the United States] work with the Soviet Union to establish a more harmonious relationship." And the new ambassador had a mandate from Reagan to do just that.[99]

From the embassy in Bonn, Burns was well placed to start a back-channel dialogue with Moscow on behalf of a Reagan administration not yet fully prepared to engage overtly. Under the terms of the four-power settlement on Berlin, the US ambassador to West Germany and the Soviet ambassador to East Germany met on occasion to discuss the city's peculiar situation, focusing primarily on air and land traffic corridors.[100] The Soviet memoranda of conversations between Burns and his Soviet counterpart, the similarly well-connected Petr Abrasimov, all begin with a statement that the two had met under those auspices.[101] But Burns's briefings for the meetings make it clear that he had no intention of discussing issues regarding the administration of Berlin.[102] And in conversation, the US ambassador constantly stressed that he spoke not only for the White House but for Reagan in particular, with whom he was in regular communication.[103] Unlike Haig's meetings with Dobrynin and Gromyko, these encounters in Berlin attracted no attention.

At their first meeting, Burns announced to an enthusiastic Abrasimov that a "new team" had taken charge of US foreign policy: the Reagan White House hoped to turn over a new leaf and move away from the distrust that had characterized the Carter years. Burns had been sent by Reagan as ambassador explicitly to work toward solving major problems in US-Soviet relations. Abrasimov affirmed that he looked forward to doing so.[104] Their second and third meetings focused on the prospects for arms control, to which both ambassadors stressed that their superiors were committed. Even when the two disagreed, they emphasized the need to find diplomatic solutions. Abrasimov would often pivot, pressing Burns for information about whether Reagan would be willing to visit the Soviet Union for a summit.[105] For example, echoing the conclusions of the December 1981 Warsaw Pact defense ministers' meeting, Abrasimov decried Washington's insistence on negotiating only from a position of strength and inflating the Soviet threat. "No responsible person," Burns countered, "seriously thought that the Soviet Union would unleash global war," yet Soviet actions around the world were cause for grave concern

44   CHAPTER 2

in Washington. Perhaps after the 1984 election, he hinted, Reagan would be in a position to openly expand contact and improve relations in the way both the president and the Kremlin hoped.[106]

After Vyacheslav Kochemasov replaced Abrasimov, Burns and his advisers had good reason to remain optimistic about this unique point of US-Soviet contact. The new Soviet ambassador to East Germany's courtesy call on the British ambassador wound up lasting two hours.[107] In his first meeting with Burns, Kochemasov insisted that the two states "must move in one direction—towards the establishment of normal and good relations"—yet he expressed doubts based on Reagan's aggressive, anti-Soviet rhetoric, which did not match the tone of their conversations in Berlin. Burns's remarkable response: "[His] behavior towards the [Soviet Union] is comparable to parents getting carried away by anger and using insulting language towards their own children."[108]

Kochemasov, like Abrasimov before him, had little inclination to discuss Berlin-specific issues with any of his Western interlocutors.[109] His preoccupation was with East-West relations as a whole.[110] The two would manage the situation in Berlin, and work to make sure that "the atmosphere of peace and cooperation . . . [would] not stay limited to West Berlin, but reach throughout Europe and even worldwide."[111] When Burns left Bonn in mid-1985, to be replaced by the former assistant secretary of state for European and Canadian affairs, Richard Burt, using the Berlin meetings for much broader discussions had become institutionalized. This time, it was Kochemasov who announced that the meetings constituted "an opportunity to discuss not only West Berlin, but also current international issues of mutual interest. He called for the continuation and expansion of this tradition."[112]

The Cold War did not end at the conference table in Berlin. But the ongoing, institutionalized back-channel dialogue between the US and Soviet ambassadors was an opportunity for two senior policy makers to speak in surprisingly frank terms about superpower relations and international stability, without the need for public posturing. Both provided consistent evidence of his government's desire for stability, counteracting the pernicious images that abounded in both Washington and Moscow depicting the other side as innately hostile and intractably warlike. And both indicated that there was a willingness to negotiate in their respective leaderships in a way that went beyond a routine desire for superpower negotiations, but rather required the initiative of leaders themselves.

"We have wasted a whole year," Haig bemoaned when he met Dobrynin again in the spring of 1982.[113] He would not have a chance to make up for lost time. In Washington, his position within the administration grew increasingly untenable. He had been chosen to counterbalance Reagan's longer-serving aides' lack of foreign-policy experience, a fact of which he was all too aware. In office, Haig's sense of his own importance in the administration (and in general) grated, and he rapidly became marginalized.[114] As secretary of state, Haig failed to build a positive relationship with Reagan—or anyone else in the White House, for that matter. He held them all in contempt, and they reciprocated.[115] He brought, according to Richard Pipes, "a sense of belligerency, [and] a kind of defensiveness about his turf."[116] Haig's response after the attempt on Reagan's life in March 1981 all but sealed his fate: alone in the White House, a frenetic Haig announced to the press that he was "in control here," a matter on which the Constitution disagreed. Haig's days were numbered, but instead of recognizing his precarious situation, he redoubled his efforts to shut others out of foreign-policy making.[117] Finally, blaming the rest of Reagan's cabinet and White House staff, Haig declared on June 24, 1982, that he could no longer function as secretary of state. In his resignation letter (rewritten four times to tone it down before he tendered it to Reagan the next day), Haig bemoaned the fact that US foreign policy would depart from the "careful course which we had laid out."[118] But to Reagan, Haig was no collaborator: "He didn't want to carry out the president's foreign policy; he wanted to formulate it and carry it out himself."[119]

Reagan had already dismissed his underperforming first national security adviser, Richard Allen, replacing him with Judge William Clark, a longtime friend, in order to bring discipline to a foreign policy—and a foreign-policy apparatus—in disarray. George P. Shultz's appointment to replace Haig was another step in that direction, and crucially, served Reagan's desire to expand dialogue with the Soviet Union.[120] Shultz was a veteran of the Nixon administration, having served as secretary of labor, director of the Office of Management and Budget, and secretary of the treasury, and was well prepared to impose discipline on foreign policy. Reagan made it clear to his aides that Shultz would be charged with crafting and implementing, alongside the president, a new approach to Moscow, even if much of the substance of that process would remain hidden from them.[121] In contrast to Haig, Shultz planned to involve Reagan directly in making foreign policy, working with him to implement both tracks of the president's Cold War grand strategy.[122] In their first meeting, Reagan and Shultz focused on the need to negotiate with the Soviets from a position of strength. Both agreed on the importance of talking to Moscow, and crucially, both saw the United States as being on the cusp of attaining such an advantage.[123]

Eastern and Western policy makers alike welcomed Shultz's appointment. The British, increasingly worried by Reagan's anti-Soviet rhetoric, applauded

CHAPTER 2

the new secretary of state's "calming influence."[124] The West German account of the first NATO foreign ministers' meeting Shultz attended is almost fawning: his "commanding, skillful, and overall masterful negotiating skills" earned him his colleagues' "high esteem and universal approbation."[125] Soviet foreign-policy makers remembered Shultz warmly from the Nixon years—Nixon was, it is safe to say, Brezhnev's favorite president—and made no secret of their pleasure at Shultz's appointment.[126] Crucially for Washington's allies, the new secretary of state at last made Reagan's thinking about the relationship between peace through strength and quiet diplomacy explicit: "He bluntly stated that strength and diplomacy are not alternatives to one another, but rather must always be used in concert. In this, Shultz was an accurate representative of the Reagan administration."[127] The new secretary of state was glad to see, when he first met with Gromyko in the autumn of 1982, that Moscow had not "written off the Reagan administration."[128] And the Soviet foreign minister went away convinced that Washington was in fact open to US-Soviet dialogue.[129]

Nearly all disapproval of Shultz's appointment came from within the White House itself. Some welcomed the arrival of a better manager and foreign-policy collaborator.[130] Others denounced him as another "Haig, only with better media instincts."[131] Shultz's arrival antagonized those in the White House who saw cooperation with the Kremlin as anathema, of which there were many. By 1982, the future course of US-Soviet relations had become the subject of significant and often hostile debate within the administration, and soon Shultz was a veritable lightning rod. His memoranda to Reagan were regularly accompanied by "a three or four page . . . memo to the president handwritten from [his national security adviser] Clark[,] pissing all over George Shultz and the State Department."[132] Clark's efforts to undermine the new secretary of state went so far that Bush intervened to let Shultz know what was happening.[133]

The Berlin back channel had developed out of Burns's desire, with Reagan's blessing, to make real progress in US-Soviet relations, but at arm's length from the president. With Shultz in office and the United States' position vis-à-vis the Soviet Union improved after a year and a half of economic recovery and military spending, Reagan became more directly involved in working with Moscow to solve common problems. Human rights issues, for instance, were a thorn in both superpowers' sides. When it came to that fraught issue, Shultz told Dobrynin that Reagan's "approach was a quiet one; he wishes to talk, not to have newspaper stories or claims of 'victory.'"[134] The president wanted to reduce US-Soviet mistrust in order to make progress on a matter of emotional significance to him.[135] Both sides likely had in mind the Siberian Seven, a group of Pentecostals who had taken refuge in the basement of the US embassy in

Moscow after the Soviet government refused to let them emigrate in June 1978. This group personified for Reagan the whole issue of human rights in the Soviet Union, and he had grown increasingly frustrated by the Kremlin's refusal "either to face reality or to show normal human feelings."[136]

Almost immediately after Reagan's inauguration, the two superpowers had agreed that the Siberian Seven were an unnecessary irritant.[137] To solve that problem, they turned to quiet diplomacy, this time in Madrid, on the fringes of the Conference on Security and Cooperation in Europe. Max Kampelman, the US ambassador to the conference, began a series of meetings with a Soviet delegate—and KGB general—Sergeĭ Kondrashev in the winter of 1980. Kondrashev stressed Brezhnev's hope for "negotiation on a serious basis and at a high political level" with the incoming administration. He insisted that he spoke with the "highest authority" when he told Kampelman that Brezhnev and the politburo "needed and wanted stability and realized that they could not achieve [it] without the United States."[138] At last, in the spring of 1983, on Shultz's watch, Kondrashev had news for Kampelman: the United States had asked for "significant gestures" on human rights, and now Moscow would allow not only the Siberian Seven but all of their close relatives to emigrate.[139]

Shultz proposed to have Dobrynin meet Reagan to finalize the arrangement.[140] He invited the Soviet ambassador to the State Department but quickly (and without forewarning) spirited him over to the White House—his first visit since Reagan took office. Tête-à-tête, the president and the Soviet ambassador finalized the agreement.[141] The Kremlin would allow the Pentecostal families to emigrate, and the United States would not make political hay "by undue publicity, by claims of credit for ourselves, or by 'crowing.'" By June 1983, after five long years spent living in the US embassy's basement, the Siberian Seven and their families had left the Soviet Union.[142] Quiet diplomacy, the president and his advisers concluded, worked.[143]

Not all diplomacy, however, was quiet—or cooperative. Early in the Reagan administration, the United States engaged the Soviet Union in "coercive diplomacy" to achieve its goals through nonmilitary means.[144] Arms control talks were a near-constant feature of the Cold War, but their common representation as an outgrowth of the real danger posed by nuclear weapons and the superpowers' shared interest in reducing—or eliminating—that danger is only part of the story.[145] Reagan did indeed understand how grave that danger was and had long believed in the need to abolish nuclear weapons.[146] But like his predecessors in the White House, Reagan saw that process of reducing that danger as one driven as much by competition and ensuring US superiority throughout as by cooperation with the Soviet Union.[147] Still, after Reagan's

48   **CHAPTER 2**

election and his unclear foreign-policy message, securing a reaffirmation of this commitment, in particular to the negotiating track, was a top priority for US allies.[148] They needed public evidence of "a modicum of agreement" with Washington to demonstrate NATO's continued strength.[149] And at home, common perceptions of the new president's "warlike tendencies" needed to be countered to ensure public support to that same end.[150]

US policy makers knew they needed to make a serious effort on arms control in order to placate their allies.[151] In fact, Reagan was prepared to continue this Carter-era commitment, which mirrored the president's own views on the importance of balancing strength and diplomacy in superpower relations.[152] On November 18, 1981, Reagan announced that the United States would return to the arms control bargaining table in Geneva to negotiate a reduction in intermediate-range nuclear forces in Europe. He read from his theretofore secret letter to Brezhnev following the attempt on his life, with its focus on US-Soviet cooperation in the name of peace. He framed the US approach to INF arms control in that same, pacific light: if only the Soviet Union would withdraw its missiles from Europe, the United States would cancel its own planned deployments.[153]

At first glance, the so-called Zero Option seemed a fair compromise: the United States would forgo future deployments (of Pershing 2 ballistic missiles and ground-launched cruise missiles) in exchange for the removal of equivalent Soviet weapons, namely the SS-20s. In reality, Reagan and his advisers designed the Zero Option to "capture world opinion" benefiting the United States regardless of the outcome. If the Kremlin accepted, US Pershing 1A nuclear weapons already in Europe would remain in place, as the Zero Option pertained only to future deployments. If it failed, as the White House anticipated it would, allied support for US deployment would increase, as the Kremlin would be held responsible for the failure to reach a negotiated solution.[154]

Tellingly, those who focused more narrowly on nuclear strategy had serious doubts about the Zero Option. It would mean that "any conflict in Europe . . . would escalate nearly at once to the intercontinental level" and require major—and costly—increases in the level of US conventional forces in Europe as a deterrent.[155] The White House certainly never saw the Zero Option as a final negotiating position, but as Reagan put it, "One should ask for the moon, and when the other fellow offers green cheese, one can settle for something in between."[156] When Gromyko accused the Reagan administration of "ensuring by hook or by crook that the NATO decision to deploy new types of nuclear weapons in Europe [would] be implemented," he was not entirely wrong.[157]

ARM TO PARLEY 49

Policy makers in Moscow and throughout Eastern Europe quickly recognized the Zero Option for what it was and rejected it.[158] They, too, saw arms control negotiations over INF as being both political and strategic, and recognized that the Zero Option would undermine their position on both fronts.[159] Moscow aimed to prevent the deployment of any US nuclear weapons, which would deny them the military advantage in Europe.[160] The new US missiles in Western Europe, Soviet policy makers believed, could reach Moscow. Though the United States insisted the missiles had only a 1,600-kilometer range, Soviet experts feared they could quickly and accurately strike targets up to 2,500 kilometers away. Soviet SS-20s in Eastern Europe, Moscow's negotiators reminded their US interlocutors, could not reach Washington.[161] This would be the perfect tool for fighting a limited nuclear war on the European continent—a "European strategic" conflict—because Moscow would be imperiled but Washington would not (or, Soviet military leaders stressed, so they thought).[162] As a result, according to Gromyko, Western Europe would become "a kind of launch pad which had been moved from US territory."[163] This had to be prevented. But the Kremlin also hoped to use the INF issue to break NATO, wielding Reagan's aggressive anti-Soviet comments and alleged unwillingness to negotiate as a wedge to divide the United States and its European allies.[164] The Kremlin needed to convince Western Europeans that Reagan merely "masquerades as an advocate of disarmament."[165]

The Soviets' own arms control plan mirrored the Zero Option as Reagan had presented it: a moratorium on new deployments of nuclear weapons to Europe, meaning that Soviet missiles already deployed would remain in place, and an exclusion regarding the Soviet Union proper. Under this agreement, then, Moscow could base further SS-20s in its westernmost regions, still within easy striking distance of Western European cities and outnumbering the existing US Pershing 1As, which could not reach Moscow.[166] The West would have none of it. Such an arrangement would, as West German Bundeskanzler Helmut Schmidt wrote to Brezhnev, merely "codify the existing imbalance in the Soviet Union's favor."[167]

Both overt and covert diplomacy played a role in arms control negotiation. Outwardly, the first round of INF talks in Geneva from November 30, 1981, to March 16, 1982, went nowhere—as both sides expected—when the US presented Reagan's Zero Option and the Soviets rejected it.[168] Despite their lack of progress, the US negotiating team managed to keep their spirits up. One mock Soviet statement drafted as a joke by US negotiators to blow off steam, for example, complimented the US embassy's meeting room: "The pictures on the wall remind us of what we are doing—playing a game. . . . This would

50   **CHAPTER 2**

all be a lot more fun if we could serve alcohol during the meetings." Similarily, their song "The Phantom TEL" told the story of a wayward transporter-erector-launcher (a self-powered vehicle capable of carrying and firing missiles including the SS-20) that became sentient and escaped US verification efforts by hiding out in the sewers under the Kremlin.[169]

Behind closed doors, however, the negotiators showed greater flexibility and enjoyed more success. Paul Nitze, the lead US negotiator, and his Soviet counterpart, Iuliĭ Kvitsinskiĭ, developed something of a friendship over the course of the talks; both spoke English, and their wives, Phyllis and Inga, both spoke French.[170] In July 1982, they took a now-famous walk in the wooded Jura Mountains by Lake Geneva. Together, they found a compromise to the arms control impasse: the United States would not deploy Pershing 2s, the Soviet Union would reduce its SS-20 deployment, and the United States would deploy as many ground-launched cruise missiles to Europe as the Soviets had SS-20s.[171] In his memoirs, Nitze describes the initiative as having had a "generally favorable" reception in Washington, failing only because of Soviet reticence.[172] However, the record shows that the Pentagon's response was anything but favorable. The initiative was a "wholly unauthorized departure from . . . instructions."[173] Weinberger led the charge himself, stating that the agreement sketched out by Nitze and Kvitsinskiĭ squandered the strong (and getting stronger, as the military buildup proceeded) US negotiating position, and that an interim deployment risked undermining already tenuous European support for a future full-scale one, abandoning the Zero Option "for nothing in return."[174] In Washington, an agreement that left any SS-20s in place was a nonstarter.[175] At Weinberger's urging, Reagan rejected the proposal.[176] Nitze is not wrong, however, in reporting on Moscow's reticence. The agreement he and Kvitsinskiĭ had crafted was unacceptable: both the deployment of any new US missiles and the exclusion of British and French nuclear weapons from the strategic equation were still anathema to the Kremlin.[177]

Whereas the Dual-Track Decision guided the Reagan administration to negotiate on INF, Reagan himself drove the decision to resume strategic arms control talks with the Soviet Union. In a heartfelt speech on May 9, 1982, at his alma mater, Eureka College, in Illinois, Reagan introduced a plan for a Strategic Arms Reduction Treaty: "The focus of our efforts will be to reduce significantly the most destabilizing systems, the ballistic missiles, the number of warheads they carry, and their overall destructive potential. . . . Why can't our peoples enjoy the benefits that would flow from real cooperation [with the Soviet Union]? Why can't we reduce the number of horrendous weapons?"[178] This was no mere rhetorical flourish. Reagan reacted viscerally to the idea of nuclear weapons and the damage they could do.[179] START reflected his long-standing desire to reduce the number of nuclear weapons in the world. Reagan had objected to the earlier Strategic Arms Limitation Talks on account of their focus on merely limiting the growth, rather than reducing the quantity, of these dangerous weapons.[180] US intelligence indicated Soviet interest in such cuts.[181] Brezhnev had made it clear that he saw lowering, not increasing, the number of weapons as the way to security.[182] Within the Kremlin, this was of course understood to mean Soviet superiority at a lower level.[183] Two days before his speech at Eureka College, Reagan had introduced the idea of START to Brezhnev in a letter. The general secretary agreed to begin negotiations that summer but made sure to blame the United States for creating the confrontational atmosphere that compelled them in the first place.[184] He also publicly lauded the START proposal as a "step in the right direction."[185] Reagan's marginalia on Brezhnev's reply illuminate the president's continued concern that the United States faced a strategic disadvantage. Where Brezhnev mentioned the "existing balance of forces," for example, Reagan corrected the record: "he means imbalance."[186]

Reagan's nuclear abolitionism alone did not motivate START. His inner circle, especially his wife, Nancy, recognized that public perceptions of the Reagan presidency as increasing the chances of nuclear war posed a serious problem for his reelection in 1984.[187] The administration needed to "stem the tide of rising skepticism" at home and abroad regarding Reagan's willingness to pursue arms control.[188] But the way Reagan spoke behind closed doors rarely invoked East-West cooperation. Through INF, START, and other diplomatic gambits, he told Schmidt in the summer of 1982, the Soviet Union could be brought to heel and back into the international community on Western terms, "just as one tries to bring an outlaw back into society before he pulls his pistol."[189]

When it came to the Soviets' so-called outlaw behavior, the ongoing crisis in Poland was at the forefront of Western policy makers' minds. Workers' strikes and general unrest in Poland already simmered at the time of Reagan's election but threatened to boil over in 1981.[190] The Solidarność trade union continued its calls for reform, which the governing PZPR resisted with increasing futility. Moscow watched the situation unfold with trepidation; Soviet defense minister Dmitriĭ Ustinov went so far as to threaten a Warsaw Pact invasion, telling Polish leaders, "Our patience is lost!"[191] On the one hand, with Warsaw Pact military exercises upcoming in Poland, Western policy makers worried that military action would soon follow, with the exercises serving as cover for mobilization, as in Czechoslovakia in 1968.[192] The Reagan administration feared that the Kremlin would go to war over the future of Poland—and that the United States would be compelled to respond.[193] On this, NATO had been

CHAPTER 2

drawing up contingency plans since December 1980.[194] On the other hand, an unmistakable sense of optimism ran through the Reagan administration's deliberations. The White House hoped to midwife "a regime not intolerable to the Russians and yet capable of further development toward democracy."[195] In London, "[Thatcher] regarded the new freedom in Poland as a gangrene in the Soviet system. She wanted it to spread."[196] US officials also observed that a Soviet military intervention would be a "golden opportunity" to strengthen NATO's defenses, be it by admitting newly democratic Spain into NATO posthaste (which it did in 1982) or by staging new US nuclear weapons in Western Europe (which it did in 1983). "I hope this memo is never declassified," William Stearman of the NSC wrote after making these suggestions.[197]

Initially, Western policy makers feared being too provocative and thereby giving Moscow a pretext to intervene in Poland.[198] Reagan's commitment to engaging the Soviet Union persisted. Poland demanded a firm response, but it did not outweigh the worldwide benefit of an improved superpower relationship.[199] Thatcher warned Haig not to call attention to the failures of the communist system; both agreed that using the Polish situation for propaganda purposes would make Moscow's intervention "more certain and more brutal."[200] In repeated public statements as well as internal discussions, the Kremlin accused the United States and the West of fomenting unrest in Poland. The last thing any foreign-policy maker wanted to do was give Moscow evidence to support these claims.[201]

Though few in the West appreciated it, the politburo had no intention of invading Poland.[202] While Warsaw may have wanted them to intervene, Andropov declared in October 1981: "We need to stick to our policy—our troops will not be sent to Poland."[203] He again made it clear in December that "[the Soviet Union] cannot risk . . . sending troops into Poland. . . . [We] do not know how things will end in Poland, but even if Poland comes to be ruled by Solidarność, then so be it."[204] Soviet leaders would have sooner suffered Eastern European governments that incorporated non-communist elements than face the consequences of an invasion. The price paid in international condemnation in both 1968 and 1979 had been too high, and Brezhnev would not pay it yet again.[205] The so-called Brezhnev Doctrine, which held that Moscow had the right to intervene militarily in any of its Warsaw Pact allies should they stray from the norms of communism as Moscow defined them was no more.[206] "It died early . . . in 1980–1981," Gen. Anatoliĭ Grybkov, chief of the Combined Staff of the Unified Armed Forces of the Warsaw Treaty Organization at the time, confirms. "The fact that we didn't send troops into Poland shows that the Brezhnev Doctrine . . . was dead."[207] But because nobody made public what the Soviets and Poles had agreed on, none of the Eastern

European leaders knew the situation had changed; the Brezhnev Doctrine died, and few knew.[208]

On December 13, 1981, the Polish prime minister, Gen. Wojciech Jaruzelski, announced that Poland would be led by a Military Council of National Salvation, with himself at the helm, and imposed martial law. Overnight, the Polish military had rounded up Solidarność's leaders, quarantined its headquarters, and erected checkpoints across the country; the crackdown took the country and the world by surprise.[209] Even the politburo in Moscow was not informed until the day before Jaruzelski's announcement.[210] The Reagan administration responded immediately, suspending agricultural aid, fishing rights, flights to the United States, and export-import credit insurance; but the main focus of the US response was the Soviet Union's planned natural gas pipeline, connecting deposits in the Iamal Peninsula of Western Siberia (later shifted to the already-tapped and more easily accessible deposits in nearby Urengoĭ) to Western European markets. The pipeline would rely heavily on Western loans and technology due to both the cost of building a 5,000-kilometer pipeline across inhospitable terrain and the advanced technology needed to extract natural gas from the permafrost. Early participants relished having a share of the largest-ever commercial venture between East and West, all the more so because the stagnant global economy of the 1970s presented few opportunities of the kind.[211] After the souring of US-Soviet relations in the late 1970s, the Carter administration sought to "restrain" the pipeline, to no avail.[212] The Reagan administration saw both the Polish crisis and the pipeline project largely in the context of Cold War competition, and used the former as grounds to punish the Soviet Union by putting a stop to the latter.[213]

Real damage could be done to the Soviet economy by halting the pipeline; as one West German diplomat put it, "Soviet energy production lives or dies with [the pipeline from] West Siberia."[214] The Soviet Union, the US intelligence community predicted, would run out of oil reserves by the mid-1980s. Without oil to export and without a pipeline to export natural gas as a substitute, the Soviet Union would be denied the hard currency it desperately needed to import commodities on which its moribund economy depended, especially consumer and high-technology goods. Rather than seizing this opportunity to inflict pain on Moscow, by constructing the pipeline, "the West is to come to [the Soviets'] rescue," Pipes bemoaned.[215] Stopping the pipeline would, in other words, force the Kremlin to make difficult choices between guns and butter. Indeed, the Soviet Union saw the solution to its own economic problems in increased revenues from the sale of its abundant natural resources. But the Eastern intelligence community did not see the pipeline as an area of vulnerability. "In the end," Andropov predicted,

54   CHAPTER 2

"business interests [in favor of the pipeline] will prove stronger than the [US] government."[216]

After Jaruzelski declared martial law, Reagan announced that the "proclamations imposed . . . by the Polish government [had been] printed in the Soviet Union"—and that Moscow would accordingly pay the price.[217] US policy makers publicly rejected any other explanation of Moscow's role.[218] Behind closed doors, Reagan focused almost exclusively on the Soviet dimension of the Polish situation: "This is the first time in 60 years that we have had this kind of opportunity. There may not be another in our lifetime. Can we afford not to go all out? . . . Cancel all licenses. Tell the allies that if they don't go along with us . . . we may have to review our alliances."[219] This response reflected Reagan's overall view of US-Soviet relations as requiring both strength and diplomacy: stopping the pipeline would reduce the growth of Soviet military spending and slow the East's acquisition of superior Western technology, thus, the White House hoped, making the Kremlin more forthcoming in arms control negotiations.[220]

Reagan may have been certain of the need to inflict maximum punishment on the Soviets, but Washington's allies remained unconvinced.[221] In a letter, the president called on Thatcher to join him in responding forcefully to this "watershed in the political history of mankind—a challenge to tyranny from within."[222] The prime minister was nonplussed. "It was so vague I didn't think it was worth reading last night," she told Carrington of Reagan's message. "There's nothing in it. . . . It seems a bit absurd if the Russians aren't actually on the front line of [the crackdown] to take it out on them. . . . It's simply an internal situation!"[223] This from the Western leader most likely to support the United States.

US economic policy was already a serious point of contention between Washington and its allies.[224] They had never been enthusiastic about punitive sanctions, seeing East-West trade as a stabilizing force and the Siberian pipeline as an opportunity to diversify Europe's energy supply in order to prevent a repeat of the oil crisis of the 1970s.[225] Moreover, despite assurances that they would be consulted, Reagan's speech on December 29, 1981, announcing the sanctions came without warning.[226] They did not like what they heard, rejecting the notion that policy makers in Washington could tell them with whom they may do business.[227] Schmidt joked to Haig that US policy makers had fetishized economic sanctions since the Boston Tea Party of 1773.[228] "The Americans just love extraterritorial laws," Allan Gotlieb, Canada's ambassador in Washington, wrote scathingly in his diary. "They must rule the world. Whatever they do, so must everyone else."[229] Washington never managed to develop the requisite "common understanding of the strategic implications of East-West trade" to secure the support of its allies.[230]

Thus, when the Kremlin decried Washington's behavior as "irresponsible," so too did US allies.[231] The decision to impose sanctions elicited "nearly unanimous and very severe criticism . . . in all Western European countries," Schmidt told Reagan.[232] His advisers went even further: "Conspiracy theories, . . . the most primitive, almost unimaginable anti-communism, and a crusader mindset" guided US policy on Poland and the pipeline.[233] Many firms defied Washington, fearful above all that having to cancel major contracts would close off the lucrative Soviet market.[234] The extent of allied opposition took Reagan by surprise. He had been under the impression that US firms were the main suppliers to the Siberian pipeline project. "Now," the president explained sheepishly, "Maggie Thatcher has made me realize that I have been wrong."[235]

In the spring of 1982, the administration sent policy makers across Europe to meet with their counterparts and encourage them to shift away from economic engagement with the Soviet Union and to support US sanctions.[236] Or, as undersecretary of state for international security affairs James Buckley, who led the initiative, put it, "to show the idiocy of subsidizing the Soviet arms buildup through credits."[237] These emissaries met a frosty reception and made no headway. Ultimately, however, the Reagan administration turned its allies' refusal to comply with restrictions on supplying the Soviet Union to its advantage: if they could do business with Moscow, they could also be a conduit for US intelligence. Acting in response to a tip about the KGB stealing software from a Canadian firm, the CIA—in cooperation with its Canadian counterparts—introduced a "Trojan horse" into the software, which controlled the pumps, turbines, and valves critical to the pipeline's safe operation. For a time, the software performed as well as Moscow had hoped, but in October 1982 it went intentionally haywire. The resulting gas explosion could be seen from outer space.[238]

Even amid the acrimony over Poland, Moscow kept up pressure for a US-Soviet summit. Georgiĭ Arbatov, the director of the Institute for US and Canadian Studies of the Russian Academy of Sciences, regularly used his position, which gave him access to Western officials and a pretext for international travel, as a back channel at the KGB's behest.[239] Arbatov pulled one unsuspecting visitor into his office and insisted—"occasionally becoming red in the face"—that the Soviet Union was not monolithic, and that without communication between the White House and the Kremlin, hard-line factions within the Soviet Union would gain ground and prevent opportunities to cooperate in the

56   CHAPTER 2

future.[240] Brezhnev was not alone in pushing for a meeting between himself and Reagan: Washington's European allies supported a summit, seeing a special role for themselves as intermediaries and interpreters between the superpowers.[241] After hosting Brezhnev in Bonn, Schmidt argued to Reagan that a face-to-face meeting would be a unique opportunity for the president to influence Soviet foreign policy. Personal impressions played a major role in shaping Brezhnev's view of the world, the Bundeskanzler rightly noted, and if Reagan would only explain US grand strategy to him, Brezhnev would learn firsthand that Reagan was no warmonger but was consistent in his foreign policy—more like Nixon than Carter. The two would at least have one thing in common, Reagan quipped when Schmidt shared this, a loathing of his predecessor—yet he would not commit to a summit.[242]

Brezhnev never got the summit he wanted; Reagan worried that US power had not yet recovered sufficiently to justify such a high-profile meeting.[243] The president did, however, offer a compromise: a non-summit meeting with Brezhnev in June 1982, to be held on the fringes of the UN Special Session on Disarmament in New York. Reagan's offer took many in the Kremlin—and, for that matter, many in his own White House—by surprise.[244] To Reagan, the time seemed ripe to begin cautious but overt dialogue with the aging Soviet leader, and key advisers—including his wife, Nancy—increasingly focused on Reagan's image and the benefit that negotiating in the open with Moscow would confer.[245] Brezhnev, however, rejected the proposal. He wanted "a real summit in Europe . . . instead of a handshake in New York."[246]

Implementing what Reagan himself described as a "policy of carrot and stick" sent conflicting messages to the Kremlin and the world.[247] US diplomats were sitting down at the bargaining table with their Soviet counterparts, though many speculated that they had no interest in actually reaching an agreement. Covert engagement, however, did bear fruit. All the while, Reagan was building up the US military to unparalleled heights and, it seemed from what he said about the Soviet Union, with malice aforethought.[248] Brezhnev could navigate these mixed signals in US policy, largely because they reflected his own approach to the Cold War, but as many had long suspected, the general secretary's window of opportunity for dialogue with the United States would soon close, and with it, an era in Soviet history. The real test of the effectiveness of Reagan's dual-track grand strategy was still to come: in its ability to navigate the crises and confrontations between the superpowers that 1983 had in store.

CHAPTER 3

Talking about Talking
Continuities and Crises

By the late summer of 1983, Maj. Gennadiĭ Osipovich had grown used to the routine of life as an interceptor pilot. Each day around dusk, a US Air Force reconnaissance aircraft flew right up to the far eastern border of the Soviet Union off the coast of Sakhalin island. MiG-31 aircraft, from the regiment of which he was deputy commander, would scramble to meet it in the skies over the Pacific. So within minutes of the alarm sounding in the early-morning hours of September 1, 1983, at Dolinsk-Sokol Airbase, Osipovich was on course to intercept the aircraft approaching Soviet territory. Somehow, the approaching aircraft—which he could barely make out—had already overflown the Kamchatka Peninsula and outrun interceptors there, and had now found a narrow channel of weak radar coverage and was about to disappear from Soviet screens.

As Osipovich approached the plane, he could see that it had two rows of illuminated windows and flashing navigational lights, like a Boeing 747. How could such a large advanced aircraft be 700 kilometers off course in restricted airspace? It was impossible. It certainly did not behave like a passenger aircraft: the pilots did not respond to radioed demands to land, and when Osipovich fired warning shots from his MiG-31's cannons, the pilots began what looked like evasive maneuvers. At night, standard operating procedure was to destroy any and all intruders—a fail-safe, at least for the Soviets—so he launched a pair of heat-seeking missiles at the aircraft. Osipovich returned to a hero's welcome

58   **CHAPTER 3**

from his fellow pilots, jealous that he had had the chance to fire on a real-life target. Of that, he was proud. "For me," he concluded, "it was a target," and one that his training had directed him to destroy.[1]

But it was not just another target. Osipovich had shot down a Boeing 747 passenger aircraft: Korean Air Lines flight 007, en route from New York to Seoul, via Anchorage to refuel, with 246 passengers and 23 crew on board. No one survived.[2] Moscow immediately denied any wrongdoing. The Soviet Air Force was fully within its rights to down a plane violating Soviet airspace, especially one that did not reply to radio contact, had no navigational lights, and, they claimed, behaved more like a military than a civilian aircraft.[3] That the aircraft had in fact had its navigational—and cabin—lights on undermined the Soviet claim. With an electric razor switched on between him and a microphone (to mimic cockpit noise) and a pack of superior officers standing over him, Osipovich lied for his country: "No, the lights are not flashing."[4] The requisite evidence had been manufactured—after the fact—to absolve Moscow of any wrongdoing. It was, Anatolii Dobrynin later conceded, a clear low point for his country.[5]

1983 was a year of extremes. It witnessed some of the largest protests in European history, as hundreds of thousands took to the streets chanting their demands that no more US nuclear weapons be deployed to their continent.[6] The superpowers only added to that cacophony; while quiet diplomacy persisted, it was a much louder form that held the public's attention. The Kremlin, West German diplomats concluded, conducted little more than "loudspeaker diplomacy."[7] Reagan, meanwhile, used his bully pulpit to condemn the Soviet Union and its system. But those same analysts in Bonn also saw a real desire for serious dialogue, both in Washington and in Moscow, as letters declaring peaceful intent flew back and forth between the White House and the Kremlin. Events, they bemoaned, kept getting in the way.[8]

Which, then, was the real Reagan—the one who wrote to Andropov privately about his desire for peace, or the one waging public ideological war and funding technologies that would enable him to wage a nuclear one, too? In times of crisis, the latter Reagan seemed to be winning out. The world watched with alarm as Osipovich shot down KAL 007, the United States invaded Grenada, and Europeans protested the deployment of INF. Through it all, however, Reagan remained committed to dialogue with the Soviet Union, and Andropov to engaging the United States. And though they suffered setbacks, US-Soviet relations never approached the brink of Armageddon. The Cold War's long peace—at least in Europe—held.[9] Explaining why requires looking past the sensational events that have come to characterize 1983; a narrow focus on crises obscures a much richer picture of US-Soviet relations.[10] Crisis

TALKING ABOUT TALKING   59

never gave way to conflagration in large part because behind the scenes, in both the Kremlin and the White House, policy makers engaged their Cold War rivals.

During the first years of the Reagan administration, as Brezhnev's poor and deteriorating health impeded diplomacy, attention gradually focused on who would succeed him. "The Soviet sweepstakes," as Richard Pipes dubbed the contest to succeed Brezhnev, were on.[11] In 1982, Andropov and Chernenko vied for position, as the "Götterdämmerung in the Kremlin," as one West German diplomat put it, continued.[12] Neither could exactly be considered an injection of fresh blood: Andropov turned sixty-eight in June, and Chernenko seventy-one in September. (Male life expectancy in the Soviet Union at the time hovered below sixty-three.)[13] Andropov and Chernenko not only closely monitored each other's political fortunes but also kept tabs on each other's health.[14] Though they were neck and neck in infirmity, Andropov emerged as the favorite. In May 1982, Brezhnev decided to throw his weight behind the KGB chair, appointing him second secretary to replace the recently deceased Mikhail Suslov.[15]

Andropov immediately began to tackle the Soviet Union's corruption problems. He directed, for example, the arrest of 159 party officials in Krasnodar and ousted the region's first secretary.[16] Andropov's politburo colleagues saw him as the type of strong leader needed for the post-Brezhnev 1980s, one who could narrow the gap between what Soviet leaders said about the country's fortunes and the reality experienced by Soviet citizens.[17] To many, Andropov embodied all of Stalin's best qualities of decisive leadership without, as the CIA deputy director for intelligence Robert Gates quipped, "the old dictator's less welcome attributes (such as a tendency to shoot his colleagues)."[18]

Brezhnev's diary for November 10, 1982, simply reads, "L[eonid] I[l'ich] is no more."[19] The US ambassador in Moscow, Arthur Hartman, cabled Washington: "The expected [had] finally happened."[20] The politburo promptly appointed Andropov to head Brezhnev's funeral commission, a clear signal to the world that he would become the next general secretary.[21] The Kremlin forbade the playing of jazz on the radio for five days following Brezhnev's death, and regular cinema schedules were superseded by a stream of patriotic and ideological films. The KGB watched closely for any signs of discontent— or glee.[22] KGB archives have yet to reveal what, if anything, was uncovered, but the East German Stasi did produce a fulsome report on a schoolboy in Potsdam overheard exclaiming, "At last, the pig is dead!"[23] Amid the orchestrated public mourning, the politburo named Andropov general secretary on November 12.

60   CHAPTER 3

The news of Brezhnev's death "evoke[d] little emotional response from the largely apolitical Soviet population."[24] The Ukrainian leadership's reflection on Brezhnev's life reads almost as self-parody when considered in light of the grim realities of Soviet life in the early 1980s. Brezhnev's "organizational talent, political wisdom, and foresight," lauded by Kyiv, were by then largely gone; his connection "by thousands of strands" to the working people of the Soviet Union had clearly frayed.[25] After all, it was during this late-Brezhnev era when one of the party's chief ideologues commented on a draft speech, "Do we really need these quotes from Lenin?"[26] Andropov's admonition to fellow funeral commission members not to repeat the mistakes of Stalin's funeral, to which mourners had flocked in such numbers that at least one hundred were trampled to death, strains credulity.[27]

Around the world, policy makers sprang into action at the news of Brezhnev's death, hoping the new general secretary—who reportedly read Shakespeare, adored Frank Sinatra, and even wrote poetry—might prove himself a "closet liberal."[28] The White House promptly sent conciliatory signals, albeit measured ones, such as Reagan's signing, in person, the condolence book at the Soviet embassy in Washington.[29] Some encouraged him to go further: Arthur Hartman stressed that attending Brezhnev's funeral would signal to a skeptical politburo Reagan's desire to improve relations.[30] But Reagan hesitated, sending George H. W. Bush and George Shultz to meet the new Soviet leader in his stead.[31] He wrote to Margaret Thatcher, expressing his hope that "there may be changes in the Soviet Union of a sort which could present the West with new opportunities."[32] Reagan had in mind improving relations not only with Andropov but also with the new, younger generation of leaders still waiting in the wings. He made no secret of this diplomatic agenda in public, citing earlier and as-yet-undisclosed quiet diplomacy. But, Reagan noted, "it takes two to tango."[33]

For the Kremlin, "continuity [was]—implicitly—the keyword," according to the West German ambassador in Moscow.[34] The CIA concurred, remarking on Moscow's studied "business-as-usual image." Yet early indicators suggested that Andropov hoped to change the course of Soviet foreign policy. He and his close advisers, one CIA assessment concluded, would not "be content simply to conduct 'Brezhnevism without Brezhnev.'"[35] Like Washington, Moscow sent conflicting signals. At the start of Brezhnev's funeral, Andropov warned that "the forces of imperialism are trying to drive the world towards hostility and military confrontation."[36] But the new general secretary's briefing papers for his meeting with Bush and Shultz described the future of East-West relations with striking optimism. The United States had made its desire to improve relations sufficiently clear, the paper explained, as had the Kremlin. Nevertheless, Andropov's advisers warned, Reagan still viewed the United States as weak in relation to the Soviet Union and might either be unwilling to make progress or, worse, take offensive action.[37]

Andropov and Bush's first meeting, accompanied by Gromyko and Shultz, is striking for its cooperative tone. Bush went so far as to describe "a friendly and jocular ambience," as the two found common ground over their shared backgrounds leading intelligence services. Few in the CIA would have been pleased by Bush's implied equivalence of their service with the KGB, but Bush had broken the ice.[38] With pleasantries (and perfunctory condolences) out of the way, the new general secretary opened by acknowledging Reagan's professed desire to improve superpower relations, and underscored his own commitment to the same. But, he bemoaned, "almost the entire stock of stability between the two countries . . . had been carelessly squandered," unsurprisingly placing the blame for this on the United States. If the two superpowers and their allies allowed this negative trend to continue, he warned, "the result could only be catastrophe." Andropov insisted that Bush convey to Reagan that the entire Soviet leadership awaited dialogue with Washington on a range of issues. Echoing earlier conversations between Haig and Dobrynin, the new general secretary stressed that the US-Soviet relationship encompassed more than just bilateral concerns: improving that relationship would benefit the whole world. "Of course," he began, "the two sides could engage in debate and even sometimes scold each other in the press or in some other forum, but when it came to specific matters it was absolutely necessary to act as soberminded and normal people."[39] The White House took particular note of this frank reminder.[40] The Cold War between them was, after all, a competition with both foreign and domestic audiences.[41] The message was clear. No matter the sometimes bellicose rhetoric out of Moscow, Andropov "wanted [Reagan] to know that he wants a dialogue."[42] Nevertheless, Shultz concluded, the new general secretary would be a formidable adversary.[43] Andropov surpassed Brezhnev in intellect, managerial skill, and worldliness. He was "a doer."[44]

The Soviet Union nevertheless had real grievances when it came to US behavior, especially Washington's "interference" in human rights issues.[45] US protestations were pure hypocrisy, as the politburo's instructions to Soviet representatives to the 1983 meeting of the UN Commission on Human Rights stated.[46] Soviet diplomats were encouraged to use the meeting to promote the Soviet Union's successes in providing for its citizens, while also highlighting US support for regimes that allegedly violated human rights, including Chile, El Salvador, Guatemala, Israel, South Africa, and South Korea.[47] This was a refrain in Soviet meetings with Western diplomats on the margins of Brezhnev's

62   CHAPTER 3

funeral as well: the West's fixation on human rights questions impeded progress in East-West relations.[48] If Reagan really hoped to move forward, Andropov exclaimed in a conversation with West German Bundespräsident Karl Carstens, he should back off from "so-called human rights."[49]

Andropov came away optimistic from the many diplomatic meetings surrounding Brezhnev's funeral. His conversations with Western leaders, including Bush and Shultz, had left a positive impression, judging by the tone in which he reported them to the politburo. Such "sad events," he noted with approval, led to a more measured and constructive Western tone. Though he reassured his politburo colleagues that he would not risk unilateral measures that might weaken the Soviet Union, the new general secretary declared his readiness to work on creating fair and balanced agreements with Washington and to work toward reducing Cold War tensions.[50]

Andropov's statements to the politburo led to complementary actions. His first foreign-policy pronouncements as general secretary focused on the imperative of improved relations with the United States. When the politburo met a week after Brezhnev's death, the entire body declared itself ready for real progress.[51] At a party plenum on November 22, Andropov called for a return to détente. "The future," he insisted, "belongs to this policy."[52] He even refrained from excoriating—or, for that matter, even criticizing—the United States, usually a hallmark of such speeches. In Washington, Dobrynin echoed these sentiments.[53] Andropov's speech commemorating the sixtieth anniversary of the Soviet Union focused on improving relations with the United States in particular, but also with former allies Albania, China, and Yugoslavia, with whom Andropov pledged to collaborate as fellow members of the "socialist world system."[54] Above all, top-level Soviet officials sent clear signals that Andropov wanted a high-profile summit with Reagan.[55]

Andropov knew all too well the real problems facing the Soviet Union. As head of the Central Committee's International Department in the late 1950s and 1960s, Andropov had surrounded himself with a group of free-thinking advisers.[56] As KGB chair, he did not shy away from acknowledging that the Soviet Union was in trouble.[57] That assessment had led him to call for restraint in Soviet foreign policy—for example, persuading his politburo colleagues that the Soviet Union could not afford military action in Poland.[58] And as much as the KGB under Andropov excelled in suppressing dissidents, senior KGB officers were also at the heart of much of the quiet diplomacy between the superpowers, with Andropov a believer in the importance of such contacts.[59] Andropov had been one of the loudest voices in the Brezhnev regime advocating for just such a policy of engagement toward the United States.[60] In 1968, with Brezhnev's blessing, Andropov dispatched KGB officer Vyacheslav

Kvorkov to set up a back channel to the West German leadership, which would be crucial to Ostpolitik and détente.[61] From 1981 to 1983, the KGB station chief in Belgrade maintained a back-channel dialogue with US embassy officials explicitly at Andropov's behest.[62] In Madrid, the overture that led to the release of the Siberian Seven came from Sergeĭ Kondrashev, a general in the KGB. Kondrashev repeatedly raised the possibility of a summit between Reagan and Andropov, making it clear that he did so on behalf of the general secretary.[63]

As general secretary, Andropov continued to encourage trusted subordinates to better understand the situation within the Soviet Union in a realistic manner.[64] Nikolaĭ Ryzhkov was one of these so-called "thinking people" (they balked at being termed "reformers"). He later recalled: "We understood that [the Soviet Union] was in a blind alley. Even if outwardly things looked okay, we, as people with certain information at our disposal, understood that it just looked that way, and that there was no gleam of hope at all."[65]

Politburo meetings under Andropov, in a departure from Brezhnev's time, became venues for heated debate and frank discussion.[66] Behind closed doors, he spoke even more candidly about the challenges facing the Soviet Union— particularly with his protégé, Mikhail Gorbachev. The two men hailed from the northern Caucasus, where Gorbachev had been party chief (based in Stavropol) and Andropov regularly vacationed in the scenic foothills. Sitting around a bonfire, the KGB chair would happily sing along with the protest music of the 1960s, as his organization sent dissidents for forced psychiatric treatment in the Soviet Union's mental hospitals.[67] Despite the elevation of Gorbachev and others, however, the Soviet leadership as a whole remained a geriatric group. "Nobody wants to talk to the weak," Andropov had maintained during his tenure as KGB chair, but now that he was general secretary, this adage seemed to describe the Soviet Union.[68]

Andropov first needed to tackle the domestic economy, not foreign policy.[69] When asked whether they approved of Andropov's appointment, virtually all Soviet citizens who responded positively cited his planned economic reforms.[70] The Kremlin had only very limited room for maneuver in the economic sphere, however, as the entire country "struggled under the burden of military expenditures," the only sector of the economy flourishing.[71] In a break from his predecessor, Andropov acknowledged and diagnosed these Soviet economic woes in a speech on November 22, just ten days after being named general secretary, in which he stressed the need for greater material incentives, managerial independence, and labor discipline.[72] This latter issue would be his priority; whereas Brezhnev envisioned a rose-colored "discipline that is not built on fear," Andropov, with his background, had other ideas about how to combat the serious problems of labor.[73] His successor as KGB chair, Viktor Chebrikov,

64   **CHAPTER 3**

told his East German counterpart Erich Mielke that at the Kremlin's behest, his organization now prioritized uncovering and prosecuting "poor leadership" within the Soviet Union, so much so that an entire new directorate had been created to deal with road, rail, sea, and air transportation as well as oil pipelines. Chebrikov summed up his marching orders from the Kremlin succinctly: "The economy has to become economic!"[74]

Andropov also purged the top leadership of policy makers who either had been in power too long, in some cases since the days of Stalin, or were too closely associated with Brezhnev.[75] In particular, he made it clear that more needed to be done to "monitor and verify the implementation" of Kremlin directives in all sectors and echelons of the Soviet Union.[76] His government made full use of the legal system to punish corruption and waste in the economy, something Brezhnev had never done for fear of undermining his popularity.[77] On instruction from the Kremlin, for example, Iuriĭ Sokolov—the former director of the Gastronom No. 1 grocery store in central Moscow and a well-known supplier of hard-to-find luxury goods (including to the Brezhnev family)—was arrested on charges of bribery and corruption, for which he received the death penalty.[78]

By 1983, Reagan had taken to asking his advisers, "When is the time to sit down and negotiate with the Soviets?"[79] They had little concrete advice to offer. William Clark, the president's national security adviser, conceded that while relations with the Soviet Union were "at the heart of [US] foreign policy and military strategy, we do not, at present, have any formal guidelines."[80] Reagan tasked his administration with identifying "political, economic, military, and ideological means" of influencing Soviet behavior.[81] Shultz responded that the White House should build on prior successes in quiet diplomacy in order to intensify dialogue, probe for Soviet flexibility, and "get Andropov to put his money where his mouth is."[82] Even Clark, who had gone to great lengths to undermine similar advice from Shultz in the past, now stressed the need for open dialogue with the Soviet Union:

> Is there a possibility of achieving a constructive change in US-Soviet relations or not? The short answer is that we don't know; in part because of the change in Soviet leadership, but also because we haven't tried. . . . What do we have to lose by trying to open some doors? Two years ago I wouldn't have said that for indeed at that point, we had a lot to lose; we would have appeared to be supplicants, rushing into a very tough card game with no winners. But that's no longer true. We're on the march, and Andropov knows it.[83]

In fact, Clark became something of an ally to Shultz in the White House battle over Soviet policy. He overruled the objections of subordinates in the NSC, such as John Lenczowski, who insisted that "the assumptions underlying [Shultz's] analysis are at best questionable and at worst (which is most of the time) faulty."[84] Reagan, Shultz, and those who shared their views gradually pushed hard-liners out of foreign-policy making.[85] Clark reminded Reagan that a president is only afforded so many opportunities for foreign-policy breakthroughs; he could demonstrate that he was "not ideologically against solving problems with the Soviet Union . . . [and was] at least willing to try."[86]

These discussions resulted in a National Security Decision Directive—the seventy-fifth of the Reagan administration—laying out the interagency approach to the Cold War going forward. The document represented some views of the administration's hard-liners—for example, insisting that "US policy must have an ideological thrust which clearly affirms the superiority of US and Western values . . . over the repressive features of Soviet communism," but this was also basic to Reagan's and Shultz's thinking.[87] NSDD 75 directed the government to pursue negotiations with Moscow, provided they served US interests and only began once the United States enjoyed a dominant position vis-à-vis the Soviet Union, making full use of both the peace-through-strength and quiet-diplomacy strategies. The time had come, Shultz counseled Reagan, for "increased diplomatic and public activism . . . including through an intensified dialogue with Moscow."[88] The secretary of state raised the possibility of an Andropov-Reagan summit with a receptive Dobrynin in February 1983, and when he wrote to Andropov to congratulate him on having been elected chair of the Presidium of the Supreme Soviet, Reagan pledged his desire to work together to promote peace and reduce both superpowers' nuclear arsenals.[89]

In the spring of 1983, Reagan concluded that the balance of power favoring the Soviet Union at the time of his election had at last tipped in the United States' favor, meaning that negotiations with the Soviet Union could be fruitful—and advantageous. Going forward, Shultz believed, the management of US-Soviet relations should center on four issue areas: human rights within the Soviet Union, regional problems (such as Afghanistan), arms control, and bilateral questions. Adhering to a broad agenda would prevent the Kremlin from focusing negotiations solely on arms control while continuing their adventurism worldwide with impunity. (To many in the Reagan administration, Moscow's ability to do just that had been the critical flaw of détente.) Continuing to build up US strength—and remaining unafraid to use it—along with overtures on a wide range of issues would, Shultz believed, lead the Kremlin "to conclude it had no alternative but to come to terms with [the United

66   **CHAPTER 3**

States . . . and opportunities for lasting and significant improvement in US-Soviet relations would be better than they had been for decades."[90] The White House even entertained the idea of sending Shultz to Moscow that very summer to reinvigorate the superpower relationship.[91]

That was a bridge too far, but clearly the time had come for bold moves. The Reagan recession had come to an end, with inflation back in the single digits, and the economy growing again.[92] More importantly, the global economy had been changing in ways that may have hurt the United States in the short run—and contributed to much of the turmoil of the 1970s—but that greatly enhanced US power in the 1980s. When the United States abandoned the gold standard and the Bretton Woods system collapsed in 1971, Washington no longer needed to stabilize the worldwide system of currency by itself. The US dollar declined as a result, yet that slip in value made US exports more competitive internationally. The doomsday scenario of the US dollar being abandoned as the global reserve currency never transpired. When in the 1970s the world economy shifted into its postindustrial phase, the plant closures dominated the headlines—and with good reason, given the damage done to communities throughout the United States—but the agility of the US economy enabled it to adapt. US financial markets attracted capital from all over the world, reenergizing the economy and giving the Reagan administration financial headroom for its massive military expenditures. Globalization gave the United States a "second wind, and diplomatic capital came with the economic rebound."[93]

To many in the White House, Shultz above all, the administration had arrested the economic, military, and political decline of the late 1970s and put the Kremlin on the defensive. It was now time to begin "intensifying the dialogue" between the superpowers. This engagement would not be devoid of Cold War competition: Washington would keep pressure on Moscow and, if the superpowers failed to make progress in negotiations, ensure that public opinion blamed the Kremlin. The United States would make no concessions just for the "privilege" of dealing with the Soviets.[94] Quietly, the NSC's Soviet staff began to explore "whether, and if so, why and how, a summit meeting should be held . . . [in order to get] the right concessions."[95] Meanwhile, Shultz and Reagan worked ever closer to shape US policy toward the Soviet Union. The secretary of state used private meetings—without opportunity for those in the bureaucracy who objected—to update the president on his proposed course of action and secure his approval. Reagan would then ensure that his full administration—which he knew was divided—followed through. "Some of the NSC staff are too hard-line [and] don't think any approach should be made to the Soviets," the frustrated president confided in his diary. "I think

I'm hard-line and will never appease but I do want to try [and] let them see there is a better world if they'll show by deed they want to get along with the free world."[96]

As more policy makers within the Reagan administration made the case for US-Soviet engagement, Washington's NATO allies worked together to push the president toward more contact with the Soviet leadership and, ideally, a US-Soviet summit.[97] To a far greater extent than they realized, they were pushing on an open door. Margaret Thatcher and Helmut Kohl, who had succeeded Helmut Schmidt as Bundeskanzler in the fall of 1982, agreed that Reagan should make diplomatic use of what they both saw as a period of newfound US strength. Thatcher in particular planned to use the upcoming G7 summit in Williamsburg, Virginia, to encourage Reagan to prepare for a meeting with Andropov in the first months of 1984.[98] That was a bridge too far—the United States would welcome a summit that promised results, not "a summit for its own sake."[99] When they met in Williamsburg in May 1983, the G7 leaders affirmed the West's readiness to work with the Soviet Union. Although they stopped short of endorsing a US-Soviet summit, they did reemphasize their commitment to modernizing US nuclear forces in Europe.[100]

How could the West be committed both to fielding missiles in Western Europe to threaten the Soviet homeland and to cooperating with the Kremlin? To many in the politburo, who saw the Williamsburg summit as the inauguration of a new, international "anti-Soviet coalition," the former was all they needed to know.[101] But Andropov and other Eastern observers noted with approbation the shift within the White House privileging those who favored diplomatic engagement with the Soviet Union.[102] In a July letter to Gromyko setting out his foreign-policy priorities, the general secretary stressed the superpowers' unique responsibility to maintain international security. Moscow's main goal should be to stop an arms race in Europe and to reduce the threat of nuclear war by coming to an arms control agreement in Geneva. He exhorted Gromyko to "respond [to Reagan] constructively. This would be of historical significance."[103] Andropov's thinking, however, outpaced that of his politburo colleagues, who feared that their country's weakening position would leave them unable to secure advantageous agreements.[104]

Such fears stemmed from Soviet domestic woes and foreign-policy challenges. Whereas a Soviet policy maker could look at the world in 1980 and believe that the balance of power favored the Kremlin, by mid-1983, that was no longer the case. An isolated Soviet Union, bogged down in Afghanistan despite massive military spending, struggling to find a balance between "guns and margarine," had no choice but to accept that the Reagan administration had the upper hand.[105] Making matters worse, Moscow's Warsaw Pact allies grew increasingly restive. Near revolt had broken out in 1983 when Moscow had informed the Eastern Europeans that they would face a 10 percent decrease in oil provided by the Soviet Union, the difference to be sold to capitalist countries for desperately needed hard-currency profits. "International solidarity in general, and in particular friendship with the Soviet Union, are fantastic in and of themselves," Georgiĭ Shakhnazarov of the Central Committee's International Department observed trenchantly, "but they are especially strong when reinforced by supplies of Soviet oil at three- or four-times lower than market prices."[106] The affected countries took matters into their own hands. East Germany, for instance, accepted a billion–Deutsche Mark loan from the West later that year.[107] For the Kohl government, as the Bundeskanzler told Andropov, extending the loan was an essential signal to East Germans that the West had not abandoned them.[108] And, as quid pro quo, the East Germans would reduce the required sum to be converted to Ostmarks (effectively a fee for entry into East Germany given the artificial exchange rate and uselessness of the currency elsewhere), facilitating freer movement of people between the two Germanies.[109] Erich Honecker, East Germany's leader, even pledged to maintain "a coalition of reason" with Kohl.[110] To the rest of the Warsaw Pact, relations between East and West Germany now seemed distinct from the wider Cold War—and, to a striking degree, from Moscow's own preferences.[111]

On March 8, 1983, Reagan addressed the annual convention of the National Association of Evangelicals in Orlando, Florida. Intended to rebuff religious organizations advocating a freeze on nuclear armaments, Reagan attacked such thinking as facile and fraudulent, but also made it clear that he shared their goal of "reductions in the world's nuclear arsenals and one day . . . their total elimination." He went on to exhort his audience not to equate East and West, morally: "I urge you to beware the temptation of pride—the temptation of blithely declaring yourselves above it all and label both sides equally at fault, to ignore the facts of history and the aggressive impulses of an evil empire, to simply call the arms race a giant misunderstanding and thereby remove yourself from the struggle between right and wrong and good and evil. . . . The reality," he concluded, "is that we must find peace through strength."[112] Reagan's reference to an "evil empire" took on a life of its own. That simple phrase, inserted by speechwriters at the last minute, transformed his pro forma remarks into a major foreign-policy statement and obscured the president's remarkable public acknowledgment of his desire to abolish nuclear weapons.[113]

Gromyko, who advocated for a softer line, following the general secretary's specific instructions, struggled to build the necessary coalition within the

Kremlin. Remarks like Reagan's in Orlando hardly helped matters; and Soviet policy makers only read excerpts of Reagan's speeches—usually truncated to feature the most aggressive passages.[114] It was not clear that the Soviet foreign minister's heart was really in it. Hearing Reagan described as "a warm-hearted and emotional person," for example, Gromyko retorted by asking if Reagan spoke of fighting a nuclear war in Europe warm-heartedly.[115] This skepticism extended throughout Eastern Europe. In Kyiv, policy makers decried the "defamatory accusations" leveled against the Soviet Union, yet wrote most such speeches off as "demagoguery."[116] East German intelligence, on the other hand, suspected that Reagan's remarks were part of an orchestrated campaign to undermine their legitimacy, and East German military units intensified their training with nuclear-armed Soviet forces in response to this pattern of "anti-Soviet defamation."[117]

Would Reagan make good on his anti-Soviet rhetoric? To Soviet observers, the substance of US national security initiatives already appeared—with good reason—calculated to enable the United States to fight and win a nuclear war. Washington would soon have the ability to launch a nuclear first strike on the East with impunity. The new, highly accurate MX and Trident D-5 missiles would mostly disarm the Soviet Union by eliminating its land-based ICBM arsenal in their silos. But it was the best-known (if also most vague) aspect of Reagan's defense buildup—the Strategic Defense Initiative—that really worried the Kremlin. The futuristic system promised the capacity to wipe out any remaining Soviet missiles that could be used to retaliate against the United States, eliminating the Soviet second-strike capability.[118]

Reagan's March 23, 1983, announcement of SDI took the world—including many in the administration—by surprise.[119] Shultz, Weinberger, and the Joint Chiefs of Staff, for example, all learned of it as a fait accompli soon to be announced by the president and had almost no opportunity to provide input.[120] As Reagan and his scientific advisers envisioned it, SDI would be a system of land- and space-based weapons designed to intercept ICBMs in flight using a range of countermeasures. These included lasers so powerful they had to be powered by nuclear explosions, magnetic rail guns firing projectiles at many times the speed of sound, and "Brilliant Pebbles"—inert tungsten projectiles scattered by a network of satellites like caltrops in the path of oncoming missiles.[121] To the president, SDI meant that the United States "could put the nuclear genie back into the bottle" by rendering nuclear weapons obsolete.[122] By his closest advisers' admission, Reagan's assessment "was surely overselling the product."[123] He saw the program romantically, believing the power of the idea of a world without nuclear weapons could overcome the real, practical obstacles to SDI. The fantastical proposed system was, in other words, "an article of faith."[124]

70   **CHAPTER 3**

The idea of US military use of outer space—particularly through satellites under Washington's control—was not new to Soviet policy makers.[125] Even the space-shuttle program begun in 1981 was, in Moscow's eyes, "a space strike weapon."[126] And the Soviet military had long been warning of the nuclear arsenal's dangerous vulnerability to incapacitation from a nuclear strike.[127] Now, their retaliatory capability risked further erosion if SDI proved viable. US policy makers were not unsympathetic to this view. SDI was, they acknowledged, easily interpreted as "an excuse for a counterforce strategy under the guise of arms reduction."[128] That was precisely the interpretation of many leading Soviet military thinkers, who even before the announcement of SDI saw the United States as fixated on creating the preconditions for first-strike impunity by downing any Soviet retaliation.[129] As Gromyko later put it to Shultz, the threat SDI posed to the Soviet Union was "clear almost to the point of being primitive."[130]

Strategic stability had long been a preoccupation of Andropov's. As KGB chair, he had feared that Washington might entertain the idea of a nuclear first strike against the Soviet Union.[131] He concluded at that time that US policy makers understood the risks. "The [United States] is preparing for war, but it is not willing to start a war," he explained to Mielke in July 1981. "They are not building factories and palaces in order to destroy them. They are striving for military superiority in order to check us and then declare checkmate against us without starting a war."[132] In 1983, the perceived US-Soviet balance of military power hovered around equality, a state considered to be especially dangerous for both sides.[133] This was certainly how leaders in the Warsaw Pact saw things: in recent years, NATO had set out to achieve superiority, and it was now on the cusp of realizing this goal.[134] Strikingly, many in the Eastern bloc intelligence community recognized Western fears that the declining Warsaw Pact might exploit a "window of vulnerability" to launch a surprise attack.[135] "The politics of confrontation and conflict in the atomic age," one Czechoslovak diplomat wrote, ascribing blame to both sides, "may serve only to bring about nuclear catastrophe and the extinction of mankind as a species."[136]

Andropov grew increasingly worried about where the arms race would lead, as he had made clear the preceding year to Bush and Shultz at Brezhnev's funeral, stressing that "the result could only be catastrophe."[137] In early 1983, he warned his Warsaw Pact colleagues of the danger of a crisis-prone leadership in the White House, reminding them that "it is in our common interest to influence the US administration away from extreme measures."[138] When W. Averell Harriman, the US ambassador to the Soviet Union between 1943 and 1946, visited the Soviet capital in June 1983, Andropov seized the opportunity to express his concerns to the high-ranking former US official. He wanted to focus Washington's attention on the dangers inherent in allowing relations to deteriorate further. Myriad "explosive issues" around the world made it dangerous and irresponsible to focus solely on the superpowers' "destructive rivalry . . . at the expense of constructive interactions."[139] "Today," Andropov elaborated to Harriman, the two superpowers "have a common foe—the threat of a war incomparable with the horrors we went through previously. This war may perhaps not occur through evil, but could happen through miscalculation. Then nothing could save mankind."[140] Aleksandr Iakovlev, a senior Soviet foreign-policy official, echoed this message in conversation with Hartman at the US embassy: the United States must "develop a more sober and realistic approach to the Soviet Union."[141] Meanwhile, official outlets denounced the United States as "preparing a crime against humanity, trying to engulf it in the flames of a third world war."[142]

In day-to-day matters, Soviet actions did little to reduce tensions. Soviet helicopters made frequent incursions into West German airspace, even flying on collision courses with NATO aircraft.[143] For its part, the United States regularly tested Soviet air defenses by flying strategic bombers toward the borders of the Soviet Union, as if to deliver their payload, only to turn away at the very last minute.[144] "These were not adolescents playing arcade games," one Canadian foreign-policy maker remarked recalling US and Soviet provocations. "These were grown men testing the outer envelope of national willpower."[145] Not everything was a result of the superpowers testing each other's limits; on September 26, 1983, for example, the Soviet Union's Oko satellite early-warning system indicated a "mass launch" of inbound ICBMs from the United States.[146] In a scenario in which every minute counted—the year-old system gave the Kremlin at most twelve minutes' warning—the watch officer, Lt. Col. Stanislav Petrov, dismissed the alarm as false.[147]

For leaders who had come of age during World War II, witnessing the disastrous consequences of Nazi Germany's 1941 surprise attack on the Soviet Union, preventing another such assault was a constant preoccupation. "The enduring trauma of Barbarossa" haunted a generation of policy makers.[148] US history being, as one Soviet officer put it, "a never-ending string of aggressive wars and imperialist pillage," there was no reason to think Washington would not stoop to the same.[149] To Soviet military observers, major US investments in precise nuclear weapons indicated a desire to launch disarming surprise attacks on Washington's enemies, Moscow included.[150]

The intelligence agencies of the Warsaw Pact therefore made gaining insight into Western intentions a priority, especially the timely detection of early preparations for a Western surprise attack.[151] At a May 1982 meeting, their leaders developed "recommendations" for cooperation on "activities in the

72   **CHAPTER 3**

field of early warning."[152] They dubbed this initiative Project RIaN (short for Raketno-Iadernoe Napadenie, or "nuclear missile attack").[153] Warsaw Pact policy makers envisioned Project RIaN as a "multi-year, complex scientific investigation" into the use of computers in intelligence analysis.[154] It focused on "theoretical reflection," housed within the KGB's Institute for Research on Operative Problems.[155] RIaN's 292 data points for predicting a surprise attack, not finalized until 1986, ranged from unusually full parking lots at the Pentagon, to major transfers of government documents to National Archives and Records Administration facilities, to the closure of museums to evacuate artifacts.[156] But skepticism abounded as to whether a computer could accurately warn of an impending strike in the first place, no matter how many data inputs.[157] At the same time, the Soviet military was working to incorporate computer modeling into war-gaming with extremely mixed results; even in the official pages of *Voennaia mysl'*, strategists were forced to acknowledge that these efforts were fruitless.[158] Markus Wolf, head of the Stasi's foreign intelligence service, deemed RIaN a "burdensome waste of time" based on a far-fetched premise.[159] And in the Soviet Union itself, "intelligence professionals . . . did not take seriously the much ballyhooed warning system."[160] By the time of the project's termination in 1991—barely a month before the collapse of the Soviet Union—RIaN had nothing to show for itself.[161]

In November 1982, ten-year-old Samantha Smith of Manchester, Maine, wrote to Andropov, expressing her fears about what she saw on the news: "I have been worrying about Russia and the United States getting into a nuclear war. Are you going to vote to have a war or not? . . . I would like to know why you want to conquer the world or at least our country."[162] Andropov responded to her in a letter with assurances that the Soviet Union wanted peace. Soviet citizens preferred to focus their energies on "growing wheat, building and inventing, writing books, and flying into space," he insisted. Seeing a possible public relations victory, he invited Smith and her parents to visit the Soviet Union.[163] To reinforce the "anti-war character of the trip," Smith spent much of her visit at Artek, the premier camp for Young Pioneers in Ukraine's Crimean Peninsula. In that same spirit of hospitality, the Ukrainian KGB turned a blind eye when Smith's father brought letters from Jewish émigrés to Andropov asking that their friends and relatives still in the Soviet Union be allowed to join them. None were granted exit visas.[164] In the United States, Smith's name has largely faded from memory, but in the Soviet Union it was synonymous with the possibility of transcending the Cold War.[165]

Across NATO, a major peace movement coalesced as citizens took to the streets to voice their fears that the planned INF deployments coupled with the visible deterioration of East-West relations would lead to a nuclear war.[166] Church organizations, trade unions, environmental groups, and others mobilized thousands of demonstrators to protest the danger of nuclear weapons and their leaders' apparent unwillingness to do anything to reduce the nuclear threat.[167] The antinuclear position had social and political traction. In the March 6, 1983, elections in West Germany, for example, Die Grünen won an unprecedented twenty-seven seats in the Bundestag, explicitly running against stationing new nuclear weapons on German soil, a political message that resonated worryingly well.[168] Kohl feared that West Germany's privileged youth were especially prone to "nihilism, skepticism, and inner emptiness"—and recruitment into domestic terrorist organizations.[169] Even West German Bundeswehr troops took to the streets in large numbers in opposition to the INF deployment, marching—in uniform—under banners declaring that "NATO Soldiers Say No to Cruise Missiles and Pershing 2s."[170]

Moscow's anti-Western propaganda grew increasingly "shrill" as the Kremlin tried to stop the INF deployments.[171] They certainly had an interest in creating the atmospherics of a "war danger."[172] Perceptions of poor US-Soviet relations encouraged public opposition to NATO's nuclear policies and increased pressure on the Reagan administration to adopt a more conciliatory approach. In the Soviet Union, that same atmosphere justified high military spending, which resulted in austerity and unpopular strict standards of labor discipline.[173] Meanwhile, Soviet policy makers accused the United States of engaging in similar behavior, using official organs such as the Voice of America radio network along with unofficial partners like the Heritage Foundation to stoke fears of war—and lay the blame on Moscow.[174] In fact, in the summer of 1983, the White House was focused on doing just the opposite. There would be no more "gratuitous hectoring" of Moscow.[175] Reagan refused a meeting with prominent Soviet dissident Aleksandr Solzhenitsyn, which members of his administration feared would be seen as "running counter to our desire for negotiations with the Soviet Union."[176] (Ironically, Reagan had lambasted Ford in July 1975 for refusing to meet with Solzhenitsyn in order to avoid "bruising the sensibilities of the Soviets.")[177] Questions about the reality of a possible upturn in US-Soviet relations now elicited a "guarded yes" from the White House.[178]

On September 1, 1983, Osipovich's interceptor aircraft shot down Korean Air Lines flight 007 as it passed through prohibited Soviet airspace en route from New York to Seoul. The Soviet Far Eastern Military District regularly witnessed US reconnaissance aircraft penetrate its airspace and, according to its commander, concluded that the off-course civilian airliner was another such flight,

CHAPTER 3

first instructing it to land and then firing on it.[179] According to a host of Soviet policy makers, this fatal error precipitated the most dangerous episode of the Cold War in the 1980s and the greatest threat to stability since the Cuban Missile Crisis some two decades earlier.[180]

US condemnation was swift—and scathing. That same day, Reagan issued a statement demanding "a full explanation for this appalling and wanton misdeed . . . inexplicable to civilized people."[181] The next day, Reagan denounced the "barbaric" act himself, asking his audience, "What can we think of a regime that . . . so callously and quickly commits a terrorist act to sacrifice the lives of innocent human beings?"[182] Three days later, Reagan made his answer clear: "This was the Soviet Union against the world and the moral precepts which guide human relations among people everywhere. It was an act of barbarism, born of a society which wantonly disregards individual rights and the value of human life and seeks constantly to expand and dominate other nations."[183] As the condemnation flowed, the Kremlin worried how far the Reagan administration would go in retaliation.[184]

The downing of KAL 007 raised questions about the internal situation in the Soviet Union. Was Andropov involved in the decision to fire? Did the Soviets recognize the Boeing 747 as a civilian aircraft?[185] But Moscow was not forthcoming. When the under secretary of state for political affairs, Lawrence Eagleburger, delivered the US démarche to Dobrynin's deputy, Oleg Sokolov, the Soviet diplomat remained silent.[186] In London and Ottawa, too, Soviet diplomats had no response.[187] Czechoslovak leaders would at least speak out, but only to denounce Reagan's "escalating arrogance and aggressiveness," as well as his "primitive and vulgar . . . anti-Soviet hysteria."[188] Washington's allies worried that Moscow's refusal to acknowledge wrongdoing would confirm the worst suspicions about the Soviet Union in the White House and deal a fatal blow to East-West relations.[189] When the ten foreign ministers of the European Economic Community met in Madrid on September 8, Hans-Dietrich Genscher lamented that "the situation is critical—as always in Washington, the local cooks are making a soup without the experience of the European chefs. The task for the European chefs now is to make sure the soup does not burn."[190]

Shultz hoped to assemble a broad international coalition to condemn the Soviet Union's actions. The State Department, however, recommended that retaliation be confined to the realm of transportation: cancellation of a planned civil aviation agreement, restriction of Aeroflot flights, and other punitive measures through the UN and its International Civil Aviation Organization. East-West relations would be damaged, but not irreparably so.[191] By contrast, Clark and the NSC urged Reagan to go on the offensive. The administration should

TALKING ABOUT TALKING   75

dispel once and for all the image of the Soviet Union as a "peacemaker."[192] They even warned of a new wave of Soviet intimidation of US allies in Asia and Europe. The deluge of telephone calls received by the White House switchboard—nearly two thousand by midday on September 2, mere hours after the news broke—all demanded a strong response.[193]

At this key moment in US-Soviet relations, Shultz's hand was strengthened by the arrival of Jack Matlock, who replaced Richard Pipes as senior director for European and Soviet affairs on the NSC. (Matlock flew from his post as US ambassador in Prague to Washington on the day after the KAL 007 tragedy.) From Prague and on frequent trips to Washington, Matlock had regularly contributed to the Reagan administration's policy-making process, suggesting ways the president might engage the Soviets.[194] In the White House debate over how to respond to KAL 007, Reagan sided with Shultz and Matlock and erred on the side of continuing to engage Moscow. To the president, the threat of nuclear war mattered above all else, especially in a time of crisis. His own instincts were to continue engaging the Soviets and not to allow the entire relationship to be derailed by the incident. He sent Paul Nitze back to the negotiating table in Geneva just three days after the massacre for exactly this reason. Knowing that Washington could "proceed in quiet ways to exact a price," Reagan told Thatcher, "now was not a time when we should isolate ourselves from the Soviet Union."[195] But quiet approaches rarely satisfied the public, and Reagan faced sharp criticism for the policy course he chose after the KAL 007 massacre, often from those who were usually allies, such as conservative columnist George Will.[196] Will was not alone. "If you say they're barbarians, how can we negotiate?" one reporter asked as Reagan publicly sent Nitze off to Geneva.[197] The president declined to answer.

At this crucial moment, Andropov's poor health kept the general secretary on the sidelines.[198] Chernenko chaired the September 2, 1983, emergency meeting of the politburo, focused on the likelihood that Washington would exploit the KAL 007 incident to undermine the Soviet Union. Gromyko warned that it would be used to gin up "anti-Soviet hysteria" and as a pretext to scrap all negotiations with Moscow. Dmitriĭ Ustinov, the minister of defense, concurred, warning that reactions to KAL 007 would distract from the Kremlin's valuable peace initiatives. He insisted that no one could prove that the Soviet Union had shot the plane down. Others believed that it was a deliberate US provocation. Nikolaĭ Tikhonov, chair of the Council of Ministers, wondered how the pilot could have allowed himself to go so far into restricted Soviet airspace when "he must have realized that this meant certain death." Viktor Chebrikov went one step further, suggesting that the aircraft flew as if it were not controlled by the pilot but remotely by US intelligence. But Gorbachev urged his colleagues not to deny the facts. The Soviet Union, he said, should make "a formal presentation" to the United States of events as they had unfolded from a Soviet perspective.[199]

Ustinov and the military won the politburo debate, prevailing on Andropov to deny responsibility outright and insist that Moscow had nothing to do with the disaster.[200] At the UN, the Soviet delegation accused the United States of "provocation," insisting that KAL 007 was an espionage flight and that a UN Security Council meeting on the subject would be "without grounds, unjustified, and unnecessary."[201] When Shultz and Gromyko met in Madrid only a week after the tragedy, Gromyko insisted that Soviet soil was sacred and that the Soviet pilot had done what needed to be done to protect it. When Shultz retorted that human life was also sacred, the Soviets walked out.[202] In a meeting with Genscher later that day, Gromyko insisted that blame for the tragedy and the passengers' deaths lay with the United States—US intelligence had framed the Soviet Union.[203] Even when the ICAO produced its final report on the incident, noting the "considerable lack of alertness and attentiveness on [the] part of [the] entire flight crew," suggesting that KAL 007 had accidentally found its way into Soviet airspace, the Soviet delegation maintained that the flight was a provocative reconnaissance mission.[204]

To Erich Mielke, Vladimir Kriuchkov—the head of the KGB's First Chief Directorate (responsible for intelligence operations overseas)—admitted that Soviet pilots had not recognized the plane as a civilian airliner. "We were absolutely convinced that the plane was on a reconnaissance mission," he concluded. "Had we known it was a passenger plane, we would not have shot it down. But everything pointed in the other direction."[205] Others went even further. *Pravda* correspondent (and KGB agent) Sergeĭ Vishnevskiĭ acknowledged that "[the Kremlin] could not have handled the KAL massacre worse." Nevertheless, the three main figures in Soviet policy making—Andropov, Gromyko, and Ustinov—all wanted to improve relations with the United States so that they could focus on domestic issues, such as the economy, "a total mess, and getting worse."[206] The Finnish president Mauno Koivisto tried to bridge the gap—at the Kremlin's behest—as Moscow realized its denial of responsibility was hurting US-Soviet relations and its own credibility worldwide. The Soviets regretted shooting down the airliner, Koivisto insisted, and now "Andropov and those around him are searching for the right thing to do."[207] "It [was] a sign of weakness that they were unable to apologize," he explained to Reagan, and could not afford to lose face even when so obviously culpable.[208] The Kremlin wanted to minimize the damage done to East-West relations.[209] Soviet diplomats indicated to their US counterparts that Moscow's hostile rhetoric was born out of frustration at the situation—

exacerbated by the policy successes of the Reagan administration. "We are . . . in for a frigid fall and winter," Hartman later elaborated, but Andropov "will recognize that circumstances . . . will never be better [for US-Soviet dialogue,] and he may not wish to lose the opportunity.[210]

"Part of the tragedy of the Korean airliner incident," Reagan told Thatcher, "was that the [Soviets] would now have to make a move before dialogue could be resumed."[211] Reagan did entertain taking a step to jump-start dialogue just over a month after the KAL 007 massacre: sending a "close associate" of his to Moscow as the new US ambassador. The two names Reagan considered were Clark, the national security adviser, and Meese, counselor to the president. Both enjoyed considerable influence in the White House as members of Reagan's inner circle for decades. The Kremlin would know that the new ambassador spoke for the president, and that they could communicate with him directly through the embassy. Matlock expected that this would be welcomed in Moscow, where Soviet officials recognized that they needed respite from international pressures in order to focus on arguably more pressing domestic issues. Ultimately, the dramatic move came to naught.[212] Clark had fallen out of favor in the White House after KAL 007 for advocating an extremely hard-line view, and soon found himself eased out of the inner circle (at Nancy Reagan's behest) and into the role of secretary of the interior.[213]

The Reagan administration did not only have to contend with events in Europe. On October 22, 1983, Reagan decided to launch a "rescue operation" to evacuate roughly one thousand US medical students from the Caribbean island of Grenada. The White House worried about increased Cuban influence after a communist-led coup had ousted and then murdered Prime Minister Maurice Bishop.[214] The next day, October 23, a suicide bomber drove an explosives-laden truck into the barracks of a contingent of US Marines deployed to Beirut, Lebanon, on a peacekeeping mission; news of the 241 deaths rocked the United States, especially after a second suicide attack struck French peacekeepers based nearby, bringing the day's death toll to 299.[215] In Washington, politicians spoke openly of "another Vietnam" in Lebanon.[216]

For all the talk of rescuing students, Grenada's significance lay in what it symbolized: that the United States had at last gotten out from the shadow of the Vietnam war."[217] Washington would project power not only with technologically advanced armaments but also with US boots on the ground.[218] As George Will, now applauding the administration, wrote in *Newsweek*: "Grenada, although small, is 15 times the size of Iwo Jima and of large symbolic value. US soldiers' boot prints on Grenada's soil have done more than the MX will do to make US power credible and peace secure. President Reagan's defense budgets are not, by themselves, a fully effective signal to the Soviet Union of US seriousness. The boot prints prove that the United States will not only procure sophisticated weapons systems but also has recovered the will to use the weapon on which its security rests: the man with a rifle."[219] Will engaged in no small amount of hyperbole. The Grenada operation had been something of a fiasco; had the 7,300 US military personnel not been up against an underequipped and undertrained Grenadian force 1,200 strong, it would likely have turned out differently.[220]

Moscow disputed the characterization of the US invasion as a rescue operation. First and foremost, purported concern over the safety of US citizens scarcely made sense, as starting a war on the island could only make matters worse. Georgiĭ Shakhnazarov of the Central Committee's International Department quipped in response to the claim that Bishop's murder justified intervention, "If the murder of a prime minister is considered sufficient reason for a foreign military intervention, then the nations of the world would have had a legitimate reason to invade the United States . . . after the assassination of President Kennedy."[221] When Iakovlev pressed Hartman in Moscow, the US ambassador gave a straightforward explanation: "As a great power the United States enjoys the right to protect its national interests, including its security interests," however it should choose to define them.[222] It was not for nothing, Shakhnazarov noted wryly, that Reagan cited Theodore Roosevelt as his favorite predecessor. The Kremlin—and the world—should be glad that "Roosevelt did not have ballistic missiles and nuclear warheads."[223] Such dark humor aside, a pessimistic few in Moscow recognized what Grenada had demonstrated: even though the Soviet Union was nominally a coequal superpower, the Kremlin could do little to deter the projection of US power around the world.[224]

After Grenada, many in the Warsaw Pact questioned their earlier assumptions about US restraint.[225] Would the United States now undertake to "widen the so-called American way of life to the entire world?" Gromyko wondered.[226] The most significant crisis triggered by the invasion, however, was in US relations with its allies.[227] Washington's lack of consultation, especially before invading a fellow member of the Commonwealth, was unacceptable in Margaret Thatcher's eyes. Deputy Secretary of State Kenneth Dam met with Thatcher, who promptly demanded assurances that Grenada "was a one-off operation" and not the beginning of a new interventionist policy. Dam assured her that the United States did not want to set a precedent that would benefit the Soviets. For her part, Thatcher saw Grenada in the context of the impending INF deployments. "People argued that if the [United States] did not consult us over Grenada," she warned Dam, "why should they do so over the firing of missiles?"[228]

Soviet policy makers remained convinced that those deployments must be stopped. If not, it would mean "the transformation of . . . [Europe] into a launching pad for US first-strike nuclear missiles," which threatened the territory—and the capital—of the Soviet Union.[229] These were "strategic armaments," the likes of which the United States would never accept so close to its own borders—as the Cuban Missile Crisis had amply demonstrated.[230] The Soviet Union employed a "complex strategy of inducements and threats" to prevent such a setback.[231] Part of this played out in Geneva at the INF negotiations; more played out on the streets of Europe. The Kremlin and its allies relied on assets within the Western European peace movement to agitate against INF.[232] Soviet policy makers took pride in their "huge propaganda campaign," but as the KGB admitted, Europeans had yet to "get it into their heads" that INF would make them "hostages."[233]

US policy makers appreciated INF's significance. It was nothing less than a "litmus test of NATO's viability." Demonstrating allied cohesion would support Reagan's push for the peace-through-strength strategy—and bring the Soviet Union to the negotiating table in earnest. INF deployment would give Washington a powerful lever.[234] The deployments were only the beginning: Reagan believed that the Soviets could not keep pace, especially with the Pershing 2s and ground-launched cruise missiles en route to Europe, whereas the United States could continue to grow its military. Moscow would need to be convinced that "the only way [to] remain equal was by negotiation."[235]

On November 22, the West German Bundestag voted to accept INF on its territory, the final obstacle to deployment.[236] The next day, as predicted, the Soviet negotiating team walked out of the talks in Geneva. Moscow hoped the move would increase pressure on Washington to offer better terms or, perhaps, even to halt the deployment. Gromyko, who devised the plan, miscalculated.[237] The Soviets saw INF as Western Europe acquiescing to US pressure, but it had also been about, as Genscher tried to explain to Kvitsinskiĭ, "fundamental European interests."[238] Moscow had been far from subtle in its interference in Western politics, and it had failed publicly when unrest on the street failed to change votes in parliament. Soviet officials, having assured their Warsaw Pact allies that the INF deployments would be prevented, failed to make good on their pledge.[239] The strategic balance tipped definitively in the West's favor; the new US weapons would be a "cocked pistol to Moscow's temple."[240]

The breakdown of US-Soviet arms control talks in Geneva marked the climax of Soviet rhetoric. The mood in Moscow was tense in late 1983 and early 1984. Reports from the Soviet capital focused on "war danger" propaganda and an atmosphere on the street of "an obsessive fear of war, and emotionalism, and a paranoia . . . that had not been present earlier."[241] As Kremlin

80   CHAPTER 3

foreign-policy official Andreĭ Aleksandrov-Agentov later summed it up, "We scared our own people."[242] The Kremlin also scared much of the rest of the world, and Reagan's admonition to look past the "awful lot of rhetoric that is delivered for home consumption" in the Soviet Union went largely unheeded worldwide.[243]

Fears of a US-Soviet military confrontation extended into popular culture. The made-for-television movie *The Day After*, which aired on November 20, 1983, depicted in graphic detail the destruction of the town of Lawrence, Kansas, as a result of a Soviet nuclear attack. Some one hundred million people watched the first broadcast, making it the most watched television movie in history. Viewers were horrified by what they saw of the realities of strategic nuclear combat.[244] In his diary, Reagan too confided that the film "left [him] greatly depressed."[245] White House officials who saw an advance version of the film went so far as to develop a full public relations strategy to assuage concerns that Reagan's foreign policy was moving the world in that direction.[246] Eastern leaders also took note. Honecker later referenced the film in a conversation with visiting members of Congress about the importance of arms control.[247] In a similar vein, the West German pop group Nena's 1983 hit song "Neunundneunzig Luftballons" told a dystopian story of errant balloons being mistaken for an incoming missile attack by war-hungry leaders, triggering a ninety-nine-year-long nuclear war.[248]

In the midst of this charged atmosphere, NATO held its annual exercises in Western Europe, collectively dubbed Autumn Forge 83, training troops (including some twenty thousand airlifted from the United States) in case of war on the continent. The final component, Able Archer 83, simulated the transition from conventional to nuclear war between November 4 and November 11.[249] To many, this episode encapsulates the tensions and dangers of what was termed the "Second Cold War."[250] The United States and the Soviet Union, so the story told by KGB defector Oleg Gordievskiĭ goes, teetered on the brink of nuclear war, as Warsaw Pact leaders believed that NATO's command-and-control exercise was cover for a surprise nuclear attack and entertained a preemptive strike of their own.[251]

Soviet and Eastern bloc policy makers gave no consideration to the possibility of a Western surprise nuclear attack masked by the exercise, nor to conducting a preemptive strike.[252] Able Archer 83 was nothing new; similar exercises occurred on an annual basis under the watchful eyes of Warsaw Pact intelligence.[253] They saw Able Archer 83 as yet another "command staff exercise," not an action involving troops but rather a rehearsal of the alliance "carrying out decisions at the highest military and political levels" to use nuclear weapons.[254] When East German military intelligence and the KGB briefed their principals on Able Archer 83, they framed it as a means of further subordinating the militaries of independent NATO members to the United States.[255] The rehearsal of nuclear war "[did] not reflect NATO's actual assessment of the international situation."[256] Rainier Rupp, the Stasi's best-placed spy at NATO in Brussels, reported that "there was no indication that NATO was preparing for war" during Able Archer 83.[257] Viktor Cherkashin of the KGB's First Chief Directorate, who was stationed in Washington at the time, agreed. "Despite the tensions, reports that Washington and Moscow came close to nuclear war are exaggerated."[258] This same sanguinity can be found in Czechoslovak military intelligence's report after the fact.[259] Viktor Esin of the Strategic Rocket Forces recounted that Soviet commanders "knew that NATO [forces] were doing an exercise, [but were] not really planning for the nuclear blow."[260] Andrian Danilevich, the chief adviser on nuclear doctrine to the Soviet General Staff, insisted that "no one believed there was a real likelihood (immediate threat) of a nuclear strike from the [United States] or NATO."[261] Vladen Smirnoff, deputy head of intelligence for the Northern Fleet at the time, recalled his staff coming to the same conclusion: "Able Archer was just a typical exercise. . . . There was nothing outstanding about it."[262] "Quite frankly," snapped Igor Kondratiev of Soviet military intelligence after a lengthy line of questioning on the subject, "I don't understand your special interest [in] this particular exercise."[263]

Able Archer 83 merited notice at the operational level, as would any significant movement of NATO forces or demonstration of NATO capabilities. At Soviet air bases in East Germany and Poland, as well as at some Soviet missile installations, alert levels did increase; but according to those who authorized them, this did not reflect serious concern over a surprise nuclear attack, nor did it extend beyond "certain military districts."[264] Those observers "did not flinch, because they knew they were monitoring an exercise."[265] They could listen to the hourly circuit-verification signal on NATO's nuclear-release communications systems and, according to the military and the KGB, recognize a release order.[266] The alerts reflect an awareness that NATO exercises were underway and a desire to remind Washington that the Soviet Union stood ready to respond to any provocation. There was nothing unusual or new about an adversary countermobilizing and countersignaling during a major military exercise.[267]

The US intelligence community concluded that "Soviet actions are not inspired by, and Soviet leaders do not perceive, a genuine danger of imminent conflict or confrontation with the United States."[268] They were "just rattling their pots and pans."[269] But reports of Soviet countersignaling reached Reagan. Talk of a Soviet "war scare" reinforced many of the president's preexisting

82 CHAPTER 3

assumptions, particularly the need for more East-West contacts and a more stable framework for superpower relations.[270] Upon hearing these accounts, Reagan confided in his diary that "the Soviets . . . [were] so paranoid about being attacked that . . . we ought to tell them no one here has any intention of doing anything like that."[271] He recalled in his memoirs how the events of that autumn encouraged him to intensify his earlier efforts at quiet diplomacy: "I began to realize that many Soviet officials feared us not only as adversaries but as potential aggressors who might hurl nuclear weapons at them in a first strike. . . . I was even more anxious to get a top Soviet leader in a room alone and try to convince him we had no designs on the Soviet Union and Russians had nothing to fear from us."[272]

As sources from the Warsaw Pact show, it is entirely possible that some in the West came to believe that Able Archer 83 almost led to a nuclear war, that there is ample documentation from Western sources to support this conclusion, and that they were entirely wrong. Even if the Soviet Union and its Warsaw Pact allies did not genuinely believe that the United States intended to attack, the atmosphere of a "war scare" encouraged Reagan to work even more closely with Shultz to implement his vision of US-Soviet relations.[273] On Reagan's instructions, a high-level working group began meeting in late 1983 to brainstorm means of jump-starting US-Soviet relations. This group of top foreign-policy officials and Reagan's close confidantes, including Bush, Shultz, Meese, and Bud McFarlane (who had replaced Clark as national security adviser in autumn 1983), had a clear objective: to develop a framework to take Reagan's quiet diplomacy public. Secretary of Defense Caspar Weinberger, an outspoken skeptic, did not an attend, though the Pentagon did send a lower-level representative.[274]

In his home office, Andropov kept a small wooden carving of Don Quixote.[275] But unlike the fictional Spanish nobleman, the general secretary's problem was not that he refused to see the world as it was. Andropov understood the real challenges facing his country up to that point. His appreciation of the fact that the United States was overtaking the Soviet Union made him especially interested in diplomatic engagement with Washington as a means of forestalling further Soviet decline.[276] And he had, as Shultz put it, "the self-confidence to . . . make his mark on history."[277] Behind closed doors, the general secretary even talked about a "reset" in US-Soviet relations.[278] Reagan shared Andropov's goals, even as he struggled to reconcile hawkish and dovish impulses. But the breakthrough they both sought in East-West relations remained out of reach. Andropov tried to balance pressing issues in both domestic and foreign policy, made worse by his own deteriorating health, which left him inca-

TALKING ABOUT TALKING 83

pacitated at key junctures.[279] And Reagan and his advisers often created new obstacles, by their own admission, sending contradictory signals such as the "evil empire" speech.[280]

1983 was a year of misfires. Neither Reagan nor Andropov accepted the other's use of a two-pronged approach to superpower relations that paired carrot and stick, despite employing such a strategy himself. Neither could overcome the year's crises to make progress in East-West relations. Internal factions in both Washington and Moscow made these differences even more difficult to surmount, working against both leaders' efforts. For all they talked about it, Reagan and Andropov never had the face-to-face meeting they envisioned, but that they kept on talking thoughout meant that a turbulent year did not become deadly. And all their talk about talking set both the United States and the Soviet Union on a course for even more overt engagement in the future. It would be up to a new Soviet leader, in this case one who craved that high visibility, to take up the challenge of turning words into deeds.

CHAPTER 4

Trial Balloons
Reaching Out and Laying Groundwork

"In the beginning were the words. . . . After the words, the walkouts. . . . Now, in silence, come the missiles, no longer metaphorical, but physical and nuclear. . . . Following the missiles, fear and alarm." The beginning of *Time*'s 1983 Men of the Year feature on Ronald Reagan and Iurii Andropov did not bode well for it being a puff piece.

Peppered with pull quotes of the two leaders' hostile rhetoric, the cover story painted a grim picture of 1983: US-Soviet hostility "overshadowed all other events." The two men were featured by the magazine not for any foreign-policy achievements but because they had the power "to decide whether there will be any future at all." Would Reagan be able to overcome the anti-Soviet and anti-communist worldview that seemed to drive US foreign policy, and would Andropov surmount the illness that made Kremlin policy making even more opaque than usual?

Time's editors expressed some hope. In an interview for the issue, for example, Reagan had conceded that he would not again describe the Soviet Union as the "focus of evil" in the world.[1] But they also had their doubts. The lengthy piece on the two leaders' actions over the course of 1983 was followed by a piece in which eight statesmen, including former president Richard Nixon and the prime ministers of Australia and Canada, Bob Hawke and Pierre Trudeau, offered their advice as to how Reagan and Andropov could do their jobs better.[2]

84

TRIAL BALLOONS 85

In a late 1983 conversation with Margaret Thatcher's predecessor, James Callaghan, Soviet Foreign Minister Andreĭ Gromyko bemoaned the fact that "there was no common language" between the two superpowers. "The Reagan administration," he charged, "was not communicating."[3] As the world watched, that changed over the course of 1984, but with the most unlikely of partners: Konstantin Chernenko, who has generally been dismissed as "a feeble, wheezing stopgap."[4] He may have lacked the menace of the former KGB chair, but Chernenko also lacked much of Andropov's gravitas. Even his own biographer argues that the West's greatest mistake was overestimating the penultimate general secretary.[5] But in a year all too often dismissed as an interregnum and under a Soviet leader regularly written off as too sick to have mattered, the two superpowers laid the groundwork for a pattern of engagement—on primarily US terms—that would characterize the end of the Cold War. Explaining this improbable—and all too often overlooked—phenomenon requires not only understanding the major structural forces at work, above all the balance of power between East and West, but also how and why leaders in Washington and Moscow perceived and responded to them as they did.

Immediately after the first Pershing 2s arrived from the United States, Bundeskanzler Helmut Kohl wrote to Andropov to reiterate that "every single [US] rocket that is now stationed [in Europe] can be dismantled"—but the Soviet Union would have to make the first move and return to the negotiating table.[6] Western publics were not willing to wait that long. The nuclear freeze movement, calling for both superpowers to halt the construction and deployment of nuclear weapons, remained a political force to be reckoned with. In the United States, for example, freeze activists had shepherded the passage of nonbinding resolutions supporting their cause in four state legislatures, the House, and the Senate.[7] Reagan's challenger in the fast-approaching 1984 presidential election, Democrat (and Jimmy Carter's former vice president) Walter Mondale, ran on a platform explicitly endorsing the freeze. Mondale's campaign returned to a theme from the 1980 campaign, dismissing Reagan as nothing more than an anti-Soviet hard-liner. If elected, Mondale promised to improve relations with the Soviet Union.[8]

Politically expedient as it may have been, Mondale's critique was out of step with the administration's actual policies. By the latter half of 1983, growing increasingly frustrated by the traction characterizations like Mondale's gained among the public, Reagan's advisers had concluded that the time had come for a major presidential address on US-Soviet relations.[9] As the year progressed, the idea took hold throughout the White House.[10] Three years of building strength in the economy, in the military, and among Washington's alliances

CHAPTER 4

augured well for an overture from the desired position of strength. Earlier episodes in 1983, such as the freeing of the Siberian Seven, had shown the White House that quiet diplomacy worked. Overt engagement was another matter; as Lawrence Eagleburger lamented, "Our dialogue is like ships passing in the night."[11] The Kremlin had to be made to see the possibility of the post-Brezhnev era becoming a turning point in Soviet foreign policy—a turning away from the costly competition with the United States, which it could ill afford. But a speech should not just address the Soviets, George Shultz urged; it should also shape public opinion at home and abroad.[12] The public needed a fuller explanation of US policy toward the Soviet Union. In one of his rare marginal notes, Reagan concurred, telling his staff that a speech should be delivered sooner rather than later.[13] And he wanted it to make a splash—the president would reject several early drafts as "pedestrian."[14] The time had come to demonstrate that the United States was not "guided by a blind and uncomprehending form of anti-Sovietism."[15]

Not everyone in the White House agreed. John Lenczowski of the NSC needed a long talking-to, explaining that the president's Soviet policy was going in a different direction to the harder line that he had been advocating.[16] Lenczowski, for example, had encouraged Reagan to make maximum propaganda use of findings that the Soviets had been violating their SALT 2 and other arms control commitments; the irony of criticizing Moscow for not complying with a deal that the Reagan administration had abandoned was apparently lost on him.[17] Instead, Reagan directed his staff to "low key it in the report" in the interests of improved relations going forward.[18]

Reagan and his team forged ahead, preparing for a presidential speech on US-Soviet relations on January 16, 1984, to, as the president put it in his diary, "reassure the eggheads and our European friends I don't plan to blow up the world."[19] As the date approached, the White House worked to ensure that the speech would have maximum effect at home and abroad. Administration officials provided advance briefings to leaders in Congress and past ambassadors to the Soviet Union.[20] US allies received advance copies of the text. Margaret Thatcher even warranted a personal visit from Shultz, who intimated that both he and Reagan expected the speech to generate considerable criticism for extending an olive branch to Moscow, but Reagan felt it necessary all the same.[21] Even Beijing received an advance briefing, indicating just how far that relationship had progressed.[22] Shultz laid the groundwork with the Soviets in a meeting with Anatolii Dobrynin, and the White House sent an advance copy of the speech to Andropov, along with a letter from Reagan expressing his desire for regular, high-level consultations.[23] Meanwhile, Reagan entertained a range of options to put his words about US-Soviet cooperation into action, including reinvigorating the Apollo-Soyuz collaboration of the mid-1970s and building a space station with the Soviet Union.[24]

On the morning of January 16, television equipment filled the East Room. The White House scheduled the speech for 10:00 a.m. to maximize news coverage across Europe and in the Soviet Union, whose residents were as much the speech's audience as were viewers in the United States.[25] Reagan pledged to build a "constructive and realistic working relationship with the Soviet Union." He explained this change in tone to be a result of the nation's increased defense spending and economic recovery. Both made the United States and the world safer. The United States' "working relationship with the Soviet Union," Reagan went on, "is not what it must be." He proposed that the two superpowers come together to discuss areas of mutual concern and examine concrete actions both could take to reduce the chances of a nuclear conflict breaking out. Reagan committed the United States to working with the Kremlin to reduce nuclear arsenals. Though he objected to the Soviet system and would not shy away from saying so, the president insisted that his "commitment to dialogue [was] firm and unshakeable. . . . We seek genuine cooperation. We seek progress for peace." Reagan communicated that sentiment, as he so often did, through a folksy story. He imagined a chance encounter between a Soviet couple and a couple from the United States:

> Just suppose with me for a moment that an Ivan and an Anya could find themselves, oh, say, in a waiting room, or sharing a shelter from the rain or a storm with a Jim and Sally, and there was no language barrier to keep them from getting acquainted. Would they then debate the differences between their respective governments? Or would they find themselves comparing notes about their children and what each other did for a living? Before they parted company, they would probably have touched on ambitions and hobbies and what they wanted for their children and problems of making ends meet. . . . They might even have decided they were all going to get together for dinner some evening soon. Above all, they would have proven that people don't make wars.[26]

Reagan had added this section himself, by hand, not long before delivering the speech.[27] Jack Matlock had edited it somewhat "to make it seem less sexist—originally [Reagan] had the men talking about their work and the women about cooking."[28]

Reagan would "[hold] the door open to the Soviets if they mean what they say about loving peace to walk in," he wrote in his diary.[29] In Stockholm, where Shultz was attending the opening of the Conference on Confidence- and Security-Building Measures and Disarmament in Europe, US allies expressed

88 CHAPTER 4

their appreciation for this new sign of openness.[30] Pierre Trudeau, in a letter to Reagan, lauded the speech as "a big step towards the constructive dialogue we both desire."[31] Moscow's initial response, by contrast, was less than encouraging. The Kremlin issued a virtually simultaneous rejoinder to the speech—it had Andropov's advance text at its disposal, after all—dismissing it as nothing more than stale propaganda. But Soviet media reported on the content of Reagan's speech all the same and in considerable detail.[32] In Stockholm, Gromyko warned the assembled policy makers that "what is needed is deeds and not verbal acrobatics."[33] When he and Shultz met in private for a lengthy discussion on January 18, Gromyko dismissed the president's "crusade against socialism" as a "false" and "illiterate" slogan.[34] He later went further, describing members of the Reagan administration to his Canadian counterpart, Allan MacEachen, as "mastodons" who seemed to "rub their hands with glee" whenever they came upon an opportunity to make East-West relations worse.[35] The Soviet account of the meeting with Shultz insisted that US calls for dialogue had not been substantiated by deeds and should not yet be taken at face value.[36] Gromyko was operating on outdated instructions, however: the politburo had drafted his brief before Reagan's speech, on December 30, 1983.[37]

In fact, to an increasing number of Soviet officials, engaging the United States simply made sense. Not doing so in previous years had gotten them nothing.[38] Behind closed doors, they "did not want to cut off the prospects [for] relations for the future."[39] Yet they still had their doubts about Reagan: "Reagan's power is that he suits mediocre Americans, that is, the majority of the country. With him, they feel at ease, without guilt and inferiority. Thus, [in him] mediocrity has a brilliant representative."[40] When Shultz met with Dobrynin on January 30 to reestablish a "private channel for confidential communications," the Soviet ambassador seemed to have more up-to-date instructions from Moscow.[41] Dobrynin passed Shultz a letter from Andropov, restating the general secretary's belief in the need for dialogue and the reduction of both superpowers' nuclear arsenals. "I will be ready to listen," Andropov assured Reagan.[42] This message encouraged the president, who noted in the margin of the translated letter: "He suggests that they want an elimination of nuclear weapons? . . . Let's take him up on that."[43]

The electoral challenge mounted by Mondale in the 1984 presidential election colored Reagan's and his advisers' thinking. Mondale's campaign had begun in earnest as early as Reagan's inauguration.[44] His critique focused on the peace-through-strength elements of the president's Soviet policy, casting it as the sum total thereof.[45] He took particular issue with the president's approach to nuclear weapons. "The highest responsibility of a president," Mondale insisted, "is to get those godawful weapons under control."[46] He supported a nuclear freeze, whereas Reagan seemed only interested in building more nuclear weapons.[47] Reagan's January 16 speech professing his commitment to US-Soviet dialogue therefore posed a unique challenge to the Mondale campaign. It undercut one of Mondale's key critiques, Reagan's intransigence, but opened the incumbent up to a new one: cynicism. Not only Carter's former vice president saw Reagan's new tone as a mere electoral ploy. "President Reagan has been nagged by his handlers to wash out his mouth when he talks about the Soviets," Mary McGrory opined in the *Washington Post*, suggesting that "he was performing a campaign chore."[48] Mondale himself went even further: "To those who welcome the new Reagan, I say this: my Dad was a Methodist minister, and he once told me, 'Son, be skeptical of deathbed conversions.' I asked why. And he said, 'because sometimes they get well.'"[49]

In his diary, Reagan lamented those who dismissed his speech as mere politicking.[50] His dual-track approach toward the Soviet Union remained consistent—there was no "Reagan reversal" in 1984—comprising both peace through strength and quiet diplomacy.[51] The balance had certainly changed, as Reagan took the latter public at the beginning of 1984, but it had changed less than was commonly thought; such is the nature of quiet diplomacy. "You do not proclaim such subjects or put them up there in the newspaper," Reagan cautioned a group of reporters in 1982. "[To] publicly discuss things of that kind makes it politically impossible to get them, whereas maybe in what I've called quiet diplomacy you secure them."[52] That certainly worried many in the White House, including Nancy Reagan, who feared that public perceptions of Reagan's presidency as increasing the chances of nuclear war posed a serious problem for his reelection.[53] But the perceived balance of power shaped US policy toward the Soviet Union more than anything. Shultz, for example, remembered nothing about overtures to the Soviet Union being politically motivated; in fact, he had expected those in Reagan's inner circle more preoccupied with the president's reelection than US foreign policy to oppose them. "After all, [Reagan] had won in 1980 blasting [the Soviets]."[54]

When Andropov took office in November 1982, the former KGB chair launched a major program of reform, but the challenges he faced proved insurmountable for a general secretary who spent as much time in the hospital as he did.[55] From the beginning, Washington had been planning for his death and what might come after.[56] On February 9, 1984, after only fifteen months in office, Andropov died "as he lived, in secret." His death would not be announced to the Soviet people for a day in order to give the politburo sufficient time to choose a successor.[57]

CHAPTER 4

Andropov himself had no doubt as to who should succeed him. In December 1983, he wrote to the Central Committee recommending Mikhail Gorbachev for the top post.[58] To Konstantin Chernenko and his supporters, this was unacceptable, as Chernenko had been passed over once already. Prime Minister Nikolaĭ Tikhonov, chief among Chernenko's supporters, intervened and had the passage excised from Andropov's report.[59] Chernenko's renewed campaign for the position of general secretary had begun not long after Andropov foiled his first effort in late 1982. Through editorials in Soviet media outlets, he cultivated an image of a talented bureaucrat genuinely concerned with the well-being of the Soviet people. Within the Kremlin, he shielded his supporters from his rival Gorbachev's efforts to oust them.[60] Those who ran afoul of Andropov's anti-corruption measures, however, Chernenko abandoned.[61]

The politburo of 1984 was a change- and risk-averse group. With more foresight than they were even aware of, many feared that Gorbachev would usher in destabilizing departures in policy; Chernenko, by contrast, promised continuity.[62] Gorbachev had not been outspoken about the need for reform. Behind closed doors and with Andropov's support, he had explored the idea, but in the politburo, he hewed a much more conservative line than that for which he is remembered today. At a party conference on ideology, he talked about the need for openness and economic restructuring—*glasnost'* and *perestroĭka*, in fact, which would become synonymous with his name but neither at length nor in depth, and nobody made much of the speech.[63] He did, however, stop short of supporting Defense Minister Dmitriĭ Ustinov's unsuccessful bid to return the city of Volgograd to its World War II–era name: Stalingrad.[64]

On his deathbed, Andropov allegedly pronounced his dying wish that Gorbachev succeed him, echoing what he had said in the letter to the Central Committee, but it was not to be.[65] Others in the upper echelons of Soviet power felt the need to reconsolidate their positions after the turbulence of the Andropov period.[66] Tikhonov nominated, Gromyko seconded, and even Gorbachev spoke out in support of the "weak and sick Chernenko," leadership continuity, and Leninist unity.[67] Gorbachev took the setback in stride; his turn would certainly come next.[68] When the Central Committee assembled on February 14, the standing ovation Chernenko doubtless hoped would greet him as the next general secretary never came. The sense of disappointment was, according to one witness, painfully obvious. Once the motions had been gone through and Chernenko formally elected general secretary, an uncomfortable silence passed before the members could bring themselves to clap.[69] Even Chernenko's wife, Anna, made her displeasure known.[70] The politburo had chosen "not the most worthy, but the most convenient."[71] This was not the outcome US observers had expected. When asked by his wife, Rebecca, if Chernenko would succeed Andropov, Matlock had answered, "No way."[72] As it turned out, "the 'old men' [were] still in control" to a greater extent than Matlock had appreciated.[73]

Chernenko faced serious problems. Gromyko and Ustinov "acted as if they owned the Kremlin" now that the powerful Andropov was dead. With the old general secretary and his bothersome, unsettling reforms out of the way, nobody paid much heed to the new old general secretary.[74] His ostensible subordinates in the politburo did not trust Chernenko to make decisions, often sending him fake work to keep him occupied and on the sidelines.[75] He commanded no respect from his colleagues, who thought him weak and utterly unprepared—despite their having supported his appointment to the highest office in the Soviet Union. That was his great appeal: he would not interfere in their personal fiefdoms as Andropov had, nor would he do anything that might imperil the rule of the party, as they feared Gorbachev would have in that position.[76]

The Soviet economy was still a shambles, cripplingly constrained by raw material shortages, transportation bottlenecks, and a dwindling labor force.[77] It had rebounded somewhat in 1983 due to favorable weather conditions, leading to a bumper crop in the agricultural sector, but there was no sustainable improvement.[78] Compared to the US economic recovery following the Reagan recession, this was a drop in the ocean. It did little to make the Soviet Union more competitive in the new, increasingly globalized world. Chernenko busied himself with the "scholastic delusion" of personally investigating whether the Soviet Union was a country of developing or developed socialism.[79] Most Soviet citizens knew the answer: their lives were getting worse, not better.[80] They spent hours waiting in the long lines spilling out of half-empty shops, many having made the long journey to Moscow, where at least something could be found on the shelves. Such was life in the land of "victorious socialism."[81]

The new general secretary was weak, as was the country he led.[82] At their December 1983 meeting, the Warsaw Pact defense ministers—dispensing with their usual pablum about Western military aggression—had a frank discussion about Western superiority and the real strategic threat posed by this new reality.[83] One Czechoslovak military intelligence study went so far as to conclude that should NATO decide to attack, the Warsaw Pact would be in no position to repel the offensive short of launching a strategic nuclear war.[84] In order to restore the military balance, the East would need to embark on an unprecedented modernization campaign that it could ill afford.[85] After all, readers of *Voennaia mysl'* were reminded, attaining technological superiority over Nazi Germany had been the decisive factor in the Soviet Union's eventual victory.

92   CHAPTER 4

It was not Soviet soldiers who won the war but rather the Soviet workers and scientists who equipped them with the latest technology.[86]

To Reagan, Chernenko coming to power presented "a chance, through quiet diplomacy, to reduce the psychological barriers that divided us."[87] Chernenko had been an outspoken proponent of détente under Brezhnev, and would now likely embrace a foreign policy along those lines. Détente had once been a slur in the Reagan White House. Now, the president and his advisers embraced the idea of engaging a new general secretary promising a return to it.[88] Chernenko proved them right. In his first foreign-policy statement to the politburo, he reaffirmed his commitment to détente, making explicit reference to Brezhnev's pronouncements at the Twenty-Sixth Party Congress in early 1981.[89] To his foreign-policy staff, Chernenko directed that "work will be done in the style of Brezhnev, as it was during the time of Leonid Il'ich."[90] Reagan's advisers encouraged the president to attend Andropov's funeral as a strong signal of his desire to engage the Soviet Union.[91] Reagan did not feel that US-Soviet relations had improved sufficiently to warrant attending, electing instead to send George H. W. Bush as his representative once more.[92] More candidly, apropos of Andropov's KGB background, the president declared that he did not "want to honor that prick."[93] Had Reagan attended, he would have been one of many Western leaders taken aback at seeing the wife of the former leader of an officially atheistic state, Tat'iana Andropova, openly make the sign of the cross as his coffin was lowered into the ground.[94]

Chernenko had a packed schedule at Andropov's funeral, but it was clear to all that he was scarcely up to it—he could barely even deliver the eulogy.[95] His meeting with Bush was primarily an exchange of statements, not a conversation in any meaningful sense. Chernenko began the meeting by reading a prepared text insisting that the Soviet Union wanted peace and stating that it believed the United States did too. Reagan, Bush responded, rejected the notion that the United States and the Soviet Union were "doomed to be in perpetual conflict." The president was ready to move from words, such as his January 16 speech, to deeds, especially regarding nuclear arms reductions. "This should be a new beginning," Bush declared, and Chernenko agreed.[96] Reagan also reached out personally to Chernenko in a letter, expressing his desire to open a dialogue.[97] In a radio address, Reagan echoed these sentiments publicly: "We would welcome negotiations. . . . We're prepared to meet the Soviets halfway in the search for mutually acceptable agreements. . . . If the Soviet government wants peace, there will be peace."[98] Chernenko's meetings with Kohl, Thatcher, and Trudeau followed a similar pattern, both in the new general secretary's strict adherence to a prepared script and in his insistence that East-West relations could—and must—be improved.[99]

Bush's report back to Reagan conveyed the vice president's optimism about the future of US-Soviet relations but also stressed Chernenko's obviously poor health and reliance on his aides to prepare his statements—and even to walk.[100] Chernenko also gave a favorable report of his meeting with Bush, looking forward to "honest, equitable, and meaningful dialogue" with the United States.[101] The Soviet foreign-policy making community concurred: the meeting portended a return to "constructive cooperation."[102]

The Reagan administration also used the occasion of Andropov's funeral to conduct some quiet diplomacy on the sidelines. On instructions from Reagan and McFarlane, Matlock met with senior party official Vadim Zagladin. Matlock emphasized that though the White House was "constantly thinking about" improving US-Soviet relations, policy makers remained unsure how their Soviet counterparts felt.[103] Washington was prepared to engage in back-channel discussions on a range of issues, but Zagladin insisted that the Kremlin needed more than just words. Reagan had given a number of speeches in the past, but hostile ones; which words should Moscow now take as indicative of US policy? The Kremlin was ready to listen but not necessarily to trust. Matlock left the meeting optimistic but not entirely sanguine: "Feel good about [the] prospects for US-Sov[iet] rel[ation]s. Worried I may be 'taken in'—not by Sov[iet]s, but by my own wishful thinking. Dangerous. Yet I do feel—almost against the logic of the situation—that there may be an opportunity. This is, after all, Chernenko's big chance. If he can preside over the 'normalization' of US-Sov[iet] rel[ation]s, [it] would be [a] real feather in his cap. But can he really get decisions? Equally relevant—can we?"[104] Chernenko's response to Reagan's letter, too, boded well. "A turn toward even and good relations between our two countries has been and continues to be our desire," he wrote, "and such a turn is quite feasible, given the same desire on the US side."[105]

Matlock's advice to Reagan for dealing with Chernenko was straightforward: "He needs you more than you need him, and he knows it." The president should push for discussions, focusing on the four key areas already identified by Shultz and the State Department for US-Soviet engagement: regional issues, arms control, human rights, and bilateral relations.[106] In the White House, those who saw dialogue as a vital part of US Cold War grand strategy were gaining ground. Even Weinberger—usually outspoken in his opposition to such outreach—now deemed it necessary "to get inside the Russian mind."[107] While policy makers entertained no illusions about Chernenko's health, they did not see him simply as a transitional figure to be waited out. Moscow, they

94   **CHAPTER 4**

believed, saw the need to negotiate in order to slow its decline, and Chernenko would be open to putting relations on "a more positive track."[108]

Despite a desire to take its quiet diplomacy public, the White House had in the past looked with skepticism on third-party efforts to mediate US-Soviet relations. When Billy Graham planned to visit Moscow in 1982, Bush spearheaded an ultimately unsuccessful campaign to dissuade him.[109] Graham felt he could not pass up a platform to advocate for peace and disarmament in the Soviet capital. Plus, he quipped, "I always wanted to preach to KGB agents."[110] Meanwhile, Armand Hammer, the CEO of Occidental Petroleum, "insist[ed] on trying to play the role of an elder statesman and intermediary." Washington was not interested, but Hammer, too, was undeterred.[111] Due to his business interests, he had long been a fixture in the Soviet Union. In Washington he was seen as a naïf at best and a traitor at worst for his frequent, highly publicized meetings with Soviet leaders.[112]

Now, in the wake of Reagan's January 16 speech, the White House noted an "upsurge in pilgrimages to the Kremlin."[113] Visits by high-ranking delegations from Canada, West Germany, Australia, the United Kingdom, and France (among others) all served as trial balloons, showing US and Soviet policy makers that their direct efforts to improve relations could bear fruit. Chernenko, inclined toward the détente-style foreign policy of Brezhnev and the prestige boost such high-profile visitors would bring, relished receiving them.[114]

Pierre Trudeau, for one, wanted to "maintain . . . a mediating position between the superpowers," according to the CIA.[115] Only the Kremlin appreciated the Canadian prime minister's good offices.[116] By late 1983, Trudeau knew his tenure would soon be at an end without a signature foreign-policy achievement since coming to office in 1968. Genuinely troubled by the state of the world, he prepared a major initiative to reduce international tensions and promote peace.[117] That the phrase "worthy Canadian initiative" had once won a contest held by the *New Republic* for most tedious headline did not deter the prime minister.[118]

Trudeau launched his self-styled peace initiative with an October 27, 1983, speech calling for a "third rail . . . of high-level political energy" in East-West relations.[119] That unfortunate metaphor would prove all too apt.[120] Two months later, in December, Trudeau visited Washington to discuss the peace initiative with Reagan. The president fulfilled his brief: to lend a sympathetic ear and little more.[121] After the meeting, Eagleburger told an audience that anyone who thought the White House would go along with Trudeau's initiative in any meaningful way "must have been smoking something pretty funny."[122] Though Eagleburger apologized for his offhand remark, policy mak-

TRIAL BALLOONS 95

ers in Ottawa knew that he spoke for many in the Reagan administration.[123] Other stops on Trudeau's world tour were no more promising: in London, Margaret Thatcher commented that flowers were growing in Hiroshima only a year after the first atomic bomb had been dropped, and in Beijing, Deng Xiaopeng noted that even if a nuclear war wiped out half of China's population, some five hundred million would still remain.[124] The peace initiative proved to be, in the undiplomatic words of Canadian diplomat Thomas Delworth, a "force de crap."[125] In February 1984, Trudeau dubiously declared his peace mission a success and left politics for good shortly thereafter.[126]

Like Canada, West Germany had a long record of engagement with the East—to the point that others saw Bonn as altogether too entrepreneurial in that regard—and had much more to show for it.[127] Eastern policy makers felt that they had more in common with Bonn than with Washington, and that West Germany was an effective intermediary between the superpowers.[128] Soon after Chernenko took office, Kohl wrote him to affirm his desire to improve East-West relations.[129] Foreign Minister Hans-Dietrich Genscher's trip to Moscow in May 1984 showed just what a challenge that would be. Gromyko confined himself to attacks on the United States in the foreign ministers' first meeting.[130] Moscow, he insisted, was ready for dialogue, but Washington offered only ultimatums.[131] Gromyko became visibly emotional and frustrated, insisting that Reagan's policy amounted to nothing more than militarism.[132]

Genscher's meeting with Chernenko was more productive. The general secretary encouraged him to use Bonn's influence to persuade Reagan to propose serious arms control talks, especially to prevent the militarization of outer space, a direct response to SDI. If this were achieved, Chernenko promised to come back to the negotiating table immediately.[133] Upon Genscher's return, West German policy makers believed his visit "made an important contribution to the maintenance and continuation of East-West dialogue and effectively represented and defended the Western position"—a relatively low bar to clear, all things considered.[134] Genscher was more candid with Shultz, explaining that Chernenko and Gromyko—notably lumping the frail general secretary and his increasingly imperious foreign minister together policy-wise—showed no flexibility beyond well-worn Soviet arguments.[135]

The Australians, too, saw an opportunity for prestige-boosting international diplomacy. The government of Bob Hawke had lifted sanctions on the Soviet Union in the spring of 1983, deciding instead to pursue a more productive bilateral relationship. To that end, Hawke sent his foreign minister, Bill Hayden, to Moscow in May 1984 in the hope of contributing to "a revision of Soviet attitudes in a more realistic, pragmatic, and positive direction."[136] Australian policy makers did not see the decline of East-West relations as solely the fault of the

96   CHAPTER 4

Soviet Union; Washington, too, bore part of the blame.[137] They nevertheless framed Hayden's visit as part of a broader Western effort to increase contacts.[138]

To spare the ailing general secretary the strain, the MID rebuffed Hayden's efforts to secure a meeting with Chernenko. He did, however, spend a marathon six hours with Gromyko. After the negative press surrounding Genscher's earlier visit, the Soviet foreign minister wanted to be seen as a reasonable negotiating partner; nevertheless, Gromyko continued his refrain that the United States alone was to blame for the downturn in US-Soviet relations. When Hayden urged him to seize the initiative and engage with Washington, Gromyko did not reply.[139] Soviet policy, Hayden observed in a letter to Shultz after the meeting, was "essentially reactive. . . . The problem may well be an absence of much creative thinking in Moscow."[140] For their part, Soviet foreign-policy makers felt more positively about Hayden's visit; he shared their view that Washington bore at least some responsibility for the decline of superpower relations, and he did not go out of his way to defend US policy, both welcome changes.[141]

Even Margaret Thatcher, who had rejected East-West engagement out of hand in 1981, was coming to see the value in opening a new dialogue with Moscow.[142] "In a cold as in a hot war it pays to know the enemy," the prime minister later recounted in her memoirs, "not least because at some time in the future you may have the opportunity to turn him into a friend."[143] To that end, she had convened a seminar of academics and policy makers on September 8, 1983, at Chequers, the prime ministerial country retreat, to discuss possibilities for East-West relations under Andropov. After hearing hours of presentations on contemporary and historical questions, she concluded that the United Kingdom must intensify its contacts with the Soviet Union, but that "there would be no public announcement of this change of policy." Although she refused to visit the Soviet Union to meet with Andropov, she hoped he could be persuaded to visit the West, ideally London.[144]

In February 1984, just days before Andropov's death, Thatcher traveled to Hungary, the first visit by a British prime minister since World War II, and her first visit east of the Iron Curtain.[145] Hungarian leader János Kádár, a close associate of Andropov, had been in power since 1956; he would surely relay her message that she and Reagan were "genuinely seeking disarmament."[146] Thatcher elaborated on her motivations in a discussion with Hungarian prime minister György Lázár: "The timing of the visit had a certain purpose. In history, opportunities for talks sometimes presented themselves. As [Thatcher] saw it, we were entering upon a period when the United States faced ten months of electioneering and the Soviet Union was in the curious situation where it had not seen its leader for a long time. These factors put a heightened responsibility on other members of alliances."[147] Lázár emphasized that

TRIAL BALLOONS   97

he too wanted to improve East-West relations; London and Budapest needed to continue their dialogue and use their influence within NATO and the Warsaw Pact to that end.[148]

Meeting with Kádár, Thatcher insisted that despite the two blocs' differences, "we need to be able to talk across the dividing line." She emphasized her close personal relationship with Reagan and his desire to create a more secure and stable world through improved relations with the Soviet Union. Kádár welcomed these remarks. Citing his close relationship with top Soviet policy makers—he was "one of the older boys," as the British notetaker put it—Kádár assured Thatcher that the Soviet leadership was ready to engage.[149] Months later, Kádár reported to Chernenko, now the general secretary, that he had been "disarmed" by Thatcher's sincerity, vitality, and informality.[150] Clearly, Washington's allies wanted to improve relations, he said, but he remained unconvinced that Reagan did as well. Thatcher was even more optimistic. She reported to Reagan that she had convinced Budapest that "the West in general and [Reagan] personally were absolutely sincere in their desire to achieve arm reductions and security at a lower level of weaponry."[151] This was just the beginning, she told Reagan, of what could be achieved in East-West relations. The visit "whetted her cautious appetite" for more engagement with the Soviet Union.[152]

Thatcher would not visit Moscow herself until the spring of 1987, but she dispatched Foreign Secretary Geoffrey Howe to the Soviet capital in July 1984, hot on Hayden's heels.[153] The visit did not go well. Howe opened a meeting with Gromyko by reiterating Thatcher's message to Kádár: Reagan sincerely wanted to improve East-West relations and eliminate nuclear weapons. Gromyko responded with an eighty-minute monologue on how Reagan's "crusade against socialism" had undone détente, consuming the rest of the meeting.[154] At lunch, Gromyko returned to this topic, insisting that Washington was "flagrantly throwing away international norms . . . not stopping short of state terrorism."[155] The Soviet foreign minister was, according to one of Howe's aides, an "adroit performer . . . [but] as he insistently played his anti-[US] gramophone record, it sounded more and more like the well-worn 78 it now is."[156]

Howe's meeting with Chernenko went no better, as the general secretary was clearly not physically equal to the occasion—a lengthy coughing fit almost ended the meeting prematurely. The British delegation reported in detail on his infirmity: "The air of abstraction and occasional bewilderment still clings to him. His reading of his prepared text was . . . disastrously bad—still the same high-speed gabble, the stumbling, the breaking of sentences (in order to breathe) often in mid-phrase; still the mechanical delivery . . . and the failure to highlight key points. In short, the same apparent lack of conviction and

98   CHAPTER 4

even, it seems at times, of comprehension."[157] With Chernenko so obviously physically incapacitated, Gromyko's control over Soviet foreign policy was at its peak. The foreign minister was not as ready to move toward a more cooperative, détente-like footing in East-West relations; in fact, he remained preoccupied with litigating the decline of détente in the first place. Howe's visit was hardly the major intervention in East-West relations for which Whitehall had hoped. The Kremlin had no interest in it being so.

French President François Mitterrand wanted to chart a distinctive course in international relations and make his own mark. With respect to the Soviet Union, he insisted French policy needed to "sober up."[158] Mitterrand's foreign-policy adviser, Jacques Attali, captured what the president meant in jokingly assuring his colleagues that they could be "forgiven for thinking that under the previous government France was on the way to joining the Warsaw Pact." This needed to be corrected.[159] In late 1983, Mitterrand had proposed that he meet with the Soviet leadership.[160] France, he believed, enjoyed "freedom of movement vis-à-vis the United States" that the rest of NATO did not.[161] Before leaving for Moscow, Mitterrand visited Reagan in Washington on March 22, 1984, during which Reagan encouraged him to convey the White House's desire for a more constructive superpower relationship. Both presidents believed that Chernenko personally wanted to improve East-West relations, even if the entire Soviet leadership—and Gromyko in particular—did not share his goals.[162]

In Mitterrand's first meeting with Chernenko on June 21, the general secretary could do little more than read from a prepared text emphasizing the Soviet Union's openness to improved relations with France, to which Mitterrand responded in kind.[163] Throughout the meeting, Chernenko struggled to speak and seemed to be under Gromyko's supervision. He sat "in the middle, like a sack, absently; nobody spoke to him, he spoke to nobody."[164] Even though they made little concrete progress, Mitterrand's primary objective—that the visit take place—had been achieved.[165]

In visit after visit, as Western policy makers descended on Moscow in order to be seen to be talking to the Kremlin, Chernenko indicated his desire to improve relations and underscored the need to negotiate in good faith.[166] But these "conversations without conversation" also brought to light serious obstacles: Gromyko's intransigence and Chernenko's frailty.[167] The combination of an incapacitated general secretary and a resistant (and frequently agitated) foreign minister made concrete improvements few and far between in the summer of 1984.[168]

On March 2, 1984, in a secret meeting with his key foreign-policy aides, Reagan declared that "the time had come to think of something between a get-acquainted meeting and a full summit with the Soviet leader."[169] He suggested, for example, inviting Chernenko to the 1984 Olympics in Los Angeles. His advisers agreed, seeing the venue as particularly propitious given the spirit of peaceful competition associated with the Olympic Games, which echoed their vision for the future of the Cold War. Reagan "thought he should show [the Soviets] that he is not the sort to eat his own young," while sending a clear signal to the rest of the world that "more is going on than you think."[170] Shultz now publicly and frequently made the case for engaging the Soviet Union from a position of strength, but there would be no formal directive to supersede NSDD 75. Such a document would almost certainly leak, giving ammunition to those who wanted to undermine the new focus on engaging the Soviet Union.[171]

Key US officials began holding meetings with their Eastern counterparts. Richard Burt, for example, met with East German politburo member Hermann Axen in Berlin because, as Burt put it, the time had come for East and West to engage in meaningful discussions. "Realism and reason," he told Axen, were the "cornerstones of the Reagan foreign policy."[172] The White House saw a host of opportunities for negotiation, especially on nuclear questions; Reagan's January 16 speech should be seen as a true reflection of the president's views, not mere propaganda. Meanwhile, officials who opposed Reagan's overtures to the Soviet Union increasingly found themselves shut out from Soviet policy.[173] John Lenczowski, for example, decried the emerging "relationship of wholesale cooperation with the Soviets." That characterization went far beyond what Reagan envisioned, but Lenczowski was nevertheless out of step with the times, something that could not escape his notice. "Perhaps," he allowed, "the strategy underlying this has appeared in secret documents which I have not seen."[174]

Their image as peacemakers in tatters after the KAL 007 massacre, Soviet diplomats faced mounting pressure to work with the Reagan administration.[175] But with a US election coming up in November, they were loath to do him any favors.[176] On March 2, Chernenko denounced Washington's using arms control talks for propaganda purposes only and insisted that US calls for dialogue could not be genuine, given US aggression worldwide.[177] On May 8, the Soviet Union announced that it would boycott the 1984 Olympics, where Reagan had envisioned meeting at last with Chernenko, in a tit-for-tat retaliation for the US boycott in 1980.[178] Reagan was undeterred. In an April 16 letter to Chernenko, he had bemoaned the difficulties both superpowers had appreciating the other's point of view. Reagan added a handwritten postscript, the same technique he had used to reach out to Brezhnev in 1981, acknowledging the massive scale of Soviet losses during World War II, and how seriously the Kremlin took any threats to national security as a result. He assured Chernenko that Washington

100   CHAPTER 4

had no aggressive designs on the Soviet Union, again pledging his "profound commitment" to reducing tensions.[179] This intransigence so soon after professions of a desire to work with the United States made sense to White House officials: they recognized the domestic audience of such speeches necessary but not meaningful for US-Soviet relations, and that their Soviet counterparts wanted to know how much they could push back in the negotiations to come.[180] Chernenko was weak, Matlock concluded, but "not a crazy."[181]

There was more to Soviet behavior than that. Chernenko delegated increasing amounts of responsibility and decision-making to his inner circle because of his health.[182] Gorbachev, for example, chaired politburo meetings in Chernenko's (frequent) absence.[183] In public, inspired by his initials K.U.Ch., Soviet citizens had taken to calling him *kucher*, or "coachman," to evoke the image of an old man struggling to control his team of horses.[184] Gromyko and others exercised authority over policy making which at times eclipsed even the general secretary's. The worse Chernenko's health became, the more Gromyko dominated foreign policy.[185] Often, Gromyko pursued his own priorities, believing Chernenko lacked the background required of a general secretary.[186] He never tired of reminding his colleagues how long he had managed to remain in the uppermost echelon of Soviet officialdom and how much experience he had in dealing with the United States.[187] As Anatoliĭ Cherniaev, a senior Central Committee foreign-policy official, remarked, at this point Gromyko was implementing a foreign policy better suited to the 1930s or 1950s than to the realities of a weakened Soviet Union, especially as compared to the United States.[188] "Soviet decision making is plagued by a number of 'really primitive people' in key positions," Matlock wrote, with Gromyko in mind. "They don't understand the West or the [United States], are convinced we are out to get them in every way we can, and are capable of reacting in truly stupid ways."[189] But younger diplomats and KGB officers made it clear to their US counterparts that they were not happy with the conduct of foreign policy under Chernenko and Gromyko thus far. Moscow, they knew, gained nothing from its refusal to reciprocate US engagement.[190]

As 1984 progressed, the overall atmosphere had grown more conducive to improving US-Soviet relations.[191] Shultz later recalled, "In the summertime, we picked up indications through these mysterious ways the Soviets communicate—they have some diplomat in Timbuktu say to somebody that something might be possible and so on. And you start to get these things filtering through."[192] Chernenko's health was improving, and with it his ability to bring Gromyko in line, working with his fellow politburo members who also found the foreign minister's intransigence counterproductive.[193] Gromyko gave in to his colleagues' pressure, agreeing to visit the United States in Sep-

TRIAL BALLOONS 101

tember 1984.[194] Attending the UN General Assembly offered a convenient pretext for such a trip.[195] "A diplomatic minuet" ensued. The White House would not invite Gromyko until they knew he would accept, and Gromyko would not indicate he would accept until a public invitation had been issued. "It's the right thing to do," Reagan insisted. "Try to work it out."[196]

The two superpowers did.[197] On September 5, Chernenko announced Gromyko's trip, casting it as an opportunity to rebuild much-needed trust between the superpowers. Three weeks later, he declared that there could be "no sensible alternative" to improving US-Soviet relations.[198] The White House staff pulled out all the stops; on September 28—"the big day," as the president wrote in his diary—Gromyko was accorded a welcome fit for a visiting head of state rather than a foreign minister.[199] "We live in one world and we must handle our competition in peace," Reagan told Gromyko. He went on to reiterate his personal commitment to reducing and eliminating nuclear weapons. If the superpowers led, Reagan argued, the rest of the world would follow. But the two rapidly descended into a fruitless debate over the origins of the Cold War. "We are offering peace as we have always offered peace," Reagan insisted, but by this point (after a lengthy, rather biased history lesson from Gromyko) he had all but given up on the meeting.[200] Nevertheless, to Reagan and Shultz, it had been time well spent in dialogue with the Soviets.[201] At the joint press conference following the meeting, Gromyko asked Nancy Reagan to whisper "peace" in the president's ear each night. "I'll whisper it in yours too," she responded, making Gromyko blush.[202]

By starting an overt dialogue, Reagan earnestly hoped "to start a process which could lead both to arms control agreements, and to an improved superpower relationship across the board."[203] Moscow had sent a range of positive signals.[204] Most strikingly, in an article featured in the military newspaper *Krasnaia zvezda* on May 9, 1984—Victory Day, on which the Soviet Union commemorated its World War II fallen—Marshal Nikolaï Ogarkov criticized both superpowers' military buildups as "senseless" in the period of relative stability. No matter how many nuclear missiles the superpowers had, the other would maintain its retaliatory capability. A limited nuclear war, the chief of the Soviet General Staff insisted—contrary to Soviet military doctrine—was "pure fantasy."[205] The Reagan administration took note, and by the autumn of 1984, Reagan concluded that the time was ripe for a major initiative on arms control.[206]

The president set a high standard for arms control agreements: "real reductions, verifiability, equality in the important measures of military capability, and [enhancing the] stability of the East-West military balance."[207] Nobody in

102   **CHAPTER 4**

the White House expected such an agreement to be easily reached, but maintaining these high standards had benefits all the same. If the Soviet Union rejected the administration's calls for an agreement, it would be they who bore the blame. "We should make our proposals general enough and ambiguous enough to provide no logical grounds for complaint," Matlock wrote. In response, the national security adviser Bud McFarlane wrote "Right on" in the margin. Either the agreements should benefit the United States, or Moscow's unwillingness to deal with Washington should be spun as intransigence.[208]

Chernenko's basic instinct, Western observers rightly concluded, was to try to be the Brezhnev to Reagan's Nixon and conclude arms control agreements for reasons of prestige and pragmatism.[209] The main obstacle to doing so: Reagan's SDI. Nobody in Moscow welcomed the prospect of an outer-space arms race, which Washington was poised to win; yet while SDI remained in its infancy, it was vulnerable.[210] Preventing the US "militarization of outer space" became the main focus of Moscow and its allies.[211] They expected that Reagan would make far-reaching concessions to demonstrate that his January 16 speech was more than just cheap talk; if talks failed to take place or collapsed, they would be vindicated in the court of public opinion, and Washington would be seen as intransigent.[212] At the United Nations, Eastern representatives made SDI their top priority, insisting that it be on the agenda for discussions on issues ranging from arms control to human rights—not dying in a nuclear war being a human right.[213] It was not just Eastern policy makers who looked askance at SDI. As Genscher asked pointedly, if the United States and the Soviet Union did in fact cooperate, as Reagan had pledged to, and render themselves impervious to nuclear weapons, where would that leave Europe?[214]

In a series of letters exchanged in the autumn of 1984, Reagan and Chernenko moved toward a new round of arms control talks. Chernenko wanted to reduce the burden of defense on the economy by negotiating reductions, but he also needed to save face after the Soviet walkout at the INF talks in November 1983.[215] Reflecting Soviet anxieties over SDI, Chernenko suggested an international conference on the militarization of outer space—or, rather, the prevention thereof.[216] Reagan countered, offering an even broader conference on the reduction of tensions "with a clear mandate to find . . . results."[217] Shultz reinforced this message in a meeting with Dobrynin, emphasizing Washington's readiness to meet without preconditions and to listen and learn about how a mutually acceptable arms control agreement might be reached.[218]

In his September 1984 speech to the UN General Assembly, Reagan proposed "to extend the arms control process to build a bigger umbrella under which it can operate," conducting talks on a range of issues concurrently.[219]

Thereafter dubbed the Umbrella Talks, Washington proposed a package to encompass outer space, INF, and START.[220] This format offered a creative means of breaking the existing deadlock on arms control, enabling US and Soviet negotiators to discuss a wide range of interrelated issues, and was the first time in over a decade that offensive and defensive systems would be discussed together. Ideally, the administration's umbrella approach would identify promising avenues for negotiation and, ultimately, the best path to an agreement. Lack of movement in one area would not prevent progress overall, which mattered to the president.[221]

Chernenko objected to the package proposal at first. He wanted the talks to focus solely on outer space; SDI, he feared, might be lost in omnibus talks.[222] In his eyes, Reagan's proposed talks appeared designed to bury the issue instead of resolving it.[223] The United States, he argued, misled international public opinion by saying it had accepted the Soviet proposal of a conference on the demilitarization of outer space while substantively rejecting it by intermingling other arms control questions.[224] Chernenko was right. Reagan may have, to his advisers, stressed the importance of empathy in dealing with the Kremlin on issues of national security, noting that in Moscow, the World War II–era barbed wire was still standing as a daily reminder of just how close Hitler had come to taking the city. "How," he asked his advisers, "do you argue with this fear?" His commitment to SDI nevertheless remained unshakeable. "No matter what happens," he concluded, "no one should consider giving away the horse cavalry."[225]

Though agreement on a new round of arms control talks remained elusive, the Kremlin grew increasingly outspoken in expressing an interest in US-Soviet engagement.[226] Valerian Zorin, a long-serving diplomat who had been Soviet ambassador to the UN during the 1962 Cuban Missile Crisis, cautioned against writing off cooperative rhetoric emanating from Washington as mere electioneering.[227] Vadim Zagladin announced to a Japanese audience that the politburo was ready and willing to make progress in the relationship, and eagerly awaited similar signs from the United States. He even went so far as to suggest that the problem in US-Soviet relations was not Reagan but rather hard-line advisers in the White House who did not share—and actively impeded—the president's own goal of improved superpower relations.[228] Nikolaï Tikhonov assured Shultz (exaggerating the actual situation) that nobody in the Kremlin opposed improving East-West relations.[229]

After Reagan's victory at the polls on November 6, 1984—reelected with 58.8 percent of the popular vote and 525 electoral votes to Mondale's 13 (he managed to carry only his home state of Minnesota and the District of Columbia)—positive signals only continued to emanate from the East.

104   **CHAPTER 4**

Chernenko, in a televised appearance on NBC after Reagan's landslide victory—in and of itself a major development—refrained from criticizing US policy or Reagan and stressed the Kremlin's preparedness to negotiate.[230] (Privately, Soviet policy makers had expressed far greater skepticism about the benefits of a Mondale presidency, given the erratic policies of the Carter administration in which he had served.)[231] Chernenko continued his "comeback," resuming public appearances and reasserting his control over foreign policy—and Gromyko, who now proposed ripping off Reagan's "peace mask"—in the Kremlin.[232] Those who recognized that the tide of global public opinion had turned against the Soviet Union, and that they increasingly appeared to be "saboteurs" of progress on arms control and East-West relations in general, gained ground. The time had come to show flexibility.[233]

On November 17, the general secretary accepted Reagan's offer to begin what had by then been dubbed the Nuclear and Space Talks. Reagan responded by underscoring both his personal investment in the success of the negotiations and the fact that he had grander designs: "eventually liquidating nuclear arms."[234] Strikingly, Chernenko replied in kind, agreeing that the "opportunity should not be lost."[235] And he meant it: the negotiating team's instructions made it clear that the Soviet Union would agree to major strategic arms reductions provided the United States signed on to a comprehensive space-weapons ban.[236] This was classic peaceful coexistence in the Soviet tradition: keep the chances of nuclear war as low as possible until socialism's triumph.[237]

In January 1985, Shultz and Gromyko met in Geneva to lay the groundwork. To demonstrate the talks' importance to the president and that the US bargaining position reflected his wishes, the White House sent McFarlane along with Shultz.[238] To Gromyko, the secretary of state stressed that Reagan believed deterrence could be maintained at much lower yet equitable levels, but that ultimately he did not accept the logic of mutually assured destruction. The president preferred defensive technologies such as SDI as a means of "eliminating nuclear weapons entirely."[239] The Soviet foreign minister remained unconvinced. The threat posed by SDI, he retorted, was "clear almost to the point of being primitive." It would enable the United States to conduct a first strike with impunity; any Soviet retaliation would be shot down in flight. "There is no room for propaganda here," Gromyko exclaimed. "We are talking here about high politics and questions of war and peace."[240] SDI would only trigger a new, destabilizing arms race. How could the United States fail to grasp this? "It must be a kind of self-hypnosis," he concluded.[241]

In spite of all this acrimony, Shultz and Gromyko agreed that the talks should go forward for March 1985. This was a foregone conclusion: both sides had clear instructions from their superiors to come to an agreement.[242] To US policy makers, it was a victory. Moscow had "caved" on issues it had used to block negotiations in the past, including SDI, and Washington had made no corresponding concessions.[243] Looking ahead to the twenty-first century, US policy makers made it known that they would work to eliminate nuclear weapons entirely.[244] To the Kremlin, the Shultz-Gromyko meetings had been "complicated."[245] Going forward, they would need to find opportunities to curtail SDI. Even Gromyko had to acknowledge, however, that this was a new type of arms control negotiation for a new era—with new threats.[246]

The Cold War was changing. Mere months earlier, US allies had made pilgrimages to Moscow to make the case for US-Soviet engagement. Now, as the superpower dialogue went public, the United States and the Soviet Union seemed to be taking to it almost too eagerly. Across Western Europe, governments began to worry what that dialogue would mean in practice. Overt superpower engagement threatened to diminish Europe's role in solving international problems, and European leaders chafed at the thought of being just another one of the "regional issues" discussed by the superpowers—on par with Africa or the Middle East. Even more sinister was the prospect of the United States and the Soviet Union going "over the heads of the Europeans" and reaching a condominium that sacrificed European interests. After all, if Washington and Moscow were each other's main opponents in competition, they would perforce be each other's main partners in cooperation. There was no indication that this was in the offing—yet—but a new, uncertain phase of the Cold War seemed to be on the horizon.[247]

On that, at least, European policy makers were in step with the superpowers. Key players in the Kremlin in particular made no secret of the fact that they looked forward to seizing new opportunities to reduce Cold War tensions in 1985.[248] It was during Chernenko's brief tenure that both superpowers received the assurances of the other's good faith, which made future progress possible. Reagan's story about Ivan and Anya and Jim and Sally reminded the Kremlin that he was not all bluster—and his electoral victory assured them that he could make good on his promises. Chernenko, even if he was motivated as much by prestige seeking as by altruism, made it clear that when his health permitted, the West had someone with whom they could negotiate in the Kremlin. But little did they know just how many opportunities the coming year would bring.

CHAPTER 5

New Departures
The Beginning of the End of the Cold War

Preparations for his summit meeting with Mikhail Gorbachev in Geneva in November 1985 must have felt familiar to Ronald Reagan, the former Hollywood star: they were, after all, strikingly similar to making a film. Locations needed to be scouted and approved, not always an easy process with the stakes so high and the personalities so strong. Nancy Reagan's astrologer had serious qualms about the Château de Belle Rive, the first location selected for the Reagans to stay in Geneva by the White House director of advance, Bill Henkel. She prevailed on him to shift their accommodations to the more auspicious Maison de Saussure, home of the Aga Khan. Once chosen, sets needed to be dressed. "Barbed wire, troops, [and anti-aircraft] guns in camouflaged pits" would ensure the president's safety. At the Château Fleur d'Eau, where Reagan would host the talks with Gorbachev, staff would prepare a pool house some two hundred yards away from the main building with a roaring fire, beside which the two could retire and converse in private, away from their teams of advisers; plus, there were "great camera angles walking down."[1]

Rehearsals were Reagan's least favorite part of the process, with Jack Matlock speaking rapid-fire Russian at him in Gorbachev's stead so that the president could get used to working with an interpreter, and twenty-one papers drafted by Soviet experts to read.[2] "I'm getting [damn] sick of cramming like a school kid," he confided to his diary in late September. "Sometimes they tell me more than I need to know."[3] Costume, too, mattered a great deal. On the first day of the long-anticipated summit, Reagan bounded out to welcome Gorbachev wearing neither coat nor hat as the general secretary emerged from his limousine bundled up against the late-autumn chill coming off Lake Geneva. Though Reagan was twenty years older than Gorbachev, to the cameras it looked the other way around.[4]

Finally, there were the often-bizarre demands of the stars, which is how Andrew Littlefair found himself wandering the streets of Geneva with a frozen dead goldfish in his pocket. Henry, the deceased, had been the pet of one of the Aga Khan's sons, whose bedroom Reagan had been using as a study. He had left clear instructions for the president of the United States regarding Henry's needs, and Reagan dutifully doled out the daily two pinches of food, but after the first full day of meetings with Gorbachev, he returned home to find Henry dead. Littlefair, a member of the advance team, secured two replacements whom Reagan was careful to feed, even if it meant interrupting meetings.[5]

All of this was comfortable to the president. "He couldn't wait for the call: lights, camera, action," his national security adviser Bud McFarlane recalled. "He was an actor, after all, and he was about to walk onto the most important sound stage of his life."[6] Reagan "enjoyed playing the part[,] and the show did have something of a happy ending."[7]

Over the course of the preceding five years, policy makers in Washington and Moscow alike struggled with the dualities of the Cold War. One, the gap between perception and reality when it came to the balance of power, had closed. Now, policy makers in both superpowers, as well as their allies, saw a strong and rising United States and a Soviet Union far worse off than it had been just five years earlier—and on a grim downward trajectory. But it remained to be seen how policy makers would turn that major structural shift into significant policy changes. Other tensions persisted. For Gorbachev, the general secretary's attention would be pulled between problems that needed to be solved at home and the prospect of creating solutions—even temporary ones—in the international sphere. And the committed anti-communist Reagan "had to keep reminding himself that these 'nice guys' . . . are the same Soviets banning Jewish emigration."[8]

By early 1985, US policy makers had observed significant changes in the Soviet Union, even compared to just a year earlier, when Konstantin Chernenko had come to power in the Kremlin.[9] But those in Washington were already looking beyond Chernenko; his health was so poor that an unlucky few in the NSC stood "death watch."[10] He was reduced to being displayed at public

108   CHAPTER 5

functions, usually heavily stage-managed for the benefit of television cameras, while rumors swirled over when he would die—or if he was in fact already dead.[11] This did not stop the general secretary from winning reelection to the Supreme Soviet on March 2, 1985, receiving 99 percent of the vote in an election with 99 percent voter turnout.[12]

In Washington, the focus was already on the next generation of Soviet leaders—Mikhail Gorbachev in particular.[13] Born in 1931 in the village of Privol'noe in the north Caucasus near Stavropol, Gorbachev's youth coincided with one of the worst periods in Soviet history: between one-third and one-half of his village died in the famine of the early 1930s; he saw family members, including both of his grandfathers, swept up in the Great Terror; and World War II brought Hitler's armies. Thanks to his academic achievements and winning the Order of the Red Banner of Labor in 1948 for working with his father to bring in a bumper grain harvest with their massive combine harvester, Gorbachev eventually secured a coveted spot at Moscow State University.[14]

At university in the early 1950s, Gorbachev asked difficult questions about the Soviet system; Stalin's death halfway through his course of study catalyzed the young man's critical thinking. It was also at Moscow State University that he met his wife, Raisa (née Titorenko). After failing to find party work in Moscow, Gorbachev returned to Stavropol, where, in an indication of things to come, his first duties included traveling throughout the region to explain Nikita Khrushchev's secret speech of February 1956 to dumbfounded Soviet citizens. As Gorbachev would later recall, these years were his "little perestroĭka."[15] Gorbachev identified as a member of the Thaw generation, which had come of political age in this ideologically turbulent time. To him, the most important struggle was not the one with the United States and capitalism; rather, it was the generational struggle within the party over control of policy. Indeed, while working in Stavropol, Gorbachev credited the region's rapid development under his leadership to the fact that he had elevated a new, younger generation to power.[16] His rise to the top of the Stavropol party organization enabled him to read widely, including the banned works of Soviet dissidents and Western literature translated into Russian by the KGB. In 1978, Gorbachev returned to Moscow as Central Committee secretary responsible for agriculture, having made a name for himself as party head in Stavropol and attracting the attention of important players in Moscow, including Leonid Brezhnev and Iuriĭ Andropov. Two years later, he joined the ranks of the politburo, the most powerful organ in Soviet policy making.[17] There, under Andropov's tutelage, Gorbachev took on increasingly diverse responsibilities.[18] He had long maintained a particular interest in learning about the world beyond Soviet borders and used travel abroad to boost his position at home. Already, the young politburo member was thinking of a future for which he would need foreign-policy bona fides.[19]

When Gorbachev remarked to a close friend of Prime Minister Pierre Trudeau that "Canada lies between the United States and Soviet Union," it was unclear whether he was referring to geography or political proclivities.[20] Still, he was eager to visit the United States' northern neighbor. When the minister of agriculture Eugene Whelan visited the Soviet Union in 1981, he invited Gorbachev to make a return visit to Canada. Aleksandr Iakovlev, the reform-minded Soviet ambassador in Ottawa, saw an opportunity to expose the up-and-coming Gorbachev to more of the world and foreign-policy makers to the man he saw as the future of the Soviet system.[21] Ottawa was all for it; the visit would be a unique opportunity to observe a top-level Soviet official at length.[22]

Iakovlev and Gorbachev worked closely to prepare for the May 1983 visit, not only crafting talking points that balanced a new level of frankness with traditional Soviet goals but forging a friendship that ensured Iakovlev would be a key adviser of Gorbachev's in the years to come.[23] Gorbachev tackled his jam-packed, seven-day program in Canada with vigor, traveling from Ottawa to the celebrated vineyards and orchards of St. Catharines, Ontario, to the cattle ranches of Alberta.[24] In Ottawa, Gorbachev addressed Canadian parliamentarians, who were especially interested to hear from a member of the politburo because, as one of them put it, "we are the meat in the sandwich between the two of you superpowers." He fielded hostile questions about Soviet foreign policy, adhering to the Kremlin line but also admitting errors—including, most strikingly, the decision to invade Afghanistan.[25] Afterwards, he watched Question Period in Parliament. Iakovlev had intended this to be a demonstration of the value of pluralism. Gorbachev, like more than a few Canadians, dismissed it as a "circus."[26]

For Canadian policy makers, the centerpiece of the trip was Gorbachev's meeting with Pierre Trudeau.[27] Initially reticent for reasons of protocol, Iakovlev persuaded his old friend Trudeau that this was his chance to meet the next general secretary.[28] Trudeau opened their first, brief meeting by invoking the progress of détente during the 1970s and reminding Gorbachev that "as a middle power, we retain a vital interest in fomenting better understanding between nations." Gorbachev agreed but bemoaned US intransigence on arms control, which he described as a "smokescreen" for Reagan's defense buildup.[29] Trudeau was not done with Gorbachev, and the two met twice more for informal discussions.[30]

Gorbachev then embarked on a cross-country tour of Canada's agricultural industry from production to retail.[31] "I would give anything to know what flashes through the mind of a politburo member . . . who, on his first visit to

110   **CHAPTER 5**

the West, wanders through a supermarket," one US policy maker mused.[32] Gorbachev certainly made no attempt to hide his awe at Canadian supermarkets and their wares, especially Canadian lobster and Canadian wine, and readily acknowledged that the situation in the Soviet Union was far inferior.[33] He would later liken Soviet meat production to the "stone age" during a politburo meeting.[34]

Some of Gorbachev's most important conversations were not with Canadians but with Iakovlev, the Soviet ambassador. The two spoke with striking frankness about the dire situation in the Soviet Union, beginning with an evening walk on the Whelans' farm. The "backwardness [and] dogmatism" of policy makers in the Kremlin rankled both, in particular Iakovlev, who saw a stark contrast with Canada and the West. Viewed from Ottawa, Iakovlev's home since 1973, Soviet policy appeared "primitive and shameful." These conversations, Iakovlev later wrote somewhat immodestly (but not erroneously), led Gorbachev to conclude that massive economic and societal reforms, glasnost' and perestroĭka, were a necessity.[35]

Gorbachev clearly enjoyed the informal conversations with Canadians he met along the way. His demeanor stood in stark contrast to past Soviet visitors: when asked hostile questions, Gorbachev stayed calm—except once, when answering a question about his future ambition to lead the Soviet Union given Andropov's poor health and likely imminent death. "I have no doubt that he might mark a refreshing, competent, and more amenable change from the elderly, conservative, and unimaginative figures now dominating the Soviet leadership," one close observer of Gorbachev in Canada wrote.[36] It was, as Iakovlev put it, Gorbachev's "best side."[37] But Canadian policy makers' later claims to have "discovered Gorbachev" rankled the general secretary.[38]

Over a year later, Gorbachev's prominence had only grown, so much so that the Reagan administration considered inviting him to visit the United States, though this plan never materialized.[39] Margaret Thatcher's government did get its chance at a preview. When Foreign Secretary Geoffrey Howe visited Moscow in July 1984, he invited Gorbachev to visit the United Kingdom as head of a Soviet parliamentary delegation, assuring him that the visit would include meetings with Thatcher.[40] French policy makers grudgingly admired the scheme to turn a parliamentary delegation into a quasi–state visit that would introduce the up-and-coming Gorbachev to Britain.[41] To Bonn, it was clear that the Kremlin would be sending "their Crown Prince."[42] Whitehall warned, however, that the hosts should not expect too much.[43]

Thatcher found otherwise. Over lunch in December of that year, she and Gorbachev sparred over the relative merits of communism and capitalism. At the end, rather than taking umbrage at her strong critiques of the Soviet system, Gorbachev declared his "great satisfaction" with the conversation.[44] He agreed enthusiastically when Thatcher bemoaned the fact that NATO and the Warsaw Pact were spending too much on their militaries—money they both agreed could be better spent on improving the lives of their citizens. But he worried that Reagan did not mean what he said about eliminating nuclear weapons. Thatcher tried to disabuse him of that notion, but Gorbachev remained unconvinced. The president's "daydreams [of] space-based systems," he insisted, remained an insurmountable obstacle.[45]

Gorbachev impressed Thatcher with his confidence, openness, affability, and lack of reliance on prepared statements. To Reagan, she wrote: "I certainly found him a man one could do business with. I actually rather liked him— there is no doubt that he is completely loyal to the Soviet system but he is prepared to listen and have a genuine dialogue and make up his own mind. I got the impression that in some ways he was using me as a stalking horse for you."

Gorbachev asked numerous questions about US foreign policy while transparently probing for areas of disagreement between London and Washington.[46] Whitehall's briefing for US and other allied officials after the visit also presented Gorbachev as "someone with whom they could do business."[47] His choice to take a sightseeing tour of central London, as opposed to the scheduled wreath laying at the grave of Karl Marx, pleased his hosts enormously.[48] In a conversation with Helmut Kohl, Thatcher described Gorbachev as "winsome" and "spontaneous" but clearly agitated—and scared—by SDI. "As you know," Kohl warned her in response, "the most charming communists are also the most dangerous."[49] Visiting Reagan at Camp David later on, Thatcher reiterated her characterization of Gorbachev as "an unusual kind of Russian."[50] US policy makers, echoing Kohl, nevertheless worried that Soviet propaganda would get a boost from Gorbachev's striking ability to "humanize" the Kremlin's policies.[51]

Washington wondered when Gorbachev's time might come. The US intelligence community gathered Soviet media footage of Chernenko, asking medical experts to diagnose the patient from afar. In the summer of 1984, one such team predicted that Chernenko would live until 1990.[52] All the while, Gorbachev grew increasingly open about his ambitions to lead the Soviet Union, complaining in private that the general secretary seemed to stay alive only to hold him back.[53]

When a delegation led by Volodymyr Shcherbyts′kyĭ, a politburo member and the Ukrainian party leader, arrived in the United States on March 4, 1985, US policy makers took it as a sign that Moscow wanted to continue engaging, but also that Chernenko's health was reasonably good, otherwise Shcherbyts′kyĭ

112   CHAPTER 5

would not dare leave the Soviet Union.[54] The delegation met with a range of US policy makers, and Shcherbyts'kyĭ himself sat down with Reagan. The president urged the Kremlin to work with him to eliminate all nuclear weapons, going well beyond his speaking notes. The two agreed that progress could be made on the issue, though mutual distrust would remain an obstacle.[55] Even the conservative Shcherbyts'kyĭ came away convinced that relations between the superpowers could be improved.[56]

On March 8, reports trickled in to the CIA that Chernenko had died. These were discounted when the media in Moscow continued its scheduled programming (as opposed to playing somber music) and Shcherbyts'kyĭ's group did not change its plans.[57] The White House nevertheless planned for an imminent announcement and returned to the question of whether Reagan should attend the funeral. "Without a KGB background," Matlock advised, remembering Reagan's earlier objections to attending Andropov's funeral, "Chernenko is marginally more savory." Attending Chernenko's funeral would bring an end to criticisms that the president did not seriously want to improve US-Soviet relations.[58] Reagan considered it at length.[59] Again, however, he elected to send George H. W. Bush in his stead, feeling that the relationship had not improved sufficiently to warrant a presidential trip to Moscow.[60]

At 2:00 p.m. on March 11, the Soviet media announced that the general secretary had died the previous day. The public greeted the news without surprise but with sneers at the Kremlin's earlier insistence on Chernenko's perfect health while, in fact, he lay dying. In so doing, they had turned the Soviet Union into a "country of fools." At the next party plenum, nobody expressed "a single gram of grief," recalled Anatoliĭ Cherniaev, a future adviser to Gorbachev.[61] An air of satisfaction, if not outright joy, pervaded the meeting. Chernenko's death meant that the Soviet Union could at last have a "real leader."[62]

Within the Kremlin, top officials wasted no time.[63] Shcherbyts'kyĭ's group, finally informed of Chernenko's death, immediately returned to Moscow. On the flight home, the planeload of top Soviet policy makers concluded that "only Gorbachev" could lead the country into the future.[64] They were not alone. Gorbachev's success, according to Georgiĭ Shakhnazarov, a close adviser, "was the will of a public opinion that, although not officially recognized, was patent all the same." Clearly, the Soviet public had grown fed up with the "shameful farce" of gerontocracy.[65]

Most politburo members had made up their minds in the twenty-four hours between Chernenko's death and the politburo's meeting to choose his successor.[66] Gorbachev had already reached an agreement with the long-serving foreign minister, Andreĭ Gromyko, who put aside concerns that Gorbachev was too inexperienced in exchange for a promise of promotion: to chair of

NEW DEPARTURES   113

the Supreme Soviet, the nominal head of state.[67] Gorbachev walked into the politburo meeting already knowing the outcome, and what followed was a torrent of approbation. "We do not, we cannot, nominate anyone but M. S. Gorbachev to the post of General Secretary," Moscow party leader Viktor Grishin declared. Viktor Chebrikov, speaking for the KGB—which, he declared, "is the voice of our people"—praised Gorbachev's "great ability to work and great erudition." "This," Konstantin Rusakov, head of the Central Committee's International Department, pronounced, "is a man with a capital M!"[68] Gorbachev's claim that all this flattery "agitated" him strains credulity; it was his triumph.[69]

Barely an hour after announcing Chernenko's death, Soviet media reported Gorbachev's appointment to head the funeral commission. To Western analysts, the announcement confirmed what they had long predicted: Gorbachev would be the Soviet Union's next (and, unbeknownst to them all, last) general secretary.[70] He was probably less than sincere when he told his new subordinates that "all of us . . . are in deep grief" at Chernenko's passing, but Gorbachev was completely honest when he pledged that "we will never sacrifice the interests of our Motherland or our allies" and his readiness to "do everything for our Soviet Motherland to become still more rich and powerful."[71]

With the support of the KGB and the military, Gorbachev quickly consolidated power in the Kremlin. His main rivals for power quickly resigned their positions (not entirely voluntarily) to enjoy a comfortable retirement.[72] The Eastern intelligence community immediately recognized that their Western counterparts saw Gorbachev as an open and worldly individual with a dynamic management style, a sharp contrast to his predecessors.[73] And within the Kremlin, policy makers could not fail to notice that the new general secretary seemed almost indefatigable.[74] One popular joke from the time imagines a man returning to his home in the provinces from a trip to Moscow. "How are things there at the centre," his neighbors ask, "do they support Gorbachev?" His answer: "No, they don't support him. Can you believe it—he walks without any support."[75]

At Chernenko's funeral, Gorbachev's eulogy focused not on Chernenko but on Andropov and his efforts to return discipline to the domestic economy. The deceased was barely mentioned. The funeral service, Thatcher remarked, had been a formality, with a "let's-get-it-over, conveyor quality about it."[76] While this did not indicate that Gorbachev would necessarily be more accommodating in East-West relations, though most in the West suspected as much, one British observer could not help remarking, "It is to the general good that the second superpower should no longer drift in the hands of a generation so

114 CHAPTER 5

obviously out of touch with the modern world."[77] Not half an hour after the ceremony ended, the flags of mourning were taken down from Red Square, and the Soviet Union looked forward.[78] So too did the rest of the world. "We have been making a concrete effort to improve relations with the Soviet Union," Reagan wrote to Helmut Kohl in Bonn. "Gorbachev's accession as General Secretary may offer an opportunity to put US-Soviet relations on a more solid footing."[79] The president had decided to waste no time in trying to get to know Gorbachev.[80] That this desire had not extended to attending Chernenko's funeral in order to meet him chafed, however, as the rest of NATO's members were represented by their head of state or government. Reagan's conspicuous absence felt like a slight.[81]

When Bush and George Shultz met with Gorbachev, Shultz quickly concluded that "he was out of a different mold."[82] Though Chernenko had not set a high bar for vigor and dynamism in a general secretary, Gorbachev's struck the US delegation. His tone was also different. Gorbachev acknowledged that nobody in the Soviet leadership was "such a madman" as to think about conflict—especially nuclear—and stressed Moscow's desire to seize opportunities for cooperation between the two superpowers.[83] He also offered a warning: if Washington wished to stress human rights issues, Moscow could point to ample cases of abuses by the United States. Meeting with Kohl, Gorbachev startled the Bundeskanzler by immediately declaring that the world was closer to war than peace. He was willing to go to great lengths to bring it back from the brink. Reagan did not seem to share this view, using negotiations for propaganda and as a "smokescreen" to overtake the Soviet Union militarily. The two did agree that the Cold War arms race was nothing more than "economic insanity," which could lead to Armageddon.[84] Thatcher's meeting with Gorbachev revisited many of the themes of their earlier conversations in London, particularly the perceived danger of SDI.[85] "Even if he wished to change matters," she worried, Gorbachev "wouldn't know how to because a rigid communist system was the only one he had ever known."[86]

Despite a record-high attendance by Moscow's Cold War rivals, Gorbachev focused more on developing ties with potential Asian partners and on loosening them with Eastern European ones.[87] Gorbachev did not pen a glowing report of his meetings with Western leaders, though he clearly appreciated their eagerness to get to know him. From the two-hour meeting with Bush and Shultz, for example, Gorbachev concluded (with good reason) that the United States was "relying on [its] huge economic potential" to best the Soviet Union. Both top US policy makers were "vague and imprecise"—except, gratifyingly, regarding Reagan's desire to meet with Gorbachev and his willingness to negotiate.[88] His most important meeting involved none of the Western visitors.[89]

To the leaders of the Warsaw Pact states, Gorbachev put into words what the Soviet nonintervention in Poland some four years earlier had hinted at: the Brezhnev Doctrine would no longer be enforced.[90] Eastern Europe was simply not a priority of Gorbachev's, and when he said otherwise, it was, according to Cherniaev, nothing more than "obligatory ritual."[91] Under his leadership, the Soviet Union would expect close and cooperative relations but would not intervene in Eastern Europeans' internal affairs. Looking back, Gorbachev identified this moment as the beginning of the process that culminated in the fall of the Berlin Wall in November 1989.[92]

On coming to power, Gorbachev knew one thing for certain from his earlier travels abroad: "We just can't go on like this."[93] His new thinking opened up policy avenues previously closed to Soviet officialdom, though many dismissed it as a mere propaganda slogan.[94] Others saw it as "a conspiracy of academicians" bent on wresting control over the Soviet Union from the bureaucracy.[95] Even Gorbachev's closest allies wondered at first whether this was genuine or just for Western consumption.[96]

New thinking required new thinkers. Reagan may have been willing to keep policy makers in his administration who openly disagreed with the president's course, but Gorbachev would not.[97] Throughout the Soviet Union, "sclerotic" officials out of step with Gorbachev's plans found themselves out of a job; younger policy makers, such as Cherniaev and Iakovlev, replaced them.[98] This was the realization of the hopes of many in the Soviet Union: to see a new generation in power that could lead the country more effectively.[99] Gorbachev also took steps to arm his advisers with the facts they needed to be effective in their roles, demanding that the provision of data for policy making not be tailored to drawing the conclusions the Kremlin wanted, obscuring flaws in the Soviet system.[100] This was a page right out of his mentor Andropov's playbook. But he also exhorted Kremlin policy makers to look outside the Soviet Union for ideas to solve long-standing problems. Abroad, Gorbachev had seen firsthand that the Soviet way of doing things was not always best. This, Andropov would have never done.[101]

As had been the case with Reagan four years earlier, foreign policy was far from Gorbachev's top priority upon assuming office; he first had to confront the "novelty and magnitude of problems facing [Soviet] society."[102] Like Andropov, he saw the domestic economy as the most pressing issue.[103] In an April 11 politburo meeting, he announced that Soviet agricultural productivity was 2.5 times lower than in capitalist countries, while hundreds of tons of produce went to waste due to spoilage resulting from inadequate transportation infrastructure.[104] At the outset, he relied on the methods of his mentor:

116   **CHAPTER 5**

deficit-financed investments in heavy industry and administrative measures to fight corruption and inefficiency. Speaking to a group of Leningrad party officials, he demanded hard work and discipline of his audience, just as Andropov might have done a few years earlier.[105] The overall state of the economy at the time was perhaps best summed up by a question one of Gorbachev's aides wrote in his notebook during a meeting with a Western counterpart: "What is a 'service sector'?"[106]

In tackling the Soviet Union's economic problems, the crisis in its oil industry significantly constrained Gorbachev's freedom of action. Production decline in 1985 outpaced even the CIA's worst-case scenario, at 500,000 barrels per day fewer than in 1984. Equipment shortages made an increase unlikely.[107] All the while, the price of oil was steadily declining. By 1985, a barrel of Soviet oil fetched only 60 percent of what it had just one year earlier.[108] It was a perfect storm. Moscow, utterly dependent on imported grain, could not simply spend less hard currency abroad—and it could scarcely export something else to make up the shortfall: nobody wanted Soviet products, only 12 percent of which, according to Moscow's own analysis, were competitive on the international market.[109] This was a new type of economic challenge: while beforehand, at the beginning of the 1980s, the Soviet economy's growth was worryingly slow, matters had seemed far worse in the West. Now, with oil prices on the decline and Western economies recovered, the Kremlin could not avoid the fact that the Soviet Union really was in decline, in both relative and actual terms.

With the economy in such a dismal state, as the State Department crassly put it, "the Soviet people have been resorting increasingly to the traditional Russian remedy for boredom and hopelessness—alcohol."[110] In early 1985, nine million drunkards had been arrested across the Soviet Union, half of them youths. Some officials, including Gorbachev, saw alcoholism as an epidemic and an existential threat to the survival of communism and pushed for at least partial prohibition.[111] Others saw it differently. As one politburo member remarked, "This is idiocy. How do you make a man whose ancestors have been drinking for centuries suddenly stop?"[112] One thing was certain: Gorbachev's anti-alcohol campaign was financially ruinous, costing the state $100 billion in lost revenue from alcohol sales. Gorbachev's first major initiative as general secretary, another continuation of the Andropov order-and-discipline line, was an abject failure.[113]

Western policy makers looked on with skepticism. "Gorbachev faces major problems, some of which he will work to solve," Hans-Dietrich Genscher pronounced, "but the basic problem, which is the [communist] system, he will not be able to solve."[114] Gorbachev took inspiration from the Japanese model for allocating investment with more of a government role than the United States, which left it up to capital markets—a model that unsurprisingly appealed much more to Soviet economists.[115] Even more intriguing were the economic reforms underway in China. Deng Xiaoping opened the country up to foreign investment, signing some twenty thousand international partnerships worth over $26 billion during the 1980s, and quadrupling the country's GDP in the process. Attracted by favorable terms in so-called special economic zones, foreign companies rushed into the Chinese market.[116] At first, to Soviet observers, this seemed a bridge too far and suspiciously un-communist; increasingly, Soviet policy makers could not deny the efficacy of such measures.[117] In the 1980s, the countries of Asia—a region, Gorbachev stressed, which included the Soviet Union—"woke up to a new life in the twentieth century" and came to represent the way forward to Soviet policy makers searching for solutions.[118]

In foreign policy, too, much of the early new thinking looked like the old. In part, this was because Soviet foreign-policy standbys such as the "peace offensive" offered useful cover for some of Gorbachev's more innovative ideas for US-Soviet relations.[119] Other aspects were nothing new: his efforts to engage the United States stemmed not from pro-Western sentiment but from a desire to compete more effectively with Moscow's Cold War rival. Yet in 1985, Gorbachev and his advisers recognized that Moscow was falling behind—and could not afford to try to make up for lost ground.[120] They could, however, work to reduce Cold War tensions—and thus expenditures—enhancing Moscow's ability to compete with the other superpower over the long term.[121] "Socialism," one of Gorbachev's foreign-policy aides wrote tellingly in his journal, "can win only in peaceful conditions."[122] Soviet history, another insisted, showed that economic development was only possible in the context of a stable international system. Reducing tensions with the United States would catalyze the development of "a new society" in the Soviet Union.[123] This had also begun under Andropov. "Maybe he was not prepared like Gorbachev to make radical steps," political commentator Fedor Burlatskiĭ recalled, "but he was going in the same direction."[124] Andropov was not compelled in the same way as Gorbachev to go so far. In 1983, US military superiority was on the horizon as the two superpowers enjoyed rough parity. In 1985, it was a reality with which the Warsaw Pact had to contend. Gorbachev may have borrowed his mentor's strategies liberally, but he played a weaker hand than Andropov's.

The West's high-technology militaries were especially troublesome to Moscow and its allies.[125] SDI remained the key issue.[126] "The so-called SDI has nothing to do with defense," Moscow's reports to its Warsaw Pact allies

118   **CHAPTER 5**

insisted.[127] It was an offensive plan to destroy the strategic balance, start a new unrestrained arms race, achieve military superiority, and secure impunity for a nuclear first strike. Stopping SDI mattered not only militarily but also economically: the Soviet Union could ill-afford a hypothetical SDI (or SDI countermeasures) of its own.[128] While most in the MID saw SDI as a fool's errand, the military took it deadly seriously. In the game of bureaucratic politics, the latter won: at this stage, Gorbachev read the generals' assessments, not the diplomats', and made policy accordingly.[129] Most Soviet leaders, including the general secretary, recognized the "senselessness and counterproductivity" of another arms race.[130] On the other side, Sergeĭ Akhromeev, who had replaced Ogarkov as chief of the General Staff in late 1984, had no patience for the idea of reducing military expenditures: "What would be done with all the weapons produced by the Soviet Union? . . . At great cost, we have created first-class factories, the equal of those in the United States. Would you order them to stop work and produce crockery? No. That is utopian."[131]

Faced with nothing but setbacks at the arms control negotiating table—the first round of the Nuclear and Space Talks had gone nowhere, thanks to Moscow's obsession with SDI—Gorbachev, too, returned to old Soviet tactics: driving a wedge between the United States and its allies.[132] In March, he wrote a highly publicized letter to the Peace Council of Heilbronn in West Germany accusing the United States of using talks as a "smokescreen" for military buildup and having "revanchist intentions."[133] In April, he denounced US aggression and militarism in a lengthy interview with *Pravda*.[134] And in May, he gave a positively "Brezhnevian" speech, full of allusions to the West's pernicious designs, to commemorate the fortieth anniversary of the end of World War II.[135] Wedge-driving remained a key aspect of Soviet foreign policy toward Europe and the United States, only now it was couched in more sophisticated language about a "growing European consciousness and a growing European identity"—in which, naturally, there was no place for the United States.[136]

In foreign policy, extricating the Soviet Union from Afghanistan was Gorbachev's top priority. In this he enjoyed the support of even the most conservative in the Kremlin—with the military in the vanguard.[137] Here again, Gorbachev was picking up where Andropov had left off. In the spring of 1983, Andropov had bemoaned the fact that "the Soviet Union had suffered nothing but casualties, expense, and international disapproval through intervening. They had no desire to stay" in order to back up a hopeless regime in Kabul.[138] Radio Moscow (the Soviet equivalent of Voice of America) had even broadcast content criticizing the decision to invade.[139] Gorbachev further relaxed rules on press coverage of the war to build public support for a complete withdrawal. Soviet television, in one 1985 broadcast, aired two and a half minutes

NEW DEPARTURES   119

of frontline footage of young Soviet Army conscripts fleeing their burning vehicles under Mujahideen attack.[140] In a secret meeting with Babrak Kamal on October 16, Gorbachev urged the Afghan leader to take all necessary measures to prepare for an imminent Soviet departure. He encouraged Kamal to return to Islamic and even capitalist values, to hold talks with rebel leaders and Afghan émigré communities, and to be prepared to share power with his noncommunist political rivals. The next day, Gorbachev announced to the politburo that he had decided to withdraw Soviet forces from Afghanistan.[141]

The way Soviet foreign-policy makers talked about their country's role in the world was beginning to change, due in large part to critical personnel shifts. Gorbachev replaced Gromyko as foreign minister in July 1985—the first time the office had changed hands since February 1957—with Eduard Shevardnadze, a provincial party leader from Georgia.[142] The two had been friends for decades, and both agreed that, as Shevardnadze put it, "everything had gone rotten" in the Soviet Union.[143] The new foreign minister forbade wanton references to Lenin and was allergic to terms like "class struggle" and "proletarian internationalism."[144] And he believed that one of the key failures of Soviet foreign policy had been to fixate on attacking the United States rather than focusing on areas of mutual interest.[145] Meanwhile, Gorbachev built a parallel foreign policy–making structure within the party, made up of officials who shared his own views and led by Anatoliĭ Dobrynin, who had returned from the embassy in Washington.[146]

The general secretary pushed this group to consider "universal human values" as the core of Soviet foreign policy, and he framed the question of relations with the United States as one of responsible behavior in light of the Soviet Union's position as a nuclear-armed superpower.[147] Preventing a nuclear war was the superpowers' chief responsibility, Gorbachev's aides stressed, and less adversarial East-West relations would go a long way toward that end.[148] Nevertheless, in letters to Reagan, many of which exceeded ten pages, Gorbachev mounted vigorous defenses of the Soviet system and launched scathing attacks of US policy.[149] He and his advisers chafed at Washington's insistence that it was the leader of the "free" world, wondering, "Who authorized the United States to take on such an august mission?"[150] Washington insisted it had the best form of government because the people chose their leaders, but Moscow contended that the people of the world had not really chosen US leadership but rather had had it foisted on them.

Soviet policy makers particularly resented US pressure on human rights issues, which they dismissed as "psychological warfare," "gross libel," and purely cynical given US support for human rights–abusing regimes, especially in Latin America.[151] As Gorbachev put it to a visiting delegation of US senators,

120   CHAPTER 5

"Human rights cannot be discussed productively" until the United States ceased its worldwide hypocrisy.[152] He would no longer let human rights be a cudgel for the United States, instructing the MID and his politburo colleagues to turn the tables on Washington.[153] The ideological competition between East and West, the Soviet military stressed, was far from over.[154]

Shifts in the balance of power, perceived in Washington and Moscow alike, predisposed the two superpowers toward a summit. Soviet diplomats were now openly telling their US counterparts that Moscow was "anxious to achieve a modus vivendi with the United States as a matter of high urgency."[155] Dating back to the years of Lenin, Soviet leaders had appreciated that being seen as equals to the capitalist powers was a critical national security concern. Moscow could not afford to isolate itself from the rest of the world, hostile though it might be. Gorbachev wanted a meeting before 1985 was through in order to take the pressure off Moscow to keep spending on arms.[156] Washington reciprocated this desire to engage—but, of course, was careful not to give the impression of being "desperate."[157]

Arranging a summit had become a complicated game of diplomatic chicken. Shultz and Gromyko squared off in Vienna in May 1985, both wanting to emerge with an agreement for their leaders to meet, but neither willing to give up anything for it. After a six-hour meeting in a stifling room in the Soviet embassy, with neither even mentioning a summit, Gromyko finally blinked. The Soviet foreign minister pulled Shultz aside, and they agreed to a Reagan-Gorbachev summit in neutral Geneva, with an agenda as yet unspecified. "The meeting had been sterile and peculiar," Shultz recalled, "but at the final moment, productive."[158] At last, after over four years in office, Reagan could look forward to meeting his Soviet counterpart on November 19, 1985.[159]

In Washington, preparations began in earnest. "The upcoming meeting with Gorbachev," the NSC advised, "poses a greater challenge to the president than any summit since the 1955 meeting between Eisenhower and Khrushchev."[160] To prepare Reagan, Matlock organized a series of seminars on the Soviet Union, "Soviet Union 101," as he called it.[161] He wrote the two most important papers himself, making a special effort to "attract Reagan's interest and appeal to his sensibilities." On Soviet psychology, Matlock warned that Gorbachev, like all Soviet and Russian leaders before him, was extremely sensitive to questions of face and legitimacy, especially as a coequal superpower with the United States. In meeting with Gorbachev, Reagan would have to take the Soviet leader's insecurities into account.[162] (A dinner with defector Arkadiĭ Shevchenko, formerly of the Soviet mission to the UN, confirmed this. In his diary, Reagan remarked that the Kremlin clearly had "an inferiority complex.")[163] On the Soviet Union's sense of its place in the world, Matlock stressed that World War II was still an open wound in the eyes of the country in general and of its leaders in particular. Richard Pipes had previously told Reagan that the war had given the Kremlin the resolve—and perhaps the willingness—to fight a nuclear war. Matlock insisted that it had actually led to a deep fear of any military conflict, especially with the United States.[164] So thorough was this preparation that on the eve of the summit, Reagan worried that he might be "overtrained" and unable to make the most of his spontaneous, personal interactions with Gorbachev.[165]

The Reagan administration did not approach the summit from the perspective of building a partnership with the Soviet leader. Rather, the summit was to be yet another forum for Cold War competition. The president professed himself "too cynical to believe" that Gorbachev was an entirely new type of leader. After all, the politburo would not have picked him if his credentials as a communist true believer were anything less than exemplary.[166] This assessment pervaded Washington, where, according to State Department official Michael Armacost, "the intelligence community was basically covering its ass with very skeptical analyses."[167] In the summer of 1985, the CIA saw Gorbachev's goal as "not radical reform" but "an attack on corruption and inefficiency." Even with this supposed aversion to reform, they warned, "he is the most aggressive and activist Soviet leader since Khrushchev."[168] Those who did see Gorbachev as a reformer concluded that he was motivated by the economic imperative to end (or at least reduce) the costly Cold War arms race, which the United States was winning—and could sustain. That meant, according to chief of staff Donald Regan, that the president "was holding the trump card."[169]

In a memorandum Reagan dictated to Matlock weeks before the summit, and seen by only a select few in the White House, he laid out his feelings on the new general secretary: "I believe Gorbachev is a highly intelligent leader totally dedicated to traditional Soviet goals. He will be a formidable negotiator and will try to make Soviet foreign and military policy more effective. He is . . . dependent on the Soviet-communist hierarchy and will be out to prove to them his strength and dedication to Soviet traditional goals." Reagan went on to conclude correctly that Gorbachev's interest in arms control was as much motivated by a desire to limit the economic consequences of trying to keep pace with the United States as by any pacific tendencies. The meeting at Geneva was first and foremost a beginning, as Reagan saw it, to a lengthy process of negotiation from which he expected to emerge the victor.[170] The summit was not meant to yield tangible results. Expectations to the contrary, leading to "a damaging cycle of euphoria and then disillusionment," should be dispelled. Meeting Gorbachev face to face would give "direction and

CHAPTER 5

momentum" to US foreign policy, making the United States a more effective Cold War competitor.[171]

Gorbachev faced serious resistance within the Kremlin in advance of his planned meeting with Reagan.[172] Soviet foreign-policy makers worried that Reagan would not be particularly forthcoming in the negotiations, making the most of US leverage over the Soviet Union.[173] Still, a face-to-face meeting between the leaders of the two superpowers could do more than decades of propaganda had done to undercut the image of a "Soviet threat" in the West.[174] Unlike previous Soviet leaders, who believed a summit had to culminate in the signing of a major agreement, Gorbachev's only goal for Geneva was to meet the president and begin to improve US-Soviet relations, even if only in atmospherics.[175] Such a shift would, the Kremlin hoped, curtail the economically "catastrophic" arms race that had Moscow spending 16 percent of its annual GDP on the military and a further 4 percent on the paramilitary KGB.[176] Gorbachev recalled the challenge he faced vividly in his memoirs: "The task was not an easy one: to find a common language not with a social democrat such as [Swedish Prime Minister Olof] Palme or a socialist like [French President François] Mitterrand, but with Ronald Reagan, who called the Soviet Union an 'evil empire,' promoted the abhorrent 'Reaganomics,' [and] invaded Grenada, among other misdeeds."[177] To Moscow's Warsaw Pact allies in Sofia, Bulgaria, Gorbachev stressed that he wanted to reduce nuclear arsenals (ideally by half), but he had no illusion that he would "meet a new Reagan at Geneva"; it would be the same Reagan who had concocted SDI and "attempts to extort us politically and economically" sitting across the table.[178]

Iakovlev penned a lengthy analysis of the president's policies, which illuminates the Kremlin's thinking on the eve of the summit. The general secretary, he wrote, should make sure Reagan did not manage to seize the initiative in East-West relations and become the "peacemaker" in global public opinion. After his military buildup, Reagan had the credibility necessary to go to the bargaining table with the Soviet Union, and he would want to make the most of it. Moreover, he had the support of US and Western public opinion to do so. Even if nothing came of the Geneva meeting, the US propaganda machine would likely be able to frame a stalemate as a victory. Nevertheless, a meeting with Reagan was undeniably "in the national interest of the Soviet Union." The Kremlin had to accept that for the next quarter century at least, the United States would be the stronger superpower. Improving US-Soviet relations would give Moscow the breathing room it desperately needed to reform the economy and compete more successfully with the West over the long term.[179] Gorbachev, for his part, highlighted four key guidelines in dealing with Reagan: not deviating from Soviet arms control positions, not ceding the right to "'solidarity' with 'freedom fighters'" worldwide, not provoking Reagan and thereby giving US hawks ammunition, and the "need to learn how to live together."[180] Thus, the politburo concluded, "the main goal of the meeting is to try to find a common language with the [president of the United States]," but not to end the war of words.[181]

Over a series of meetings in autumn 1985, the two superpowers moved toward finalizing the program for the Reagan-Gorbachev summit. On September 16, Dobrynin informed Shultz that Gorbachev hoped to reach agreements in Geneva on reducing offensive weapons or, at the very least, lay the groundwork for real results, and shocked his US interlocutors by announcing that the general secretary would accept US "fundamental research" on SDI.[182] Eastern intelligence predicted that Reagan would be willing to make a distinction between research and deployment and forgo the latter, at least for the time being, stalling SDI until the early 1990s.[183] Later that month, Shultz met Shevardnadze in New York, where the Soviet foreign minister was attending the UN General Assembly. "We far prefer to rely on lower levels of forces," Shultz told his Soviet counterpart on September 26, "and this can only happen through arms control."[184] With an overabundance of nuclear weapons and a dearth of trust, mistakes or misperceptions could trigger a devastating war. Reagan reinforced this message in a personal meeting with Shevardnadze the next day. "We need to get beyond stereotypes," he insisted, "to explore constructively what we can achieve together."[185] Like Reagan, Shevardnadze said, Gorbachev saw the elimination of the threat of nuclear war as his main duty. The two met again on October 24, agreeing that Reagan and Gorbachev had "no right to disappoint the world" by failing to make the most of their long-awaited summit.[186]

Finally, on November 2, Shultz and McFarlane arrived in Moscow to meet with Gorbachev for final preparations, the summit just two weeks away. The White House kept this trip hidden even from Caspar Weinberger, who made no secret of his fears that Reagan and Shultz would give up too much at Geneva, to prevent him from undermining the effort. In his meetings with Shultz and McFarlane, Gorbachev was "very, very feisty." He insisted that the Kremlin wanted better relations, but the US lack of respect for Moscow as a superpower made that increasingly difficult. Not relying on talking points or his advisers, Gorbachev excoriated US foreign policy in front of two of its chief architects. "George and I just kind of sat there," McFarlane recalled, "somewhat astonished really." At least when Shultz stressed Reagan's respect for the Soviet Union and the superpowers' joint responsibilities, Gorbachev seemed receptive. It was clear to the two visitors that Gorbachev's aim, however, was to "repair [the Soviet] system, not replace it."[187]

"Discussions in Moscow were tough," Shultz reported to Reagan.[188] Gorbachev displayed intellectual agility and rhetorical prowess not seen for a long time in the Kremlin's highest office, yet he remained a deft user of the "blunt, sometimes browbeating style" of Soviet leaders before him. Or, as Arthur Hartman put it from the US embassy in Moscow, using a Hollywood analogy befitting the Reagan administration, "[Gorbachev] could be played convincingly by George C. Scott but not by Jimmy Stewart."[189] Neither the new general secretary nor the new coterie of advisers he had elevated wanted to squander Soviet power. Gorbachev was a committed communist, motivated by a desire to compete more effectively with the United States in the long run. He was not about to make concessions on issues of grave concern, particularly SDI.[190] That, Reagan predicted, would "be a case of an irresistible force meeting an immovable object."[191]

In a November 1981 conversation with Helmut Schmidt, Margaret Thatcher had suggested that "President Brezhnev might be surprised when he met President Reagan. He might find that they understood each other more easily than he might have expected."[192] Four years—and three general secretaries—later, with Gorbachev leading the Kremlin, she was proven right in the first US-Soviet summit since June 1979.

Already on the eve of the Geneva summit, both Reagan and Gorbachev saw encouraging signs. Eastern intelligence reports highlighted that Radio Free Europe and Radio Liberty broadcasts pertaining to the Soviet Union had softened their tone.[193] Before taking off for Geneva, Reagan learned that Moscow had allowed several Soviets married to US citizens to emigrate and reunite with their spouses.[194] The Kremlin timed the release for maximum effect: the public relations battle between the superpowers was as important, according to the MID, as those set to take place in Geneva over warhead levels and SDI.[195]

Gorbachev's aides were confident that the general secretary would "outdo [and] intimidate that actor-cowboy."[196] In hindsight, foreign-policy adviser Andreĭ Aleksandrov-Agentov admitted, the MID, the Kremlin, and even the general secretary himself had all underestimated Reagan.[197] So too did Reagan's own secretary of defense. Weinberger penned a letter to the president, urging him to stand firm against Gorbachev in Geneva—and promptly leaked it to the *New York Times*. Reagan did not appreciate the implication that he was captive to the "McFarlane-Shultz cabal," and while another president might have changed the leadership in the Pentagon, discipline had never been Reagan's strong suit.[198] Weinberger's insubordination notwithstanding, Reagan met Gorbachev with considerable support at home. No less than 83 percent of the US public, according to one poll, approved of the president's summit with the new Soviet general secretary.[199] The pre-summit mood in Washington, as the French ambassador Emmanuel Jacquin de Margerie cabled to Paris, was one of "febrile agitation at the State Department, sulky quiet at the Pentagon, [and] firm resolve on the part of the White House."[200]

On the morning of November 19, 1985, Reagan, Gorbachev, and only one interpreter sat down across from one another in the Château Fleur d'Eau. This first private meeting was only scheduled to last fifteen minutes. To the surprise and confusion of both US and Soviet officials "waiting [and] wondering" outside the closed doors, they spoke for an hour.[201] The two leaders' conversation went from being between "communist number one" and "imperialist number one," as Gorbachev recounted in his memoirs, to a businesslike dialogue between statesmen.[202] Both came from humble backgrounds and had risen to high office, Reagan emphasized. They led the most powerful countries in the world: the only ones who could start a third world war and the only ones who could prevent it. Reagan had taken to heart advice regarding the Soviets' sense of inferiority and was trying to make Gorbachev feel like his equal from the outset. "Young people were wondering about whether they would be alive or not," Gorbachev reminded Reagan. If the two left Geneva without making progress, he went on, the world would be rightly disappointed. In this first conversation, it became clear that both of them would be disappointed as well.[203]

Translating that enthusiasm and personal connection into progress proved easier said than done, especially in front of all their advisers. Over two plenary sessions, Reagan and Gorbachev rehashed their previous correspondence. While the meetings were businesslike, that was the best that could be said of them.[204] Reagan declared that when it came to the US nuclear arsenal, he "was willing to give it up," but that was nothing new, and the Soviets had serious doubts whether he really meant it.[205] On SDI, Washington had heard rumblings that it was not Gorbachev but the Soviet military who felt threatened by the program. The general secretary wasted no time making it clear how wrong that information was.[206] SDI, he insisted, only made sense if it was meant to give the United States first-strike impunity: "Weinberger has said that if the [Soviet Union] had such a defense first, it would be bad. If we go first, you feel it would be bad for the world, feeding mistrust. We cannot accept the rationale which says it is good if you do it and bad if we do it. . . . We will have to frustrate this plan, and we will build up in order to smash your shield."[207] All Reagan could do was to ask the Soviets to trust him and to work with the United States to liberate themselves from mutually assured destruction. Gorbachev and his advisers were, unsurprisingly, not ready to take that leap of faith.[208]

126   **CHAPTER 5**

Open formats like that, Reagan's advisers recognized, were unlikely to bear fruit. Instead, they steered the two leaders toward the carefully staged pool house, where they talked together by the fire. Afterwards, Reagan remarked that Gorbachev was almost a different person one on one. "You could almost like the guy—but I keep telling myself I must not do it, because he could turn." The two remained at loggerheads over SDI. At one point, Reagan even offered to give the Soviets access to the technology. Gorbachev refused. He appreciated that SDI appealed to Reagan personally but remained convinced of the program's destabilizing nature. "Layer after layer of offensive weapons, Soviet as well as US weapons, would appear in outer space," he warned, "and only God himself would know what they were."[209] It was not an auspicious end to the day. Over dinner, however, Gorbachev gave Reagan a glimpse of something else the two had in common when he stressed the importance of "family values," an encouraging sign.[210]

The next morning, Reagan broached the vexed question of human rights in the Soviet Union. If Gorbachev would make some concessions, Reagan assured him, mindful of the earlier successes of quiet diplomacy, Washington "would never boast that the Soviet side had given in."[211] Gorbachev was not interested—he remained fixated on SDI.[212] "It is not convincing, it is emotional, a dream," he exclaimed. "You intend to launch space weapons—not toys. . . . We are accusing you of not wanting peace."[213] After the session ended, a shaken Reagan talked the SDI issue over with Shultz and McFarlane. The three agreed to hold the line, even if it meant the summit ended without agreement. Outwardly, Reagan stressed that SDI was a key catalyst for the eventual elimination of nuclear weapons. But behind closed doors, Reagan and his advisers also stressed the value of SDI as a means of exerting pressure on the Soviets, who would be loath to face the cost of competing with the United States in yet another high-technology arms race.[214]

A final meeting between the leaders and their advisers concluded the first superpower summit in over half a decade. Reagan and Gorbachev patted themselves on the back for having met at all—an achievement in its own right given the history of the preceding half decade.[215] Over dinner, Gorbachev even "half apologized" for his earlier outburst over SDI.[216] Reagan proposed that the two "say, 'to hell with the past, we'll do it our way and get something done!'"[217] After dinner, the two delegations worked until 5:00 a.m. on a joint communiqué. Reagan got what he wanted: no mention of SDI (and no limits thereon) and one sentence on human rights issues in the Soviet Union. The next morning, as the two leaders signed it, Reagan joked to Gorbachev, "Your hard liners and my hard liners are going to swallow very hard seeing us up here shaking hands and smiling." "You're so right," the general secretary replied. "They won't like it."[218]

Reading the record of Reagan and Gorbachev's conversations in Geneva, it is difficult to appreciate the extent to which the summit was, in Gorbachev's words, a "breakthrough."[219] Little of what the president had to say went beyond "pieties lifted from election stump speeches."[220] The summit's value was not in policy proposals aired and debated but in something much less tangible: personal rapport and chemistry between its participants.[221] Neither leader foresaw the competitive nature of the Cold War dissipating—in fact, both saw the summit as a means of competing more successfully in the future—but they also hoped to imbue it with a degree of trust that neither side would go beyond peaceful competition.

Reagan then took his "victory lap."[222] From Geneva, he traveled to a special meeting of the North Atlantic Council in Brussels, where he reported that the summit was "an important step forward in our efforts to build a basis for more stable and constructive East-West relations," something for which many of Washington's NATO allies had long lobbied and which fit squarely within the president's own dual-track framework for US-Soviet relations.[223] Reagan then returned to the United States to address a joint session of Congress. He framed the meeting with Gorbachev as the culmination of the past four years of quiet diplomacy and peace through strength, making the most of the chance to highlight his own foreign-policy successes: "We met, as we had to meet. I called for a fresh start—and we made a fresh start. . . . I gained a better perspective; I feel that [Gorbachev] did too. . . . Preparations for the summit began five years ago when . . . we began strengthening our economy, restoring our national will, and rebuilding our defenses and alliances."[224] Reagan felt confident his audiences in Brussels and Washington were persuaded. In his diary, the president quipped, "I haven't gotten such a reception since I was shot."[225] Actually, US policy makers were now worried that Gorbachev's stock was rising faster than Reagan's—especially as the president's conservative allies were far from laudatory of his meeting with the Soviet general secretary.[226] Leading Republican Congressman Newt Gingrich, for example, derided the summit as "the most dangerous summit for the West since Adolf Hitler met with Neville Chamberlain in 1938 in Munich."[227]

Throughout the Soviet Union, policy makers and the general public were relieved to see a Soviet general secretary who could actually engage the president of the United States as an equal. That alone would make the Soviet Union a more effective Cold War competitor.[228] In public, Gorbachev put a cooperative spin on the meeting, speaking without polemics about the

128   **CHAPTER 5**

opening made at Geneva.[229] The politburo went even further, dubbing the summit "the most consequential political event in international life during 1985." The Soviet Union's top leadership looked forward to a much-needed relaxation of tensions with the United States and worldwide.[230] In large part, this was because the US leader had been humanized in their eyes. Anatoliĭ Adamishin, who in late 1984 had bemoaned that nobody took him seriously when he likened the president to Adolf Hitler, now, after just a handshake in Geneva, confessed that he found Reagan "simpatico."[231] The Supreme Soviet—now chaired by Andreĭ Gromyko, who had so ardently opposed a summit during his final years as foreign minister—applauded Gorbachev for continuing the "Leninist, peaceful policy of the Soviet Union."[232]

To a gathering of Soviet diplomats, Gorbachev declared that "halting the nuclear arms race" was now the Kremlin's "highest of high priorities" in order to shift spending away from defense and toward the starved civilian sector.[233] In private, Gorbachev's language focused much more on competition. He congratulated himself for having boxed Reagan into publicly committing to continuing to negotiate with the Soviet Union going forward, a small victory, to be sure.[234] He warned his politburo colleagues that Reagan was "a creature of the military-industrial complex," who would not be willing to make a fundamental change in superpower relations. Going forward, Soviet economic and military recovery would be "the holy of holies."[235]

Kremlin policy makers congratulated themselves on demonstrating that they would neither back down on Soviet interests in the face of continued US anti-communism nor be taken in by Reagan's assurances on SDI. Now was the time to ratchet up pressure on Washington. It was not, Georgiĭ Kornienko of the MID stressed, a new phase of superpower cooperation, and his office focused on how Geneva could help the Gorbachev-led Soviet Union put the United States on the defensive.[236] Accordingly, the general secretary launched into a series of meetings to explore how SDI might be countered with top Soviet scientists and defense officials.[237] In March 1986, he went so far as to assure the politburo that SDI could, in fact, be disabled—through atmospheric nuclear explosions that would disable the satellites on which it relied to detect missiles in flight.[238]

As the United States and the Soviet Union looked ahead to a future that looked very different from the vantage points of the Kremlin and the White House, Eastern policy makers turned to the language of the past. One Czechoslovak diplomat, for example, praised "the vigorous pursuit of détente" resumed at Geneva.[239] Several others in the MID referred to an emerging "spirit of Geneva," harking back to the rhetoric that followed the 1955 summit there, when

British, French, Soviet, and US leaders had convened for the first time in the Cold War.[240] Tellingly, in order to describe what already seemed to the participants to be a new phase of the Cold War (though not yet obviously the beginning of its end), they referenced policies predicated on the continuation of Cold War competition and intended by the Soviet Union to best the United States. Overt engagement between East and West might keep it under control, but competition would not cease to be a fact of life in the Cold War.[241]

The Reagan-Gorbachev summit in Geneva, generally presented as a new beginning, also signified an end. In 1981, leaders in both Washington and Moscow perceived the Soviet Union to be stronger than the United States. By 1985, that had reversed. Equally important, however, the commitment of actors like Reagan, Gorbachev, and some of their advisers to reducing superpower tensions remained constant. The new realities of the post-1985 Cold War emboldened Reagan and Gorbachev alike to engage, but both did so with an eye toward the competition ahead. Now, however, Western policy makers readied themselves to press their advantage.[242] "The US position is strong," Matlock summed up, "and the momentum in the balance of power is with the [United States]."[243] To be sure, something was new in 1985. As "they got to know each other, studied each other, [and] 'adjusted' to each other," policy makers including Reagan and Gorbachev reimagined the future of the Cold War—but neither changed their ultimate goal.[244] Going forward, Reagan and Gorbachev would become, at once, partners and rivals in shaping its end.

Conclusion
Winners and Losers

To thunderous applause, George H. W. Bush strode into the chamber of the House of Representatives on January 28, 1992, to deliver his report on the state of the union. Up for reelection that November, Bush was determined to make the most of his moment. His popularity after the successful Persian Gulf War was on the wane as the United States fell into a recession. He (and his speechwriters) needed a win. Having watched the Soviet Union collapse, with the hammer and sickle lowered for the last time at the Kremlin on Christmas Day 1991, they believed they had one. "The biggest thing that has happened in the world in my life, in our lives, is this," Bush proclaimed. "By the grace of God, America won the Cold War."[1] There would be no more strategic bombers on twenty-four-hour alert, no more air raid drills in schools, and no more nightmares of nuclear Armageddon. The United States was now the world's sole superpower. In late 1989, Bush had famously admonished his press secretary, Marlin Fitzwater, "I'm not going to dance on the Berlin Wall. The last thing I want to do is brag about winning the Cold War."[2] Now, just over two years later, he was dancing on the Soviet Union's grave.

Such an outcome was far from clear when Ronald Reagan and Mikhail Gorbachev parted ways in Geneva in November 1985. That Cold War endgame was a highly contingent, frequently chaotic process. Nothing about the Cold War's largely peaceful conclusion was inevitable. But by late 1985, it was possible to imagine an eventual end state along the lines Bush described without

130

CONCLUSION 131

being laughed out of the room. At the beginning of the 1980s, however, such a prognosis would have been dismissed as a flight of fancy.

As president, Ronald Reagan made several key decisions that moved the conflict in that direction. He conceived of a dual-track grand strategy toward the Soviet Union that used the proverbial carrot and stick to their fullest. The first track, peace through strength, asserted that US national security also provided international security, and that a weak United States led to an unstable world. The second, quiet diplomacy, used outreach to the Soviet Union not only to keep the East-West relationship on a stable footing but also to make it possible for US policy makers to turn that advantage into diplomatic bargains favoring the United States. In engaging the Soviet Union, Reagan did not wait for a promising or at least sympathetic interlocutor like Mikhail Gorbachev to begin. After his first letter to Leonid Brezhnev from his hospital bed, Reagan tried to make common cause with Brezhnev, Iurii Andropov, and Konstantin Chernenko, no matter that the odds of success seemed slim. Even the Gorbachev of the mid-1980s was a far cry from the Gorbachev of the decade's end; when he came to power, the man who would be the last general secretary looked a great deal like his predecessors to the White House.

Policy makers had ample opportunity to make choices that would have taken the course of international events in a very different direction. The rejection of violence and the practice of "hippocratic diplomacy" by actors in both superpowers and their allies made all the difference in bringing the Cold War to a peaceful conclusion.[3] So too did the global trends recognized by all in 1985: the rise of the United States from the perceived lows of the previous decade and the corresponding decline of the Soviet Union. This shift in the perceived balance of power took place over the first half of the 1980s. Over the decade's latter half and into the next, the gap between the superpowers only widened. The decisive shift—the beginning of the end of the Cold War—occurred well before the Cold War ended.

That shift consisted of two elements. First, both the real and the perceived balance of power in the world, specifically between the two superpowers and the blocs they led, shifted from one that favored the Soviet Union to one that decisively favored the United States. As Western economies emerged from the doldrums of the 1970s at the dawn of a new decade and began the process of adjusting to the new, globalized world economy, they outpaced the centrally planned economies of the East. Investments in US and NATO military forces, especially in high-technology (and, in the case of SDI, fantastical) weapons systems, put the Warsaw Pact at a disadvantage. Whatever confidence Soviet and Eastern European leaders may have had in 1980, it had vanished by 1985; they could not keep up. Emboldened, US and Western policy makers pressed

132   **CONCLUSION**

their advantage, but they did so above all in the diplomatic domain. Second, the nature of US-Soviet diplomatic engagement shifted from covert to overt. US-Soviet contacts continued throughout the first half of the 1980s, though much of that dialogue took place in clandestine channels. From 1985 on, that changed, as superpower summitry and leader-to-leader engagement replaced back-channel talks by lower-profile officials. In Washington, Reagan and his advisers believed that they could engage overtly and risk their efforts coming to naught if the prize was agreements that benefited the United States. In Moscow, Gorbachev and his circle believed that they had to engage overtly to bring down superpower tensions in order to shift focus from costly armaments programs to vital domestic economic restructuring—from tanks and ICBMs to perestroĭka and glasnost'. The first half of the 1980s witnessed the transformation of both perceptions and realities in leadership circles on both sides of the Iron Curtain.

That shift shaped not only how policy makers behaved but also how they thought—above all, in terms of time.[4] Early in the 1980s, the Reagan administration's foreign-policy aim had been "to buy time" and to deal with the Soviets from a position of strength later on.[5] By the end of the decade, it was Gorbachev who wanted "a long period of peace" to rebuild Soviet capabilities.[6] Washington, however, was in no rush; US policy makers operated with a long time horizon. The United States could afford to wait and would likely benefit from doing so, as Soviet problems only mounted. Gorbachev, on the other hand, operated on a short timeline, growing increasingly desperate for results and respite abroad, as he found neither at home. Gorbachev may have complained that US policy makers wanted him to "show his cards," but Washington knew he had a bad hand, which was only getting worse.[7]

Reagan did a great deal right—especially when it came to US-Soviet relations—but in many senses, he was pushing on an open door. "It is impossible to understand how the Cold War came to an end," one of Gorbachev's biographers, Archie Brown, cautions, "without an understanding of the Soviet domestic political context."[8] On the first anniversary of his becoming general secretary, Gorbachev, by his own admission, did not have much to show for himself when it came to improving the Soviet Union's economic footing. At the Twenty-Seventh Party Congress, he acknowledged "the unfavorable tendencies in the economy and the social and moral sphere[s]."[9] To the Central Committee, he openly bemoaned the fact that despite the party's efforts, "the country is rife with confusion and problems!"[10] Just a month later, on the night of April 26, 1986, at the Chornobyl' Nuclear Power Station north of Kyiv, Ukraine, the world saw just how much. A safety test went horribly wrong, triggering an

CONCLUSION   133

explosion in one reactor and unleashing radioactive material not just on the neighboring town of Pripiat' but across the Soviet Union and Europe.[11] To the politburo, Gorbachev put it best: "They all fucked up."[12] Gorbachev himself later observed that his life could be divided into two phases: before and after Chornobyl'.[13] "In just one breath," he told the politburo, "we learned what nuclear war was"—and that "we need negotiations."[14]

Soon after, the global price of oil fell yet again, along with the Soviet Union's output thereof. The combination threw the economy into even deeper crisis: Gorbachev did not have the funds to follow through on his commitment to major state investments in the economy, a key aspect of his flagship program, perestroĭka, nor to finance the military's ongoing but seemingly vain efforts to keep up with the West.[15] Already at the Twenty-Seventh Party Congress, Gorbachev had declared that the Soviet military would have to settle for what he termed "reasonable sufficiency."[16]

In curbing the Soviet Union's military spending after Chornobyl', Gorbachev's hand was strengthened by the most unlikely of events. On May 28, 1987, a West German amateur pilot and peace activist named Mathias Rust took off from Helsinki, Finland, flying due southeast, and landed his small Cessna aircraft in the heart of the Soviet capital. "It is an absolute disgrace," Gorbachev declared. "This is even worse than Chornobyl'."[17] It was a humiliation, to be sure, but one that could be turned to the general secretary's advantage. He and his advisers decided to "punish those who were directly guilty, but also those who had indirect responsibility."[18] This expansive definition brought down some 150 senior leaders in the largest single purge in the history of the Soviet military, Stalin's included.[19] By late 1988, Gorbachev announced to the UN General Assembly that Moscow would unilaterally reduce its military forces by some 500,000—50,000 of them (along with 5,000 tanks) coming from Soviet forces deployed to Warsaw Pact member states.[20] While Gorbachev was retrenching, as Secretary of the Navy John Lehman later put it, the United States "continued [its] full-court press."[21]

Increasingly, however, Gorbachev could and would do little to push back. The Reykjavík Summit between him and Reagan in October 1986, for example, broke down because the two could not find common ground on SDI. Reagan's insistence that he would share the technology with the Soviets strained Gorbachev's credulity; if the United States would not share milking technology, the general secretary doubted Washington would ever be more forthcoming when it came to that required to shoot down ICBMs mid-flight.[22] Neither would budge, and SDI, which still caused so much disquiet in the Kremlin, remained on the table.[23] A year later, by contrast, Gorbachev had little choice but to accommodate. The INF Treaty, signed in Washington on December 8,

134 CONCLUSION

1987, eliminated intermediate-range weapons, which Gorbachev had previously insisted would only be possible if the United States abandoned SDI. Now, Gorbachev needed the economic flexibility that a reduction in spending on nuclear weapons would bring, and he needed the boost that signing a major agreement with Reagan would give him at home and abroad as perestroĭka foundered and opposition, emboldened by glasnost', mounted.[24]

Washington knew exactly what it was doing. "US policy is one of extorting more and more concessions," Gorbachev complained to George Shultz. "I'm weeping for you," the secretary of state responded sardonically.[25] "Your navy and bases surround my country and threaten the security of the Soviet Union," Marshal Sergeĭ Akhromeev declared to his US counterpart, the chair of the Joint Chiefs of Staff. "I'm very pleased to hear that," Adm. William J. Crowe replied.[26]

When Bush succeeded Reagan in January 1989, this pattern continued. The new administration worried that "the Soviet Union was making a virtue out of its growing relative weakness," buying time to rebuild Soviet strength and undermining the West's will to challenge Moscow.[27] The Bush administration also worried that Reagan had gone too far in accommodating the Soviet Union during its decline in the preceding years. Brent Scowcroft, the new national security adviser, led a review of US policy toward the Soviet Union that effectively froze superpower relations for months.[28] Gorbachev seethed but could do little about it, having next to no leverage over the White House by the end of the 1980s.[29]

Ultimately, the greatest challenge to the political strength of the Soviet Union came from within, not from the West. One of the great ironies of Soviet history is that as Gorbachev transformed his country, he could not transform himself. As glasnost' and perestroĭka made the country more liberal, and opposition to the Kremlin's course mounted, Gorbachev grew increasingly authoritarian. "Glasnost' ended at the Kremlin's edge," his biographer William Taubman sums up, but the damage it did to central control ricocheted throughout the Soviet Union.[30]

The opening salvo of the conservative opposition to Gorbachev came from Nina Andreeva, a chemistry professor from Leningrad. In a March 13, 1988, article titled "I Cannot Forsake My Principles," she—and the politburo members who backed her—spoke out against the challenging of Soviet orthodoxies unleashed by glasnost'.[31] The criticism continued until August 1991, when a group of politburo members demanded Gorbachev's resignation so that they could reverse the effects of glasnost' and perestroĭka. At the time, Gorbachev and his family were vacationing at the general secretary's villa in Foros, on Ukraine's Crimean Peninsula. In a televised press conference two days after

CONCLUSION 135

announcing the emergency measures, two of the coup's ringleaders were visibly drunk for all to see. Things only went downhill from there. The putsch finally unraveled when the military refused to obey orders and use force on the crowds gathering in Moscow in protest.[32]

For others, glasnost' did not go far enough, fast enough. Boris Yeltsin, the party head in Moscow, wanted Gorbachev to go further in his reforms—and was not shy about making his criticisms of the general secretary known.[33] The two clashed at politburo meetings with increasing frequency, culminating in a marathon dressing-down of the troublesome member during an October 1987 session.[34] After that, Yeltsin had a minor breakdown, half-heartedly attempting to take his own life, but his and Gorbachev's simmering disagreement had become a seething, self-destructive hatred for both. As Gorbachev went forward with his glasnost' reforms, he strengthened Yeltsin's hand. In December 1986, for example, he invited Andreĭ Sakharov to return to Moscow from his exile in Gor'kiĭ to bolster reforms. Sakharov's preferred means of aiding Gorbachev was to castigate the Kremlin and to demand more liberalization and democratization at every turn.[35] Gorbachev saw glasnost' as vital to building support for perestroĭka, but ultimately recognized that it undermined that and all his other reform efforts by weakening the Kremlin's authority and ability to implement them.[36] This became increasingly difficult as nationalism—which offered an alternative vision for the future to communism—came to dominate conversations, ultimately becoming a powerful force in the unraveling of the Soviet Union, as glasnost' fanned its flames.[37]

Beyond the borders of the Soviet Union, citizens throughout Eastern Europe craved liberalization. When Gorbachev visited East Germany in October 1989, it became clear to him that the leadership in East Berlin was not equal to the task of managing its citizens' demands for change.[38] On the night of November 9, 1989, Gorbachev's misgivings proved accurate as East German politburo spokesman Günter Schabowski accidentally indicated that free travel through the Berlin Wall would be permitted immediately. Thousands of East Berliners, watching the press conference on pirated West German television, rushed to the border. At 10:30 p.m., the first of them crossed at Bornholmer Straße, whose unsuspecting outnumbered guards chose to open the gates rather than open fire on their fellow citizens. That night, at just that post, twenty thousand East Germans crossed into the West.[39] Gorbachev made good on his declaration at Chernenko's funeral years earlier and left the Eastern European regimes to their own devices. The next month, when he and Bush met at Malta, he promulgated the Sinatra Doctrine, which superceded Brezhnev's, and promised that the Eastern Europeans would be permitted to "go their own way"—a move Andreĭ Gromyko denounced as the "Maltese Munich."[40] One

136 **CONCLUSION**

by one, communist regimes collapsed as Eastern Europeans demanded freedom—and took it. From within and without, the Soviet Union and its empire were being pulled apart. Gorbachev could not stop the process that "had all begun at Geneva."[41] On December 25, 1991, the final day of the Soviet Union's existence, Jack Matlock, the ambassador to the Soviet Union, wrote a poignant "autopsy" for the departed: "The deceased was a being of vicious habits that his physicians set out to cure. They managed to alleviate the patient's paranoia and curb his aggressive behavior, but the drugs administered undermined his immune system, and he eventually died from the spread of infections that would not be life threatening to a healthy body."[42]

One man had a front-row seat to the massive dislocations at the end of the Cold War: Lt. Col. Vladimir Putin, a KGB officer posted to East Germany's third-largest city, Dresden. What he saw playing out before him was, as Putin later put it, the "greatest geopolitical catastrophe of the [twentieth] century"—and far from inevitable.[43] In retrospect, it is tempting to see the collapse of the Soviet Union otherwise, knowing that it would indeed fall apart by 1991 and with its structural weaknesses in plain view. Russia's reduced stature after the Cold War, then, might be seen as no more than what its citizens should have expected: a harsh reality, but one to which they should have been ready to adjust. After all, the United States had won the Cold War, and the Soviet Union had lost.

This is not how Putin and millions of other Soviet citizens saw things. He and his generation "came of age at the zenith of Soviet socialism, only to see the system crumble."[44] At the dawn of the 1980s, they believed themselves to be at that high point, ascendant, with the West at a disadvantage and capitalism in crisis. For upwardly mobile citizens like Putin, the future looked bright. In the span of a short half decade, that changed dramatically. The heady days of the early 1980s in the Soviet Union had been illusory. Few knew how quickly that outlook would be proven to have been more perception than reality, as the Soviet Union collapsed under the weight of its own contradictions, its decline accelerated by policies designed to "consolidate [US] gains" at Moscow's expense.[45] And few were ready to accept so abrupt a reversal of fortunes, from the confidence at the beginning of the decade to the collapse of Moscow's sphere of influence at the end.

From Putin's vantage point, the fall of the Berlin Wall on November 9, 1989, gave way to chaos. Living in an apartment complex for Stasi officials and their Soviet partners in Dresden, panic swirled around him and his then wife, Liudmila. Barely a month later, events went from bad to worse. On December 5, angry crowds surrounded the Stasi headquarters, within which the KGB's own offices were located. They stormed the Stasi complex, stopping the employees

CONCLUSION   137

from destroying more evidence of the East German state's repression and large-scale surveillance, and then turned on the KGB annex. For a time, Putin and his colleagues held them off by "demonstrating [their] readiness to defend [the] premises," but they needed support from the massive Soviet Army contingent in the country if they were to hold out much longer, lest their bluff be called. That help took hours to arrive. "I got the feeling then that the country no longer existed," Putin recalled on the eve of his own accession to power in the Kremlin. "It was clear that the [Soviet] Union was ailing. And it had a terminal disease without a cure, namely paralysis. Paralysis of power."[46]

Bush had spoken in 1989 of a "Europe whole and free" to come, but the dominant experience in Russia was one of rending.[47] Yeltsin may have gotten his wish and become the first president of an independent, non-communist Russia, but in order for that to happen, millions of his fellow compatriots had to become orphans. In 1991, they had been citizens of the Soviet Union, certainly not a flawless country but one of which they felt they could be proud. In their eyes, just because communist ideology had come to an end did not mean that Russia's status as one of the world's preeminent powers had to as well. But in 1992 it did, and quickly. Economic "shock therapy" visited decades' worth of inflation on Russians virtually overnight, having been bottled up over years of the Soviet Union printing money with abandon but not raising prices.[48] As many watched their life savings evaporate, a new class of oligarchs became fantastically wealthy, mostly through underhanded means and usually first and foremost at the public's expense.[49]

Abroad, Russia fared little better. The Soviet Army, once spread across Eastern Europe as the backbone of the Warsaw Pact, standing "on guard for peace and socialism," came home, but thousands of troops lived in squalid tent cities, as there was no infrastructure to reabsorb them.[50] Meanwhile, their old barracks in the former East Germany came under NATO control as a unified Germany took its place in the alliance in 1990. The Russian Federation's first major military effort, a campaign to restrain the breakaway province of Chechnya in the north Caucasus from 1994 to 1996, killed and displaced hundreds of thousands of Chechen civilians. Russia was now one of the world's democracies, but most Western observers saw more of the old Soviet Union in the brutal Chechen War than the promise of a new Russia. "I tell you it was the right thing to do," Yeltsin's liberal-minded foreign minister, Andreĭ Kozyrev, declared of the Chechnya operation. "How it was done is not my business."[51]

NATO did not stop its growth at the eastern border of unified Germany, whatever assurances Gorbachev may have believed himself to have received.[52] By the end of the 1990s, the Czech Republic, Hungary, and Poland also joined the alliance, with more former Warsaw Pact members to follow in the new

138 CONCLUSION

millennium. "Hallelujah," the US secretary of state Madeleine Albright famously exclaimed, while her Russian counterparts fumed.[53] In 1999, Yeltsin demanded that this newly enlarged NATO not intervene militarily to halt the ongoing genocide in Kosovo being perpetrated by the Serbian forces of Slobodan Milošević. Bush's successor in the White House, Bill Clinton, ignored him; NATO airstrikes went ahead regardless of Russian opposition and the threats of its leaders. During the Soviet years, such disregard would have been unthinkable. Now, it was the new normal.[54]

By the end of the 1990s, Russians were exhausted, not least Yeltsin himself. His heart—and drinking—problems were catching up with him. Already in 1996, the Communist Party had nearly won the presidency back, on a platform promising that a vote for their candidate, Gennadiĭ Ziuganov, would mean there would be no need to ever vote again. An influx of cash from the oligarchs who had accumulated enormous wealth—and political power—amid the aftershocks of the Soviet collapse saved Yeltsin's skin, but only for the time being.[55] Resigning the presidency at the end of the millennium, Russia's first president did not go out on a high note: "I want to ask your forgiveness—for the dreams that have not come true, and for the things that seemed easy but turned out to be so excruciatingly difficult. I am asking your forgiveness for failing to justify the hopes of those who believed me when I said that we would leap from the grey, stagnating totalitarian past into a bright, prosperous and civilized future."[56]

Enter President Vladimir Putin. He had spent the 1990s in relative obscurity, first in St. Petersburg, managing the city's foreign economic relations, and later in Moscow in the Presidential Administration, as director of the Federal Security Service (the heir to his old employer, the KGB), and finally from August 16, 1999, as prime minister. When, some four months later, Yeltsin resigned, Putin became Russia's second president by dint of the constitutional line of succession—as well as his background in the security services, which meant he could guarantee Yeltsin's safety in retirement—and he was elected to the post on March 26, 2000. Putin's first priority was to restore what he referred to as "the executive vertical"—in other words, Kremlin control.[57] During the late 1980s, when glasnost' ran amok, it had been absent.[58] So too during the 1990s, when Moscow could not even collect taxes reliably and Yeltsin shelled the Russian parliament to impose his will on the legislature.[59] As Putin saw it, a loss of central control first in the Soviet Union and then in the Russian Federation had had disastrous consequences. It is not for nothing that when Russia hosted the 2014 Winter Olympics in Sochi, the opening ceremonies—usually a spectacular, and spectacularly rose tinted, telling of the host country's history—stopped with Iuriĭ Gagarin's spaceflight in 1961.[60]

CONCLUSION   139

Russia's president does not want to revive the Soviet Union, but he does want to restore Russia to the position of international influence and respect—*derzhavnost'*—the Soviet Union once enjoyed and, over the course of the 1980s, began to lose.[61] What Putin mourns the loss of is Soviet power, not the Soviet system itself. Of the latter, he has been explicitly critical, denouncing it as "historic futility" and "a blind alley" whose result was "dooming our country to lag behind . . . far away from the mainstream of world civilization."[62] To German journalists, he summed up how many Russians felt: "Those who do not regret the collapse of the Soviet Union have no heart, but those that do regret it have no brain."[63]

To Putin, who had served as a KGB officer in East Germany, the decision by the new Yeltsin administration to "just drop everything and leave," abandoning the Soviet Union's position in Europe, was "what hurt."[64] What perhaps hurt even more is who came in to fill the vacuum. Putin has made no secret of how dissatisfied he is with the "unipolar moment" of unquestioned and unchallenged US supremacy, and of Washington declaring even the former Soviet space to be within its sphere of influence.[65] Speaking to the 2007 meeting of the Munich Security Conference, he denounced Washington's "unrestrained hyper-use of force" in the post–Cold War world, which instead of solving problems only created new ones and caused further suffering. In such a world, he spat at his stunned audience, "no one feels safe!"[66]

A broader view of the end of the Cold War, taking the power shift of the first half of the 1980s into account, changes the story of that transformational episode in international relations. It also changes the story of its legacy and the origins of today's renewed tensions between Washington and Moscow. The Soviet Union's international influence is not a distant memory to Putin or his coterie. After all, as recently as 1980, a balance of power favoring the Soviet Union was the common perception in the East. Within the span of just five short years, it came crashing down before their eyes, the perception of Soviet strength giving way to the harsh realities of Soviet decline and years of seemingly futile efforts to revive the system that unleashed chaos. This is not ancient history to these policy makers but a relatively recent reversal of fortunes. "Things developed so swiftly," Putin later recalled of the Cold War's aftermath, when explaining the Russian annexation of Crimea in 2014, "that few people realized how truly dramatic those events and their consequences would be."[67] Many fought bitterly, hoping to arrest the Soviet Union's (and later Russia's) decline. Many still do. It is no surprise that Russia's current leaders want to return to the position of international influence they enjoyed as Soviet citizens—and intend to rebuild and hold on to it for themselves, whatever the cost.

NOTES

Introduction

1. Adams, *Tiny Revolutions in Russia*, 114. This and other jokes even reached the attention of the US intelligence community's uppermost leaders. CIA memorandum, "Soviet Jokes for the DDCI," NARA, CREST, doc. CIA-RDP89G00720R 000800040003-6.

2. Yurchak, *Everything Was Forever*, 257.

3. Bush, *All the Best*, 321.

4. Reagan remarks, Washington, D.C., 29 Jan. 1981, in Greene et al., *Public Papers of the Presidents: Ronald Reagan, 1981*, 57.

5. Reagan remarks, Notre Dame University, Notre Dame, Ind., 17 May 1981, in Greene et al., *Public Papers of the Presidents: Ronald Reagan, 1981*, 431–435.

6. Reagan remarks, Palace of Westminster, London, United Kingdom, 8 June 1982, in Greene, Mellody, and Payne, *Public Papers of the Presidents: Ronald Reagan, 1982*, 1:742–748.

7. Reagan remarks, Annual Convention of the National Association of Evangelicals, Orlando, Fla., 8 Mar. 1983, in Hill and Kevan, *Public Papers of the Presidents: Ronald Reagan, 1983*, 1:359–364.

8. Andropov, "Zaiavlenie Generalnogo sekretaria TsK KPSS Predsedatelia Prezidiuma Verkhovnogo Soveta SSSR Iu.V. Andropov," 1.

9. Kostikov, "Protiv iadernogo bezumiia," 5.

10. Kurdiumov, "Politika terrorizma," 5.

11. Gaddis, "On Starting All Over Again," 3.

12. Kennedy, *Rise and Fall of the Great Powers*, 514.

13. The February 1988 pogroms in Sumgait, Azerbaijan, the April 1989 massacre in Tbilisi, Georgia, the January 1990 massacre in Baku, Azerbaijan, and the crackdowns in Rīga, Latvia and Vilnius, Lithuania, for example, all being important exceptions.

14. Hayward, *The Age of Reagan*; Kengor, *The Crusader*; Marlo, *Planning Reagan's War*; Schweizer, *Victory*; Schweizer, *Reagan's War*. So much has been written advancing this triumphalist narrative of US and Western military, economic, and moral victory that the body of literature has spawned its own body of literature. Fischer, *The Myth of Triumphalism*; Matlock, *Superpower Illusions*; Prados, *How the Cold War Ended*; Schrecker, ed., *Cold War Triumphalism*.

15. Jentleson, *The Peacemakers*; Taubman, *Gorbachev*.

16. Evangelista, *Unarmed Forces*; Freeman, "Looking over the Horizon"; Snyder, *Human Rights Activism and the End of the Cold War*.

142   **NOTES TO PAGES 2–7**

17. Bartel, "The Triumph of Broken Promises"; Brooks and Wohlforth, "Power, Globalization, and the End of the Cold War"; Brands, *Making the Unipolar Moment*; De Groot, "Disruption"; Sargent, *A Superpower Transformed*; Westad, *The Cold War*; cf. English, "Power, Ideas and New Evidence on the Cold War's End."

18. Ikenberry, *After Victory*; Kydd, *Trust and Mistrust in International Relations*; Glaser, *Rational Theory of International Politics*; Yarhi-Milo, *Knowing the Adversary*.

19. Halliday, *Making of the Second Cold War*, 3; Rossinow, *The Reagan Era*, 101.

20. Fischer, *The Reagan Reversal*, 2–3.

21. Wilson, *The Triumph of Improvisation*; Wilson, "How Grand Was Reagan's Strategy?"

22. Brown, *The Gorbachev Factor*; Leffler, "Ronald Reagan and the Cold War."

23. Bange, "'Keeping Détente Alive'"; Békés, "Why Was There No 'Second Cold War' in Europe?"; Kieninger, *Diplomacy of Détente*; Villaume and Westad, "The Secrets of European Détente"; Wenkel, "Overcoming the Crisis of Détente, 1979–1983."

24. Reagan diary entry, 6 Apr. 1983, in Brinkley, *The Reagan Diaries*, 1:212–213; Reagan to Vaschenko, 11 Oct. 1984, in *Life in Letters*, 380.

25. Reagan remarks, 19 Oct. 1980, LOC, AMHP, box 131, folder 8.

26. Shultz remarks, Senate Foreign Relations Committee, Washington, D.C., 26 Apr. 1983, RRPL, JFMP, box 41, folder: "US-USSR Relations Apr. 1983 2."

27. Gorbachev, *Zhizn' i reformy*, 1:218.

28. Kotkin, *Armageddon Averted*, 49–54; Suny, *Soviet Experiment*, 449–451. Garthoff, *Great Transition*; Haslam, *Russia's Cold War*; Zubok, *Failed Empire*.

29. Smith, "New Bottles for New Wine."

30. Garton Ash, *The File*.

31. Kotkin, *Magnetic Mountain*, 118.

32. Stalin, "O nekotorykh voprosakh istorii Bol'shevizma," in Stalin, *Sochineniia* 13:96.

33. Shifrinson, *Rising Titans, Falling Giants*.

34. Clausewitz, *On War*, 127–132.

35. Herz, "Idealist Internationalism and the Security Dilemma"; Jervis, *Perception and Misperception in International Politics*.

36. Wendt, "The Agent-Structure Problem in International Relations Theory."

37. Blainey, *The Causes of War*; Copeland, *The Origins of Major War*; Gilpin, *War and Change in World Politics*; Organski and Kugler, *The War Ledger*; Van Evera, *Causes of War*.

38. Taubman, *Gorbachev*, 1.

39. Bacon and Sandle, *Brezhnev Reconsidered*; Khinshtein, *Skazka o poteriannom vremeni*; Maisurian, *Drugoĭ Brezhnev*; Morgan, *The Final Act*; Raleigh, "'Soviet' Man of Peace."

40. Soldatov and Borogan, *New Nobility*, 91–100.

41. Grinevskiĭ, *Taĭny sovetskoĭ diplomatii*, 131; Iakovlev, *Sumerki*, 568; Wolford, "Turnover Trap." The encounter was characterized by uncomfortable small talk, not scheming. Taubman, *Gorbachev*, 160–161.

42. Brezhnev remarks, KPSS Politburo, 6 July 1968, *General'nyĭ sekretar' L.I. Brezhnev*, 70–79.

43. Brezhnev had used similar circumstances created by his predecessor, Nikita Khrushchev, to mount a successful coup in 1964. Miles, "Envisioning Détente."

44. Gaidar, *Collapse of an Empire*, xviii.

NOTES TO PAGES 8–12   143

45. Mann, *Rebellion of Ronald Reagan*, 346.

46. Gotlieb diary entry, 18 May 1983, in Gotlieb, *The Washington Diaries*, 157–158. The comments in question were a commitment by Reagan to tackle the issue of acid rain.

47. Matlock, *Reagan and Gorbachev*, 326.

48. Therefore, adherents of this view go so far as to suggest, those who characterize Reagan as an effective grand strategist are guilty of "intellectual malpractice." Rossinow, "The Legend of Reagan the Peacemaker," 57; Prados, *How the Cold War Ended*, 178.

49. Longley et al., *Deconstructing Reagan*, 121–126.

50. MNO memorandum, no. 4 (244), "Hlavní rysy zahraniční a vojenské politiky nové americké vlády," 1981, ABS, ZSGŠ, PM, box 106; ISKRAN memorandum, "Nekotorye osobennosti voennoĭ politiki administratsii Reĭgana," 25 Mar. 1985, ARAN, fond 2021, opis' 2, delo 3; Njølstad, "Carter Legacy," 197. Some US allies came to the same conclusion. Stabreit memorandum, "Rede Präsident Reagans vor der UN-Vollversammlung," 28 Sept. 1983, BA, B 136/29797.

51. Allen, "Ronald Reagan," 52. On Reagan as a grand strategist, see Nitze, "Reagan as Foreign Policy Strategist."

52. IFPAB memorandum, 25 Dec. 1980, HIA, WJCP, box 300, folder: "Interim Foreign Policy Advisory Board"; Brands, *What Good Is Grand Strategy?*, 103, 127; cf. Leffler, "Ronald Reagan and the Cold War," 80–81.

53. Ronald Reagan, *American Life*, 605.

54. Cannon, *President Reagan*, 183.

55. Nancy Reagan, *My Turn*, 106.

56. Stearman, *American Adventure*, 218.

57. Leffler, *For the Soul of Mankind*, 462; Leffler, "Ronald Reagan and the Cold War," 84–85.

58. Shevardnadze, *Moĭ vybor*, 131.

59. Greiner, "Angst im Kalten Krieg," 17–21.

60. Wacker, *America's Pastor*, 242.

61. Cowie, *Stayin' Alive*, 310.

62. Brands, *Latin America's Cold War*, 189.

63. Not all are welcoming of this "Reagan revisionism," which uses newly accessible archives to craft balanced accounts of the fortieth president. Hayward, "Reagan Reclaimed."

64. Krauthammer, "The Unipolar Moment," 23.

1. Red Star Rising

1. Heigerson, *Getting to Know the President*, 111–113.

2. Turner, *Burn Before Reading*, 192.

3. Arbel and Edelist, *Western Intelligence and the Collapse of the Soviet Union*, 152.

4. Church, "Can Capitalism Survive?," 52.

5. Sayle, *Enduring Alliance*, 191–211.

6. Reagan remarks, Republican National Convention, Detroit, Mich., 17 July 1980, LOC, CWWP, box 551, folder: "Ronald Reagan Campaign 1980 3."

7. Van Cleave memorandum, "Defense Policy Briefing Book: 1980 Campaign," LOC, CWWP, box 572, folder: "Campaign Defense Policy Briefing Book"; Malone to

144 **NOTES TO PAGES 13–15**

Shakespeare, "ACDA Transition Team Final Report," 18 Dec. 1980, HIA, RVAP, box 35, folder 8; Nitze to Iklé, 23 Dec. 1980, LOC, PHNP, pt. 1, box 144, folder 3.

8. CIA memorandum, "The Development of Soviet Military Power: Trends since 1965 and Prospects for the 1980s," Apr. 1981, NARA, RG 263, PUC, box 12, folder 21977.

9. Adamishin diary entry, 19 Mar. 1980, HIA, ALAP, box 1, folder: "1980"; Schmidt–Bahr memorandum of conversation, 20 Apr. 1980, PAdAA, B 150/477; Schmidt–Giscard d'Estaing memorandum of conversation, 24 Apr. 1980, PAdAA, B 150/477.

10. CIA memorandum, "Soviet and US Defense Activities, 1971–80: A Dollar Cost Comparison," Jan. 1981, LOC, PHNP, pt. 1, box 151, folder 9; NIE, no. 11-14-81, "Warsaw Pact Forces Opposite NATO," 7 July 1981, NARA, RG 263, NIE, box 18, folder 51.

11. Esin interview, 2007, LHCMA, BOA 2/1; SED memorandum, "Stenografische Niederschrift der Tagung des Politischen Beratenden Ausschusses der Teilnehmerstaaten des Warschauer Vertrages am 14. und 15. Mai 1980 in Warschau," SAPMO, DY 30/2351.

12. Caryl, *Strange Rebels*, 229–242; Cogan, "Desert One and Its Disorders," 201–216.

13. Powell memorandum, "The Declarations of Algiers," 21 Jan. 1981, BCA, ESMP, SOS, box 12, folder 2. It was Reagan who welcomed them home in an emotional ceremony at the White House just a week after his inauguration. Reagan diary entry, 27 Jan. 1981, in Brinkley, *The Reagan Diaries*, 1:15.

14. Grinevskiĭ, *Taĭny sovetskoĭ diplomatii*, 169–170.

15. Jacobs, *Panic at the Pump*, 207–218; Sargent, *Superpower Transformed*, 273–285.

16. KPSS memorandum, "K polozheniiu v 'A,'" 12 Dec. 1979, RGANI, fond 89, opis' 14, delo 31; Khristoforov, *Afganistan*, 22–23; Grinevskiĭ, *Taĭny sovetskoĭ diplomatii*, 179, 311.

17. Vance, *Hard Choices*, 386–394.

18. Reagan diary entry, 28 Jan. 1981, in Brinkley, *The Reagan Diaries*, 1:15.

19. Ronald Reagan, *American Life*, 238–239.

20. Brands, *Latin America's Cold War*, 189.

21. Johnson to Marrell, "Operation Commonsense," 6 Jan. 1981, NAUK, FCO 105/544.

22. Van Cleave memorandum, "Defense Policy Briefing Book: 1980 Campaign," LOC, CWWP, box 572, folder: "Campaign Defense Policy Briefing Book."

23. Franks to Carter, "Reagan Research," 26 June 1980, JCPL, CSF, HJCF, box 79, folder: "Reagan, Ronald"; Aronson to Mondale, 29 Dec. 1981, MNHS, WFMP, loc. 146.L.10.1B, folder: "Aronson, Bernie."

24. Carter remarks, Washington, D.C., 15 July 1979, in Mellody et al., *Public Papers of the Presidents: Jimmy Carter, 1979*, 2:1235–1241; Evans memorandum, "Opinion Survey of Publishers of Major Daily Newspapers of America on 1980 Presidential Election," JCPL, CSF, HJCF, box 79, folder: "Polls."

25. Jacobs, *Panic at the Pump*, 207–218; Sargent, *Superpower Transformed*, 273–285.

26. Perry, "Please, Japan, Return the Favor: Occupy Us," A1; McKevitt, *Consuming Japan*, 15; Jennifer Miller, *Cold War Democracy*, 281.

27. Biven, *Jimmy Carter's Economy*, 3.

28. USICA memorandum, "French and West Germans Have Markedly Different Views from Americans on East-West Relations," 16 Apr. 1981, RRPL, DCBF, box 4, folder: "Public Diplomacy March 1981–June 1981."

NOTES TO PAGES 15-17   145

29. MAÉ memorandum, "Équilibre stratégique et relations sovieto-américaines," 17 Jan. 1980, AD, 91 QO/924, "Relations avec les pays de l'Est, 1980 janvier–juin" folder; Bone to Coles, "Arms Control and Disarmament," 29 Nov. 1982, PREM 19/693; Wieck memorandum, "Die Lage der Sowjetunion an der Schwelle der achtziger Jahre," 9 Jan. 1980, BA, B 136/16696. French analysts also noted the extent to which the Reagan administration's perception of the United States as weak was a self-fulfilling prophesy: Laboulaye to François-Poncet, "Danger soviétique," 5 Feb. 1981, AD, 91 QO/925, folder: "Relations du pays avec l'URSS et pays de l'Est, 1981 janvier–avril."

30. Schmidt-Thatcher memorandum of conversation, 16 Nov. 1980, PAdAA, B 150/491.

31. Kampelman to Eagleburger, 11 Nov. 1981, MNHS, MMKP, loc. 151.C.5.2F, folder: "Department of State Staff Correspondence, 1980–1983."

32. Garthoff, *Détente and Confrontation*, 935–957.

33. Elmes to Eizenstat, "Communicating the Administration's Theme to the Public," 15 Aug. 1979, JCPL, CSF, LBSF, box 100, folder: "Foreign Policy Political Working Group, 8/15/79–9/19/80."

34. Caddell memorandum, "General Election Strategy," 25 June 1980, JCPL, JLPP, SF, box 20, folder: "General Election Strategy, 6/25/80."

35. Biven, *Jimmy Carter's Economy*, 1–3.

36. Caddell memorandum, "Results of Miscellaneous Questions on the February 1979 DNC Survey," 24 May 1979, JCPL, CSF, HJSF, box 33, folder: "Caddell, Patrick 2."

37. Palumbo to Muskie, 11 Nov. 1980, BCA, ESMP, SOS, box 12, folder 7; Trubowitz, *Defining the National Interest*, 169–176.

38. Pipes interview, 21 Sept. 1990, LHCMA, TNA 11/95; Adelman interview, 21 Sept. 1990, LHCMA, TNA 11/2. They accordingly embarked on a remarkable effort to solidify Carter's image as an inept and ineffectual president while they served his successor.

39. IFPAB memorandum, 25 Dec. 1980, HIA, WJCP, box 300, folder: "Interim Foreign Policy Advisory Board"; Gray to Casey, 18 Oct. 1980, HIA, WJCP, box 292, folder: "Foreign Policy 5"; Gergen to Casey, 24 Sept. 1980, HIA, WJCP, box 292, folder: "Foreign Policy 4."

40. Reagan, "Communism, the Disease," May 1975, in Skinner, Anderson, and Anderson, *In His Own Hand*, 10–12.

41. Deaver interview, 6 June 2000, HIA, HIGFC, box 1, folder 13. This mirrored the attitude of British foreign secretary Ernest Bevin, who, during his tenure as leader of the Transport and General Workers' Union, had become equally concerned over efforts by the communist left to penetrate the labor movement. Bullock, *Ernest Bevin*, 106.

42. Reagan, "A Time for Choosing," 27 Oct. 1964, in Baltizer and Bonetto, *A Time for Choosing*, 39–57.

43. Cannon, *Governor Reagan*, 399.

44. Lasault memorandum, GFPL, PFCR, box A4, folder: "Reagan, Ronald."

45. Reagan remarks, 31 Mar. 1976, GFPL, RNP, box 39, folder: "Reagan Nationwide TV Address." Reagan was one of many in Washington who believed that the foreign-policy establishment—Republican and Democratic alike—no longer appreciated the gravity of the Soviet threat. Ford responded to such critics by sharing the raw intelligence that went into the administration's national intelligence estimates with an independent group of outside experts, dubbed Team B. Though it claimed to be an attempt to inject diversity in assessments of the Soviet Union, the experts who

146 **NOTES TO PAGES 17–19**

made up Team B held uniformly hawkish views. They reached the unsurprising conclusion that the intelligence community had indeed downplayed the Soviet threat. PFIAB memorandum, "Intelligence Community Experiment in Competitive Analysis: Soviet Strategic Objectives," Dec. 1976, NARA, RG 263, SOT, box 1, folder: "Team B."

46. Cheney to Gergen, "Data on Détente," 11 Mar. 1976, GFPL, RMF, box 1, folder: "Foreign Policy"; Ford remarks, University of Hawaii, Manoa, Hawaii, 7 Dec. 1975, in Donohoe et al., *Public Papers of the Presidents: Gerald R. Ford, 1975*, 2:1950–1955.

47. Reagan remarks, 13 Mar. 1980, in Skinner, Anderson, and Anderson, *In His Own Hand*, 471–479.

48. Reagan remarks, 19 Oct. 1980, LOC, AMHP, box 131, folder 8.

49. Lettow, *Ronald Reagan and His Quest*, 3–4.

50. Reagan to Landers, 20 May 1982, in Skinner, Anderson, and Anderson, *Reagan: A Life in Letters*, 406; Reed, *At the Abyss*, 254–255.

51. Reagan diary entry, 7 June 1981, in Brinkley, *The Reagan Diaries*, 1:46; Cannon, *President Reagan*, 288–290.

52. Lettow, *Ronald Reagan and His Quest*, 22–23.

53. Gray to Casey, 18 Oct. 1980, HIA, WJCP, box 292, folder: "Foreign Policy 5"; Matlock, *Reagan and Gorbachev*, 3.

54. Ra'anan to Iklé, "Toward the Evolution of a 'Reagan Doctrine' on Global Strategy: Some Considerations," 26 May 1980, HIA, FCIP, box 14, folder: "Soviet Union File."

55. Gray to Casey, 18 Oct. 1980, HIA, WJCP, box 292, folder: "Foreign Policy 5"; Matlock, *Reagan and Gorbachev*, 3.

56. Rowny memorandum, "Integrating US Defense and Arms Control Policies," 14 Nov. 1980, HIA, WJCP, box 300, folder: "Arms Control." Nixon, who offered unsolicited advice to the Reagan campaign and transition team on a regular basis (in addition to purporting to speak on their behalf with the Soviets), suggested that Reagan should tackle the economy first, leaving foreign policy until the economic situation improved. This advice corroborated public opinion polls and Reagan's own priorities. Nixon to Reagan, 17 Nov. 1980, HIA, JMP, box 55; Kunz, *Butter and Guns*, 284–285.

57. RNC memorandum, "National Defense and American Jobs," RRPL, 1980 CP, box 461, folder: "Task Force on Defense and Foreign Policy." Among those who would benefit the most were those in the Sunbelt, precisely the voters who had delivered the White House for Reagan. Trubowitz, *Defining the National Interest*, 225–232.

58. IFPAB memorandum, "Foreign Policy Advisory Board Summary Report," Jan. 1981, HIA, FCIP, box 15, folder: "Interim Foreign Policy Advisory Board File."

59. IFPAB memorandum, 25 Dec. 1980, HIA, WJCP, box 300, folder: "Interim Foreign Policy Advisory Board."

60. Nitze to Iklé, 23 Dec. 1980, LOC, PHNP, pt. 1, box 144, folder 3.

61. Reagan remarks, Los Angeles, Calif., 12 Oct. 1972, in Baltizer and Bonetto, *A Time for Choosing*, 103–104.

62. Engel, *When the World Seemed New*, 24.

63. Pipes, *Vixi*, 152.

64. Brauer, *Presidential Transitions*, 227.

65. Ronald Reagan, *American Life*, 254.

66. Inboden, "Grand Strategy and Petty Squabbles," 157–166.

67. Weinberger, *Fighting for Peace*, 29.

68. Fitzpatrick, *Spy in the Archives*, 47.

NOTES TO PAGES 19–21 147

69. Pipes, *Vixi*, xi, 129.

70. Pipes to Lenz, "State Meetings with Dobrynin," 20 May 1981, RRPL, REPF, box 9, folder: "05/18/1981–05/20/1981"; Pipes to Allen, "'Reagan Soviet Policy' Paper," 21 Aug. 1981, RRPL, REPF, box 11, folder: "08/21/1981"; Stearman, *American Adventure*, 211.

71. Deaver interview, 8 May 1990, SMML, DOP, box 2, folder 12. In a conversation with Helmut Schmidt, for example, Reagan warned that a worldwide economic recession could lead to a worldwide depression, which, in the experience of his childhood, had led to Hitler's rise—of which the West German Bundeskanzler presumably did not need to be reminded. Schmidt-Reagan memorandum of conversation, 4 Jan. 1982, PAdAA, B 150/522.

72. Gaddis, *On Grand Strategy*, 14–16.

73. Dupont to François-Poncet, "M. Brejnev, réélu président du Présidium," 18 Apr. 1979, AD, 1929INVA/4731, folder: "Présidium du Soviet Suprême."

74. Lever to Cartledge, "Call on the Prime Minister by HM Ambassador, Moscow," 9 Aug. 1979, NAUK, PREM 19/926.

75. Genscher-Mladenov memorandum of conversation, 8 July 1981, PAdAA, B 150/507.

76. Thatcher-Kohl memorandum of conversation, 19 Oct. 1982, NAUK, PREM 19/735.

77. Brezhnev diary entry, 19 Dec. 1981, in Brezhnev, *Rabochie i dnevnikovye zapisi*, 1:1122; Brezhnev diary entry, 25 Jan. 1982, in Brezhnev, *Rabochie i dnevnikovye zapisi*, 1:1136; Chazov, *Zdorov'e i vlast'*, 116–117.

78. Vladimir Medvedev, *Chelovek za spinoĭ*, 148.

79. Brezhnev diary entry, 28 July 1979, in Brezhnev, *Rabochie i dnevnikovye zapisi*, 1:962; Brezhnev diary entry, 3 Dec. 1979, in Brezhnev, *Rabochie i dnevnikovye zapisi*, 1:980; Brezhnev diary entry, 13 Feb. 1980, in Brezhnev, *Rabochie i dnevnikovye zapisi*, 1:999; Brezhnev diary entry, 19 Dec. 1981, in Brezhnev, *Rabochie i dnevnikovye zapisi*, 1:1122.

80. Gromyko, *Andreĭ Gromyko*, 48, 55; Grishin, *Ot Khrushcheva do Gorbacheva*, 61.

81. Brutents, *Tridtsat' let na staroĭ ploshchadi*, 495.

82. Casey to Rowen, "Succession in USSR," 18 Sept. 1981, NARA, CREST, doc. CIA-RDP88B00443R001103890087-8.

83. CIA memorandum, "USSR," 26 Nov. 1980, JCPL, RAC, doc. NLC-23-68-1-5-6.

84. Laboulaye to François-Poncet, "M. Brejnev et la succession en URSS," 8 Nov. 1979, AD, 91 QO/924, folder: "Relations avec l'URSS et Satellites."

85. Arnot memorandum, "Überlegungen zur Breschnew-Nachfolge," 6 Apr. 1982, BA, B 136/16697.

86. CIA memorandum, "Soviet Leader Chernenko: An Emerging Political Profile," 10 Aug. 1979, JCPL, RAC, doc. NLC-23-67-9-10-3.

87. Pribytkov, *Apparat*, 41–54; Zemtsov, *Chernenko*, 15–54; Shakhnazarov, *S vozhdiami i bez nikh*, 215.

88. Zemtsov, *Chernenko*, 157; Grachev, *Kremlevskaia khronika*, 79.

89. Davis, *Myth Making in the Soviet Union and Modern Russia*, 66.

90. Gorbachev, *Naedine s soboĭ*, 302.

91. Khlobustov, *Neizvestnyĭ Andropov*, 16–18; Roĭ Medvedev, *Iuriĭ Andropov*, 22–30.

92. Burovskiĭ, *Velikiĭ Andropov*, 126–150; Sidorenko, *Andropov*, 273–284.

93. Roĭ Medvedev, *Iuriĭ Andropov*, 105–108, 144–165.

148   NOTES TO PAGES 21–24

94. CIA memorandum, "USSR: Candidates for the Succession," 4 May 1982, RRPL, JFMF, box 36, folder: "USSR Succession 1"; Vogel memorandum, "Veränderungen in der sowjetischen Führungsspitze," 25 May 1982, BA, B 136/16697.

95. Zimianin interview, 14 July 1990, BLPES, 2RR 1/1/3.

96. CIA memorandum, "Prospects for Brezhnev's Retirement," 6 July 1982, RRPL, JFMF, box 34, folder: "Soviet Leadership Transition CPPG 2"; Miles, "Envisioning Détente," 728.

97. Pipes to Clark, "Talking Points for Your Meeting with Ambassador Hartman," 28 Sept. 1982, RRPL, REPF, box 15, folder: "09/28/1982 2."

98. Haig to Reagan, "Kremlin Succession Politics Heating Up," 9 Mar. 1982, RRPL, REPF, box 13, folder: "03/09/1982–03/10/1982"; DIA memorandum, "USSR: Leadership Succession Issue," 20 May 1982, RRPL, JFMF, box 36, folder: "USSR Succession 1"; Pipes to Clark, "Talking Points for Your Meeting with Ambassador Hartman," 28 Sept. 1982, RRPL, REPF, box 15, folder: "09/28/1982 2."

99. Roĭ Medvedev, *Iuriĭ Andropov*, 313–317; Grishin, *Ot Khrushcheva do Gorbacheva*, 59.

100. Kissinger, *White House Years*, 788–789.

101. Meyer-Landrut memorandum, "Gespräch mit AM Gromyko am 11.5.1981," 11 May 1981, PAdAA, B 150/503.

102. Aleksandrov-Agentov, *Ot Kollontai do Gorbacheva*, 268; Savel'yev and Detinov, *Big Five*, 9–11.

103. Černý memorandum, "Informace o konzultaci s. nám. M. Jablonského na MZV SSSR," 12 Nov. 1980, AMZV, TOT, 1980–1989, SSSR, box 1, folder 1; Falin, *Bez skidok na obstoiatel'stva*, 362; Gromyko, *Andreĭ Gromyko*, 56–57.

104. SED memorandum, "Stenografische Niederschrift der Tagung des Politischen Beratenden Ausschusses der Teilnehmerstaaten des Warschauer Vertrages am 14. und 15. Mai 1980 in Warschau," SAPMO, DY 30/2351; Vasil'chenko, "Operativnaia podgotovka ob"edinennykh vooruzhennykh sil NATO v 1980 godu," 62.

105. Merkulov and Kondriatiuk memorandum, "O besede s chlenom palaty predstaviteleĭ kongressa SShA S. Solarzom," 15 Oct. 1980, TsDAHO, fond 1, opis' 25, sprava 2136.

106. Adamishin diary entry, 6 May 1980, HIA, ALAP, box 1, folder: "1980"; Adamishin diary entry, 5 June 1980, HIA, ALAP, box 1, folder: "1980."

107. Brutents, *Tridtsat' let na staroĭ ploshchadi*, 308.

108. PD, no. 59, "Nuclear Weapons Employment Policy," 25 July 1980, JCPL, ZBC, box 23, folder: "Muskie/Brown/Brzezinski, 7/80–9/80."

109. Keefer, *Harold Brown*, 142–144.

110. Christopher to Shulman, "Izvestiya on PD-59," 23 Sept. 1980, BCA, ESMP, SOS, box 12, folder 7.

111. Muskie-Genscher memorandum of conversation, 2 July 1980, NARA, RG 59, SFESM, box 2, folder: "ESM Eyes Only."

112. Muskie-Spasowski memorandum of conversation, 19 May 1980, NARA, RG 59, SFESM, box 2, folder: "ESM Eyes Only."

113. Muskie-Gromyko memorandum of conversation, 25 Sept. 1980, NARA, RG 59, SFESM, box 2, folder: "Memoranda 1980–1981 2."

114. Froment-Meurice to François-Poncet, "La press soviétique et la campagne electoral américaine," 14 Apr. 1980, AD, 91 QO/924, folder: "Relations avec les pays de l'Est, 1980 janvier–juin."

NOTES TO PAGES 24–26 149

115. Jakubik memorandum, "K niektorým aktuálnym otázkam US zahraničnej politiky," 15 Dec. 1980, AMZV, TOT, 1980–1989, SSA, box 1, folder 1; Fedorchuk memorandum, "Dokladnaia zapiska o prebyvanii v g. Kieve amerikanskoĭ delegatsii Assotsiatiia sodeĭstviia OON v SShA," 21 Nov. 1980, HDASBU, fond 16, opis' 1, sprava 1084.

116. Kukan memorandum, "Výsledky prezidentských volieb v USA," 19 Nov. 1980, AMZV, TOT, 1980–1989, SSA, box 4, folder 21.

117. Froment-Meurice to François-Poncet, "Élection de M. Reagan: déclaration de M. Brejnev," 18 Nov. 1980, AD, 1929 INVA/4786, folder: "Relations avec les États-Unis."

118. Cuvillier memorandum, "Les relations américano-soviétiques à la veille de l'entrée en fonction de la nouvelle administration républicaine," 12 Dec. 1980, AD, 91 QO/925, folder: "Relations avec les pays de l'Est, 1980 juillet–décembre."

119. MAÉ memorandum, "URSS/États-Unis," 27 Nov. 1980, AD, 1929 INVA/4786, folder: "Relations avec les États-Unis"; Braunmühl to Genscher, 11 Nov. 1980, PAdAA, B 150/495.

120. Dobrynin, *Sugubo doveritel'no*, 481.

121. Goldgeier, *Leadership Style and Soviet Foreign Policy*, 76, 86, 94; Raleigh, "'Soviet' Man of Peace," 867.

122. MfS memorandum, "Erste Einschätzung zum Ausgang der Präsidentschaftswahlen 1980 in den USA," 20 Nov. 1980, BStU, SED–KL, no. 3186; Shakhnazarov, *S vozhdiami i bez nikh*, 225.

123. SED memorandum, "Stenografische Niederschrift der Tagung des Politischen Beratenden Ausschusses der Teilnehmerstaaten des Warschauer Vertrages am 14. und 15. Mai 1980 in Warschau," SAPMO, DY 30/2351; MNO memorandum, no. 9 (233), "Perspektivy vojenskopolitického vývoje v NATO v osmdesátých letech," 1980, ABS, ZSGŠ, PM, box 102; MNO memorandum, no. 4 (244), "Hlavní rysy zahraniční a vojenské politiky nové americké vlády," 1981, ABS, ZSGŠ, PM, box 106.

124. MfS memorandum, "Erste Einschätzung zum Ausgang der Präsidentschaftswahlen 1980 in den USA," 20 Nov. 1980, BStU, SED–KL, no. 3186.

125. Jakubik memorandum, "Ideovopolitická situácia v USA v druhej polovici roku 1980," 2 Dec. 1980, AMZV, TOT, 1980–1989, SSA, box 4, folder 21; MNO memorandum, no. 4 (244), "Hlavní rysy zahraniční a vojenské politiky nové americké vlády," 1981, ABS, ZSGŠ, PM, box 106.

126. Mielke-Andropov memorandum of conversation, 11 July 1981, BStU, ZAIG, no. 5382.

127. Dobrynin, *Sugubo doveritel'no*, 483.

128. Voigt-Arbatov memorandum of conversation, 13 Oct. 1980, BA, B 136/17484.

129. Žlábek memorandum, "Některé poznatky z diplomatického sboru v Berlíně k politice Reaganovy vlády," 25 Mar. 1981, AMZV, TOT, 1980–1989, NDR, box 1, folder 2.

130. Chňoupek to Husák, 9 Dec. 1980, NAČR, fond 1261/0/44, box 444, folder 12511.

131. Dobrynin, *Sugubo doveritel'no*, 482. Tellingly, Nixon's exact phrasing regarding an improved détente-like atmosphere was "relations no worse than they had been with him."

132. Ford to MacGuigan, "Soviet-American Relations and Poland," 9 Dec. 1980, LAC, RG 25, vol. 16021, file 20-USA-1-3-USSR, pt. 11.

133. Liakhovskiĭ, *Tragediia i doblest' Afgana*, 109–110.

134. Salmin, *Internatsionalizm v deĭstvii*, 66–67.

135. Adamishin diary entry, 1 Jan. 1981, HIA, ALAP, box 1, folder: "1980."

150   NOTES TO PAGES 26–29

136. Sakharov, *Vospominaniia*, 2:450–468.

137. Adamishin diary entry, 4 Dec. 1981, HIA, ALAP, box 1, folder: "1981"; Liakhovskiĭ, *Plamia Afgana*, 271.

138. CIA memorandum, "The Soviet Leadership: Second Thoughts on Afghanistan," Feb. 1980, JCPL, RAC, doc. NLC-12-1-3-9-5; Roĭ Medvedev, *Iuriĭ Andropov*, 280; Grachev, *Kremlevskaia khronika*, 67.

139. Muskie-Vrhovec memorandum of conversation, 23 Sept. 1980, NARA, RG 59, SFESM, box 2, folder: "Memoranda 1980–1981 2."

140. Kornienko interview, BLPES, 2RR 1/3/13.

141. Allison to Muskie, "Two Cents' Worth for Your Meeting with Gromyko on Thursday, September 25," 23 Sept. 1980, BCA, ESMP, SOS, box 12, folder 7.

142. PZPR Politburo meeting record, 14 Aug. 1980, *PZPR a Solidarność*, 83–86.

143. PZPR Politburo meeting record, 18 July 1980, *PZPR a Solidarność*, 76–77.

144. KPSS Politburo meeting record, 25 Aug. 1980, RGANI, fond 89, opis' 42, delo 22; Mukha to Shcherbitskiĭ, "Ob obstanovke v respublike v sviazi s sobytiiami v Pol'she," 26 Aug. 1980, HDASBU, fond 16, sprava 1082.

145. Brzezinski to Carter, "NSC Weekly Report #160," 12 Dec. 1980, JCPL, RAC, doc. NLC-128-10-4-4-1; Brement to Brzezinski, "Soviet Options in Poland: An Alternate Scenario," 9 Dec. 1980, JCPL, RAC, doc. NLC-23-50-5-5-1.

146. Suslov memorandum, 28 Aug. 1980, LOC, DAVP, box 27, folder 5.

147. Honecker-Brezhnev memorandum of conversation, 16 May 1981, SAPMO, DY 30/2379.

148. Snyder, *Human Rights Activism and the End of the Cold War*, 8–13, 69–71.

149. Tismaneanu, *Stalinism for All Seasons*, 187–189.

150. Adamishin diary entry, 1 Apr. 1980, HIA, ALAP, box 1, folder: "1980."

151. Chen, "Defying Moscow," 260–261.

152. Eichengreen, *European Economy since 1945*, 296–301.

153. Honecker-Brezhnev memorandum of conversation, 3 Aug. 1981, SAPMO, DY 30/11853.

154. CIA memorandum, "USSR: The Cost of Aid to Communist States," June 1981, NARA, CREST, doc. CIA-RDP83M00914R001900220025-5.

155. Schalck-Golodkowski and Volpert memorandum, "Zur Vermeidung ökonomischer Verluste und zur Erwirtschaftung zusätzlicher Devisen im Bereich Kommerzielle Koordinierung des Ministeriums für Außenwirtschaft der Deutschen Demokratischen Republik," May 1979, BStU, JHS, no. 24672.

156. Thatcher-Solzhenytsin memorandum of conversation, 11 May 1983, NAUK, PREM 19/1103.

157. Karpov interview, 11 Jan. 1990, SMML, DOP, box 1, folder 10.

158. Adamishin diary entry, 9 Dec. 1980, HIA, ALAP, box 1, folder: "1980."

159. Gorbachev, *Zhizn' i reformy*, 2:58–59.

160. Kornienko interview, 19 Jan. 1990, SMML, DOP, box 1, folder 12.

161. Meshcheriakov, "Strategicheskaia razvedka SShA," 15.

162. Mielke-Andropov memorandum of conversation, 11 July 1981, BStU, MfS, ZAIG, no. 5382; Adamishin diary entry, 13 May 1980, HIA, ALAP, box 1, folder: "1980"; Hanson, *Rise and Fall of the Soviet Economy*, 135, 149–154.

163. Gaidar, *Collapse of an Empire*, 74–79.

NOTES TO PAGES 29–30 151

164. Gregory, "Productivity, Slack, and Time Theft in the Soviet Economy," 255–259.

165. Zaslavskaia, "The Novosibirsk Report," 88–108.

166. Hanson, *Rise and Fall of the Soviet Economy*, 139.

167. Gurov, "Rost ekonomicheskogo potentsiala razvitogo sotsialisticheskogo obshchestva," 62–63, 68; Bondarenko, "XXVI s″ezd KPSS o nauchnom potentsiale razvitogo sotsializma," 53.

168. Andropov memorandum, "O meropriyatiiakh v otnoshenii organizatsii 'Mezhdunarodnaia amnistiia,'" 24 July 1984, LOC, DAVP, box 28, folder 3.

169. Hanson, *Rise and Fall of the Soviet Economy*, 130–131, 154–155.

170. CIA memorandum, "Prospects for Soviet Oil Production," Apr. 1977, NARA, CREST, doc. CIA-RDP08S01350R000602080002-0; CIA memorandum, "Prospects for Soviet Oil Production: A Supplemental Analysis," July 1977, NARA, CREST, doc. CIA-RDP79B00457A000600090001-8; Gaidar, *Collapse of an Empire*, 103, 105–106.

171. Černý memorandum, "Některá názory v moskevském diplomatickém sboru v předvečer XXVI. sjezdu KSSS," 20 Feb. 1981, AMZV, TOT, 1980–1989, SSSR, box 1, folder 3; Brzezinski to Carter, "Daily Report," 14 Jan. 1981, JCPL, RAC, doc. NLC-1-18-4-8-9.

172. Adamishin diary entry, 22 Mar. 1981, HIA, ALAP, box 1, folder: "1981."

173. KPSS memorandum, "O novykh ideaiakh dlia mezhdunarodnogo razdela doklada," 9 Jan. 1981, RGANI, fond 80, opis′ 1, delo 125; Ruth memorandum, "Deutschamerikanische Konsultation über die Weiterführung der Rüstungskontrollpolitik im Bündnis," 25 Feb. 1981, PAdAA, B 150/497; Grabowski memorandum, "Information über die außenpolitischen Aktivitäten der UdSSR zur Umsetzung der Friedensinitiativen der 26. Parteitages der KPdSU," 9 Apr. 1981, SAPMO, DY 30/IV 2/2.035/63.

174. MNO memorandum, no. 6 (230), "Nové jevy ve světové vojenskopolitické situaci," 1980, ABS, ZSGŠ, PM, box 102.

175. Andropov to Brezhnev, 10 Jan. 1981, RGANI, fond 80, opis′ 1, delo 125. The idea of a "peace offensive" is most closely associated with Brezhnev's predecessor, Nikita Khrushchev, and his fondness for foreign travel, summitry, and spontaneous engagement with the foreign press. Taubman, *Khrushchev*, 400 401.

176. Pearson to MacGuigan, "USA/USSR Relations," 12 Feb. 1981, LAC, RG 25, vol. 16021, file 20-USA-1-3-USSR, pt. 11.

177. Matlock to Shultz, "Pravda Editorial on Soviet Foreign Policy on the Eve of the XXVI Party Congress," 18 Feb. 1981, RRPL, JFMF, box 26, folder: "USSR General 1981–1983 1."

178. Brezhnev remarks, Twenty-Sixth KPSS Congress, Moscow, Soviet Union, 23 Feb. 1981, *Leninskim kursom*, vol. 8, 633–728.

179. Pipes to Allen, "26th Congress," 26 Feb. 1981, RRPL, REPF, box 9, folder: "02/05/1981–02/28/1981."

180. Raleigh, "'Soviet' Man of Peace," 842–843; Suri, *Power and Protest*, 5.

181. Zagladin-Voigt memorandum of conversation, 16 Oct. 1980, AGF, fond 3, opis′ 1, delo 14974.

182. Genscher-Brezhnev memorandum of conversation, 3 Apr. 1981, PAdAA, B 150/501.

183. Leclercq to Giscard d'Estaing, "Discours de M. Brejnev," 24 Feb. 1981, AN, 5 AG 3/1095, folder: "1981"; MAÉ memorandum, "L'offensive diplomatique de l'URSS,"

152   **NOTES TO PAGES 30–35**

18 Mar. 1981, AD, 91 QO/925, folder: "Relations du pays avec l'URSS et pays de l'Est, 1981 janvier–avril."

184. SED memorandum, "Brief des ZK der KPdSU an sozialistische bzw. sozialdemokratische Parteien zu Fragen des Kampfes und Frieden, Entspannung und Abrüstung," 15 June 1981, SAPMO, DY 30/IV 2/2.035/71.

185. MfAA memorandum, "Schlußfolgerungen aus dem XXVI. Parteitag der KPdSU für die Außenpolitik der DDR," 6 Mar. 1981, PAdAA, M 1, ZR 442/87.

186. MfAA memorandum, "Information über die Einschätzung sowjetischer Genossen zur Formierung der Reagan-Administration und ihrer Politik," 30 Dec. 1980, PAdAA, M 1, ZR 562/86; MNO memorandum, no. 4 (244), "Hlavní rysy zahraniční a vojenské politiky nové americké vlády," 1981, ABS, ZSGŠ, PM, box 106.

187. Reagan remarks, Washington, D.C., 20 Jan. 1981, in Greene et al., *Public Papers of the Presidents: Ronald Reagan, 1981*, 1–4.

188. NSC meeting record, 6 Feb. 1981, RRPL, ES–NSC, MF, box 1, folder: "NSC #1 1."

189. McFarlane, *Special Trust*, 216.

190. Preble, "'Who Ever Believed in the Missile Gap?,'" 810–812.

191. Trachtenberg, "Assessing Soviet Economic Performance during the Cold War," 77, 93.

192. Ronald Reagan, *American Life*, 342.

193. Bremer to Allen, 14 July 1981, RRPL, REPF, box 5, folder: "Soviet NSSD 1."

194. Laboulaye to François-Poncet, "Entretien avec M. Dobrynine le 24 avril: les relations américano-soviétiques," 24 Apr. 1981, AD, 91 QO/925, folder: "Relations du pays avec l'URSS et pays de l'Est, 1981 janvier–avril."

195. BKA memorandum, "Die sowjetische Führung," 19 Nov. 1981, BA, B 136/17365.

2. Arm to Parley

1. Reagan remarks, AFL-CIO, Washington, D.C., 30 Mar. 1981, in Greene et al., *Public Papers of the Presidents: Ronald Reagan, 1981*, 306–310.

2. Ronald Reagan, *American Life*, 259.

3. Nancy Reagan, *My Turn*, 6.

4. Ronald Reagan, *American Life*, 36.

5. Reagan to Brezhnev, 24 Apr. 1981, RRPL, ES–NSC, HSF, box 38, folder: "Brezhnev 8190204, 8190205."

6. Ronald Reagan, *American Life*, 269.

7. Nitze to Iklé, 23 Dec. 1980, LOC, PHNP, pt. 1, box 144, folder 3.

8. Gala, "Euromissile Crisis and the Centrality of the 'Zero Option,'" 162; Rossinow, "Legend of Reagan the Peacemaker," 61. Reagan wanted to rid the world of nuclear weapons, but he wanted to do so on terms most favorable to the United States, a competitive approach to arms control dated back to criticisms of the Eisenhower administration's limitations on defense spending, particularly on the US nuclear arsenal. Maurer, "Divided Counsels," 357–364; Lettow, *Ronald Reagan and His Quest*.

9. Henderson to Bullard, "US Foreign Policy," 7 Aug. 1981, NAUK, FCO 28/4372.

10. Zagladin-Cobb memorandum of conversation, 8 June 1981, AGF, fond 3, opis' 1, delo 15412.

NOTES TO PAGES 35–37   153

11. MfAA memorandum, "Information über die Einschätzung sowjetischer Genossen zur Formierung der Reagan-Administration und ihrer Politik," 30 Dec. 1980, PAdAA, M 1, ZR 562/86; Kukan memorandum, "Porada zástupcov velvyslancov socialistických krajín vo Washingtone," 16 Feb. 1981, AMZV, TOT, 1980–1989, SSA, box 1, folder 1.

12. Johanes memorandum, "Dosavadní politika Reaganovy administrativy," 30 Apr. 1981, AMZV, TOT, 1980–1989, SSA, box 4, folder 22; Žlábek memorandum, "Hodnocení politiky USA vládními kruhy NSR," 26 June 1981, AMZV, TOT, 1980–1989, NDR, box 1, folder 2; MNO memorandum, no. 11 (251), "Nové poznatky o ozbrojených silách Severoatlantického paktu," 1981, ABS, ZSGŠ, PM, box 107.

13. Kapto memorandum, "O besede s sekretarem po mezhdunarodnym voprosam Pravleniia Sotsialisticheskoĭ partii Avstrii V. Khakkerom," 24 Mar. 1981, TsDAHO, fond 1, opis' 25, sprava 2294; MfS memorandum, "Information vom Politbüro des ZK der SED," 28 Sept. 1982, BStU, ZAIG, no. 7172.

14. Dobrynin, *Sugubo doveritel'no*, 500; Froment-Meurice to François-Poncet, "L'URSS et la nouvelle administration américaine: de l'expectative au skepticisme," 17 Jan. 1981, AD, 91 QO/925, folder: "Relations du pays avec l'URSS et pays de l'Est, 1981 janvier–avril."

15. Černý memorandum, "Politika USA a sovětsko-americké vztahy," 17 Feb. 1982, AMZV, TOT, 1980–1989, SSSR, box 9, folder 53.

16. Honecker-Brezhnev memorandum of conversation, 3 Aug. 1981, SAPMO, DY 30/11853.

17. Meyer-Landrut memorandum, "Äußerungen Gromykos zur Politik der neuen US-Administration," 24 Mar. 1981, PAdAA, B 150/500; Adamishin diary entry, 23 Dec. 1981, HIA, ALAP, box 1, folder: "1981."

18. Grabowski memorandum, "Information über das außenpolitische Vorgehen der Reagan-Administration und über die Beziehungen zwischen der UdSSR und den USA," 19 Feb. 1981, PAdAA, M 1, ZR 562/86; Johanes and Kukan memorandum, "Předpokládané zaměřeni zahranični politiky Reaganovy administrativy," 27 Feb. 1981, AMZV, TOT, 1980–1989, SSA, box 4, folder 22.

19. MNO memorandum, no. 4 (244), "Hlavní rysy zahranični a vojenské politiky nové americké vlády," 1981, ABS, ZSGŠ, PM, box 106.

20. Adamishin diary entry, 23 Mar. 1982, HIA, ALAP, box 1, folder: "1982."

21. Vessey remarks, Schofield Barracks, Hawaii, 30 June 1983, NDUA, PJWV, box 96, folder 18.

22. NSDD, no. 32, "US National Security Strategy," 20 May 1982, RRPL, ES–NSC, box 2, folder: "NSDD 32 1."

23. DOD, *Soviet Military Power*, 99.

24. Memorandum, "Foreign Policy Talking Points," JCPL, CSF, GDMSF, box 193, folder: "Foreign Policy Working Group."

25. Keefer, *Harold Brown*, 548–549.

26. Weinberger, *Fighting for Peace*, 39–79.

27. Reagan remarks, Washington, D.C., 5 Feb. 1981, in Greene et al., *Public Papers of the Presidents: Ronald Reagan, 1981*, 79–83.

28. Volcker, *Keeping at It*, 2018.

29. Reagan remarks, Washington, D.C., 18 Feb. 1981, in Greene et al., *Public Papers of the Presidents: Ronald Reagan, 1981*, 108–115.

154 **NOTES TO PAGES 37–38**

30. Van Cleave memorandum, "Defense Policy Briefing Book: 1980 Campaign," LOC, CWWP, box 572, folder: "Campaign Defense Policy Briefing Book."

31. Heefner, *Missile Next Door*, 134–136.

32. Weinberger-Thatcher memorandum of conversation, 27 Feb. 1981, NARA, CREST, doc. CIA-RDP84B00049R001403560041-3; Weinberger, *Fighting for Peace*, 57. Weighing these options became the task of a blue-ribbon commission headed by Ford's former national security adviser, Brent Scowcroft. Sparrow, *The Strategist*, 220–243.

33. Černý memorandum, "Pokračující militaristické tendence v USA a perspektivy sovětsko-amerického dialogu," 23 July 1981, AMZV, TOT, 1980–1989, SSSR, box 9, folder 52; MfNV memorandum, "Information über den Zustand der strategischen Kernwaffeneinsatzkräfte der NATO und ihrer Mitgliedstaaten sowie über ihre zu erwartende Entwicklung bis in die 90er Jahre," 22 Jan. 1982, MA, DVW 1/94239.

34. Baturin, "Nauchno-tekhnicheskaia revoliutsiia i voennye prigotovleniia SShA," 75–76; Korochianskiĭ, "Narushenie voenno-strategicheskogo ravnovesiia," 15–16.

35. Petrov, "O iadernoĭ strategii SShA," 14–15.

36. Wade-Gery to Coles, "Trident," 26 Feb. 1982, NAUK, PREM 19/649.

37. Thatcher, *Downing Street Years*, 212.

38. Plaisant to Cheysson, "Nouvelle doctrine stratégique américaine—d'une guerre et demie à deux guerres," 19 June 1981, AD, 91 QO/926, folder: "Relations avec les pays de l'Est, 1981 mai–août."

39. Radchenko, *Two Suns in the Heavens*, 206; Westad, *Restless Empire*, 341.

40. Chňoupek memorandum, "Informácia o priebehu a výsledkoch pracovného stretnutia ministra zahraničných vecí ČSSR s. B. Chňoupka s členom politického byra ÚV KSSZ a ministrom zahraničných vecí ZSSR s. A.A. Gromykom," 31 Mar. 1980, NAČR, fond 1261/0/7, box P136/80, folder I1; Dobrynin, *Sugubo doveritel'no*, 515–516; Roĭ Medvedev, *Iuriĭ Andropov*, 275; Falin, *Bez skidok na obstoiatel'stva*, 360.

41. Odom to Brzezinski, "Princeton Meeting on Soviet Studies," 28 Aug. 1980, JCPL, RAC, doc. NLC-12-12-4-6-5.

42. Reagan remarks, Los Angeles, Calif., 25 Aug. 1980, LOC, AMHP, box 131, folder 8.

43. Haig to Reagan, "Second Soviet Demarche on our Relations with China," 7 July 1981, RRPL, REPF, box 10, folder: "07/02/1981–07/07/1981."

44. Adamishin diary entry, 23 Dec. 1981, HIA, ALAP, box 1, folder: "1981"; Andropov to Brezhnev, "Otchet o rabote Komiteta gosudarstvennoĭ bezopasnosti SSSR za 1980 god," 31 Mar. 1981, LOC, DAVP, box 28, folder 3; Johanes memorandum, "Problémy súčasných americko-činskych vzťahov," 5 June 1981, AMZV, TOT, 1980–1989, SSA, box 4, folder 22; MfS memorandum, "Erste Einschätzung zum Ausgang der Präsidentschaftswahlen 1980 in den USA," 21 Nov. 1980, BStU, SED–KL, no. 3186.

45. Pipes to Allen, "NSC Meeting of July 13: Soviet Demarches on China," 8 July 1981, RRPL, REPF, box 10, folder: "07/08/1981–07/15/1981"; Pipes to Allen, "Suggested Revision of the Paper on 'US Military Sales to China,'" 21 Aug. 1981, RRPL, REPF, box 11, folder: "08/21/1981."

46. Kropáč memorandum, "Názory sovětských soudruhů na vývoj sovětsko-čínských vztahů," 16 May 1983, AMZV, TOT, 1980–1989, SSSR, box 2, folder 7; ISKRAN memorandum, "Razvitie kitaĭsko-amerikanskikh otnoshcheniĭ i ikh mesto v strategii amerikanskogo imperializma," 12 Mar. 1985, ARAN, fond 2021, opis' 2, delo 2; ISKRAN memorandum, "Sostoyanie i perspektivy amerikano-kitaĭskikh otnosheniĭ," Dec. 1986, ARAN, fond 2021, opis' 2, delo 34.

NOTES TO PAGES 38-39   155

47. Kruchinin, "Partnerstvo imperializma i pekinskovo gegemonizma," 52–53.

48. Schmidt-Reagan memorandum of conversation, 4 Jan. 1982, PAdAA, B 150/522. Even the later Iran-Contra imbroglio, charitably interpreted, indicates such an open-mindedness.

49. NVA memorandum, "Protokoll der Sitzung des Komitees der Vertaudigungsminister der Teilnehmerstaaten des Warschauer Vertrages," 4 Dec. 1981, MA, DVW 1/71039.

50. NVA memorandum, "Analyse des Zustandes und der Tendenzen der Entwicklung der Streitkräfte des aggressiven NATO-Blocks," Dec. 1981, MA, DVW 1/71039.

51. NVA memorandum, "Bericht über die wichtigsten Ergebnisse der 14. Sitzung des Komitees der Verteidigungsminister der Teilnehmerstaaten des Warschauer Vertrages in Moskau," Dec. 1981, MA, DVW 1/71039; NVA memorandum, "Thesen zum Vortrag des Chefs der Hauptverwaltung Aufklärung des Generalstabes der Streitkräfte der UdSSR, Armeegeneral P.E. Iwaschutin," Dec. 1981, MA, DVW 1/71039.

52. MNO memorandum, no. 6 (246), "Vojenské výdaje státu Severoatlantického paktu v roce 1981," 1981, ABS, ZSGŠ, PM, box 107.

53. SED memorandum,"Vorlag für die Außenpolitische Kommission beim Politbüro des ZK der SED: Zur Stellung der Sozialdemokratie in der internationalen Kassenauseinandersetzung," 6 Nov. 1981, SAPMO, DY 30/11636.

54. MfNV memorandum, "Information über den Zustand der strategischen Kernwaffeneinsatzkräfte der NATO und ihrer Mitgliedstaaten sowie über ihre zu erwartende Entwicklung bis in die 90er Jahre," 22 Jan. 1982, MA, DVW 1/94239.

55. MNO memorandum, no. 15 (255), "Vojenskopolitická situace na jižním křídle Severoatlantického paktu," 1981, ABS, ZSGŠ, PM, box 106; MNO memorandum, no. 14 (254), "Zásady použití ozbrojených sil NATO ve strategické operaci na středoevropském válčišti s důrazem na stupeň skupiny armád a spojeneckého taktického leteckého velitelství," 1981, ABS, ZSGŠ, PM, box 106.

56. Genscher-Mladenov memorandum of conversation, 28 Jan. 1982, PAdAA, B 150/524.

57. MfAA memorandum, "Zur ideologischen Kriegsführung der Reagan-Administration gegen die sozialistischen Staaten," PAdAA, M 1, ZR 562/86.

58. Grabowski memorandum, "Information über das außenpolitische Vorgehen der Reagan-Administration und über die Beziehungen zwischen der UdSSR und den USA," 19 Feb. 1981, PAdAA, M 1, ZR 562/86.

59. Mielke-Andropov memorandum of conversation, 11 July 1981, BStU, ZAIG, no. 5382; Brutents, *Nesbyvsheesia*, 125.

60. Reagan remarks, Washington, D.C., 29 Jan. 1981, in Greene et al., *Public Papers of the Presidents: Ronald Reagan, 1981*, 57.

61. Reagan remarks, Palace of Westminster, London, United Kingdom, 8 June 1982, in Greene, Mellody, and Payne, *Public Papers of the Presidents: Ronald Reagan, 1982*, 1:742–748. Reagan's speech in London led to the founding of the National Endowment for Democracy, to, as Reagan put it, "make clear to those who cherish democracy throughout the world that we mean what we say." Reagan remarks, Washington, D.C., 16 Dec. 1983, in Hill and Kevan, *Public Papers of the Presidents: Ronald Reagan, 1983*, 2:1708–1709.

62. Thatcher-Reagan memorandum of conversation, 9 June 1982, NAUK, PREM 19/943. West German Bundespräsident, Karl Carstens, applauded Reagan's

156   NOTES TO PAGES 40–41

plain-speaking and forthright condemnation of totalitarianism. Carstens-Reagan memorandum of conversation, 9 June 1982, BA, B 122/25580.

63. Clark to Reagan, "Moscow's Reactions to Your June 8 London Speech," 15 June 1982, RRPL, REPF, box 14, folder: "06/13/1982–06/16/1982."

64. Thatcher-Reagan memorandum of conversation, 9 June 1982, NAUK, PREM 19/943; Henderson to Carrington, "President Reagan's Visit," 23 Mar. 1982, NAUK, PREM 19/942.

65. Pipes to Allen, "The Impact of US-China Accords on the Soviet Union," 29 June 1981, RRPL, REPF, box 10, folder: "06/29/1981–06/30/1981."

66. McFarlane interview, 26 Sept. 1990, LHCMA, TNA 11/73.

67. Keeble-Gromyko memorandum of conversation, 18 Mar. 1981, NAUK, FCO 28/4593.

68. Ernst to Inman, "The DIA Assessment of the Impact of the US Grain Embargo," 20 Apr. 1981, NARA, CREST, doc. CIA-RDP83M00914R002700090023-3; Pipes to Allen, "Grain Embargo," 20 Apr. 1981, RRPL, REPF, box 9, folder: "04/20/1981–04/26/1981."

69. Gaidar, *Collapse of an Empire*, 95.

70. NSC memorandum, "Summary of Conclusions: Mini-SCC Meeting on Possible Economic Countermeasures Against the USSR," 17 Dec. 1980, JCPL, RAC, doc. NLC-132-124-7-4-6; CIA memorandum, "USSR: Impact of Economic Denial Measures," Feb. 1981, NARA, RG 263, PUC, box 12, folder 22167.

71. Feith to Allen, "The US Grain Embargo and Economic Threats," 15 May 1981, RRPL, JFMF, box 27, folder: "Grain Embargo 1981 4."

72. Haig to Carrington, 22 Apr. 1982, NAUK, PREM 19/924.

73. Kukan memorandum, "Schôdzka zástupcov titulárov ZÚ socialistických krajín vo Washingtone," 30 Apr. 1981, AMZV, TOT, 1980–1989, SSA, box 1, folder 1; Lequertier memorandum "Les relations américano-soviétiques," 6 Apr. 1981, AD, 91 QO/925, folder: "Relations du pays avec l'URSS et pays de l'Est, 1981 janvier–avril."

74. Giffard to Henderson, "The 'Transatlantic Crisis,'" 5 Mar. 1982, NAUK, FCO 28/4719.

75. BKA memorandum, "Amerikanisch-sowjetische Beziehungen," 3 Sept. 1981, BA, B 136/17054.

76. Haig to Reagan, "My Meeting with Ambassador Dobrynin, July 2, 1981," 7 July 1981, RRPL, JFMF, box 22, folder: "USSR Diplomatic Contacts 1."

77. Haig, *Caveat*, 105.

78. Haig to Reagan, "My Meetings with Soviet Foreign Minister Gromyko September 23 and 28," 10 Nov. 1981, RRPL, WPCF, box 3, folder: "Haig-Gromyko Meetings 09/23/1981 & 09/28/1981."

79. Haig to Reagan, "My Forthcoming Meetings with Soviet Foreign Minister Gromyko," 18 Sept. 1981, RRPL, ES–NSC, HSF, box 37, folder: "Brezhnev 8105567, 1805658."

80. Blair and Pipes to Allen, "Press Backgrounder on President's Letter to Brezhnev, 22 September 1981," 21 Sept. 1981, RRPL, ES–NSC, HSF, box 37, folder: "Brezhnev 8105567, 1805658."

81. Haig-Gromyko memorandum of conversation, 14:00–16:50, 23 Sept. 1981, RRPL, WPCF, box 3, folder: "Haig-Gromyko Meetings 09/23/1981 & 09/28/1981"; Haig-Gromyko memorandum of conversation, 16:50–18:15, 23 Sept. 1981, RRPL, WPCF, box 3, folder: "Haig-Gromyko Meetings 09/23/1981 & 09/28/1981."

NOTES TO PAGES 41–43

82. Haig-Gromyko memorandum of conversation, 14:00–18:00, 28 Sept. 1981, RRPL, WPCF, box 3, folder: "Haig-Gromyko Meetings 09/23/1981 & 09/28/1981"; Haig-Gromyko memorandum of conversation, 18:00–19:00, 28 Sept. 1981, RRPL, WPCF, box 3, folder: "Haig-Gromyko Meetings 09/23/1981 & 09/28/1981."

83. Genscher-Carrington-Cheysson-Haig memorandum of conversation, 23 Sept. 1981, PAdAA, B 150/513.

84. Haig to Reagan, "Brezhnev's October 15 Letter," RRPL, RPF, box 12, folder: "11/06/1981–11/12/1981."

85. Beauchataud to Cheysson, "URSS–États-Unis: entretien au MID," 16 Oct. 1981, AD, 91 QO/926, folder: "Relations avec les pays de l'Est, 1981 septembre–décembre."

86. Keeble to Broomfield, 3 Dec. 1981, NAUK, FCO 28/4583.

87. Pipes to Allen, "Approaches to a Summit Meeting," 26 Feb. 1981, RRPL, REPF, box 9, folder: "02/05/1981–02/28/1981."

88. Shultz interview, 12 July 1989, SMML, DOP, box 3, folder 2.

89. Harel to Cheysson, "Relations américano-soviétiques," 13 May 1982, AD, 1930 INVA/5670, folder: "URSS-USA 1982."

90. Dobrynin, *Sugubo doveritel'no*, 518–519.

91. Froment-Meurice to François-Poncet, "Depart de l'ambassadeur des États-Unis," 6 Jan. 1981, AD, 91 QO/925, folder: "Relations du pays avec l'URSS et pays de l'Est, 1981 janvier–avril."

92. Froment-Meurice to Cheysson, "États-Unis/URSS," 10 Nov. 1981, AD, 1930 INVA/5670, folder: "URSS-USA 1981."

93. Zagladin-Hartman memorandum of conversation, 4 Dec. 1981, AGF, fond 3, opis' 1, delo 15416.

94. MZV memorandum, "Zpráva o návštěvě bývalého prezidenta USA R. Nixona v ČSSR ve dnech 2.–4. 7. 1982," 22 July 1982, NAČR, fond 1261/0/44, box 444, folder 12513.

95. Allen to Reagan, "Analysis of Brezhnev Proposal for a Summit," 2 Mar. 1981, GBPL, VPR, NSA, DPGF, CF, OA/ID 19768, folder: "USSR 1981 1."

96. Reagan to Burns, 13 Mar. 1981, RRBML, AFBP, box 3, folder: "Reagan to Burns"; Reagan to Burns, 14 Feb. 1981, RRBML, AFBP, box 3, folder: "Reagan to Burns."

97. Hartman interview, 3 Nov. 1989, SMML, DOP, box 2, folder 16.

98. Burns to Reagan, 31 Aug. 1981, RRBML, AFBP, box 3, folder: "Burns to Reagan."

99. Burns remarks, Chamber of Industry and Commerce, West Berlin, Federal Republic of Germany, 27 Nov. 1984, *Department of State Bulletin* 85, no. 2094, 20–23.

100. Sarotte, *Dealing with the Devil*, 114–123.

101. Abrasimov-Burns memorandum of conversation, 19 Oct. 1981, SAPMO, DY 30/IV 2/2.035/67.

102. Lissfelt to Burns, "Your Luncheon with Abrasimov November 24 in Berlin," 20 Nov. 1981, GFPL, AFBP, box T6, folder: "Berlin, Frankfurt 11/21–24/81."

103. Abrasimov-Burns memorandum of conversation, 13 Dec. 1982, SAPMO, DY 30/IV 2/2.035/67; Kochemasov-Burns memorandum of conversation, 23 Sept. 1983, SAPMO, DY 30/IV 2/2.035/67.

104. Abrasimov-Burns memorandum of conversation, 19 Oct. 1981, SAPMO, DY 30/IV 2/2.035/67.

105. Abrasimov-Burns memorandum of conversation, 24 Nov. 1981, SAPMO, DY 30/IV 2/2.035/67; Abrasimov-Burns memorandum of conversation, 16 Apr. 1982, SAPMO, DY 30/IV 2/2.035/67.

158 **NOTES TO PAGES 44–46**

106. Abrasimov-Burns memorandum of conversation, 13 Dec. 1982, SAPMO, DY 30/IV 2/2.035/67.

107. Barkley to Burns, "Your Meeting with Soviet Ambassador Kochemasov," 22 Sept. 1983, GFPL, AFBP, box T10, folder: "Berlin, 9/23–24/83."

108. Kochemasov-Burns memorandum of conversation, 23 Sept. 1983, SAPMO, DY 30/IV 2/2.035/67.

109. Weston to Burns, "Your Lunch with Ambassador Kochemasov on December 23," 22 Dec. 1983, GFPL, AFBP, box T12, folder: "Hamburg, Berlin, 12/22–26/83."

110. Barkley to Burns, "Your May 24 Luncheon with Ambassador Kochemasov," 23 May 1984, GFPL, AFBP, box T14, folder: "Berlin, 5/24–27/84"; Ledsky to Burns, "Your May 24 Luncheon with Soviet Ambassador Kochemasov," 23 May 1984, GFPL, AFBP, box T14, folder: "Berlin, 5/24–27/84."

111. Kochemasov-Burns memorandum of conversation, 24 May 1984, SAPMO, DY 30/IV 2/2.035/67.

112. Kochemasov-Burt memorandum of conversation, 5 Nov. 1985, SAPMO, DY 30/IV 2/2.035/67.

113. Haig to Reagan, "My Meeting with Soviet Ambassador Dobrynin March 16," 17 Mar. 1982, RRPL, REPF, box 13, folder: "03/15/1982–03/23/1982."

114. Von Damm to Reagan, 25 June 1982, RRPL, RCMF, box 1, folder: "Sensitive Chron. 1982 1."

115. Inboden, "Grand Strategy and Petty Squabbles," 151.

116. Pipes interview, 21 Sept. 1990, LHCMA, TNA 11/95. This critique applied as much to Pipes as Haig.

117. Cannon, *President Reagan*, 199.

118. Haig to Reagan, 25 June 1982, RRPL, WPCF, box 3, folder: "Haig Resignation Classified Documents"; Reagan diary entries, 24–25 June 1982, in Brinkley, *The Reagan Diaries*, 1:139. Haig expands on this theme of policy divergence at length in his memoir about his time in the Reagan White House. Haig, *Caveat*, 353–358.

119. Ronald Reagan, *American Life*, 270.

120. Inboden, "Grand Strategy and Petty Squabbles," 159.

121. Deaver interview, 8 May 1990, SMML, DOP, box 2, folder 12.

122. Shultz interview, 11 July 1989, SMML, DOP, box 3, folder 2.

123. Clark to Reagan, "Discussion with George Shultz," 26 June 1982, RRPL, RCMF, box 1, folder: "Sensitive Chron. 1982 1."

124. Wright to Acland, "George Shultz: The Calming Influence," 28 Dec. 1982, NAUK, PREM 19/1656. Shultz's appointment also caused some consternation in Whitehall, as spelling his name proved a challenge for some. "The author of the strip cartoon 'Peanuts' is spelled 'Shulz.' The American Secretary of State is spelled 'Shultz.' I am still unsure as to who Mr. Schultz is, who seems to be so widely referred to in current FCO documents and telegrams. Would it be worth a circular to find out?" Weston to Berry, "Very Important Persons," 16 Sept. 1982, NAUK, FCO 82/1196.

125. Staden memorandum, "Gymnich-type Treffen der Außenminister der Mitgliedstaaten der Atlantischen Allianz in La Sapinière, Kanada, am 2. und 3. Oktober 1982," 3 Oct. 1982, PAdAA, B 150/546.

126. Kornienko interview, 19 Jan. 1990, SMML, DOP, box 1, folder 12; Stoessel-Dobrynin memorandum of conversation, 9 July 1982, RRPL, JFMF, box 22,

folder: "USSR Diplomatic Contacts 1"; Raleigh, "'I Speak Frankly Because You Are My Friend,'" 181–182.

127. Dobrynin, *Sugubo doveritel'no*, 533.

128. Shultz to Reagan, "My Meeting with Gromyko September 28," 29 Sept. 1982, NARA, CREST, doc. CIA-RDP84B00049R001403480015-1.

129. Gromyko-Shultz memorandum of conversation, 28–29 Sept. 1982, SAPMO, DY 30/IV 2/2.035/70.

130. McFarlane to Clark, "The President's Discussion with Secretary-Designate Shultz," 26 June 1982, RRPL, RCMF, box 1, "Sensitive Chron. 1982 1" folder.

131. Von Damm to Reagan, 25 June 1982, RRPL, RCMF, box 1, "Sensitive Chron. 1982 1" folder.

132. Deaver interview, 8 May 1990, SMML, DOP, box 2, folder 12.

133. Shultz interview, 11 July 1989, SMML, DOP, box 3, folder 2.

134. Shultz-Dobrynin memorandum of conversation, 15 Feb. 1983, RRPL, RCMF, box 4, folder: "Soviet Union Sensitive File 1983."

135. Snyder, "'No Crowing,'" 42.

136. Hartman interview, 3 Nov. 1989, SMML, DOP, box 2, folder 16.

137. Haig to Reagan, "Meeting with Dobrynin," 3 Apr. 1981, RRPL, REPF, box 9, folder: "03/26/1981–03/30/1981."

138. Kampelman-Kondrashev memorandum of conversation, 18 Dec. 1980, MNHS, MMKP, loc. 151.C.4.6F, folder: "CSCE Correspondence, 9/1980–10/1982."

139. Kampelman-Kondrashev memorandum of conversation, 5 May 1983, MNHS, MMKP, loc. 151.C.5.2F, folder: "Department of State Staff Correspondence, 1980–1983."

140. Shultz interview, 11 July 1989, SMML, DOP, box 3, folder 2.

141. Dobrynin, *Sugubo doveritel'no*, 544–549.

142. Matlock, *Reagan and Gorbachev*, 54–59. Around the same time, the government in Prague released the Czech dissident playwright Václav Havel from prison. Matlock diary entry, 9 Mar. 1983, RRBML, JRMP, box 1, folder: "1983 1."

143. Meeting record, 6 Apr. 1983, RRPL, WCF, box 8, folder: "US-Soviet Relations Papers 4."

144. George, *Forceful Persuasion*, 4–7.

145. Evangelista, *Unarmed Forces*, 7–8; Garthoff, *Détente and Confrontation*, 8–11.

146. Lettow, *Ronald Reagan and His Quest*, 3–41.

147. Gavin, "Strategies of Inhibition," 19–24.

148. Ruth memorandum, "Deutsch-amerikanische Konsultation über die Weiter-führung der Rüstungskontrollpolitik im Bündnis," 25 Feb. 1981, PAdAA, B 150/497.

149. Haig memorandum, "US-Soviet Joint Statement on TNF Negotiations: Briefing the Allies," 25 Sept. 1981, NARA, CREST, doc. CIA-RDP84B00049R001203100005-5.

150. Genscher-Bush memorandum of conversation, 10 Mar. 1981, BA, B 136/16822.

151. Weinberger-Thatcher memorandum of conversation, 27 Feb. 1981, NARA, CREST, doc. CIA-RDP84B00049R001403560041-3; Henderson to Carrington, "TNF," 8 July 1981, NAUK, FCO 28/4320; BKA memorandum, "Ihr Gespräch mit Richard V. Allen am 4. September 1981, 16.30 Uhr," 4 Sept. 1981, BA, B 136/17053.

152. Genscher-Reagan memorandum of conversation, 9 Mar. 1981, PAdAA, B 150/498; Reagan to Thatcher, 10 Sept. 1983, CAC, THCR 3/1/33, pt. 1; Allen to Reagan, 30 Apr. 1981, RRPL, ES–NSC, MF, box 1, folder: "NSC #8 1."

160   NOTES TO PAGES 48–49

153. Reagan remarks, National Press Club, Washington, D.C., 18 Nov. 1981, in Greene et al., *Public Papers of the Presidents: Ronald Reagan, 1981*, 1062–1067.

154. NSC meeting record, 13 Oct. 1981, RRPL, ES–NSC, MF, box 3, folder: "NSC #22"; Haig memorandum, "US-Soviet Joint Statement on TNF Negotiations: Briefing the Allies," 25 Sept. 1981, NARA, CREST, doc. CIA-RDP84B00049R001203100005-5.

155. Rostow memorandum, "INF Policy," 5 Oct. 1982, RRPL, RFLF, box 9, folder: "INF Material 2"; Iklé interview, 27 Sept. 1990, LHCMA, TNA 11/58.

156. NSC meeting record, 12 Nov. 1981, RRPL, ES–NSC, MF, box 3, folder: "NSC #25."

157. Haig-Gromyko memorandum of conversation, 10:00–12:40, 26 Jan. 1982, RRPL, WPCF, box 3, folder: "Haig-Gromyko Meetings 01/26/1982 10:00am"; Haig-Gromyko memorandum of conversation, 14:00–19:00, 26 Jan. 1982, RRPL, WPCF, box 3, folder: "Haig-Gromyko Meetings 01/26/1982 2:00pm."

158. MZV memorandum, "O výsledcích sovětsko-amerických jednání o omezení jaderných zbraní v Evropě, která proběhla od 30. 11. do 17. 12. 1981 v Ženevě," NAČR, fond 1261/0/8, box P28/82, folder I13; NVA memorandum, "Bericht über die wichtigsten Ergebnisse der 14. Sitzung des Komitees der Verteidigungsminister der Teilnehmerstaaten des Warschauer Vertrages in Moskau," Dec. 1981, MA, DVW 1/71039; Dobrynin, *Sugubo doveritel'no*, 521.

159. Jakubik memorandum, "Přístupy administrativy prezidenta Reagana k otázke kontroly zbrojenia," 22 July 1981, AMZV, TOT, 1980–1989, SSA, box 4, folder 22; Winkelmann to Honecker, 26 Nov. 1981, SAPMO, DY 30/2379.

160. SED memornadum, "Information über die Ergebnisse der sowjetisch-amerikanischen Verhandlung über die Begrenzung der nuklearen Rüstungen in Europa vom 30. November bis 17. Dezember 1981 in Genf," 4 Jan. 1982, SAPMO, DY 30/IV 2/2.035/156; MZV memorandum, "O výsledkoch posledného kola sovietsko-amerických rokovaní o obmedzení jadrových zbraní v Európe, ktoré sa uskutočnili od 12. januára do 16. marca 1982 v Ženeve," 16 Apr. 1982, NAČR, fond 1261/0/8, box P37/82, folder I11.

161. Savel'yev and Detinov, *Big Five*, 57. Soviet officials were not alone in thinking the Pershing 2 could strike Moscow; even Schmidt believed this to be within the system's capabilities. Thatcher-Schmidt memorandum of conversation, 11 May 1979, NAUK, PREM 19/15.

162. Berkutov, "Iadernye sredstva NATO na Evropeĭskom teatre voĭny," 53–54, 56.

163. Haig-Gromyko memorandum of conversation, 10:00–12:40, 26 Jan. 1982, RRPL, WPCF, box 3, folder: "Haig-Gromyko Meetings 01/26/1982 10:00am"; Haig-Gromyko memorandum of conversation, 14:00–19:00, 26 Jan. 1982, RRPL, WPCF, box 3, folder: "Haig-Gromyko Meetings 01/26/1982 2:00pm."

164. KPSS Politburo meeting record, 9 Sept. 1982, LOC, DAVP, box 24, folder 14; Korneenko memorandum, "Zvit pro robotu delegatsiï URSR na sesiiakh Pidgotovchogo komitety dlia drugoï spetsial'noï sesiï General'noï Asambleï OON po rozzbroenniu i Komisiï OON po rozzbroenniu," 30 June 1981, TsDAHO, fond 1, opis' 25, sprava 2601.

165. MZV memorandum, "O výsledcích sovětsko-amerických jednání o omezení jaderných zbraní v Evropě, která proběhla od 30. 11. do 17. 12. 1981 v Ženevě," NAČR, fond 1261/0/8, box P28/82, folder I13.

NOTES TO PAGES 49–51

166. KPSS memorandum, "O novykh ideaiakh dlia mezhdunarodnogo razdela doklada," 9 Jan. 1981, RGANI, fond 80, opis' 1, delo 125.

167. Schmidt to Brezhnev, 4 May 1981, PAdAA, B 150/503.

168. SED memorandum, "Information über die Ergebnisse der letzten sowjetisch-amerikanischen Verhandlungsrunde zur Begrenzung der Kernwaffen in Europa, die im 1. Quartal d. J. in Genf stattfand," 12 Apr. 1982, SAPMO, DY 30/IV 2/2.035/156; Glitman, *Last Battle of the Cold War*, 70–71; Savel'yev and Detinov, *Big Five*, 61–63.

169. Meeting record, 12 Mar. 1982, LOC, PHNP, pt. 1, box 114, folder 3.

170. Nitze, *From Hiroshima to Glasnost*, 370–371.

171. Nitze memorandum, LOC, PHNP, pt. 2, box 103, folder 3.

172. Nitze, *From Hiroshima to Glasnost*, 386–389.

173. Perle to Weinberger, 20 Aug. 1982, RRPL, RFLF, box 9, folder: "INF Materials 5."

174. Weinberger to Clark, "INF Negotiations," 4 Aug. 1982, RRPL, RFLF, box 9, folder: "Nitze Initiative 1"; Weinberger to Reagan, "Response to Your Question About Cruise Missiles vs. Ballistic Missiles in the Nitze Package," 20 Aug. 1982, RRPL, RFLF, box 9, folder: "Nitze Initiative 1."

175. Iklé interview, 27 Sept. 1990, LHCMA, TNA 11/58.

176. Rostow memorandum, "INF Policy," 5 Oct. 1982, RRPL, RFLF, box 9, folder: "INF Materials 2."

177. Savel'yev and Detinov, *Big Five*, 65.

178. Reagan remarks, Eureka College, Eureka, Ill., 9 May 1982, in Greene, Mellody, and Payne, *Public Papers of the Presidents: Ronald Reagan, 1982*, 1:580–586.

179. Lettow, *Ronald Reagan and His Quest*, 59–61, 70–72.

180. Pipes to Rostow, "Preliminary START Discussions," 29 July 1981, RRPL, REPF, box 11, folder: "07/25/1981–07/31/1981."

181. CIA memorandum, "Are the Soviets Interested in Deep Reductions in Strategic Forces?," Apr. 1982, NARA, CREST, doc. CIA-RDP84B00049R000501050002-4.

182. Carstens-Brezhnev memorandum of conversation, 24 Nov. 1981, BA, B 122/27259.

183. MZV memorandum, "O výsledcích řádného kola sovětsko-amerického jednání o omezení a snížení strategických zbraní, které proběhlo v Ženevě od 2. února do 31. března 1983," 6 May 1983, NAČR, fond 1261/0/8, box P68/83, folder I1; Černý memorandum, "Některé názory v moskevském diplomatickém sboru na současnou situaci ve světě v souvislosti s návštěvou s. L.I. Brežněva v NSR," 1 Dec. 1981, AMZV, TOT, 1980–1989, SSSR, box 1, folder 3.

184. Clark to Reagan, "Brezhnev's Letter of May 20," 26 May 1982, RRPL, REPF, box 14, folder: "05/07/1982–05/11/1982"; Bremer to Clark, "Brezhnev's Reply to the President's May 7 Letter," 21 May 1982, RRPL, REPF, box 14, folder: "05/07/1982–05/11/1982."

185. Ruth memorandum, "Sitzung des Bundessicherheitsrats am 26. Mai 1982," 19 May 1982, PAdAA, B 150/536.

186. Brezhnev to Reagan, 20 May 1982, RRPL, ES-NSC, HSF, box 38, folder: "Brezhnev 8290289, 8290342."

187. Nancy Reagan, *My Turn*, 63.

188. Fischer to Haig, "Addressing Nuclear Issues," 2 Apr. 1982, RRPL, DCBF, box 4, folder: "Public Diplomacy April 1982."

162   **NOTES TO PAGES 51–53**

189. Schmidt-Reagan memorandum of conversation, 9 June 1982, PAdAA, B 150/537.

190. PZPR Politburo meeting record, 26 Jan. 1981, *PZPR a Solidarność*, 394–404; Honecker-Brezhnev memorandum of conversation, 3 Aug. 1981, SAPMO, DY 30/11853.

191. Zubok, *Failed Empire*, 267.

192. CIA memorandum, "SOYUZ-81—Backdrop for a Declaration of National Emergency and Confrontation with Solidarity?," 12 Mar. 1981, NARA, CREST, doc. CIA-RDP83B01027R000100110031-1; Spiers to Haig, "Poland: Soviet Military Options," 3 Apr. 1981, NARA, CREST doc. CIA-RDP84B00049R000601530017-4; Prozumenščikov, "Die Entscheidung im Politbüro der KPdSU," 205–241.

193. NSC meeting record, 21 Dec. 1981, RRPL, ES–NSC, MF, box 4, folder: "NSC #33."

194. Haig to Reagan, "Meeting with Dobrynin," 3 Apr. 1981, RRPL, REPF, box 9, folder: "03/26/1981–03/30/1981"; Chiampan, "'Those European Chicken Littles,'" 685–686.

195. Allen to Bush, "Your Meeting with Polish First Deputy Prime Minister Mieczyslaw Jagielski," 1 Apr. 1981, RRPL, REPF, box 9, folder: "03/26/1981–03/30/1981."

196. Thatcher-Haig memorandum of conversation, 29 Jan. 1982, NAUK, PREM 19/873.

197. Stearman to Allen, "Reflections on Unilateral Measures," 3 Apr. 1981, RRPL, PJDF, box 3, folder: "Crisis Management 4."

198. Bearg Dyke to Bush, "Vice Presidential Attendance at Cardinal Wyszynski's Funeral," 28 May 1981, GBPL, VPR, NSA, DPGF, CF, OA/ID 19768, folder: "Poland 1981 2."

199. Reagan to Mitterrand, 24 Dec. 1981, AD, 91 QO/926, folder: "Relations avec les pays de l'Est, 1981 septembre–décembre."

200. Thatcher-Haig memorandum of conversation, 10 Apr. 1981, NAUK, PREM 19/944.

201. AA memoandum, "Antwortbrief Gromykos auf Haig-Brief vom 23.1.1981," PAdAA, B 150/496; MNO memorandum, no. 11 (251), "Nové poznatky o ozbrojených silách Severoatlantického paktu," 1981, ABS, ZSGŠ, PM, box 107.

202. Stearman, *American Adventure*, 211.

203. KPSS Politburo meeting record, 29 Oct. 1981, RGANI, fond 89, opis' 42, delo 48.

204. KPSS Politburo meeting record, 10 Dec. 1981, RGANI, fond 89, opis' 42, delo 6.

205. Dobrynin, *Sugubo doveritel'no*, 522.

206. Kovalev, "Suverenitet i internatsional'nye obiazannosti sotsialisticheskikh stran," 4.

207. Ouimet, *Rise and Fall of the Brezhnev Doctrine*, 242.

208. Brezhnev remarks, Fifth PZPR Congress, Warsaw, Poland, 12 Nov. 1968, *Leninskim kursom*, vol. 2, 324–336.

209. PZPR Politburo meeting record, 13 Dec. 1981, *PZPR a Solidarność*, 800–813.

210. KPSS Politburo meeting record, 13 Dec. 1981, RGANI, fond 89, opis' 66, delo 4.

211. Bonin, "Business Interests versus Geopolitics," 235–241.

212. Brzezinski to Carter, "Daily Report," 18 Dec. 1980, JCPL, RAC, doc. NLC-128-11-8-5-5.

NOTES TO PAGES 53–55   163

213. NSC meeting record, 21 Dec. 1981, RRPL, ES–NSC, MF, box 4, folder: "NSC #33"; Thatcher-Carrington memorandum of conversation, 29 Dec. 1981, NAUK, PREM 19/871; Jentleson, *Pipeline Politics*, 175.

214. Meyer-Landrut memorandum, "Die sowjetische Energiepolitik," 5 Mar. 1981, BA, B 136/16697. The Soviet Union also had major coal reserves in eastern Siberia, but lacked the requisite transport infrastructure to sell them.

215. Pipes to Bailey, "Siberian Gas Pipeline Project," 7 July 1981, RRPL, REPF, box 10, folder: "07/02/1981–07/07/1981"; Reagan to Thatcher, 13 Jan. 1982, CAC, THCR 3/1/18; Henderson to Carrington, "US Response on Poland," 5 Feb. 1982, NAUK, PREM 19/873.

216. Mielke-Andropov memorandum of conversation, 11 July 1981, BStU, ZAIG, no. 5382.

217. Reagan remarks, Washington, D.C., 23 Dec. 1981, in Greene et al., *Public Papers of the Presidents: Ronald Reagan, 1981*, 1185–1188.

218. Henderson to Carrington, "Poland," 16 Dec. 1981, NAUK, PREM 19/561.

219. NSC meeting record, 21 Dec. 1981, RRPL, ES–NSC, MF, box 4, folder: "NSC #33."

220. Casey to Reagan, "Siberian Pipeline," 9 July 1981, NARA, CREST, doc.CIA-RDP84B00049R000400810009-5.

221. Allen to Reagan, "Status of Preparations/Contingency Planning on Poland," 19 Feb. 1981, RRPL, REPF, box 9, folder: "02/19/1981–02/22/1981"; Clark to Reagan, "Haig's Memorandum 'Poland—Working with the Allies,'" 6 Jan. 1982, RRPL, REPF, box 12, folder: "01/06/1982–01/07/1982."

222. Reagan to Thatcher, 19 Dec. 1981, THCR 3/1/17.

223. Thatcher-Carrington memorandum of conversation, 20 Dec. 1981, NAUK, PREM 19/871.

224. Schmidt-Reagan memorandum of conversation, 21 May 1981, PAdAA, B 150/504; Schmidt-Reagan memorandum of conversation, 19 July 1981, PAdAA, B 150/508.

225. Thatcher-Haig memorandum of conversation, 29 Jan. 1982, NAUK, PREM 19/873; Richards to Coles, "Poland," 5 Feb. 1982, NAUK, PREM 19/873.

226. Pfeffer and Fischer memorandum, "Brief Außenminister Haigs an Bundesminister vom 29.12.1981," 29 Dec. 1981, PAdAA, B 150/521; Reagan remarks, Washington, D.C., 29 Dec. 1981, in Greene et al., *Public Papers of the Presidents: Ronald Reagan, 1981*, 1209.

227. Schmidt-Mitterrand memorandum of conversation, 11 Jan. 1982, PAdAA, B 150/522.

228. Schmidt-Haig memorandum of conversation, 6 Jan. 1982, PAdAA, B 150/522.

229. Gotlieb diary entry, 4 July 1982, in Gotlieb, *The Washington Diaries*, 75.

230. SNIE, no. 3-11/2-82, "The Soviet Gas Pipeline in Perspective," 21 Sept. 1982, NARA, RG 263, NIE, box 6, folder 49.

231. Cherniaev diary entry, 22 Jan. 1982, in Cherniaev, *Sovmestnyĭ iskhod*, 471–473.

232. Schmidt to Reagan, 24 June 1982, BA, B 136/17057.

233. BKA memorandum, "Gespräch mit Reagan: Politische Fragen," 4 Jan. 1982, PAdAA, B 150/522.

234. Richardson to Pownall, "Siberian Gas Pipeline," 22 Jan. 1982, NAUK, BT 241/3244; McInnes to Pownall, "Siberian Pipeline," 8 July 1982, NAUK, BT 241/3245.

164   **NOTES TO PAGES 55–58**

235. NSC meeting record, 26 Feb. 1982, RRPL, ES–NSC, MF, box 5, folder: "NSC #43."

236. Clark to Bush, "High Level Mission to Europe," 1 Mar. 1982, RRPL, REPF, box 13, folder: "03/01/1982–03/02/1982."

237. NSC meeting record, 25 Mar. 1982, RRPL, ES–NSC, MF, box 5, folder: "NSC #44."

238. Reed, *At the Abyss*, 268–269; Weiss, "Duping the Soviets," 125.

239. Mitrokhin notes, CAC, MITN 1/6/1.

240. Webster memorandum, "US-USSR Relations: Comments of Georgi Arbatov, Director, Institute for the Study of United States of America and Canada, Moscow, USSR," 5 May 1981, RRPL, REPF, box 9, folder: "05/05/1981–05/12/1981."

241. Genscher-Haig memorandum of conversation, 9 Mar. 1981, PAdAA, B 150/498; Schmidt-Reagan memorandum of conversation, 21 May 1981, PAdAA, B 150/504; Von der Gablentz memorandum, "Vermerk für die Kabinettssitzung am Mittwoch, 25. November 1981," 24 Nov. 1981, BA, B 136/17362; Maubert memorandum, "Relations Est-Ouest," 4 Dec. 1981, AD, 91 QO/926, folder: "Relations avec les pays de l'Est, 1981 septembre–décembre."

242. Schmidt-Reagan memorandum of conversation, 25 Nov. 1981, BA, B 136/17363. Raleigh, "'I Speak Frankly Because You Are My Friend,'" 152–153.

243. Allen to Reagan, "Analysis of Brezhnev Proposal for a Summit," 2 Mar. 1981, GBPL, VPR, NSA, DPGF, CF, OA/ID 19768, folder: "USSR 1981 1."

244. Clark to Reagan, "Brezhnev Invitation," 16 Apr. 1982, RRPL, REPF, box 13, folder: "05/25/1982–05/26/1982"; Haig to Reagan, "Extending Brezhnev an Invitation to Meet With You at the SSOD," 16 Apr. 1982, RRPL, REPF, box 13, folder: "04/08/1982–04/13/1982."

245. Nancy Reagan, *My Turn*, 63.

246. Stearman to Clark, "Observations on a US-Soviet Summit," 21 Apr. 1982, RRPL, REPF, box 14, folder: "05/07/1982–05/11/1982"; Dobrynin, *Sugubo doveritel'no*, 526.

247. Genscher-Reagan memorandum of conversation, 9 Mar. 1982, PAdAA, B 150/528.

248. Craig and Logevall, *America's Cold War*, 322.

3. Talking about Talking

1. Osipovich interview, 2007, LHCMA, BOA 2/9.

2. Neal memorandum, "Korean Airliner," 6 Dec. 1983, NAUK, AVIA 120/37.

3. Shinn to Shultz, "Korean Airlines Incident Explained to Soviet Lecture Audience," 4 Sept. 1983, RRPL, ES–NSC, SF, box 43, folder: "Korean Airline Shootdown 6."

4. Osipovich interview, 2007, LHCMA, BOA 2/9.

5. Dobrynin, *Sugubo doveritel'no*, 540.

6. Colbourn, "Defining Détente," 228–250.

7. AA memorandum, "Anmerkung zum Stil außenpolitischer Initiativen der Soviet Union," 24 Sept. 1982, BA, B 136/16698. This comment, perhaps unwittingly, illustrated Lev Trotskiĭ's 1917 quip that Soviet foreign policy amounted to nothing more than issuing proclamations, though in fact Trotskiĭ's role as foreign minister extended much further. Service, *Trotsky*, 191–198.

NOTES TO PAGES 58–60   165

8. BKA memorandum, "Amerikanisch-sowjetische Beziehungen," 3 Sept. 1981, BA, B 136/17054.

9. Gaddis, "Long Peace," 120–123; cf. Chamberlin, *Cold War's Killing Fields*, 2.

10. Ambinder, *The Brink*, 10–11; Downing, *1983*, 16.

11. Pipes to Clark, "Soviet Succession," 27 May 1982, RRPL, REPF, box 14, folder: "05/27/1982–05/31/1982"; Chazov, *Zdorov'e i vlast'*, 154; Gorbachev, *Naedine s soboĭ*, 288; Medvedev, *Iuriĭ Andropov*, 311.

12. AA memorandum, "Anmerkung zum Stil außenpolitischer Initiativen der Soviet Union," 24 Sept. 1982, BA, B 136/16698.

13. Ryan, "Life Expectancy and Mortality Data from the Soviet Union," 1513.

14. Chazov, *Zdorov'e i vlast'*, 104.

15. Kevorkov, *Taĭnyĭ kanal*, 275.

16. Vorotnikov, *A bylo eto tak*, 14.

17. Artizov and Tomilina, *Andropov*, 186; Kevorkov, *Taĭnyĭ kanal*, 153; Medvedev, *Iuriĭ Andropov*, 324–333; Gromyko, *Andreĭ Gromyko*, 48–49, 52.

18. Gates to Casey, "Andropov: His Power and Program," 20 Nov. 1983, RRPL, JFMF, box 20, folder: "Andropov 6."

19. Brezhnev diary entry, 10 Nov. 1982, in Brezhnev, *Rabochie i dnevnikovye zapisi*, 2:1119.

20. Hartman to Shultz, "Brezhnev's Death," 11 Nov. 1982, RRPL, JFMF, box 34, folder: "Soviet Leadership Transition CPPG 1."

21. Hartman to Shultz, "Andropov Named Chairman of Brezhnev Funeral Commission," 11 Nov. 1982, RRPL, JFMF, box 34, folder: "Soviet Leadership Transition CPPG 1."

22. Brezhnev funeral commission meeting record, 11 Nov. 1982, *General'nyĭ sekretar' L.I. Brezhnev*, 196–200.

23. Glaser memo, "Information über eine negative Reaktion eines Schülers der POS 12 im Zusammenhang mit dem Amlemen des Genossen Breschnew," 12 Nov. 1982, BStU, BVP, Abt. 19, no. 795.

24. CIA memorandum, "USSR: After Brezhnev," RRPL, JFMF, box 34, folder: "Soviet Leadership Transition CPPG 1"; Yurchak, *Everything Was Forever*, 256–259.

25. KPU Politburo meeting record, 11 Nov. 1982, TsDAHO, fond 1, opis' 11, sprava 427.

26. Zagladin memorandum, 23 Apr. 1982, RGANI, fond 80, opis' 1, delo 196.

27. Brezhnev funeral commission meeting record, 11 Nov. 1982, in Kudriashov, *General'nyĭ sekretar' L.I. Brezhnev*, 196–200; Taubman, *Khrushchev*, 244.

28. BKA memorandum, "Sowjetunion nach Breschnews Tod," 23 Nov. 1982, PAdAA, B 150/151; CIA memorandum, "Andropov in the Western Press," 14 June 1982, RRPL, JFMF, box 36, folder: "USSR Succession 1"; Sell, *From Washington to Moscow*, 119–120.

29. Pipes to Clark, "Background Paper for Your Thursday Meeting with Shultz and Weinberger," 17 Nov. 1982, RRPL, REPF, box 16, folder: "11/10/1982–11/17/1982."

30. Hartman to Shultz, "Brezhnev's Death," 11 Nov. 1982, RRPL, JFMF, box 34, folder: "Soviet Leadership Transition CPPG 1."

31. Ronald Reagan, *American Life*, 559.

32. Reagan to Thatcher, 12 Nov. 1982, NAUK, PREM 19/1033.

33. Reagan remarks, Washington, D.C., 11 Nov. 1982, in Greene, Mellody, and Payne, *Public Papers of the Presidents: Ronald Reagan, 1982*, 2:1452.

166   **NOTES TO PAGES 60–62**

34. Meyer-Landrut memorandum, "Ableben Leonid I. Breschnews," 11 Nov. 1982, BA, B 136/16698; BKA memorandum, "Gespräch des Bundespräsidenten und BM mit GS Andropow und AM Gromyko," 23 Nov. 1982, PAdAA, B 150/551.

35. CIA memorandum, "USSR: The Immediate Post-Brezhnev Policy Agenda," Nov. 1982, NARA, CREST, doc. CIA-RDP83T00853R000200100002-2.

36. Andropov remarks, Moscow, Soviet Union, 15 Nov. 1982, in Andropov, *Iu.V. Andropov*, 207–208.

37. KPSS memorandum, "K besede s Bushem i Shul'tsem," Nov. 1982, RGANI, fond 82, opis' 1, delo 36.

38. Bush interview, 7 May 1990, SMML, DOP, box 2, folder 6.

39. Andropov-Bush memorandum of conversation, 15 Nov. 1982, RGANI, fond 82, opis' 1, delo 36; Bush-Andropov memorandum of conversation, 15 Nov. 1982, RRPL, REPF, box 16, folder: "11/18/1982."

40. Dobriansky to Wheeler, "Briefing of Former Presidents," 14 Dec. 1982, RRPL, REPF, box 18, folder: "12/13/1982."

41. Putnam, "Diplomacy and Domestic Politics," 427–460.

42. Shultz to Reagan, "Our Meeting with Andropov—November 15," 16 Nov. 1982, RRPL, JFMF, box 20, folder: "Andropov 8."

43. Shultz interview, 11 July 1989, SMML, DOP, box 3, folder 2.

44. Gates to Casey, "Andropov: His Power and Program," 20 Nov. 1982, RRPL, REPF, box 18, folder: "12/13/1982."

45. Shultz to Reagan, "Our Meeting with Andropov—November 15," 16 Nov. 1982, RRPL, JFMF, box 20, folder: "Andropov 8."

46. Chňoupek memorandum, "Informace o průběhu a výsledcích pracovního setkání člena ÚV KSČ a ministra zahraničních věcí USSR s. B. Chňoupka se členem politického byra ÚV KSSS a ministrem zahraničních věcí SSSR s. A.A. Gromykem," 31 Mar. 1982, NAČR, fond 1261/0/8, box P36/82, folder I6.

47. KPSS memorandum, "Direktivy delegatsii SSSR na XXXVIII sessii Komissii OON po pravam cheloveka," 1983, RGANI, fond 89, opis' 19, delo 21.

48. Meyer to Smith, "US/Soviet Relations," 18 Nov. 1982, NAUK, FCO 82/1204.

49. Andropov-Carstens memorandum of conversation, 15 Nov. 1982, RGANI, fond 82, opis' 1, delo 37; Carstens-Andropov memorandum of conversation, 15 Nov. 1982, PAdAA, B 150/550.

50. Andropov memorandum, "K itogam besed s nekotorymi inostrannymi delegatsiiami, pribyvshimi na pokhorony L.I. Brezhneva," 18 Nov. 1982, RGANI, fond 82, opis' 1, delo 2.

51. KPSS Politburo meeting record, 18 Nov. 1982, LOC, DAVP, box 25, folder 1.

52. Andropov remarks, KPSS Plenum, Moscow, Soviet Union, 22 Nov. 1982, in Andropov, *Iu.V. Andropov*, 209–218.

53. Shultz to Reagan, "My Luncheon with Soviet Ambassador Dobrynin, November 23," 24 Nov. 1982, RRPL, REPF, box 16, folder: "11/23/1982–11/25/1982"; Shultz to Reagan, "US-Soviet Dialogue: Dec. 6 Dobrynin Demarche," 7 Dec. 1982, RRPL, REPF, box 16, folder: "12/01/1982–12/12/1982."

54. Andropov remarks, KPSS Supreme Soviet, Moscow, Soviet Union, 21 Dec. 1982, in Andropov, *Iu.V. Andropov*, 5–19.

55. Kohl-Mitterrand memorandum of conversation, 22 Nov. 1982, PAdAA, B 150/551.

NOTES TO PAGES 62–64   167

56. Roĭ Medvedev, *Iuriĭ Andropov*, 84–87. This group's influence on Soviet policy making would peak in the late 1980s; they were, in retrospect, "'Team Gorbachev' in training." Taubman, *Gorbachev*, 141.

57. Bobkov, *KGB i vlast'*, 214; Roĭ Medvedev, *Iuriĭ Andropov*, 340–341; Pikhoia, *Sovetskiĭ soiuz*, 376; Volkogonov, *Sem' vozhdeĭ*, 2:136; Wolf, *Man without a Face*, 219.

58. KPSS Politburo meeting record, 29 Oct. 1981, RGANI, fond 89, opis' 42, delo 48; KPSS Politburo meeting record, 10 Dec. 1981, RGANI, fond 89, opis' 42, delo 6. When Gorbachev, who was present for the politburo's deliberations over Poland, reflected on Andropov's hard-line bona fides in his memoirs, he cited only Hungary, Czechoslovakia, and Afghanistan. Gorbachev, *Naedine s soboĭ*, 357.

59. Kevorkov, *Taĭnyĭ kanal*, 154.

60. Zubok, *Failed Empire*, 210–215. This is a far cry from the common perception of Andropov as the ultimate hard-liner, based primarily on his time as ambassador in Budapest during the 1956 Hungarian Revolution. Sayle, "Andropov's Hungarian Complex," 428–429; Sell, *From Washington to Moscow*, 119.

61. Kevorkov, *Taĭnyĭ kanal*, 24–25.

62. Sell, *From Washington to Moscow*, 119.

63. Kampelman-Kondrashev memorandum of conversation, 5 May 1983, MNHS, MMKP, loc. 151.C.5.2F, folder: "Department of State Staff Correspondence, 1980–1983."

64. Adamishin diary entry, 15 Jan. 1985, HIA, ALAP, box 1, folder: "1985."

65. Ryzhkov interview, BLPES, 2RR 1/2/1.

66. Cherniaev diary entry, 20 Dec. 1982, in Cherniaev, *Sovmestnyĭ iskhod*, 523–525.

67. Gorbachev, *Zhizn' i reformy*, 1:148; Gorbachev, *Naedine s soboĭ*, 357; Taubman, *Gorbachev*, 138–144.

68. Chazov, *Zdorov'e i vlast'*, 90.

69. Arnot memorandum, "Osteuropäische Beratungen auf die Veränderungen in der sowjetischen Führung," 23 Dec. 1982, BA, B 136/16698; Roĭ Medvedev, *Iuriĭ Andropov*, 345–348; Pikhoia, *Sovetskiĭ soiuz*, 377.

70. Bobkov, *KGB i vlast'*, 214.

71. Vadim Medvedev, *V komande Gorbacheva*, 6–7.

72. Andropov remarks, KPSS Plenum, Moscow, Soviet Union, 22 Nov. 1982, in Andropov, *Iu.V. Andropov*, 209–218.

73. Clark, *Crime and Punishment in Soviet Officialdom*, 159–163; Shkadov, "Povyshat' otvetstvennost' i distsiplinu, sovrshenstvovat' stil' raboty rukovodiashchikh voennykh kadrov," 3.

74. Mielke-Chebrikov memorandum of conversation, 9 Feb. 1983, BStU, Abt. 10, no. 1863; Macrakis, *Seduced by Secrets*, 1.

75. Prozorov, *Rassekrechennyĭ Andropov*, 62.

76. KPSS Politburo meeting record, 7 Dec. 1982, RGANI, fond 82, opis' 1, delo 2.

77. KPSS memorandum, "Ob usilenii raboty po ukrepleniiu sotsialisticheskoĭ distsipliny truda," 28 July 1983, RGANI, fond 89, opis' 7, delo 3.

78. Drozdov and Fartyshev, *Na puti k vozrozhdeniiu*, 89.

79. NIE, no. 11/4-82, "The Soviet Challenge to US Security Interests," NARA, CREST, doc. CIA-RDP85T00176R000400010001-7.

80. Clark to Reagan, "Terms of Reference for NSSD on 'US Policy toward the Soviet Union,'" RRPL, REPF, box 15, folder: "08/05/1982–08/16/1982."

168 NOTES TO PAGES 64–67

81. NSSD, no. 11-82, "US Policy toward the Soviet Union," 21 Aug. 1982, RRPL, REPF, box 5, folder: "Soviet NSSD 3."

82. Shultz to Reagan, "US-Soviet Relations in 1983," 19 Jan. 1983, RRPL, JFMF, box 41, folder: "US-USSR Relations Jan.–Feb. 1983."

83. Clark to Reagan, "The Prospects for Progress in US-Soviet Relations," 4 Feb. 1983, RRPL, WPCF, box 8, folder: "US-Soviet Relations Papers 2."

84. Lenczowski to Clark, "The Memorandum to the President on US-Soviet Relations," 7 Feb. 1983, RRPL, JFMF, box 41, folder: "US-USSR Relations Jan.–Feb. 1983."

85. McFarlane to Clark, 23 Mar. 1983, RRPL, WPCF, box 8, folder: "US-Soviet Relations Papers 4."

86. Clark to Reagan, "The Prospects for Progress in US-Soviet Relations," 4 Feb. 1983, RRPL, WPCF, box 8, folder: "US-Soviet Relations Papers 2."

87. NSDD 75, "US Relations with the USSR," 17 Jan. 1983, RRPL, ES–NSC, NSDD, box 5, folder: "NSDD 75 1."

88. Shultz to Reagan, "US-Soviet Relations in 1983," 19 Jan. 1983, RRPL, JFMF, box 41, folder: "US-USSR Relations Jan.–Feb. 1983."

89. Shultz-Dobrynin memorandum of conversation, 15 Feb. 1983, RRPL, RCMF, box 4, folder: "Soviet Union Sensitive File 1983"; Reagan to Andropov, 17 June 1983, RGANI, fond 82, opis′ 1, delo 83.

90. Shultz to Reagan, "USG-Soviet Relations—Where Do We Want to Be and How Do We Get There?," 3 Mar. 1983, RRPL, RCMF, box 4, folder: "Soviet Union Sensitive File 1983."

91. Matlock diary entry, 26 May 1983, RRBML, JRMP, box 1, folder: "1983 1."

92. Volcker, *Keeping at It*, 116, 138.

93. Brands, *Making the Unipolar Moment*, 57–61.

94. Matlock memorandum, "US-Soviet Relations: The Next Year," RRPL, JFMF, box 34, folder: "Saturday Group Notes Jan.–Feb. 1983."

95. McFarlane to Matlock, 16 June 1983, RRPL, WPCF, box 9, folder: "US-Soviet Relations Papers 14."

96. Reagan diary entry, 6 Apr. 1983, in Brinkley, *The Reagan Diaries*, 1: 212–213.

97. MAÉ memorandum, "L'arrivée au pouvoir de M. Andropov et les relations est-ouest," 30 Nov. 1983, AD, 1930 INVA/5856, folder: "Notes du département."

98. Kohl-Thatcher memorandum of conversation, 21 Apr. 1983, PAdAA, B 150/562.

99. Arnot memorandum, "Gipfelbegegnungen Ost–West," 28 Apr. 1983, PAdAA, B 150/562.

100. Memorandum, "Williamsburg Economic Summit Conference Statement on Security Issues," 29 May 1983, in Hill and Kevan, *Public Papers of the Presidents: Ronald Reagan, 1983*, 1:795.

101. KPSS Politburo meeting record, 31 May 1983, RGANI, fond 89, opis′ 42, delo 53.

102. Švec memorandum, "Zpráva o některých subjektivních aspektech utváření zahraniční politiky admin. Reagana v současném období k výměně Clarka McFarlanem," 8 Nov. 1983, AMZV, TOT, 1980–1989, SSA, box 4, folder 23.

103. Andropov to Gromyko, 22 July 1983, RGANI, fond 82, opis′ 1, delo 47.

104. Chňoupek memorandum, "Informace o průběhu a výsledcích pracovního setkání člena ÚV KSČ a ministra zahraničních věcí USSR s. B. Chňoupka se členem politického byra ÚV KSSS a ministrem zahraničních věcí SSSR s. A.A. Gromykem," 31 Mar. 1982, NAČR, fond 1261/0/8, box P36/82, folder I6.

NOTES TO PAGES 67–70   169

105. Cobb to Clark, "Soviet-American Relations at the Crossroads," 9 June 1983, RRPL, WPCF, box 9, folder: "US-Soviet Relations Papers 8."

106. Shakhnazarov, *S vozhdiami i bez nikh*, 119.

107. Kohl, *Erinnerungen*, 2:175–183.

108. Kohl-Andropov memorandum of conversation, 5 July 1983, PAdAA, B 150/570.

109. SED Politburo meeting record, 15 Aug. 1983, SAPMO, DY 30/J IV 2/2015.

110. Honecker to Kohl, 5 Oct. 1983, BA, B 136/20632.

111. Rejlek memorandum, "Poznámky ke vztahům HDR-NSR po rozmístění raket USA v ITSR a po 7. plénu ÚV SED," 5 Dec. 1983, AMZV, TOT, 1980–1989, NDR, box 1, folder 4.

112. Reagan remarks, Annual Convention of the National Association of Evangelicals, Orlando, Fla., 8 Mar. 1983, in Hill and Kevan, *Public Papers of the Presidents: Ronald Reagan, 1983*, 1:359–364.

113. Shultz, *Turmoil and Triumph*, 266–267.

114. Kornienko interview, 19 Jan. 1990, SMML, DOP, box 1, folder 12.

115. Kohl-Gromyko memorandum of conversation, 18 Jan. 1983, PAdAA, B 150/555.

116. Mukha memorandum, "Informatsionnoe soobshchenie," 18 June 1982, HDASBU, fond 16, opis' 1, sprava 1095.

117. NVA memorandum, "Informationsbericht Ergebnisse der Waffenbrüderschaftsbeziehungen im Ausbildungsjahr 1982/83," 20 Oct. 1983, MA, DVH 10-1/180107.

118. MNO memorandum, no. 15 (255), "Vojenskopolitická situace na jižním křídle Severoatlantického paktu," 1981, ABS, ZSGŠ, PM, box 106; MNO memorandum, no. 14 (254), "Zásady použití ozbrojených sil NATO ve strategické operaci na středoevropském válčišti s důrazem na stupeň skupiny armád a spojeneckého taktického leteckého velitelství," 1981, ABS, ZSGŠ, PM, box 106; MNO memorandum, no. 9 (314), "Vojenské rozpočty států Severoatlantického pakty v roce 1985—základní údaje," 1985, ABS, ZSGŠ, PM, box 123; Dobrynin, *Sugubo doveritel'no*, 554. In fact, second-strike forces had been far more vulnerable during the Cold War than strategists appreciated. Long and Green, "Stalking the Secure Second Strike," 65.

119. Reagan remarks, Washington, D.C., 23 Mar. 1983, in Hill and Kevan, *Public Papers of the Presidents: Ronald Reagan, 1983*, 1:437–443.

120. Inboden, "Grand Strategy and Petty Squabbles," 171–172; Nitze, *From Hiroshima to Glasnost*, 401.

121. Teller, *Memoirs*, 525–540.

122. NSC meeting record, 30 Nov. 1982, ES–NSC, MF, box 10, folder: "NSC #96 2."

123. McFarlane interview, 26 Sept. 1990, LHCMA, TNA 11/73.

124. Pipes interview, 21 Sept. 1990, LHCMA, TNA 11/95.

125. Mashchenko and Dmitriev, "Primenenie kosmicheskikh sistem gidrometeorologicheskoĭ razvedki SShA v voennykh tseliakh," 76.

126. Aleksandrov, "O dolgosrochnoĭ voennoĭ programme NATO," 79.

127. Dmitriev memorandum, "O rabotakh po proverb stoĭkosti voennoĭ tekhniki k porazhaiushchim faktoram iadernoho vzryva," Mar. 1982, HIA, VLKP, box 5, folder 8.

128. Matlock diary entry, 24 Mar. 1983, RRBML, JRMP, box 1, folder: "1983 1."

129. Popov, "Sostoianie i perspektivy razvitiia v SShA kosmicheskoĭ sistemy nabliudeniia za zapuskami ballisticheskikh raket," 68.

170   NOTES TO PAGES 70–72

130. Shultz-Gromyko memorandum of conversation, 15:35–18:55, 7 Jan. 1985, RRPL, JFMF, box 8, folder: "March 1985 1"; Gromyko, *Andreĭ Gromyko*, 94.

131. Wolf, *Man without a Face*, 221.

132. Mielke-Andropov memorandum of conversation, 11 July 1981, BStU, ZAIG, no. 5382.

133. Organski and Kugler, *The War Ledger*, 206–207; Gilpin, *War and Change in World Politics*, 197–198.

134. MNO memorandum, no. 12 (284), "Nové jevy světové vojenskopolitické situaci," 1983, ABS, ZSGŠ, PM, box 114; NVA memorandum, "Bericht über die wichtigsten Ergebnisse der 16. Sitzung des Komitees der Verteidigungsminister der Teilnehmerstaaten des Warschauer Vertrages in Sofia," Dec. 1983, MA, DVW 1/71041.

135. MNO memorandum, "Strategický systém velení, řízení, spojení a vojenského zpravodajství v ozbrojených silách USA," 1984, ABS, ZSGŠ, PM, box 117.

136. Kukan memorandum, "Výsledky prezidentských volieb v USA," 19 Nov. 1980, AMZV, TOT, 1980–1989, SSA, box 4, folder 21.

137. Sutherland to Pym, "US/Soviet Relations," 16 Nov. 1982, NAUK, PREM 19/1033.

138. Andropov remarks, Warsaw Pact Political Consultative Committee, Prague, Czechoslovakia, 5 Jan. 1983, SAPMO, DY 30/IV 2/2.035/31.

139. KPSS memorandum, "K besede s A. Garrimanom," June 1983, RGANI, fond 82, opis' 1, delo 36.

140. Andropov-Harriman memorandum of conversation, 2 June 1983, RGANI, fond 82, opis' 1, delo 36; Harriman-Andropov memorandum of conversation, 2 June 1983, RRPL, JFMF, box 20, folder: "Andropov 5."

141. Iakovlev-Hartman memorandum of conversation, 20 Oct. 1983, GARF, fond 10063, opis' 1, delo 101.

142. Chervov, "Ravnestvo i odinakovaia bezopasnost'," 18.

143. BKA memorandum, "Luftraumverletzungen durch sowjetische Hubschrauber am 25. Februar, 29. März, 12. Mai und 08. Juni 1983," 22 July 1983, BA, B 136/30420.

144. Kriuchkov interview, 2007, LHCMA, BOA 3/5; Schweizer, *Victory*, 8.

145. Head and Trudeau, *Canadian Way*, 298.

146. Votintsev, "Neizvestnye voĭska ischeznuvsheĭ sverkhderzhavy," pt. 3, 38.

147. Petrov interview, 2007, LHCMA, BOA 2/5; Hoffman, *Dead Hand*, 6–11.

148. Sell, *From Washington to Moscow*, 16–17.

149. Kostenko, "O vnezapnosti v vooruzhennoĭ bor'b," 70.

150. Afinov, "Razvitie v SShA vyzokotochnogo oruzhiia i perspektivy sozdaniia razvedyvatel'no-udarnykh kompleksov," 63.

151. Andropov to Brezhnev, "Otchet o rabote Komiteta gosudarstvennoĭ bezopasnosti SSSR za 1980 god," 31 Mar. 1981, LOC, DAVP, box 28, folder 3; Andropov to Brezhnev, "Otchet o rabote Komiteta gosudarstvennoĭ bezopasnosti SSSR za 1981 god," 13 Apr. 1982, LOC, DAVP, box 28, folder 3; Chebrikov to Andropov, "Otchet o rabote Komiteta gosudarstvennoĭ bezopasnosti SSSR za 1982 god," 15 Mar. 1983, LOC, DAVP, box 28, folder 3; Mitrokhin notes, CAC, MITN 1/6/3.

152. MfS memorandum, "Bericht über die Entwicklung und den erreichten Stand der Albeit our Frühkennerung gegenerischer Angriffs- und Überraschungsabsichten (Komplex RJAN)," 23 Apr. 1986, BStU, Arbeitsgruppe des Ministers (AGM), no. 1021.

NOTES TO PAGES 72-73   171

153. The project is sometimes referred to as VRIaN, the "V" standing for *vnezapnoe* (surprise).

154. MfNV memorandum, "Die Schaffung einheitliche Dokumente für die schnelle Aufdeckung und zuverlässige Beurteilung von Maßnahmen der NATO zur Überführung ihrer Mitgliedstaaten und Streitkräfte von Friedens- in den Kriegszustand sowie zur Erhöhung ihrer Kriegsbereitschaft in Krisensituation," Feb. 1983, MA, DVW 1/94471.

155. MfS memorandum, "Zu den Gesprächen mit Genossen W.A. Krjutschkow," 4 Oct. 1983, BStU, Abt. 10, no. 2020; Wolf to Irmler, "Vermerk über die Ergebisse der Konsultationen mit Genossen Generalmajor Schapkin, Stellvertreter des Leiters der I. Hauptverwaltung der KfS und zwei Experten zur Problematik RJAN," 29 Aug. 1984, BStU, ZAIG, no. 5384.

156. MfS memorandum, "Merkmale zur Erkennung der gegnerischen Vorbereitung auf einen überraschenden Raketenkernwaffenangriff," 26 Nov. 1984, BStU, HA 3, no. 11792; MfS memorandum, "Bericht über die Entwicklung und den erreichten Stand der Albeit our Frühkennerung gegenerischer Angriffs- und Überraschungsabsichten (Komplex RJAN)," 23 Apr. 1986, BStU, AGM, no. 1021.

157. MfNV memorandum, "Die Schaffung einheitliche Dokumente für die schnelle Aufdeckung und zuverlässige Beurteilung von Maßnahmen der NATO zur Überführung ihrer Mitgliedstaaten und Streitkräfte von Friedens- in den Kriegszustand sowie zur Erhöhung ihrer Kriegsbereitschaft in Krisensituation," Feb. 1983, MA, DVW 1/94471; Zagladin memorandum, "Kak odolet' iadernuiu ugrozu," 1985, AGF, fond 1, opis' 8, delo 17757.

158. Pavlovskiĭ and Kariakin, "Ob opyte primeneniia matematicheskikh modeleĭ," 54, 57.

159. Wolf, *Man without a Face*, 222; Wolf to Irmler, "Vermerk über die Ergebisse der Konsultationen mit Genossen Generalmajor Schapkin, Stellvertreter des Leiters der I. Hauptverwaltung der KfS und zwei Experten zur Problematik RJAN," 29 Aug. 1984, BStU, ZAIG, no. 5384.

160. Gordievsky, *Next Stop Execution*, 261; Gordievskiĭ interview, 2007, LHCMA, BOA 3/3; Ermarth, "Observations on the 'War Scare' of 1983." At the same time, the Republic of Korea was attempting to develop a similar capacity for computer analysis; in Washington, policy makers were highly skeptical of the enterprise and doubted it could be completed on time and on budget, if at all. Oswald to Ambrose, "Comparison of the Korean Intelligence Support System (KISS) and the All Source Analysis System (ASAS) Requirements," 15 Sept. 1982, LOC, WEOP, pt. 1, box 11, folder 1.

161. Umbach, *Das rote Bündnis*, 331.

162. Smith to Andropov, Nov. 1982, RGANI, fond 82, opis' 1, delo 61.

163. Andropov to Smith, 19 Apr. 1983, RGANI, fond 82, opis' 1, delo 61.

164. Mukha memorandum, "Informatsionnoe soobshchenie," 14 July 1983, HDASBU, fond 16, opis' 1, sprava 1101.

165. Peacock, "Samantha Smith in the Land of the Bolsheviks," 419.

166. Wittner, *Struggle against the Bomb*, 3:130–168.

167. Pym to Thatcher, "Nuclear Weapons and Public Opinion," 7 Jan 1983, NAUK, PREM 19/1690; Guasconi, "Public Opinion and the Euromissile Crisis," 275–279.

168. Kohl-Bush memorandum of conversation, 15 Apr. 1983, PAdAA, B 150/562.

169. Kohl-Bush memorandum of conversation, 31 Jan. 1983, PAdAA, B 150/555; Kohl to Reagan, 8 Feb. 1983, PAdAA, B 150/556.

170. Sonne, *Leben mit der Bombe*, 171.

171. Meyer-Landrut memorandum, "Amerikanische Nuklearstrategie," 24 Aug. 1982, PAdAA, B 150/543.

172. CIA memorandum, "Soviet Thinking on the Possibility of Armed Confrontation with the United States," 30 Dec. 1983, RRPL, JFMF, box 3, folder: "January 1984 2."

173. CIA memorandum, "Andropov's Leadership Style and Strategy," 3 Feb. 1984, RRPL, JFMF, box 20, folder: "Andropov 1."

174. Gurov memorandum, "'Khertiedzh Faundeĭtsn'—Odin iz tsentrov antisovetskoĭ propagandy v SShA," 12 July 1984, HDAMZS, fond 1, opis' 3, sprava 5084.

175. Matlock to Clark, "Soviet Calls for Normalization and Peaceful Coexistence," 28 June 1983, RRPL, JFMF, box 1, folder: "June 1983."

176. Matlock to Clark, "Appointment Request for Solzhenitsyn," 13 July 1983, RRPL, JFMF, box 1, folder: "July 1983 1." Hard-liners in the administration protested this decision vociferously and unsuccessfully. Lenczowski to Clark, "Invitation to Solzhenitsyn," 15 July 1983, RRPL, JFMF, box 1, folder: "July 1983 2."

177. Snyder, "'Jerry, Don't Go,'" 76.

178. Matlock diary entry, 1 Aug. 1983, RRBML, JRMP, box 1, folder: "1983 1."

179. Tretyak interview, 2007, LHCMA, BOA 2/8; Osipovich interview, 2007, LHCMA, BOA 2/9.

180. Akhromeev and Kornienko, *Glazami marshala i diplomata*, 10–53; Aleksandrov-Agentov, *Ot Kollontai do Gorbacheva*, 275–285; Brutents, *Tridtsat' let na Staroĭ ploshchadi*, 486–495; Dobrynin, *Sugubo doveritel'no*, 497–580; Gorbachev, *Naedine s soboĭ*, 318–357; Kevorkov, *Taĭnyĭ kanal*, 273–291; Grishin, *Ot Khrushcheva do Gorbacheva*, 57–66; Kornienko, *Kholodnaia voĭna*, 263–310; Sukhodrev, *Iazik moĭ—drug moĭ*, 421–422; Vorotnikov, *A bylo eto tak*, 39.

181. Speakes remarks, Santa Barbara, Calif., 1 Sept. 1983, in Hill and Kevan, *Public Papers of the Presidents: Ronald Reagan, 1983*, 2:1221.

182. Reagan remarks, Point Mugu Naval Air Station, Calif., 2 Sept. 1983, in Hill and Kevan, *Public Papers of the Presidents: Ronald Reagan, 1983*, 2:1223–1224.

183. Reagan remarks, Washington, D.C., 5 Sept. 1983, in Hill and Kevan, *Public Papers of the Presidents: Ronald Reagan, 1983*, 2:1227–1230.

184. Cherniaev diary entry, 6 Sept. 1983, in Cherniaev, *Sovmestnyĭ iskhod*, 536–537.

185. Shultz to Reagan, "US Response to Soviet Attack on Korean Airliner: Current Status and Next Steps," 1 Sept. 1983, RRPL, JFMF, box 28, folder: "KAL 1."

186. DOS memorandum, "Working Group on KAL Incident: Situation Report No. 2," 1 Sept. 1983, RRPL, ES–NSC, SF, box 43, folder: "Korean Airline Shootdown 1."

187. Streator to Shultz, "Shooting Down of Korean Airliner: British Foreign Secretary's Meeting with Soviet Ambassador," 2 Sept. 1983, RRPL, ES–NSC, SF, box 43, folder: "Korean Airline Shootdown 2"; Hancock to Mawhinney, "Conversation with A.P. Makarov, Soviet Embassy," 6 Sept. 1983, LAC, RG 25, vol. 8800, file 20-1-2-USSR, pt. 46.

188. Chňoupek memorandum, "Informace o průběhu a výsledcích pracovního setkání člena ÚV KSS a ministra zahraničních věcí ČSSR s. B. Chňoupka se členem politického byra ÚV KSSS, I. náměstkem předsedy rady ministrů SSSR a ministrem zahraničních věcí SSSR s. A.A. Gromykem," 4 Oct. 1983, NAČR, fond 1261/0/8, box P83/83, folder I2.

NOTES TO PAGES 74–76   173

189. AA memorandum, "Abschuß einer Südkoreanischen Verkehrsmaschine durch sowjetische Jäger," PAdAA, B 150/573.

190. AA memorandum, Mittagessen der AM der Zehn; 8.9.1983 in Madrid," 8 Sept. 1983, PAdAA, B 150/573.

191. Shultz to Reagan, "US Response to Soviet Attack on Korean Airliner: Current Status and Next Steps," 1 Sept. 1981, RRPL, JFMF, box 28, folder: "KAL 1"; Matlock diary entry, 3 Sept. 1983, RRBML, JRMP, box 1, folder: "1983 2."

192. Clark to Reagan, "NSPG Meeting: Soviet Shoot-Down of KAL Airliner," 2 Sept. 1983, RRPL, CMC–NSC, box 2, folder: "KAL 007 1."

193. Higgins to Reagan, "Public Response to Soviet Attack on Korean Airliner," 2 Sept. 1983, RRPL, AVHF, box 75, folder: "Soviet Attack."

194. Matlock diary entry, 2 Sept. 1983, RRBML, JRMP, box 1, folder: "1983 2" As ambassador, Shultz and Dobrynin agreed, Matlock had demonstrated "that agreements could be struck even when relations were not all that they could be" between East and West. Shultz-Dobrynin memorandum of conversation, 15 Feb. 1983, RRPL, RCMF, box 4, folder: "Soviet Union Sensitive File 1983."

195. Thatcher-Reagan memorandum of conversation, 29 Sept. 1983, NAUK, PREM 19/1153; Matlock diary entry, 3 Sept. 1983, RRBML, JRMP, box 1, folder: "1983 2"; Reagan diary entry, 3 Sept. 1983, in Brinkley, *The Reagan Diaries*, 1:259; Shultz, *Turmoil and Triumph*, 365.

196. Reagan diary entry, 17–18 Sept. 1983, in Brinkley, *The Reagan Diaries*, 1:264–265.

197. Reagan remarks, Washington, D.C., 3 Sept. 1983, in Hill and Kevan, *Public Papers of the Presidents: Ronald Reagan, 1983*, 2:1226.

198. Kliuiukov interview, 2007, LHCMA, BOA 3/6.

199. KPSS Politburo meeting record, 2 Sept. 1983, LOC, DAVP, box 25, folder 4.

200. Kornienko interview, 19 Jan. 1990, SMML, DOP, box 1, folder 12.

201. Kirkpatrick to Shultz, "Soviet Stonewalling in the Security Council," 3 Sept. 1983, RRPL, ES–NSC, SF, box 43, folder: "Korean Airline Shootdown 6."

202. Shultz, *Turmoil and Triumph*, 369–370; Matlock diary entry, 8 Sept. 1983, RRBML, JRMP, box 1, folder: "1983 2."

203. Genscher-Gromyko memorandum of conversation, 8 Sept. 1983, PAdAA, B 150/573.

204. Singh memorandum, "Summary Report by the Air Navigation Commissioner," NAUK, AVIA 120/37; Neal memorandum, "Korean Airliner," 6 Dec. 1983, NAUK, AVIA 120/37.

205. Mielke-Kriuchkov memorandum of conversation, 19 Sept. 1983, BStU, ZAIG, no. 5306; MfS memorandum, "Flugzeugprovokation gegen die Sowjetunion am 31. August 1983," 28 Sept. 1983, BStU, ZOS, no. 2654.

206. Matlock-Vishnevskiĭ memorandum of conversation, 11 Oct. 1983, RRPL, JFMF, box 2, folder: "October 1983 2"; Matlock diary entry, 11 Oct. 1983, RRBML, JRMP, box 1, folder: "1983 2."

207. Bush to Shultz and Clark, "Meeting with President Koivisto of Finland," 26 Sept. 1983, RRPL, JFMF, box 1, folder: "September 1983." Bush's account makes it clear how taken aback the vice president was by this arrangement: "President Koivisto took a folded paper from his back pocket which turned out to be notes on things the Russians wanted him to observe while in Washington. Koivisto said that he had been

174   **NOTES TO PAGES 76–79**

asked to give an assessment [of the prospects of repairing US-Soviet relations, and in particular a summit] on his return."

208. Reagan-Koivisto memorandum of conversation, 27 Sept. 1983, RRPL, JFMF, box 1, folder: "September 1983."

209. Kriuchkov interview, 2007, LHCMA, BOA 3/5; Dobrynin, *Sugubo doveritel'no*, 568.

210. Hartman to Shultz, "US-Soviet Relations after KAL—the View from the Kremlin," 1 Oct. 1983, RRPL, JFMF, box 41, folder: "US-USSR Relations July–Aug. 1983 2."

211. Thatcher-Reagan memorandum of conversation, 29 Sept. 1983, NAUK, PREM 19/1153.

212. Matlock diary entires, 11–12 Oct. 1983, RRBML, JRMP, box 1, folder: "1983 2."

213. Stearman, *American Adventure*, 217.

214. Shultz, *Turmoil and Triumph*, 324–332.

215. Geraghty, *Peacekeepers at War*, 91–95.

216. Ronald Reagan, *American Life*, 451.

217. Ronald Reagan, *American Life*, 451.

218. CIA memorandum, "Soviet Thinking on the Possibility of Armed Confrontation with the United States," 30 Dec. 1983, RRPL, JFMF, box 3, folder: "January 1984 2."

219. Will, "The Price of Power," 142.

220. Raines, *Rucksack War*, 515–524.

221. Shakhnazarov memorandum, "Kommentarii po povodu agressii SShA protiv Grenady," 1983, AGF, fond 5, opis' 1, delo 17861.

222. Iakovlev-Hartman memorandum of conversation, 20 Oct. 1983, GARF, fond 10063, opis' 1, delo 101.

223. Shakhnazarov memorandum, "Kommentarii po povodu agressii SShA protiv Grenady," 1983, AGF, fond 5, opis' 1, delo 17861.

224. Cherniaev diary entry, 27 Oct. 1983, *Sovmestnyĭ iskhod*, 541.

225. Kolačkovský memorandum, "Záznam z besedy vel'vyslancov ZSS s 1. zástupcom vedúceho odboru informácií ÚV KSSZ s. Četverikovom N.N.," 10 Jan. 1984, AMZV, TOT, 1980–1989, SSSR, box 2, folder 9.

226. MID memorandum, "Informace o setkání A. A. Gromyka s ministrem zahraničních věcí NSR H.D. Genscherem, které se konalo 15. až 16. října 1983," Oct. 1983, AMZV, TOT, 1980–1989, SSSR, box 2, folder 8.

227. Shultz interview, 12 July 1989, SMML, DOP, box 3, folder 2.

228. Thatcher-Dam memorandum of conversation, 7 Nov. 1983, NAUK, PREM 19/1151.

229. KPSS memorandum, "Material k besede s G. Kolem," 4 June 1983, RGANI, fond 82, opis' 1, delo 37.

230. Dam to Reagan, "My Meeting with Dobrynin—May 5, 1983," RRPL, JFMF, box 22, folder: "USSR Diplomatic Contacts 3"; Kohl-Gromyko memorandum of conversation, 18 Jan. 1983, PAdAA, B 150/555.

231. CIA memorandum, "Soviet Strategy to Derail US INF Deployment," Feb. 1983, NARA, RG 263, PUC, box 17, folder 22355.

232. MfAA memorandum, "Information über die Entwicklung der Beziehungen zwischen der DDR und der UdSSR im Jahre 1983 sowie Schlußfolgerungen für ihre weitere Gestaltung," 1 Nov. 1983, PAdAA, M 1, ZR 1074/85; Mitrokhin notes, CAC, MITN 1/6/5; Savel'yev and Detinov, *Big Five*, 65–66.

NOTES TO PAGES 79–80

233. Mielke-Kriuchkov memorandum of conversation, 19 Sept. 1983, BStU, ZAIG, no. 5306.

234. Dobriansky to Clark, "Cable from Ambassador to Hartman," 28 Jan. 1983, RRPL, JFMF, box 22, folder: "USSR Diplomatic Contacts 2." Soviet intelligence understood this thinking from its sources in the West German government. MfS memorandum, "SPD-Einchatzungen zu den Ergebnissen der Reisen des SPD-Kanzlerkandidaten Vogel in die USA und die UdSSR," 1983, BStU, AS, no. 136/86.

235. Thatcher-Reagan memorandum of conversation, 29 Sept. 1983, NAUK, PREM 19/1153.

236. Kohl to Reagan, 1 Dec. 1983, PAdAA, B 150/582; Kohl, *Erinnerungen*, 2:191–202.

237. Karpov interview, 11 Jan. 1990, SMML, DOP, box 1, folder 10; Savel'yev and Detinov, *Big Five*, 67–68.

238. Genscher-Kvitsinskiĭ memorandum of conversation, 3 Feb. 1983, PAdAA, B 150/556.

239. MfS memorandum, "Aufstellung neuer amerikanischer Mittelstreckenraketen," 28 Nov. 1983, BStU, ZAIG, no. 7171.

240. Votintsev, "Neizvestnye voĭska ischeznuvsheĭ sverkhderzhavy," pt. 2, 34.

241. CIA memorandum, "Soviet Thinking on the Possibility of Armed Confrontation with the United States," 30 Dec. 1983, RRPL, JFMF, box 3, folder: "January 1984 2."

242. Aleksandrov-Agentov interview, 15 Jan. 1990, SMML, DOP, box 1, folder 2.

243. Reagan remarks, Williamsburg, Va., 31 May 1983, in Hill and Kevan, *Public Papers of the Presidents: Ronald Reagan, 1983*, 1:802. This echoed Andropov's reminder to Bush at Brezhnev's funeral that neither superpower should allow strong rhetoric for domestic consumption influence the substance of international relations.

244. Hänni, "Chance for a Propaganda Coup?," 116.

245. Reagan diary entry, 10 Oct. 1983, in Brinkley, *The Reagan Diaries*, 1:273.

246. NSC memorandum, "Public Affairs Strategy for 'The Day After,'" RRPL, RFLF, box 12, folder: "Nuclear Weapons Effects."

247. SED memorandum, "Gespräch des Honecker mit der Delegation des Repräsentantenhauses des USA-Kongress," 10 Jan. 1986, SAPMO, DY 30/2492.

248. Franke and Schiltz, "'They Don't Really Care about Us!,'" 117.

249. MNO memorandum, no. 1 (294), "Podzimní série cvičení ozbrojených sil NATO 'AUTUMN FORGE-83,'" 1984, ABS, ZSGŠ, PM, box 117.

250. Halliday, *Making of the Second Cold War*.

251. Andrew and Gordievsky, *KGB*, 492–507; Brook-Shepherd, *Storm Birds*, 266–279; Gordievsky, *Next Stop Execution*, 272. This interpretation has become standard in accounts of the Cold War during the early 1980s. Ambinder, *The Brink*, 194–201; Brands, *What Good Is Grand Strategy?*, 104; Cimbala, "Revisiting the Nuclear 'War Scare' of 1983," 234–253; DiCicco, "Fear, Loathing, and Cracks in Reagan's Mirror Images," 253–274; Downing, *1983*, 222–249; Jones, *Able Archer 83*, 1–59; Beth Fischer, *Reagan Reversal*, 122–140; Gaddis, *Strategies of Containment*, 360; Hoffman, *Dead Hand*, 94–100; Manchanda, "When Truth is Stranger than Fiction," 111–133; Mann, *Rebellion of Ronald Reagan*, 42, 77; Oberdorfer, *From the Cold War to a New Era*, 65–68; Pry, *War Scare*, 33–44; Rossinow, *Reagan Era*, 101–118; Scott, "Intelligence and the Risk of Nuclear War," 5–23; Suri, "Explaining the End of the Cold War," 63–72; Wilson, *Triumph of Improvisation*, 78–81; Winik, *On the Brink*, 289–291.

176 **NOTES TO PAGES 80–82**

252. Barras, "Able Archer 83"; Kramer, "Die Nicht-Krise um 'Able Archer 1983'"; Mastny, "How Able Was 'Able Archer'? "; Miles, "War Scare That Wasn't."

253. MNO memorandum, no. 3 (243), "Podzimní série cvičení ozbrojených sil NATO 'AUTUMN FORGE-80,'" 1980, ABS, ZSGŠ, PM, box 103; NVA memorandum, "Aufklärungssammelbericht zum zur Kommandostabsübung 'Able Archer 81' im Bereich des NATO-Oberkommandos Europa vom 02.11.1981 bis 06.11.1981," 17 Nov. 1981, MA, DVW 1/94228.

254. MNO memorandum, no. 1 (294), "Podzimní série cvičení ozbrojených sil NATO 'AUTUMN FORGE-83,'" 1984, ABS, ZSGŠ, PM, box 117; MfNV memorandum, "Information über die bevorstehende strategische NATO-Kommandostabsübung 'Wintex/Cimex 83,'" MA, DVW 1/94469.

255. Hoffmann to Honecker, 14 Sept. 1983, MA, DVW 1/115702; Cherkashin interview, 2007, LHCMA, BOA 3/1.

256. MfNV memorandum, "Information über die bevorstehende strategische NATO-Kommandostabsübung 'Wintex/Cimex 83,'" MA, DVW 1/94469.

257. Barrass, "Able Archer 83," 19; Wolf, *Man without a Face*, 299–301.

258. Cherkashin, *Spy Handler*, 144; Cherkashin interview, 2007, LHCMA, BOA 3/1. Cherkashin was at the time the KGB handler of two of the United States' worst traitors, Aldrich Ames and Robert Hanssen.

259. MNO memorandum, no. 1 (294), "Podzimní série cvičení ozbrojených sil NATO 'AUTUMN FORGE-83,'" 1984, ABS, ZSGŠ, PM, box 117.

260. Esin interview, 2007, LHCMA, BOA 2/1.

261. Danilevich interview, 18 Dec. 1990, in Hines, Mishulovich, and Shull, *Soviet Intentions, 1965–1985*, 2:26; Danilevich interview, 24 Sept. 1992, in Hines, Mishulovich, and Shull, *Soviet Intentions, 1965–1985*, 2:42.

262. Smirnoff interview, 2007, LHCMA, BOA 2/5.

263. Kondratiev interview, 2007, LHCMA, BOA 3/2.

264. Wohlforth, *Witnesses to the End of the Cold War*, 72–73; Barrass, *Great Cold War*, 300; Garthoff, "Soviet Leaders, Soviet Intelligence, and Changing Views of the United States," 45.

265. Barrass, *Great Cold War*, 301.

266. Batenin interview, 6 Aug. 1993, in Hines, Mishulovich, and Shull, *Soviet Intentions, 1965–1985*, 2:8; Kriuchkov interview, 2007, LHCMA, BOA 3/5; Lehman, *Oceans Ventured*, 129.

267. Benjamin Fischer, "Scolding Intelligence," 107; Hart, "Soviet Approaches to Crisis Management."

268. SNIE, no. 11-10-84/JX, "Implications of Recent Soviet Military-Political Activities," NARA, CREST, doc. CIA-RDP09T00367R000300330001-9. A later assessment by the president's Foreign Intelligence Advisory Board disputes these sanguine conclusions. PFIAB memorandum, "The Soviet 'War Scare,'" 15 Feb. 1990, GBPL, PR, PFIAB, SF, OA/ID 85010, folder: "War Scare Report 1990."

269. Ermarth, "Observations on the 'War Scare' of 1983."

270. McFarlane interview, 18 Oct. 1989, SMML, DOP, box 2, folder 22.

271. Reagan diary entry, 18 Nov. 1983, in Brinkley, *The Reagan Diaries*, 1:289–290. Reagan went on to wonder "what the [hell] have they got that anyone would want?"

272. Ronald Reagan, *American Life*, 588–589.

273. Deaver interview, 8 May 1990, SMML, DOP, box 2, folder 12.

NOTES TO PAGES 82–86   177

274. Meeting record, 19 Nov. 1983, RRPL, JFMF, box 34, folder: "Saturday Group Notes Nov.–Dec. 1983."

275. Artizov and Tomilina, *Andropov*, 224.

276. Pikhoia, *Sovetskiĭ soiuz*, 376; Volkogonov, *Sem' vozhdeĭ*, 2:136.

277. Wright to Howe, "Mr. Heseltine's Meeting with Shultz," 15 Sept. 1983, NAUK, PREM 19/1404.

278. Genscher-Semenov memorandum of conversation, 17 Dec. 1984, PAdAA, B 150/609.

279. Hermes memorandum, "Andropov," 13 Dec. 1983, PAdAA, B 150/583.

280. Shultz, *Turmoil and Triumph*, 266–267.

4. Trial Balloons

1. Church, "Men of the Year," 16–35.

2. Elson and Muller, "Some Practical and Realistic Advice," 38–40. In a similar vein, the *Bulletin of the Atomic Scientists* moved the hands of its "doomsday clock," a representation of the threat of nuclear war, forward by one minute, pronouncing it a mere three minutes to midnight. Holdren, Holloway, and Shapley, "Three Minutes to Midnight," 2.

3. Jamieson to Trudeau, "Callaghan Visit to USSR," 25 Oct. 1983, LAC, RG 25, vol. 25336, file 28-6-1-TRUDEAU PEACE MISSION, pt. 3.

4. Bothwell and Granatstein, *Pirouette*, 363.

5. Zemtsov, *Chernenko*, 197.

6. Kohl to Andropov, 14 Dec. 1983, PAdAA, B 150/583; MAÉ memorandum, "Relations est-ouest," 19 Nov. 1984, AD, 1930 INVA/5856, folder: "Notes du département."

7. Caldicott, *A Desperate Passion*, 214.

8. On Mondale's electoral challenge and critiques of the Reagan administration, particularly regarding foreign policy, see Miles, "Domestic Politics of Superpower Rapprochement."

9. Cobb to Clark, "Soviet-American Relations at the Crossroads," 9 June 1983, RRPL, WPCF, box 9, folder: "US-Soviet Relations Papers 8."

10. Matlock diary entry, 12 Oct. 1983, RRBML, JRMP, box 1, folder: "1983 2"; Matlock to Kimmitt, "Draft Speech by Deputy Secretary Dam," 27 Oct. 1983, RRPL, JMP, box 2, folder: "October 1983 3."

11. Meeting record, 19 Nov. 1983, RRPL, JFMF, box 34, folder: "Saturday Group Notes Nov.–Dec. 1983."

12. Shultz to Reagan, "Speech on US-Soviet Relations," RRPL, JFMF, box 41, folder: "US-USSR Relations Jul.–Aug. 1983 1."

13. Clark to Reagan, "Proposed Speech on US-Soviet Relations," 23 Aug. 1983, RRPL, JFMF, box 41, folder: "US-USSR Relations Jul.–Aug. 1983 2."

14. Deaver and McFarlane to Reagan, "Your Speech on US-Soviet Relations," 5 Jan. 1984, RRPL, JFMF, box 31, folder: "Presidential Address US-Soviet Relations Background Materials 1."

15. Fortier to McFarlane, "Soviet Speech," 7 Jan. 1984, RRPL, JFMF, box 31, folder: "Presidential Address US-Soviet Relations."

16. Matlock diary entry, 7 Jan. 1984, RRBML, JRMP, box 1, folder: "1984 Jan.–Mar."

178   NOTES TO PAGES 86–88

17. NSC memorandum, "Decision Measures: US Policy to Soviet Violations," 6 Jan. 1984, RRPL, ES–NSC, MF, box 10, folder: "NSC #99 1."

18. Reagan diary entry, 9 Jan. 1984, in Brinkley, *The Reagan Diaries*, 1:306; Matlock diary entry, 9 Jan. 1984, RRBML, JRMP, box 1, folder: "1984 Jan.–Mar."

19. Reagan diary entry, 6 Jan. 1984, in Brinkley, *The Reagan Diaries*, 1:305.

20. Matlock to McFarlane, "Action Plan for President's Speech," 12 Jan. 1984, RRPL, JFMF, box 31, folder: "Presidential Address US-Soviet Relations Background Materials 4"; Matlock diary entries, 13–14 Jan. 1984, RRBML, JRMP, box 1, folder: "1984 Jan.–Mar."

21. Thatcher-Shultz memorandum of conversation, 15 Jan. 1984, NAUK, PREM 19/1656.

22. Matlock diary entry, 9 Jan. 1984, RRBML, JRMP, box 1, folder: "1984 Jan.–Mar."

23. Shultz to Reagan, "My Meeting with Dobrynin, January 3, 1983," 4 Jan. 1984, RRPL, JFMF, box 31, folder: "Presidential Address US-Soviet Relations Background Materials 2"; Matlock to McFarlane, "Draft Presidential Letter to Andropov," 19 Dec. 1983, RRPL, JFMF, box 2, folder: "December 1983 2."

24. Matlock diary entry, 3 Jan. 1984, RRBML, JRMP, box 1, folder: "1984 Jan.–Mar."; Ezell and Ezell, *The Partnership*, 317–357.

25. Reagan diary entry, 6 Jan. 1984, in Brinkley, *The Reagan Diaries*, 1:305; Reagan diary entry, 16 Jan. 1984, in Brinkley, *The Reagan Diaries*, 1:308–309; Vernier-Palliez to Cheysson, "Relations américano-soviétiques—discours du Président Reagan," 16 Jan. 1984, AD, 1930 INVA/5671, folder: "URSS-USA 1984."

26. Reagan remarks, Washington, D.C., 16 Jan. 1984, in Greene and Banks, *Public Papers of the Presidents: Ronald Reagan, 1984*, 1:40–44.

27. NSC memorandum, "Presidential Address: US-Soviet Relations," 6 Jan. 1984, RRPL, JFMF, box 3, folder: "January 1984 1." The memorandum is marked "RR's changes" at the top.

28. Matlock, *Reagan and Gorbachev*, 83.

29. Reagan diary entry, 16 Jan. 1984, in Brinkley, *The Reagan Diaries*, 1:308–309.

30. Hill to McFarlane, "Further Foreign Reaction to the President's Speech on US-Soviet Relations," 19 Jan. 1984, RRPL, JFMF, box 3, folder: "January 1984 2."

31. Trudeau to Reagan, 19 Jan. 1984, LAC, RG 25, vol. 26956, file 28-6-1-TRUDEAU PEACE MISSION, pt. 23.

32. Hill to McFarlane, "International Reaction to President's Speech on US-Soviet Relations," 17 Jan. 1984, RRPL, JFMF, box 3, folder: "January 1984 2." Most Eastern European countries followed the Soviet line, though the Hungarian press printed the president's speech without commentary, which the White House saw as a positive step.

33. Hill to McFarlane, "International Reaction to President's Speech on US-Soviet Relations," 17 Jan. 1984, RRPL, JFMF, box 3, folder: "January 1984 2."

34. Shultz-Gromyko memorandum of conversation, 18 Jan. 1984, RRPL, JFMF, box 3, folder: "January 1984 3"; Matlock diary entry, 18 Jan. 1984, RRBML, JRMP, box 1, folder: "1984 Jan.–Mar."

35. MacEachen-Gromyko memorandum of conversation, 19 Jan. 1984, LAC, RG 25, vol. 8800, file 20-1-2-USSR, pt. 47.

36. MZV memorandum, "Informace o setkání A.A. Gromyka se státním tajemníkem USA G. Shultzem," 10 Feb. 1984, NAČR, fond 1261/0/8, box P96/83, folder I4.

37. Dobrynin, *Sugubo doveritel'no*, 573–574.

NOTES TO PAGES 88–90   179

38. Iakovlev memorandum, "Deciatiletie trudnoe i trevozhnoe," 1984, GARF, fond 10063, opis' 1, delo 114.

39. Aleksandrov-Agentov interview, 15 Jan. 1990, SMML, DOP, box 1, folder 2.

40. Adamishin diary entry, 20 Feb. 1984, HIA, ALAP, box 1, folder: "1984."

41. Shultz to Reagan, "My Meeting with Dobrynin, January 30," 30 Jan. 1984, RRPL, RCMF, box 4, folder: "Soviet Union Sensitive File 1984."

42. Andropov to Reagan, 28 Jan. 1984, RRPL, ES–NSC, HSF, box 38, folder: "Andropov 8391507, 8490115"; McFarlane to Reagan, "Letter from Andropov and Shultz Meeting with Dobrynin," RRPL, RCMF, box 4, folder: "Soviet Union Sensitive File 1984."

43. McFarlane to Reagan, "Letter from Andropov and Shultz Meeting with Dobrynin," RRPL, RCMF, box 4, folder: "Soviet Union Sensitive File 1984."

44. Aronson to Mondale, 29 Dec. 1981, MNHS, WFMP, loc. 146.L.10.1B, folder: "Aronson, Bernie."

45. Mondale campaign memorandum, "Debate Materials," 1984, MNHS, WFMP, loc. 146.L.9.1B, folder: "Briefing Book Part 2-I."

46. Mondale remarks, Chicago Council on Foreign Relations, Chicago, Ill., 14 Mar. 1984, MNHS, WFMP, loc. 146.L.9.7B, folder: "Platform Briefing Materials Book."

47. Mondale remarks, George Washington University, Washington, D.C., 25 Sept. 1984, MNHS, WFMP, loc. 148.J.17.10F, folder: "Mondale / Ferraro Issue Papers Book."

48. Beth Fischer, *Reagan Reversal*, 51–57.

49. Mondale remarks, George Washington University, Washington, D.C., 25 Sept. 1984, MNHS, WFMP, loc. 148.J.17.10F, folder: "Mondale / Ferraro Issue Papers Book."

50. Reagan diary entry, 16 Jan. 1984, in Brinkley, *The Reagan Diaries*, 1:308–309.

51. Brands, *Making the Unipolar Moment*, 94; Beth Fischer, *Reagan Reversal*, 141–143; Mann, *Rebellion of Ronald Reagan*, 78–81; Wilson, *Triumph of Improvisation*, 81–86.

52. Reagan remarks, Versailles, France, 21 May 1982, in Greene, Mellody, and Payne, *Public Papers of the Presidents: Ronald Reagan, 1982*, 1:697–698.

53. Nancy Reagan, *My Turn*, 63.

54. Shultz interview, 13 July 1989, SMML, DOP, box 3, folder 2.

55. Pikhoia, *Moskva, Kreml', vlast'*, 678; Hartman to Shultz, "The Soviet Union Under Andropov: A Year Later," 15 Nov. 1983, RRPL, JFMF, box 20, folder: "Andropov 4."

56. Matlock diary entry, 6 Feb. 1984, RRBML, JRMP, box 1, folder: "1984 Jan.–Mar."

57. Pribytkov, *Apparat*, 131; Zemtsov, *Chernenko*, 190.

58. Gorbachev, *Naedine s soboĭ*, 355; Roĭ Medvedev, *Iuriĭ Andropov*, 406; Prozorov, *Rassekrechennyĭ Andropov*, 67; Sidorenko, *Andropov*, 198; Volkogonov, *Sem' vozhdeĭ*, 2:199.

59. Taubman, *Gorbachev*, 191.

60. Zemtsov, *Chernenko*, 178–186.

61. Pribytkov, *Apparat*, 199–200.

62. Prozorov, *Rassekrechennyĭ Andropov*, 68; Gromyko, *Andreĭ Gromyko*, 25.

63. Gorbachev remarks, KPSS Central Committee Plenum, Moscow, Soviet Union, 10 Dec. 1984, in Gorbachev, *Sobranie sochineniĭ*, 2:77–114.

64. Pikhoia, *Moskva, Kreml', vlast'*, 683–685; Taubman, *Gorbachev*, 190.

65. Gorbachev, *Naedine s soboĭ*, 395.

66. Aleksandrov-Agentov, *Ot Kollontaĭ do Gorbacheva*, 283–284; Clark, *Crime and Punishment in Soviet Officialdom*, 196–197; Ryzhkov, *Perestroĭka*, 58.

180   **NOTES TO PAGES 90–92**

67. Ryzhkov, *Perestroĭka*, 54–57; Zemtsov, *Chernenko*, 186–189; Volkogonov, *Sem' vozhdeĭ*, 2:201–202.

68. Taubman, *Gorbachev*, 192.

69. Cherniaev diary entry, 14 Feb. 1984, in Cherniaev, *Sovmestnyĭ iskhod*, 550–553.

70. Pribytkov, *Apparat*, 64–65.

71. Pikhoia, *Moskva, Kreml', vlast'*, 698.

72. Matlock diary entry, 10 Feb. 1984, RRBML, JRMP, box 1, folder: "1984 Jan.–Mar."

73. Odom to Marsh, "More on Andropov's Successor," 10 Feb. 1984, LOC, WEOP, box 14, folder 25.

74. Service, *End of the Cold War*, 104–105.

75. Cherniaev diary entry, 30 Jan. 1985, in Cherniaev, *Sovmestnyĭ iskhod*, 597–598; Pribytkov interview, 25 June 1990, BLPES, 2RR 1/1/9.

76. Zimyanin interview, 14 July 1990, BLPES, 2RR 1/1/3; Volkogonov, *Sem' vozhdeĭ*, 2:203–204; Gromyko, *Andreĭ Gromyko*, 129.

77. CIA memorandum, "Andropov's Legacy and the Future," 10 Feb. 1984, NARA, CREST, doc. CIA-RDP90B01370R000100130012-4.

78. CIA memorandum, "USSR: Economic Projections Through 1990—a New Look," Feb. 1984, NARA, RG 263, PUC, box 12, folder 21926.

79. Pikhoia, *Moskva, Kreml', vlast'*, 699.

80. Matlock diary entry, 6 Apr. 1984, RRBML, JRMP, box 1, folder: "1984 Apr.–May"

81. Volkogonov, *Sem' vozhdeĭ*, 2:205.

82. Adamishin diary entry, 21 Aug. 1984, HIA, ALAP, box 1, folder: "1984."

83. NVA memorandum, "Bericht über die Wichtigsten Ergebnisse der 15. Sitzung des Komitees der Verteidigungsminister der Teilnehmerstaaten des Warschauer Vertrages in Prag," Nov. 1983, MA, DVW 1/71040.

84. MNO memorandum, "Operační závěry o možnostech použití ozbrojených sil států NATO na středoevropském válčišti a proti ČSSR," 1983, ABS, ZSGŠ, PM, box 114.

85. NVA memorandum, "Protokoll der Sitzung des Komitees der Verteidigungsminister der Teilnehmerstaaten des Warschauer Vertrages," 7 Dec. 1983, MA, DVW 1/71041; NVA memorandum, "Über die Einführung neuer Bewaffnung und Militärtechnik in den Armeen der Teilnehmerstaaten des Warschauer Vertrages," Nov. 1983, MA, DVW 1/71040; Zemtsov, *Chernenko*, 297.

86. Ivashov, "Dostizhenie voenno-tekhnicheskogo prevoskhodstva nad fashistskoĭ Germanieĭ vazhneĭshiĭ faktor pobedy v Velikoĭ Otechestvennoĭ voĭne," 42. US analysts thought very little of Eastern efforts to improve the technological sophistication of their militaries. Odom to Marshall, 15 Oct. 1984, LOC, WEOP, pt. 1, box 14, folder 22.

87. Ronald Reagan, *American Life*, 592.

88. Hartman to Shultz, "Konstantin Chernenko as General Secretary: His Role, Views and Prospects," 13 Feb. 1984, RRPL, JFMF, box 21, folder: "Chernenko 1"; Odom to Marsh, "More on Andropov's Successor," 10 Feb. 1984, LOC, WEOP, box 14, folder 25; Matlock diary entry, 16 Feb. 1984, RRBML, JRMP, box 1, folder: "1984 Jan.–Mar."

89. KPSS Politburo meeting record, 23 Feb. 1984, LOC, DAVP, box 25, folder 4; Zemtsov, *Chernenko*, 283–286, 291.

90. Aleksandrov-Agentov, *Ot Kollontaĭ do Gorbacheva*, 284. Though he did not have this in mind, in practice it meant a general secretary reliant on large-print, preprepared statements. Volkogonov, *Sem' vozhdeĭ*, 2:247; Zemtsov, *Chernenko*, 207–209.

91. Shultz to Reagan, "Substantive Approach to New Soviet Leadership," RRPL, JFMF, box 20, folder: "Andropov 2"; Matlock diary entry, 6 Feb. 1984, RRBML, JRMP, box 1, folder: "1984 Jan.–Mar."

92. Ronald Reagan, *American Life*, 592. Reagan's decision suited those members of the NSC who warned of the "deleterious consequences" of him traveling to Moscow and "coddling" the Soviets. Lenczowski to McFarlane, "Andropov's Funeral and US-Soviet Relations," 10 Feb. 1984, RRPL, JFMF, box 20, folder: "Andropov 2."

93. Matlock, *Reagan and Gorbachev*, 87.

94. Matlock diary entry, 5 Mar. 1984, RRBML, JRMP, box 1, folder: "1984 Jan.–Mar."; Hartman to Shultz, "Andropov Funeral: Chernenko Bilaterals," 15 Feb. 1984, RRPL, JFMF, box 21, folder: "Chernenko 1." This was all the more surprising as, until recently, Western policy makers believed that Andropov's wife had predeceased her husband. Hill to McFarlane, "Soviet New Year's Greetings to President and Mrs. Reagan," 30 Dec. 1983, RRPL, JFMF, box 3, folder: "January 1984 1."

95. Zemtsov, *Chernenko*, 194–195; Matlock diary entry, 14 Feb. 1984, RRBML, JRMP, box 1, folder: "1984 Jan.–Mar."

96. Chernenko-Bush memorandum of conversation, 14 Feb. 1984, RGANI, fond 83, opis' 1, delo 190; Bush to Reagan, "My Meeting with Chernenko, February 14, 1984," 15 Feb. 1984, GBPL, VPR, NSA, DPGF, FTF, OA/ID 19807, folder: "Vice President's Trip to Europe and the USSR: Post-Trip."

97. Reagan to Chernenko, 11 Feb. 1984, RRPL, ES–NSC, HSF, box 39, folder: "Chernenko 8401238."

98. Reagan remarks, Rancho del Cielo, Santa Barbara, Calif., 11 Feb. 1984, in Greene and Banks, *Public Papers of the Presidents: Ronald Reagan, 1984*, 1:191–192.

99. Kohl-Chernenko memorandum of conversation, 14 Feb. 1984, PAdAA, B 150/587; Thatcher-Chernenko memorandum of conversation, 14 Feb. 1984, NAUK, PREM 19/1646; Chernenko-Trudeau memorandum of conversation, 15 Feb. 1984, RGANI, fond 83, opis' 1, delo 167.

100. Bush to Reagan, "My Meeting with Chernenko, February 14, 1984," 15 Feb. 1984, GBPL, VPR, NSA, DPGF, FTF, OA/ID 19807, folder: "Vice President's Trip to Europe and the USSR: Post-Trip."

101. Chernenko-Castro memorandum of conversation, 15 Feb. 1984, RGANI, fond 83, opis' 1, delo 178; KPSS memorandum, "O polozhenii na Kube i sovetsko-kubinskikh otnosheniiakh," RGANI, fond 83, opis' 1, delo 178.

102. MID memorandum, "Über die Gespräche Tschernenkos mit Bush, Kohl, Maroy, und Thatcher anlässlich der Ablebens von Andropow," 22 Feb. 1984, SAPMO, DY 30/IV 2/2.035/70.

103. Zagladin-Matlock memorandum of conversation, 15 Feb. 1984, AGF, fond 3, opis' 1, delo 15130; Matlock-Zagladin memorandum of conversation, 15 Feb. 1984, RRPL, RCMF, box 4, folder: "Soviet Union Sensitive File 1984."

104. Matlock diary entry, 15 Feb. 1984, RRBML, JRMP, box 1, folder: "1984 Jan.–Mar."

105. Chernenko to Reagan, 23 Feb. 1984, RRPL, ES–NSC, HSF, box 39, folder: "Chernenko 8490236, 8490283, 8490304."

106. Matlock memorandum, "US-Soviet Relations: A Framework for the Future," RRPL, JFMF, box 3, folder: "February 1984 2"; Matlock diary entry, 2 Mar. 1984, RRBML, JRMP, box 1, folder: "1984 Jan.–Mar."

182 **NOTES TO PAGES 93-95**

107. Heseltine-Weinberger memorandum of conversation, 28 Feb. 1984, NAUK, PREM 19/1404.

108. Matlock memorandum, "US-Soviet Relations: A Framework for the Future," RRPL, JFMF, box 3, folder: "February 1984 2."

109. Bearg Dyke to Bush, "Talking Points for Meeting with Dr. Billy Graham," 25 Feb. 1982, GBPL, VPR, NSA, DPGF, CF, OA/ID 19771, folder: "USSR 1982: Billy Graham Visit to Moscow."

110. Wacker, *America's Pastor*, 239–241.

111. Pipes to Clark, "Response to Armand Hammer Letter," 17 Mar. 1982, RRPL, REPF, box 13, folder: "03/17/1982."

112. Weinberg, *Armand Hammer*, 44, 317–328.

113. Shultz to Reagan, "Forthcoming Visits to Moscow," 19 Mar. 1984, RRPL, JFMF, box 3, folder: "March 1984 3"; Colbourn, "Defining Détente," 259–271.

114. Aleksandrov-Agentov, *Ot Kollontaĭ do Gorbacheva*, 286; Vorotnikov, *A bylo eto tak*, 53; Volkogonov, *Sem' vozhdeĭ*, vol. 2, 247; Zemtsov, *Chernenko*, 231, 296–297.

115. CIA memorandum, "Allied Responses to a Soviet Invasion of Poland," 10 Dec. 1980, JCPL, RAC, doc. NLC-2-33-5-1-7.

116. Tarasiuk memorandum, "O pozitsiĭ Kanady po osnovnym voprosam, rassmatrivavshimsia v khode raboty 38-ĭ sessii General'noĭ Assemblei OON," 12 Apr. 1984, HDAMZS, fond 1, opis' 3, sprava 5107; Iakovlev, *Sumerki*, 350.

117. Head and Trudeau, *Canadian Way*, 295–296.

118. Bothwell, *Your Country, My Country*, 2.

119. Trudeau remarks, University of Guelph, Guelph, Ont., 27 Oct. 1983, *Department of External Affairs Statements and Speeches*, no. 83/18.

120. Colbourn, "'Cruising toward Nuclear Danger,'" 30; Colbourn, "The Elephant in the Room."

121. Dam to Reagan, "Your Meeting with Pierre Elliott Trudeau, Prime Minister of Canada, December 15, 1983," 12 Dec. 1983, RRPL, ESAD–NSC, box 1, folder: "Canada 12/83"; Trudeau-Reagan memorandum of conversation, 15 Dec. 1983, LAC, RG 25, vol. 25338, file 28-6-1-TRUDEAU PEACE MISSION, pt. 16; Reagan diary entry, 15 Dec. 1984, in Brinkley, *The Reagan Diaries*, 1:298–299.

122. John English, *Life of Pierre Elliott Trudeau*, 2:600.

123. DEA memorandum, "Eagleburger's Remarks on PM Trudeau Peace Initiative," 22 Dec. 1983, LAC, RG 25, vol. 25339, file 28-6-1-TRUDEAU PEACE MISSION, pt. 18.

124. Delvoie interview, 6 Oct. 1987, in Bothwell and Granatstein, *Trudeau's World*, 357.

125. Delworth interview, 26 Oct. 1987 and 19 Feb. 1988, in Bothwell and Granatstein, *Trudeau's World*, 368. This was a play on the French term for their nuclear arsenal, the force de frappe.

126. John English, *Life of Pierre Elliott Trudeau*, 2:602–603.

127. Brunet to François-Poncet, "Voyage à Moscou de M. Genscher," 30 Mar. 1981, AD, 1930 INVA/4906, folder: "Dossier générale"; Genscher-Gromyko memorandum of conversation, 5 Oct. 1982, PAdAA, B 150/546.

128. Černý memorandum, "Politika NSR a situace v sovětsko-západoněmeckých vztazích," 21 June 1982, AMZV, TOT, 1980–1989, SSSR, box 1, folder 5; Vogel to Gen-

NOTES TO PAGES 95–97   183

scher, "Ihre Einladung durch AM Gromyko zu einem Besuch der SU am 21. und 22.05.1984," 9 Mar. 1984, PAdAA, B 150/589.

129. Roßbach memorandum, "Schreiben des Bundeskanzlers an Generalsekretär Tschernenko," 23 Mar. 1984, BA, B 136/30420.

130. Kastl memorandum, "Tischrede Gromyko am 21.5.1984," 21 May 1984, BA, B 136/30154.

131. Meyer-Landrut memorandum, "1. Besuchstag—Übersicht," 21 May 1984, BA, B 136/30154.

132. Kastl memorandum, "2. Delegationsgespräch—thematische Übersicht," 23 May 1984, BA, B 136/30154.

133. Chernenko-Genscher memorandum of conversation, 22 May 1984, RGANI, fond 83, opis' 1, delo 193; Genscher-Chernenko memorandum of conversation, 22 May 1984, PAdAA, B 150/595; Meyer-Landrut memorandum, "Gespräch BM–GS Tschernenko," 22 May 1984, BA, B 136/30154.

134. Wieck memorandum, "Unterrichtung des NATO-Rats am 25.05.1984," 25 May 1984, BA, B 136/30154.

135. Genscher to Shultz, 23 May 1984, PAdAA, B 150/595.

136. DFA memorandum, "Briefing Notes on Bilateral Relations for Mr. Bill Hayden MP, Minister for Foreign Affairs: Visit to Europe and the Soviet Union, 11 May–2 June 1984," May 1984, NAA, series A2539, no. B1984/000277.

137. Hawke, *The Hawke Memoirs*, 204.

138. Laurie to Costello, "Mr. Hayden's Visit to Moscow," 9 Apr. 1984, NAA, series A1838, no. 69/1/3/6/22, pt. 1.

139. Laurie to Pocock, 26 July 1984, NAA, series A1838, no. 69/1/3/6/22, pt. 4.

140. Hayden to Shultz, NAA, series A1838, no. 69/1/3/6/22, pt. 4.

141. MID memorandum, "Information über die Einschatzung der Ergebnisse des offiziellen besucht des Außenministers Australiens, W. Hayden, in der Sowjetunion vom 26. Mai bis 2. Juni 1984," 7 June 1984, SAPMO, DY 30/IV 2/2.035/68.

142. Thatcher-Haig memorandum of conversation, 10 Apr. 1981, NAUK, PREM 19/944. "I am very unhappy indeed," Thatcher had remarked on a memorandum encouraging the intensification of Anglo-Soviet contacts in early 1981. Walden to Alexander, "Anglo-Soviet Contacts," 16 Mar. 1981, NAUK, PREM 19/926.

143. Thatcher, *Downing Street Years*, 451.

144. Coles to Fall, "Policy on East/West Relations," 12 Sept. 1983, NAUK, PREM 19/1033.

145. FCO memorandum, "Visit of the Prime Minister to Hungary: 2–4 February 1984," 26 Jan. 1984, NAUK, PREM 19/1534.

146. Thatcher, *Downing Street Years*, 454–455.

147. Thatcher-Lázár memorandum of conversation, 9:15–10:05, 3 Feb. 1984, NAUK, PREM 19/1534.

148. Thatcher-Lázár memorandum of conversation, 10:10–11:20, 3 Feb. 1984, NAUK, PREM 19/1534.

149. Thatcher-Kádár memorandum of conversation, 3 Feb. 1984, NAUK, PREM 19/1534.

150. Chernenko-Kádár memorandum of conversation, 13 July 1984, RGANI, fond 83, opis' 1, delo 144.

184   **NOTES TO PAGES 97–99**

151. Thatcher to Reagan, 8 Feb. 1984, NAUK, PREM 19/1534.

152. Howe, *Conflict of Loyalty*, 353.

153. Sutherland to Howe, "Your Visit to Moscow, 1–3 July: General Impressions," 3 July 1984, NAUK, PREM 19/1394.

154. Sutherland to Howe, "Secretary of State's Visit to Moscow: First Session of Talks with Gromyko," 2 July 1984, NAUK, PREM 19/1394.

155. Sutherland to Howe, "Secretary of State's Visit to Moscow: Gromyko's Speech on East/West and Anglo/Soviet Relations," 2 July 1984, NAUK, PREM 19/1394.

156. Sutherland to Howe, "Your Visit to Moscow, 1–3 July: General Impressions," 3 July 1984, NAUK, PREM 19/1394.

157. Bishop to Broomfield, "A View of Chernenko on 3 July 1984," 4 July 1984, NAUK, PREM 19/1394.

158. Grosser, "Serrer le jeu sans le fermer," 253.

159. Hibbert to Bullard, 22 Dec. 1981, NAUK, FCO 28/4358; Arnaud to Cheysson, "Plan d'action," 22 Sept. 1982, AD, 1930 INVA/5690, folder: "Plan d'action."

160. Petrie to Howe, "Mitterrand: East/West and Defence Issues," 17 Nov. 1983, NAUK, PREM 19/1182.

161. Thatcher-Mitterrand memorandum of conversation, 23 Jan. 1984, NAUK, PREM 19/1242.

162. Matlock memorandum, "Talking Points for Mitterrand," RRPL, JFMF, box 4, folder: "April 1984 2"; MAÉ memorandum, "Situation au Kremlin, fin 1984," 30 Nov. 1984, AD, 1930 INVA/5617, folder: "Déroulement des évènements, 1984."

163. Chernenko-Mitterrand memorandum of conversation, 21 June 1984, RGANI, fond 83, opis' 1, delo 204; Mitterrand-Chernenko memorandum of conversation, 21 June 1984, AD, 1930 INVA/5698, folder: "Visite de M. François Mitterrand en URSS."

164. MAÉ memorandum, "Sommet franco-soviétique: quelques impressions sur les dirigeants soviétiques," 28 June 1984, AN, 5 AG 4/PM/98, folder 1; Védrine, *Les mondes de François Mitterrand*, 266.

165. Arnaud to Cheysson, "Visite de M. le Président de la République en Union Soviétique: information des Dix," 22 June 1984, AD, 1930 INVA/5698, folder: "Visite de M. François Mitterrand en URSS."

166. Arnot memorandum, "Akzentverschiebungen in der sowjetischen Westpolitik," 18 July 1984, BA, B 136/27052.

167. Volkogonov, *Sem' vozhdeĭ*, 2:249–250.

168. Volkogonov, *Sem' vozhdeĭ*, 2:249–250; Zemtsov, *Chernenko*, 230–231, 285–286, 290–292.

169. Meeting record, "Private Meeting on US-Soviet Relations," 2 Mar. 1984, RRPL, JFMF, box 42, folder: "US-USSR Relations Mar. 1984 1."

170. Reagan diary entry, 2 Mar. 1984, in Brinkley, *The Reagan Diaries*, 1:324.

171. Matlock diary entry, 22 Feb. 1984, RRBML, JRMP, box 1, folder: "1984 Jan.–Mar."; McFarlane interview, 18 Oct. 1989, SMML, DOP, box 2, folder 22.

172. Axen-Burt memorandum of conversation, 21 Feb. 1984, SAPMO, DY 30/13660.

173. Poindexter to Matlock, "John Lenczowski," 26 Mar. 1984, RRPL, JFMF, box 42, folder: "US-USSR Relations Mar. 1984 1."

174. Lenczowski to McFarlane, "Reactivation of US-USSR Environmental Agreement," 8 May 1984, RRPL, JFMF, box 4, folder: "May 1984 1."

NOTES TO PAGES 99–101   185

175. Matlock diary entry, 20 Mar. 1984, RRBML, JRMP, box 1, folder: "1984 Jan.–Mar."

176. Volkogonov, *Sem' vozhdeĭ*, 2:247.

177. Chernenko remarks, Moscow, Soviet Union, 2 Mar. 1984, in Chernenko, *Narod i partiia ediny*, 9–23.

178. Kornienko interview, 19 Jan. 1990, MML, DOP, box 1, folder 12; Dobrynin, *Sugubo doveritel'no*, 582.

179. Reagan to Chernenko, 16 Apr. 1984, RRPL, ES–NSC, HSF, box 39, folder: "Chernenko 8490448, 8490546." When Kohl visited Washington the month before, the two discussed a possible meeting with Chernenko. Kohl emphasized the Soviet sense of insecurity, dating back to World War II. In his diaries, Reagan noted that "they still preserve the tank traps and barb[ed] wire that show how close the Germans got to Moscow." Reagan diary entry, 5 Mar. 1984, in Brinkley, *The Reagan Diaries*, 1:325.

180. Matlock to McFarlane, "US-Soviet Relations: Thoughts on Where We Stand," 19 Mar. 1984, RRPL, JFMF, box 42, folder: "US-USSR Relations Mar. 1984 1"; Matlock diary entry, 19 Mar. 1984, RRBML, JRMP, box 1, folder: "1984 Jan.–Mar."

181. Matlock diary entry, 3 Apr. 1984, RRBML, JRMP, box 1, folder: "1984 Apr.–May."

182. Chazov, *Zdorov'e i vlast'*, 296.

183. Vorotnikov, *A bylo eto tak*, 48.

184. Zemtsov, *Chernenko*, 208.

185. Aleksandrov-Agentov, *Ot Kollontaĭ do Gorbacheva*, 285.

186. Pribytkov, *Apparat*, 135; Zemtsov, *Chernenko*, 283.

187. Shakhnazarov, *S vozhdiami i bez nikh*, 235.

188. Cherniaev diary entry, 7 Dec. 1983, in Cherniaev, *Sovmestnyĭ iskhod*, 544–545.

189. Matlock diary entry, 3 Apr. 1984, RRBML, JRMP, box 1, folder: "1984 Apr.–May."

190. AA memorandum, "Vierer-Gespräche der Politischen Direktoren am 19.07.1984 in Paris," 20 July 1984, PAdAA, B 150/599.

191. AA memorandum, "Sowjetische Politik gegenüber den USA und Westeuropa," 3 May 1984, BA, B 136/30154.

192. Shultz interview, 12 July 1989, SMML, DOP, box 3, folder 2.

193. Matlock to McFarlane, "The Soviets: Where We Stand," 6 July 1984, RRPL, JFMF, box 5, folder: "July 1984 1"; Dam to Reagan, "US-Soviet Bilateral Relations: Possible Soviet Policy Decision," 14 July 1984, RRPL, JFMF, box 5, folder: "July 1984 1"; Zemtsov, *Chernenko*, 289.

194. Dobrynin, *Sugubo doveritel'no*, 588.

195. Matlock to McFarlane, "The Soviets: Where We Stand," 6 July 1984, RRPL, JFMF, box 5, folder: "July 1984 1."

196. Shultz, *Turmoil and Triumph*, 480.

197. Genscher-Shultz memorandum of conversation, 25 Sept. 1984, PAdAA, B 150/603.

198. NIC memorandum, "Upbeat View on Gromyko's Mission," 25 Sept. 1984, NARA, CREST, doc. CIA-RDP86M00886R001000010006-7.

199. Shultz, *Turmoil and Triumph*, 483; Reagan diary entry, 28 Sept. 1984, in Brinkley, *The Reagan Diaries*, 1:386–387.

200. Reagan-Gromyko memorandum of conversation, 28 Sept. 1984, RRPL, JFMF, box 6, folder: "September 1984 5."

186   NOTES TO PAGES 101–102

201. Reagan diary entry, 28 Sept. 1984, in Brinkley, *The Reagan Diaries*, 1:386–387; Shultz, *Turmoil and Triumph*, 487.

202. Leffler, *For the Soul of Mankind*, 364; Matlock, *Reagan and Gorbachev*, 101. Gromyko clearly relished recounting this story to the politburo on his return. Dobrynin, *Sugubo doveritel'no*, 589.

203. Wright to Howe, "Shultz at Chevening: East-West Relations and Arms Control," 5 Dec. 1984, NAUK, PREM 19/1184.

204. Shultz to Weinberger et al., "A Reordering of Soviet Military Priorities," 2 July 1984, NARA, CREST, doc. CIA-RDP86B00420R000901750001-9.

205. Ogarkov, "Zashchita sotsializma," 2–3.

206. Reagan to Thatcher, 22 Nov. 1984, NAUK, PREM 19/1184; Matlock diary entry, 30 Jan. 1984, RRBML, JRMP, box 1, folder: "1984 Jan.–Mar."

207. Shultz to Reagan, "USG-Soviet Relations—Where Do We Want to Be and How Do We Get There?," 3 Mar. 1983, RRPL, RCMF, box 4, folder: "Soviet Union Sensitive File 1983."

208. Matlock to McFarlane, "The Soviets: Where We Stand," 6 July 1984, RRPL, JFMF, box 5, folder: "July 1984 1."

209. Genscher-Shultz memorandum of conversation, 7 May 1984, PAdAA, B 150/593; Zemtsov, *Chernenko*, 286, 296–297.

210. SED memorandum, "Information zur ersten Runde der sowjetisch-amerikanischen Verhandlungen über nukleare und Weltraumwaffen (Genf, 12. März bis 23. April)," 10 May 1985, SAPMO, DY 30/IV 2/2.035/156.

211. Balcar memorandum, "K některým aspektům sovětské zahraniční politiky," 13 July 1984, AMZV, TOT, 1980–1989, SSSR, box 2, folder 9; MID memorandum, "Informatsiia o soveshchanii zamestiteleĭ ministrov inostrannykh del sotsialisticheskikh stran po voprosam podgatovki k 39-ĭ sessii General'noĭ Assamblei OON," 7 Sept. 1984, HDAMZS, fond 1, opis' 3, sprava 5107. The Soviet Union also began to explore a range of countermeasures in case these efforts proved unsuccessful, including hardening warheads against lasers; basing ICBMs on mobile launchers, which could be fielded across the vast Soviet Union wherever the SDI satellites' coverage was weakest; and, the most likely option, simply building more missiles to overwhelm SDI. Savel'yev and Detinov, *Big Five*, 86.

212. KPSS Politburo meeting record, 31 May 1983, RGANI, fond 89, opis' 42, delo 53; ISKRAN memorandum, "Sdvigi v rasstanovke sil v SShA po voprosam vneshneĭ i voennoĭ politiki, zatragivaiushchi interesy SSSR," 30 Sept. 1985, ARAN, fond 2021, opis' 2, delo 12.

213. Kravets memorandum, "Otchet o rabote delegatsii Ukrainskoĭ SSR na 39-ĭ sessii General'noĭ Assamblei OON," 10 Jan. 1985, TsDAHO, fond 1, opis' 25, sprava 2891; Bykov and Darusenkov memorandum, "O rassmotrenii v tret'em komitete 38-ĭ sessii General'noĭ Assamblei OON voprosa prava cheloveka," 16 Dec. 1983, HDAMZS, fond 1, opis' 3, sprava 5127.

214. Genscher-Eagleburger memorandum of conversation, 5 May 1984, PAdAA, B 150/593.

215. Karpov interview, 11 Jan. 1990, SMML, DOP, box 1, folder 10; Pribytkov, *Apparat*, 169; Zemtsov, *Chernenko*, 296–297.

216. Chernenko to Reagan, 6 June 1984, RRPL, ES–NSC, HSF, box 39, folder: "Chernenko 8490695 1."

NOTES TO PAGES 102–104   187

217. Reagan to Chernenko, 2 July 1984, RRPL, ES–NSC, HSF, box 39, folder: "Chernenko 8490757, 8490769, 8490793."

218. Shultz to Reagan, "Breakfast Meeting with Ambassador Dobrynin," 3 July 1984, RRPL, JFMF, box 42, folder: "US-USSR Relations Jul. 1984 1."

219. Reagan remarks, UN General Assembly, New York, N.Y., 24 Sept. 1984, in Greene and Banks, *Public Papers of the Presidents: Ronald Reagan, 1984*, 2:1355–1361.

220. NSDD, no. 148, "The US Umbrella Talks Proposal," 26 Oct. 1984, RRPL, ES–NSC, NSDD, box 7, folder: "NSDD 148."

221. McFarlane to Reagan, "Conversation with Dobrynin at Barbecue Today," RRPL, JFMF, box 5, folder: "June 1984 4"; Matlock, *Reagan and Gorbachev*, 104; Glitman, *Last Battle of the Cold War*, 107–116.

222. Dam to Reagan, "Chernenko's Response to Your July 2 Letter on the Vienna Talks," 7 July 1984, RRPL, ES–NSC, HSF, box 39, folder: "Chernenko 8490757, 8490769, 8490793."

223. Chernenko to Reagan, 7 July 1984, RRPL, ES–NSC, HSF, box 39, folder: "Chernenko 8490757, 8490769, 8490793."

224. Chernenko to Reagan, 31 July 1984, RRPL, ES–NSC, HSF, box 39, folder: "Chernenko 8490847, 8490154."

225. Linhard to McFarlane, "Minutes for September 18 NSPG Meeting," 25 Oct. 1984, RRPL, ES–NSC, NSPGF, box 3, folder: "NSPG #96 1." Reagan's remarks about the barbed wire came, nearly verbatim, from an earlier conversation with Kohl (see note 187). Reagan diary entry, 5 Mar. 1984, in Brinkley, *The Reagan Diaries*, 1:325.

226. FBIS memorandum, "Chernenko Continues Gradual Reorientation of Public Posture," 23 Oct. 1984, RRPL, JFMF, box 7, folder: "Signals Oct.–Dec. 1984 3."

227. FBIS memorandum, "Soviet Commentators Raise Possibility of Altered US Course," 11 Oct. 1984, RRPL, JFMF, box 7, folder: "Signals Oct.–Dec. 1984 1."

228. Mansfield to Shultz, "Soviet Spokesman Calls for Improved US-Soviet Ties," 1 Nov. 1984, RRPL, JFMF, box 7, folder: "Signals Oct.–Dec. 1984 3."

229. Shultz-Tikhonov memorandum of conversation, 3 Nov. 1984, RRPL, JFMF, box 22, folder: "USSR Diplomatic Contacts 8."

230. Hartman to Shultz, "Chernenko NBC Interview: Upbeat on Prospects for US-Soviet Relations," 19 Nov. 1984, RRPL, JFMF, box 21, folder: "Chernenko 3."

231. Sokol memorandum, "Zpráva o některých aspektech Reaganovy presidentské kandidatury," 12 Sept. 1983, AMZV, TOT, 1980–1989, SSA, box 4, folder 23.

232. CIA memorandum, "Chernenko's Comeback," 30 Nov. 1984, NARA, CREST, doc. CIA-RDP85T00287R001401120001-4; Bil'ak memorandum, "Informace o přátelské pracovní návštěvě člena předsednictva a tajemníka ÚV KSČ s. V. Bil'aka v SSSR," 18 Mar. 1985, NAČR, fond 1261/0/8, box P129/85, folder 6; Zemtsov, *Chernenko*, 289.

233. Cherniaev diary entry, 4 July 1984, in Cherniaev, *Sovmestnyĭ iskhod*, 563; Savel'yev and Detinov, *Big Five*, 121–122.

234. Shultz to Reagan, "Letter to Chernenko," RRPL, JFMF, box 7, folder: "December 1984 2."

235. Chernenko to Reagan, 20 Dec. 1984, RRPL, ES–NSC, HSF, box 39, folder: "Chernenko 8491334."

236. Savel'yev and Detinov, *Big Five*, 87; Zemtsov, *Chernenko*, 316–317.

237. Taubman, *Khrushchev*, 349–360.

188 **NOTES TO PAGES 104–108**

238. Matlock to McFarlane, "Geneva and Beyond: Your Discussions with Secretary Shultz," 28 Dec. 1984, RRPL, JFMF, box 7, folder: "December 1984 5."

239. Shultz-Gromyko memorandum of conversation, 9:40–13:00, 7 Jan. 1985, RRPL, JFMF, box 8, folder: "March 1985 1."

240. Shultz-Gromyko memorandum of conversation, 15:35–18:55, 7 Jan. 1985, RRPL, JFMF, box 8, folder: "March 1985 1."

241. Shultz-Gromyko memorandum of conversation, 9:30–12:00, 8 Jan. 1985, RRPL, JFMF, box 8, folder: "March 1985 2."

242. Shultz-Gromyko memorandum of conversation, 15:35–18:55, 8 Jan. 1985, RRPL, JFMF, box 8, folder: "March 1985 2"; Shultz, *Turmoil and Triumph*, 517–519; Dobrynin, *Sugubo doveritel'no*, 598.

243. Matlock to McFarlane, "Organizing for Arms Reduction Negotiations with the Soviets," 12 Jan. 1985, RRPL, JFMF, box 7, folder: "January 1985 2."

244. Kohl-Nitze memorandum of conversation, 10 Jan. 1985, PAdAA, B 150/610.

245. Suja memorandum, "Informácia o priebehu a výsledkoch rozhovorov ministra zahraničných vecí ZSSR A.A. Gromyka a štátneho tajomníka USA G. Shultza v Ženeve 7.–8. 1. 1985," 19 Jan. 1985, AMZV, TOT, 1980–1989, SSA, box 1, folder 2.

246. Genscher-Gromyko memorandum of conversation, 4 Mar. 1985, PAdAA, B 150/614.

247. Braunmühl memorandum, "Bewertung des wiederaufgenomen Großmächte-Dialogs für Europa," 4 Oct. 1984, PAdAA, B 150/604. Such an arrangement excluding—or abandoning—Europe had long been a fear of Washington's allies. Schulz and Schwartz, "Superpower and the Union in the Making," 359.

248. Genscher-Semenov memorandum of conversation, 17 Dec. 1984, PAdAA, B 150/609.

5. New Departures

1. Regan memorandum, "Summit Notes," LOC, DTRP, box 215, folder 3; Regan, *For the Record*, 300, 308–309.

2. Matlock, *Reagan and Gorbachev*, 134–135.

3. Reagan diary entry, 26 Sept. 1985, in Brinkley, *The Reagan Diaries*, 1:499–500.

4. Regan memorandum, "Summit Notes," LOC, DTRP, box 215, folder 3; Regan, *For the Record*, 305.

5. Regan memorandum, "Summit Notes," LOC, DTRP, box 215, folder 3; Regan, *For the Record*, 300.

6. McFarlane, *Special Trust*, 317.

7. Reagan to Murphy, 19 Dec. 1985, in Skinner, Anderson, and Anderson, *Reagan: A Life in Letters*, 415–416.

8. Regan memorandum, "Summit Notes," LOC, DTRP, box 215, folder 4.

9. Wieck memorandum, "Die Lage des Bündnisses 1985 und Betrachtungen zur Orientierung der Deutschen Politik im Bündnis," 4 Jan. 1985, PAdAA, B 150/610; Kohl-Nitze memorandum of conversation, 10 Jan. 1985, PAdAA, B 150/610.

10. Lucas to McFarlane, "Chernenko Chronology," 30 Aug. 1984, RRPL, JFMF, box 21, folder: "Chernenko 3."

11. Cherniaev, *Shest' let s Gorbachevym*, 27.

12. Gorbacheva, *Ia nadeius'*, 130; Gromyko, *Andreĭ Gromyko*, 139.

NOTES TO PAGES 108–110   189

13. McFarlane to Reagan, "US-Soviet Relations: Toward Defining a Strategy," 6 Feb. 1984, RRPL, JFMF, box 3, folder: "February 1984 2."

14. Taubman, *Gorbachev*, 11–19, 22–27, 41–42.

15. Taubman, *Gorbachev*, 57–67, 78.

16. Slavin, *Neokonchennaia istoriia*, 15–16; Raleigh, *Russia's Sputnik Generation*, 16; Zubok, *Zhivago's Childern*, 60–87.

17. Taubman, *Gorbachev*, 127, 158–162, 173–174.

18. Cherniaev diary entry, 8 Mar. 1985, in Cherniaev, *Sovmestnyĭ iskhod*, 606–608; Kornienko interview, 19 Jan. 1990, SMML, DOP, box 1, folder 12.

19. Blagovolin interview, 19 Jan. 1990, SMML, DOP, box 1, folder 3; Arbatov, *Zatianuvsheesia vyzdorovlenie*, 335.

20. Gorbachev-Gordon memorandum of conversation, 10 July 1983, AGF, fond 3, opis' 1, delo 13675.

21. Delworth to MacEachen, "Visit to Canada by Mikhail Gorbachev, Member of the Politburo of the USSR," 21 Jan. 1983, LAC, R12298, box 609, folder 13.

22. McLaine to Christensen, 11 May 1983, LAC, RG 25, vol. 9216, file 20-USSR-9, pt. 13.

23. Shulgan, *Soviet Ambassador*, 249; Shakhnazarov, *S vozhdiami i bez nikh*, 278; Gorbachev, *Naedine s soboĭ*, 342.

24. Whelan, *Whelan*, 257. Gorbachev had initially planned to spend ten days, but Andropov insisted he condense the visit. Taubman, *Gorbachev*, 184.

25. Gorbachev remarks, Standing Committee on External Affairs and National Defense, Ottawa, Ont., 18 May 1983, in Gorbachev, *Sobranie sochineniĭ*, 1:456–461; Shulgan, *Soviet Ambassador*, 255.

26. Gorbachev, *Naedine s soboĭ*, 342.

27. Mace to Trudeau, 16 May 1983, LAC, RG 25, vol. 8704, file 20-USSR-9, pt. 14.

28. Trudeau interview, 30 June 1988, in Bothwell and Granatstein, *Trudeau's World*, 380–382; Iakovlev, *Sumerki*, 353; Shulgan, *Soviet Ambassador*, 248. Trudeau was not exactly hidebound when it came to protocol, as Queen Elizabeth II had discovered when he performed a black tie–clad pirouette in her presence in 1977. John English, *Life of Pierre Elliott Trudeau*, 2:349–350.

29. Trudeau-Gorbachev memorandum of conversation, 18 May 1983, LAC, RG 25, vol. 8704, file 20-USSR-9, pt. 14.

30. Iakovlev, *Sumerki*, 354.

31. Shulgan, *Soviet Ambassador*, 263–273.

32. Meyer to Gates, 8 June 1983, NARA, CREST, doc. CIA-RDP85T00153R000300060040-9.

33. Whelan, *Whelan*, 256–257, 260.

34. Cherniaev diary entry, 22 Jan. 1985, in Cherniaev, *Sovmestnyĭ iskhod*, 596.

35. Iakovlev, *Sumerki*, 354; Iakovlev interview, 14 July 1990, BLPES, 2RR 1/2/7. In late 1972, as head of the KPSS Department of Ideology and Propaganda, he had published an article highly critical of nationalism (and Russian nationalism in particular) and was removed from that post and dispatched to Canada as a result. Iakovlev, *Sumerki*, 324–326; Iakovlev, "Protiv antiistorizma," 4–5.

36. McLaine to Clark, "Mikhail Gorbachev: Personal Reflections," 3 Dec. 1984, LAC, RG 25, vol. 8704, file 20-USSR-9, pt. 14.

37. Iakovlev, *Sumerki*, 353.

190 **NOTES TO PAGES 110–112**

38. Gorbachev, *Naedine s soboĭ*, 342.

39. Matlock to McFarlane, "Suggestion Regarding Gorbachev–Vice President Meeting," 21 June 1984, RRPL, JFMF, box 5, folder: "June 1984 5."

40. Howe, *Conflict of Loyalty*, 357. Gorbachev was chosen over two other possible future Soviet leaders—politburo members Viktor Grishin and Grigoriĭ Romanov—after an intervention by Trudeau (at Iakovlev's behest), making the case that of the three, Gorbachev was most likely to eventually lead the Soviet Union. Iakovlev, *Sumerki*, 354.

41. Arnaud to Dumas, "M. Gorbatchev à Londres," 17 Dec. 1984, AD, 1930 INVA/5227, folder: "Visite de M. Gorbatchev en Grande-Bretagne."

42. Kohl-Fabius memorandum of conversation, 6 Feb. 1985, PAdAA, B 150/612.

43. Cradock to Powell, "Talking to Gorbachev," 11 Dec. 1984, NAUK, PREM 19/1394.

44. Thatcher-Gorbachev memorandum of conversation, 12:30–15:00, 16 Dec. 1984, NAUK, PREM 19/1394.

45. Thatcher-Gorbachev memorandum of conversation, 15:00–17:50, 16 Dec. 1984, NAUK, PREM 19/1394. Gorbachev again identified SDI as the most important issue in US-Soviet relations and an insurmountable obstacle to nuclear arms reductions in a meeting with Howe. Price to Shultz, "FCO Debrief on Gorbachev Visit," 20 Dec. 1984, RRPL, JFMF, box 7, folder: "Signals Oct.–Dec. 1984 3"; Gorbachev, *Naedine s soboĭ*, 469.

46. Thatcher memorandum, "Meeting with President Reagan: Gorbachev," 22 Dec. 1984, NAUK, PREM 19/1394.

47. Price to Shultz, "FCO Impressions of Gorbachev," 20 Dec. 1984, RRPL, JFMF, box 7, folder: "Signals Oct.–Dec. 1984 3."

48. AA memorandum, "Reise von Politbüro-Mitglied Gorbatschow nach Großbritannien (15.–22.12.1984)," 20 Dec. 1984, PAdAA, B 150/609.

49. Kohl-Thatcher memorandum of conversation, 18 Jan. 1985, PAdAA, B 150/611.

50. Thatcher-Reagan memorandum of conversation, 10:30–11:15, 22 Dec. 1984, NAUK, PREM 19/1656. Nancy Reagan would come to strongly disagree with Thatcher's positive assessment of Raisa Gorbacheva, however. Nancy Reagan, *My Turn*, 338–340.

51. Matlock diary entry, 3 Jan. 1985, RRBML, JRMP, box 2, folder: "1985 1."

52. Matlock to Lucas, "US-Soviet Relations: Leadership Situation," 27 Aug. 1984, RRPL, JFMF, box 5, folder: "August 1984 3."

53. Aleksandrov-Agentov, *Ot Kollontaĭ do Gorbacheva*, 287.

54. Matlock diary entry, 4 Mar. 1985, RRBML, JRMP, box 2, folder: "1985 Jan.–Apr."

55. Reagan-Shcherbyts'kyĭ memorandum of conversation, 8 Mar. 1985, RRPL, JFMF, box 47, folder: "Memcons—President with Shcherbitsky"; Matlock diary entry, 6 Mar. 1985, RRBML, JRMP, box 2, folder: "1985 Jan.–Apr."

56. Shcherbyts'kyĭ memorandum, "Otchet o poezdke delegatsii Verkhovnogo Soveta SSSR v SShA," 27 Mar. 1985, TsDAGO, fond 1, opis' 25, sprava 2886.

57. CIA memorandum, "Reports That Chernenko Has Died," 8 Mar. 1985, RRPL, JFMF, box 8, folder: "March 1985 3."

58. Matlock to McFarlane, "Report of Chernenko Death," 8 Mar. 1985, RRPL, JFMF, box 21, folder: "Chernenko Death."

59. Matlock diary entry, 10 Mar. 1985, RRBML, JRMP, box 2, folder: "1985 Jan.–Apr."

60. Ronald Reagan, *American Life*, 612.

NOTES TO PAGES 112–114   191

61. Cherniaev, *Shest' let s Gorbachevym*, 29.

62. Cherniaev diary entry, 11 Mar. 1985, in Cherniaev, *Sovmestnyĭ iskhod*, 608–610.

63. Ryzhkov, *Perestroĭka*, 78.

64. Arbatov interview, 1989, BLPES, 2RR 1/4/4.

65. Shakhnazarov, *S vozhdiami i bez nikh*, 292.

66. Kornienko interview, 19 Jan. 1990, SMML, DOP, box 1, folder 12; Zimyanin interview, 14 July 1990, BLPES, 2RR 1/1/3; Vorotnikov interview, 26 June 1990, BLPES, 2RR 1/1/19; Brutents, *Nesbyvsheesia*, 66.

67. Boldin, *Krushenie p'edestala*, 86–89; Gromyko, *Andreĭ Gromyko*, 146, 157–165.

68. Taubman, *Gorbachev*, 210.

69. Gorbachev, *Zhizn' i reformy*, vol. 1, 270.

70. CIA memorandum, "Gorbachev Named Funeral Commission Chairman," 11 Mar. 1985, RRPL, JFMF, box 21, folder: "Chernenko Death"; Heyken memorandum, "Tod Tschernekos," 11 Mar. 1985, PAdAA, B 150/614.

71. Gorbachev remarks, KPSS Central Committee Plenum, Moscow, Soviet Union, 11 Mar. 1985, in Gorbachev, *Sobranie sochineniĭ*, 2:158–163.

72. Gorbachev, *Zhizn' i reformy*, 1:265–270. Grishin had nothing but contempt for Gorbachev as a result, dismissing him as "cowardly" and a "traitor" in his memoirs. Grishin, *Ot Khrushcheva do Gorbacheva*, 71.

73. MfS memorandum, "Hinweise dir Reaktion der Bevölkerung der DDR zum Ableben des Tschernenko un dir Wahl des Genossen Gorbatschow in diese Funktion," 15 Mar. 1985, BStU, ZAIG, no. 4190.

74. Aleksandrov-Agentov interview, 15 Jan. 1990, MML, DOP, box 1, folder 2.

75. Gorbacheva, *Ia nadeius'*, 167.

76. Thatcher memorandum, "Return to Moscow," 16 Mar. 1985, CAC, THCR 1/20/5.

77. Sutherland to Howe, "The Funeral of President Chernenko," 14 Mar. 1985, NAUK, PREM 19/1646; Gorbachev remarks, Moscow, Soviet Union, in Gorbachev, *Sobranie sochineniĭ*, 2:164–166.

78. Cherniaev diary entry, 13 Mar. 1985, in Cherniaev, *Sovmestnyĭ iskhod*, 610.

79. Reagan to Kohl, 25 Sept. 1985, PAdAA, B 150/627.

80. Ronald Reagan, *American Life*, 612.

81. Boulder to Raimond, "Informations d'origins américaine," 30 Apr. 1985, AD, 1930 INVA/5672, folder: "URSS-USA 1985."

82. Shultz, *Turmoil and Triumph*, 533.

83. Gorbachev-Bush memorandum of conversation, 13 Mar. 1985, AGF, fond 3, delo 1, opis' 4763.

84. Kohl-Gorbachev memorandum of conversation, 14 Mar. 1985, PAdAA, B 150/614.

85. Thatcher-Gorbachev memorandum of conversation, 13 Mar. 1985, NAUK, PREM 19/1646. After the meeting, the Soviet Foreign Ministry became convinced that Thatcher hoped to use her established relationship with Gorbachev to leapfrog Reagan as the key player in East-West relations. Cherniaev diary entry, 14 Mar. 1985, in Cherniaev, *Sovmestnyĭ iskhod*, 610–611.

86. Thatcher memorandum, "Return to Moscow," 16 Mar. 1985, CAC, THCR 1/20/5.

87. Radchenko, *Unwanted Visionaries*, 1–3.

192   NOTES TO PAGES 114–116

88. KPSS memorandum, "Soveshchanie sekretareĭ TsK KPSS, sostoiavsheesia u General'nogo sekretaria TsK KPSS tovarishcha Gorbacheva M.S.," 15 Mar. 1985, LOC, DAVP, box 25, folder 11.

89. Kornienko, *Kholodnaia voĭna*, 357.

90. Gorbachev, *Zhizn' i reformy*, 2:311–312.

91. Grachev, *Gorbachev's Gamble*, 114; Cherniaev, *Shest' let s Gorbachevym*, 81.

92. Gorbachev interview, 1994, LHCMA, FOTW 3/18

93. Gorbachev, *Ia nadeius'*, 14.

94. Gromyko, *Andreĭ Gromyko v labirintakh Kremliia*, 133–137.

95. Robert English, *Russia and the Idea of the West*, 195.

96. Cherniaev diary entry, 22 Feb. 1985, in Cherniaev, *Sovmestnyĭ iskhod*, 602–604; Cherniaev diary entry, 8 Dec. 1985, in Cherniaev, *Sovmestnyĭ iskhod*, 658–659.

97. Robert English, *Russia and the Idea of the West*, 194–195; Shultz, *Turmoil and Triumph*, 536.

98. MAÉ memorandum, "Situation intériure de l'URSS en septembre 1985," 9 Sept. 1985, AD, 1930 INVA/5617, folder: "Déroulement des évènements, 1985."

99. Leonov, *Likholet'e*, 175.

100. Falin interview, 11 Jan. 1990, SMML, DOP, box 1, folder 6.

101. Cherniaev, *Shest' let s Gorbachevym*, 9.

102. Gorbachev remarks, KPSS Plenum, Moscow, 23 Apr. 1985, in Cherniaev, *V Politbiuro TsK KPSS*, 15–17; Cherniaev diary entry, 17 Mar. 1985, in Cherniaev, *Sovmestnyĭ iskhod*, 611–612; Aleksandrov-Agentov, *Ot Kollontaĭ do Gorbacheva*, 287.

103. Taubman, *Gorbachev*, 213–214.

104. Cherniaev diary entry, 11 Apr. 1985, in Cherniaev, *Sovmestnyĭ iskhod*, 619–621.

105. Gorbachev remarks, Leningrad, Soviet Union, 17 May 1985, in Gorbachev, *Sobranie sochineniĭ*, 2:253–269; Taubman, *Gorbachev*, 213–214.

106. Stepanov-Mamaladze notes, 9 Nov. 1985, HIA, TGSMP, box 1, folder 3.

107. Hoffmann to Meyer, "Soviet Oil: Gorbachev's Alternatives," 2 Oct. 1985, NARA, CREST, doc. CIA-RDP87T00759R000100130020-1; Low memorandum, "Soviet Oil Problems," 11 Sept. 1985, NARA, CREST, doc. CIA-RDP87T00759R000100120013-0.

108. CIA memorandum, "Lower Oil Prices: Impact on the Soviet Union," 13 Feb. 1985, NARA, CREST, doc. CIA-RDP87T00759R000100040026-5.

109. Adamishin diary entry, 23 Feb. 1985, HIA, ALAP, box 1, folder: "1985"; Gaidar, *Collapse of an Empire*, 122–123.

110. Goble memorandum, "USSR: The Problem of Alcoholism," 10 Mar. 1985, RRPL, JFMF, box 49, folder: "Geneva Meeting Background Papers for Mrs. Reagan 1."

111. KPSS Politburo meeting record, 4 Apr. 1985, LOC, DAVP, box 25, folder 12; Cherniaev diary entry, 6 Apr. 1985, in Cherniaev, *Sovmestnyĭ iskhod*, 617–618; Vorotnikov interview, 26 June 1990, BLPES, 2RR 1/1/19. Cherniaev could name a dozen Kremlin officials who habitually came to work drunk or missed multiple days of work per week because of their drinking binges. Cherniaev diary entry, 2 Mar. 1985, in Cherniaev, *Sovmestnyĭ iskhod*, 605–606.

112. Aliev interview, BLPES, 2RR 1/4/2.

113. Taubman, *Gorbachev*, 232–233.

114. Genscher-Shultz memorandum of conversation, 2 May 1985, PAdAA, B 150/618; CIA memorandum, "Gorbachev's Domestic Challenge: The Looming Problems," Feb. 1985, NARA, CREST, doc. CIA-RDP08S01350R000300960001-9.

NOTES TO PAGES 117–118 193

115. Chris Miller, *Struggle to Save the Soviet Economy*, 20–23.

116. Westad, *Restless Empire*, 377.

117. Chris Miller, *Struggle to Save the Soviet Economy*, 40, 50–51.

118. Gorbachev remarks, 28 July 1986, Vladivostock, Soviet Union, in Gorbachev, *Sobranie sochineniĭ*, 4:350–377.

119. Taubman, *Gorbachev*, 263.

120. ISKRAN memorandum, "Rol' sovetsko-amerikanskikh otnosheniĭ v sovremennom mire i vozmozhnosti dostizheniia cer'eznykh dogovorennosteĭ mezhdu Moskvoĭ i Vashingtonom," 15 Nov. 1985, ARAN, fond 2021, opis' 2, delo 14; MNO memorandum, no. 9 (314), "Vojenské rozpočty států Severoatlantického pakty v roce 1985—základní údaje," 1985, ABS, ZSGŠ, PM, box 123.

121. Iakovlev memorandum, "Imperativ politicheskogo razvitiia," 25 Dec. 1985, GARF, fond 10063, opis' 1, delo 380; Balcar memorandum, "K sovětsko-americkým vztahům," 18 Jan. 1985, AMZV, TOT, 1980–1989, SSSR, box 2, folder 11; Iakovlev, *Sumerki*, 385; Wohlforth, *Witnesses to the End of the Cold War*, 15.

122. Stepanov-Mamaladze notes, 6 Oct. 1985, HIA, TGSMP, box 1, folder 2.

123. Shakhnazarov memorandum, "Vneshniaia politika SSSR na sovermennom etape," AGF, fond 5, opis' 1, delo 17828.

124. Burlatskiĭ interview, 25 Jan. 1990, SMML, DOP, box 1, folder 5.

125. MNO memorandum, "Využití nových technologií—hlavní prostředek zvyšování bojových možností ozbrojených sil NATO," 1985, ABS, ZSGŠ, PM, box 122; MfS memorandum, "Einschatzung von USA-Experten zu Fragen der Elektronischen Kampfführung," 1985, BStU, AS, no. 68/88; Zhuravlev, "O povyshenii effektivnosti voenno-nauchnykh issledovani," 43–44. Gorbachev tasked East Germany with spearheading rapid development in high-technology fields, but the East Germans preferred to steal, rather than autonomously develop, these capabilities: Honecker-Gorbachev memorandum of conversation, 5 May 1985, SAPMO, DY 30/2381; Macrakis, *Seduced by Secrets*, 1.

126. Zagladin memorandum, "Kak odolet' iadernuiu ugrozu," 1985, AGF, fond 1, opis' 8, delo 17757; Shakhnazarov memorandum, "Ne dopustit' militarisatsii kosmosa," 6 Feb. 1985, AGF, fond 5, opis' 1, delo 17855; Dvinina, "'Zvezdnye voĭny," 15, 28.

127. MfS memorandum, "Information zur ersten Runde der sowjetisch-amerikanischen Verhandlungen über nukleare und Weltraumwaffen," 10 May 1985, BStU, ZAIG, no. 7155; MfS memorandum, "SPD-Führungskreise zur Haltung der USA- und BRD-Regierung zum amerikanischen Welraumrüstungsprogramm," 1985, BStU, AS, no. 68/88.

128. Hager-Meehan memorandum of conversation, 18 Oct. 1985, SAPMO, DY 30/27192.

129. Haslam, *Russia's Cold War*, 355.

130. Savel'yev and Detinov, *Big Five*, 121; Grachev, *Gorbachev's Gamble*, 46.

131. Shakhnazarov, *Tsena svobody*, 86.

132. Savel'yev and Detinov, *Big Five*, 125; Genscher-Tower-Glitman memorandum of conversation, 2 Apr. 1985, PAdAA, B 150/616.

133. Weiß memorandum, "Antwortschreiben Gorbatschows an den Friedensrat von Heilbronn," 29 Mar. 1985, PAdAA, B 150/615. Heilbronn was not selected at random; the city was home to a Pershing 2 base and surrounded by other US military installations.

194   **NOTES TO PAGES 118–120**

134. Pfeffer and Hartmann memorandum, "Prawda-Interview Gorbatschows vom 08.04.85," 9 Apr. 1985, PAdAA, B 150/616.

135. Brutents, *Nesbyvsheesia*, 127; Gorbachev remarks, Moscow, Soviet Union, 9 May 1985, in Gorbachev, *Sobranie sochineniĭ*, 2:250–252.

136. Genscher-Shevardnadze memorandum of conversation, 1 Aug. 1985, PAdAA, B 150/624; Cherniaev, *Shest' let s Gorbachevym*, 78.

137. Zimyanin interview, 14 July 1990, BLPES, 2RR 1/1/3; Taubman, *Gorbachev*, 272.

138. KPSS Politburo meeting record, 10 Mar. 1983, RGANI, fond 89, opis' 42, delo 51; Parsons to Coles, "The Russians," 30 Mar. 1983, NAUK, PREM 19/1033.

139. Margerie to Cheysson, "Les mystères de Radio Moscou," 26 May 1983, AD, 1930 INVA/5683, folder: "Correspondence Moscou et pays de l'Est."

140. Cherniaev diary entry, 4 Apr. 1985, in Cherniaev, *Sovmestnyĭ iskhod*, 617; Kalinovsky, *Long Goodbye*, 80–90.

141. Cherniaev diary entries, 16–17 Oct. 1985, in Cherniaev, *Sovmestnyĭ iskhod*, 649–650; Aleksandrov-Agentov interview, 15 Jan. 1990, SMML, DOP, box 1, folder 2. Gorbachev did not, as is often alleged, surge Soviet troops at the same time to enable the military to quickly declare victory and then withdraw, though he did fear the consequences for Soviet influence in the Third World if Moscow abandoned its ally and the Kabul regime fell. Kalinovsky, *Long Goodbye*, 87–88.

142. Palazhchenko, *My Years with Gorbachev and Shevardnadze*, 30–31.

143. Ekedahl and Goodman, *Wars of Eduard Shevardnadze*, 30.

144. Robert English, *Russia and the Idea of the West*, 209.

145. Shevardnadze, *Moĭ vybor*, 152.

146. Gorbachev, *Zhizn' i reformy*, 2:12; Dobrynin, *Sugubo doveritel'no*, 635–637.

147. Akhromeev interview, 10 Jan. 1990, SMML, DOP, box 1, folder 1; ISKRAN memorandum, "Rol' sovetsko-amerikanskikh otnosheniĭ v sovremennom mire i vozmozhnosti dostizheniia cer'eznykh dogovorennosteĭ mezhdu Moskvoĭ i Vashingtonom," 15 Nov. 1985, ARAN, fond 2021, opis' 2, delo 14.

148. Iakovlev memorandum, "Desiat' let v Kanade,"15 Mar. 1984, GARF, fond 10063, opis' 1, delo 20; Zagladin memorandum, "Kak odolet' iadernuiu ugrozu," 1985, AGF, fond 1, opis' 8, delo 17757.

149. Ronald Reagan, *American Life*, 617.

150. Shakhnazarov memorandum, "O rukovodstve mirom," 5 Feb. 1985, AGF, fond 5, opis' 1, delo 17854.

151. Polishchuk memorandum, "Prava cheloveka i ideologicheskaia bor'ba," 12 Apr. 1984, HDAMZS, fond 1, opis' 3, sprava 5131; ISKRAN memoranum, "Polozhenie v oblasti prav cheloveka v SShA," 11 Feb. 1985, ARAN, fond 2021, opis' 2, delo 1; ISKRAN memorandum, "Kritika v SShA tsentral'noamerikanskoĭ politike administratsii Reĭgana," 9 Oct. 1985, ARAN, fond 2021, opis' 2, delo 13; ISKRAN memorandum, "Vashington i prava cheloveka: uiazvimye pozitsii vashingtonsoĭ administratsii," 22 Aug. 1985, ARAN, fond 2021, opis' 2, delo 10.

152. NSC memorandum, "Meeting with General Secretary Gorbachev, September 3, 1985," 4 Sept. 1985, RRPL, DTRF, box 7, folder: "Gorbachev Meeting with Senators."

153. Cherniaev diary entry, 9 June 1985, in Cherniaev, *Sovmestnyĭ iskhod*, 630–631.

154. Zaĭnullin, "Ideologicheskoe protivoborstvo dvukh sistem," 63.

NOTES TO PAGES 120–122   195

155. Rostow-Parastaev memorandum of conversation, 11 Feb. 1985, RRPL, JFMF, box 8, folder: "February 1985 3."

156. Ulam, *Lenin and the Bolsheviks*, 412–413.

157. Matlock diary entry, 2 Apr. 1985, RRBML, JRMP, box 2, folder: "1985 Jan.–Apr."

158. Shultz, *Turmoil and Triumph*, 563–564; Matlock diary entry, 14 May 1985, RRBML, JRMP, box 2, folder: "1985 Apr.–Jun."

159. Reagan diary entry, 22 May 1985, in Brinkley, *The Reagan Diaries*, 1:461–462.

160. Lenczowski to McFarlane, "Reagan-Gorbachev Meeting: The Question of Objectives," 10 Oct. 1985, RRPL, JLF, box 9, folder: "Summit Geneva 4."

161. Matlock diary entry, 1 June 1985, RRBML, JRMP, box 2, folder: "1985 Apr.–June"; Matlock, *Reagan and Gorbachev*, 133–135.

162. Matlock memorandum, "Soviet Russian Psychology: Some Common Traits," RRPL, JFMF, box 47, folder: "Briefing Material for President Reagan—Gorbachev Meeting 2."

163. Reagan diary entry, 26 May 1985, in Brinkley, *The Reagan Diaries*, 1:463.

164. Matlock memorandum, "Russia's Place in the World: The View from Moscow," RRPL, JFMF, box 47, folder: "Briefing Material for President Reagan—Gorbachev Meeting 2."

165. Reagan diary entry, 18 Nov. 1985, in Brinkley, *The Reagan Diaries*, 2:541.

166. Reagan diary entry, 24 June 1985, in Brinkley, *The Reagan Diaries*, 1:474–475; Ronald Reagan, *American Life*, 614–615.

167. Armacost interview, 20 Apr. 1989, SMML, DOP, box 2, folder 3.

168. CIA memorandum, "Gorbachev, the New Broom," 27 June 1985, NARA, CREST, doc. CIA-RDP88B00443R001704320004-4.

169. Regan, *For the Record*, 296–297.

170. Reagan memorandum, "Gorbachev," 13 Oct. 1985, LOC, DTRP, box 215, folder 4; Matlock to Ermarth, "Odds and Ends," 31 Dec. 1986, RRPL, JFMF, box 27, folder: "Important History Pre-1987."

171. NSDD 183, "Meeting with Soviet Leader in Geneva," 8 Aug. 1985, RRPL, ES–NSC, NSDD, box 8, folder: "NSDD 183."

172. Kornienko, *Kholodnaia voĭna*, 358; Palazhchenko, *My Years with Gorbachev and Shevardnadze*, 41.

173. ISKRAN memorandum, "Administratsiia R. Reĭgana i sovetsko-amerikanskie ekonomicheskie i nauchno-tekhnicheskie sviazi," 15 Feb. 1985, ARAN, fond 2021, opis' 2, delo 1.

174. Gorbachev, *Zhizn' i reformy*, 2:12; Cherniaev diary entry, 27 Aug. 1985, in Cherniaev, *Sovmestnyĭ iskhod*, 643–645.

175. Dobrynin, *Sugubo doveritel'no*, 605.

176. Cherniaev diary entry, 15 Feb. 1985, in Cherniaev, *Sovmestnyĭ iskhod*, 597–598; Shakhnazarov, *S vozhdiami i bez nikh*, 304.

177. Gorbachev, *Zhizn' i reformy*, 2:11.

178. Gorbachev remarks, Warsaw Pact Political Consultative Committee, Sofia, 22 Oct. 1985, AGF, fond 5, opis' 1, delo 20667; SED memorandum, "Niederschrift des treffen der Generalsekretäre und Ersten Sekretäre der Zentralkomitees der Bruderpartei der Teilnehmerstaaten des WV am 23. Oktober 1985 in Sofia," SAPMO, DY 30/2352.

179. Iakovlev to Gorbachev, "O Reĭgane," 12 Mar. 1985, GARF, fond 10063, opis' 1, delo 379.

196 **NOTES TO PAGES 123–125**

180. Cherniaev diary entry, 12 Nov. 1985, in Cherniaev, *Sovmestnyĭ iskhod*, 655.

181. Dobrynin, *Sugubo doveritel'no*, 622.

182. Shultz to Reagan, "Dobrynin Meeting," 17 Sept. 1985, RRPL, RFLF, box 18, folder: "Summit III 9."

183. MfS memorandum, "Zur Vorbereitung des Gipfeltreffens UdSSR-USA," 13 Sept. 1985, BStU, AS, no. 72/88; ISKRAN memorandum, "Nekotorye osobennosti upravleniia nauchnym obespecheniem Stratekicheskoĭ Oboronnoĭ Initsiativy administratsii Reĭgana," 27 Nov. 1985, ARAN, fond 2021, opis' 2, delo 14.

184. DOS memorandum, "Talking Points for Secretary's September 25 and 27 Meetings with Shevardnadze," RRPL, RFLF, box 18, folder: "Summit III 7."

185. Reagan-Shevardnadze memorandum of conversation, 27 Sept. 1985, RRPL, JFMF, box 47, folder: "Memcons—President with Shevardnadze."

186. Reagan-Shevardnadze memorandum of conversation, 24 Oct. 1985, RRPL, JFMF, box 47, folder: "Memcons—President with Shevardnadze"; Reagan diary entry, 24 Oct. 1985, in Brinkley, *The Reagan Diaries*, 1:509.

187. McFarlane interview, 7 Nov. 1989, SMML, DOP, box 2, folder 22; Shultz, *Turmoil and Triumph*, 589–596. The Kremlin did not appreciate the extent to which the Reagan administration remained split over East-West relations: ISKRAN memorandum, "Rasstanovka politicheskikh sil v SShA posle vyborov 1984 g.," 29 Mar. 1985, ARAN, fond 2021, opis' 2, delo 3.

188. Shultz to Reagan, "Your Meetings with Gorbachev in Geneva," RRPL, RFLF, box 18, folder: "Summit I 2."

189. Hartman to Shultz, "Gorbachev and the Geneva Meeting," 11 Nov. 1985, RRPL, JFMF, box 47, folder: "Briefing Material for President Reagan—Gorbachev Meeting 3."

190. Shultz to Reagan, "What to Expect from Gorbachev in Geneva," 12 Nov. 1985, RRPL, JFMF, box 47, folder: "Briefing Material for President Reagan—Gorbachev Meeting 3"; Shultz to Reagan, "Your Meetings with Gorbachev in Geneva," RRPL, RFLF, box 18, folder: "Summit I 2."

191. Reagan diary entry, 5 Nov. 1985, in Brinkley, *The Reagan Diaries*, 2:536.

192. Thatcher-Schmidt memorandum of conversation, 18 Nov. 1981, NAUK, PREM 19/766.

193. MfS memorandum, "Neue Erkenntnisse über Vorbereitungen auf das sowjetisch-amerikanische Gipfeltreffen und über die Aufnahme der neuen sowjetischen Abrustungs-vorschläge," 28 Oct. 1985, BStU, AS, no. 72/88.

194. Ronald Reagan, *American Life*, 633–634.

195. Stepanov-Mamaladze notes, 6 Oct. 1985, HIA, TGSMP, box 1, folder 2.

196. Cherniaev diary entry, 20 June 1985, in Cherniaev, *Sovmestnyĭ iskhod*, 634–635.

197. Aleksandrov-Agentov, *Ot Kollontaĭ do Gorbacheva*, 289.

198. McFarlane, *Special Trust*, 316–317.

199. Kalb to Shultz, "American Attitudes Toward USSR on Eve of Summit," 31 Oct. 1985, RRPL, SFKF, box 91043, folder: "Geneva 1."

200. Margerie to Dumas, "À huit jours du sommet Reagan-Gorbatchev," 13 Nov. 1985, AD, 1930 INVA/5672, folder: "Sommet de Genève."

201. Regan memorandum, "Summit Notes," LOC, DTRP, box 215, folder 3.

202. Gorbachev, *Zhizn' i reformy*, 2:14.

203. Reagan-Gorbachev memorandum of conversation, 10:20–11:20, 19 Nov. 1985, RRPL, RELF, box 7, folder: "Geneva Summit Records 1"; Iakovlev memorandum,

"Vstrecha v Zheneve," 19–20 Nov. 1985, GARF, fond 10063, opis' 1, delo 115; Regan memorandum, "Summit Notes," LOC, DTRP, box 215, folder 3.

204. Dobrynin, *Sugubo doveritel'no*, 624–628.

205. Reagan-Gorbachev memorandum of conversation, 11:27–12:15, 19 Nov. 1985, RRPL, RELF, box 7, folder: "Geneva Summit Records 2"; Iakovlev memorandum, "Vstrecha v Zheneve," 19–20 Nov. 1985, GARF, fond 10063, opis' 1, delo 115.

206. Matlock diary entry, 12 Oct. 1985, RRBML, JRMP, box 2, folder: "1985 Sept.–Dec."

207. Reagan-Gorbachev memorandum of conversation, 14:30–15:40, 19 Nov. 1985, RRPL, RELF, box 7, folder: "Geneva Summit Records 2."

208. Grachev, *Gorbachev's Gamble*, 64.

209. Reagan-Gorbachev memorandum of conversation, 15:40–16:45, 19 Nov. 1985, RRPL, RELF, box 7, folder: "Geneva Summit Records 3"; Regan memorandum, "Summit Notes," LOC, DTRP, box 215, folder 3; Palazhchenko, *My Years with Gorbachev and Shevardnadze*, 43.

210. Reagan-Gorbachev memorandum of conversation, 20:00–22:30, 19 Nov. 1985, RRPL, RELF, box 7, folder: "Geneva Summit Records 3."

211. Reagan-Gorbachev memorandum of conversation, 10:15–11:25, 20 Nov. 1985, RRPL, RELF, box 7, folder: "Geneva Summit Records 3."

212. Iakovlev memorandum, "Vstrecha v Zheneve," 19–20 Nov. 1985, GARF, fond 10063, opis' 1, delo 115; Dobrynin, *Sugubo doveritel'no*, 624–628.

213. Reagan-Gorbachev memorandum of conversation, 11:30–12:40, 20 Nov. 1985, RRPL, RELF, box 7, folder: "Geneva Summit Records 3"; Regan memorandum, "Summit Notes," LOC, DTRP, box 215, folder 4.

214. Regan memorandum, "Summit Notes," LOC, DTRP, box 215, folder 4; Lettow, *Ronald Reagan and His Quest*, 186–188.

215. Reagan-Gorbachev memorandum of conversation, 14:45–15:30, 20 Nov. 1985, RRPL, RELF, box 7, folder: "Geneva Summit Records 4."

216. Regan memorandum, "Summit Notes," LOC, DTRP, box 215, folder 3.

217. Reagan-Gorbachev memorandum of conversation, 20:00–22:30, 20 Nov. 1985, RRPL, RELF, box 7, folder: "Geneva Summit Records 4"; Iakovlev memorandum, "Vstrecha v Zheneve," 19–20 Nov. 1985, GARF, fond 10063, opis' 1, delo 115.

218. Regan memorandum, "Summit Notes," LOC, DTRP, box 215, folder 3.

219. Gorbachev, *Zhizn' i reformy*, 2:21; Taubman, *Gorbachev*, 283.

220. Taubman, *Gorbachev*, 284.

221. Reagan interview, 27 Mar. 1990, MML, DOP, box 2, folder 28; Aleksandrov-Agentov, *Ot Kollontaï do Gorbacheva*, 290; Shevardnadze interview, 17 Jan. 1990, SMML, DOP, box 1, folder 21; Regan, *For the Record*, 317.

222. McFarlane, *Special Trust*, 44.

223. Brown to Platt, "NATO Consultations: Memcon," 30 Nov. 1985, RRPL, RELF, box 7, folder: "Geneva Summit Records 4"; Memorandum, "Themes on Geneva Meeting," RRPL, LJKF, box 11518, folder: "Gorbachev Summit November 1985."

224. Reagan remarks, Washington, D.C., 21 Nov. 1985, *Public Papers of the Presidents: Ronald Reagan, 1985*, 2:1411–1415.

225. Reagan diary entry, 21 Nov. 1985, in Brinkley, *The Reagan Diaries*, 2:543.

226. Matlock diary entry, 4 Mar. 1986, RRBML, JRMP, box 3, folder: "1986 1."

198   NOTES TO PAGES 127-132

227. Abrams, "Gingrich and Reagan." As Abrams puts it, "Gingrich was voluble and certain in predicting that Reagan's policies would fail."

228. Kornienko, *Kholodnaia voĭna*, 361; Palazhchenko, *My Years with Gorbachev and Shevardnadze*, 45.

229. Raimond to Dumas, "Voeux au corps diplomatique: discours de M. Gorbatchev," 27 Dec. 1985, AD, 1930 INVA/5607, folder: "Discours."

230. KPSS memorandum, "Nekotorye dannye o deiatel'nosti Politbiuro i Sekretariata TsK KPSS v 1985 godu," 30 Dec. 1985, LOC, DAVP, box 25, folder 11; Cherniaev diary entry, 24 Nov. 1985, in Cherniaev, *Sovmestnyĭ iskhod*, 657.

231. Adamishin diary entry, 29 Aug. 1984, HIA, ALAP, box 1, folder: "1984"; Adamishin diary entry, 24 Nov. 1985, HIA, ALAP, box 1, folder: "1985."

232. Gromyko memorandum, "Predstavliaetsia informatsiia ob itogakh deyatel'nosti Verkhovnogo Soveta SSSR v 1985 godu," 5 Feb. 1986, RGANI, fond 89, opis' 30, delo 2.

233. Gorbachev remarks, Ministry of Foreign Affairs, Moscow, Soviet Union, in Gorbachev, *Sobranie sochineniĭ*, 4:124–134; Bierbaum memorandum, "Leiterinformation zu den Differenzierungsprozessen in der Administration und Politischen Kreisen der USA nach dem Genfer Treffen," 29 Nov. 1985, BStU, ZAIG, no. 6263; NVA memorandum, "Protokoll der Sitzung des Komitees der Verteidigungsminister der Teilnehmerstaaten des Warschauer Vertrages," 5 Dec. 1985, MA, DVW 1/71044.

234. Gorbachev remarks, KPSS Central Committee, 28 Nov. 1985, in Cherniaev, *V Politbiuro TsK KPSS*, 22–23.

235. Vorotnikov, *A bylo eto tak*, 79.

236. Adamishin diary entries, 24–25 Nov. 1985, HIA, ALAP, box 1, folder: "1985."

237. Akhromeev and Kornienko, *Glazami marshala i diplomata*, 72.

238. KPSS Politburo meeting record, 20 Mar. 1986, in Cherniaev, *V Politbiuro TsK KPSS*, 31–32.

239. Suja memorandum, "Zpráva o vnitropolitické situaci a zahraniční politice USA v 2. pol. r. 1985," 29 Nov. 1985, AMZV, TOT, 1980–1989, SSA, box 5, folder 26.

240. Aleksandrov-Agentov, *Ot Kollontaĭ do Gorbacheva*, 290; Stepanov-Mamaladze notes, 18 Jan. 1986, HIA, TGSMP, box 1, folder 4.

241. Zubok, *Failed Empire*, 107–109, 204–205.

242. Shultz, *Turmoil and Triumph*, 690–691; Lehman, *Oceans Ventured*, 176.

243. Matlock to McDaniel, "Poindexter Tasking on US-Soviet Relations," 29 May 1986, RRPL, JFMF, box 44, folder: "US-USSR Relations March–May 1986 2."

244. Gorbacheva, *Ia nadeius'*, 210.

Conclusion

1. Bush remarks, Washington, D.C., 28 Jan. 1992, in Ashlin, *Public Papers of the Presidents: George H. W. Bush, 1992–1993*, 1:156–163.

2. Fitzwater, *Call the Briefing!*, 261.

3. Engel, *When the World Seemed New*, 6.

4. Edelstein, *Over the Horizon*.

5. Nitze to Iklé, 23 Dec. 1980, LOC, PHNP, pt. 1, box 144, folder 3.

6. Bush and Scowcroft, *A World Transformed*, 28.

7. KPSS Politburo meeting record, 14 Aug. 1986, in Cherniaev, *V Politbiuro TsK KPSS*, 77.

NOTES TO PAGES 132–136

8. Brown, *Seven Years That Changed the World*, 253.

9. Gorbachev remarks, Twenty-Seventh KPSS Plenum, Moscow, Soviet Union, 25 Feb. 1986, in Gorbachev, *Sobranie sochineniĭ*, 3:286–392.

10. Gorbachev remarks, KPSS Central Committee, Moscow, Soviet Union, 10 Mar. 1986, in Gorbachev, *Sobranie sochineniĭ*, 3:415–418.

11. Plokhy, *Chernobyl*, 75–86.

12. KPSS Politburo meeting record, 3 July 1986, in Cherniaev, *V Politbiuro TsK KPSS*, 60–66.

13. Gorbachev, *Naedine s soboĭ*, 442.

14. KPSS Politburo meeting record, 8 May 1986, in Cherniaev, *V Politbiuro TsK KPSS*, 42–43.

15. Gaidar, *Collapse of an Empire*, 122, 137.

16. Gorbachev remarks, Twenty-Seventh KPSS Plenum, Moscow, Soviet Union, 25 Feb. 1986, in Gorbachev, *Sobranie sochineniĭ*, 3:286–392.

17. Haslam, *Russia's Cold War*, 361.

18. Akhromeev oral history, BLPES, 2RR 1/4/12.

19. Odom, *Collapse of the Soviet Military*, 110.

20. Gorbachev remarks, UN General Assembly, New York, N.Y., 7 Dec. 1988, in Gorbachev, *Sobranie sochineniĭ*, 13:18–37. These troops would come chiefly from specialized units with an offensive posture—for example, those trained and equipped for riverine assault to spearhead an invasion westward.

21. Lehman, *Oceans Ventured*, 219.

22. Reagan-Gorbachev memorandum of conversation, 15:30–17:40, 11 Oct. 1986, in Savranskaya and Blanton, *The Last Superpower Summits*, 191.

23. Gorbachev, *Zhizn' i reformy*, 2:31.

24. Charles, "Gorbachev and the Decision to Decouple the Arms Control Package," 68.

25. Shultz, *Turmoil and Triumph*, 894; Savel'yev and Detinov, *Big Five*, 136–137.

26. Lehman, *Oceans Ventured*, 236.

27. Shifrinson, *Rising Titans, Falling Giants*, 129.

28. Engel, *When the World Seemed New*, 86–99.

29. Grachev, *Gorbachev's Gamble*, 177.

30. Taubman, *Gorbachev*, 330.

31. Andreeva, "Ne mogu postupat'sia printsipami," 3; Taubman, *Gorbachev*, 337, 342–346.

32. Taubman, *Gorbachev*, 605–616.

33. Colton, *Yeltsin: A Life*, 130–132.

34. Cherniaev diary entry, 21 Oct. 1987, in Cherniaev, *Sovmestnyĭ iskhod*, 727–731.

35. Sakharov, *Vospominaniia*, 3:427–433.

36. Gorbachev, *Zhizn' i reformy*, 1:318.

37. Suny, *Revenge of the Past*, 138–145.

38. Gorbachev, *Zhizn' i reformy*, 2:410–412.

39. Sarotte, *1989*, 36–47.

40. Gromyko, *Andreĭ Gromyko*, 321.

41. Reagan-Gorbachev memorandum of conversation, 13:05–13:30, 7 Dec. 1988, in Savranskaya and Blanton, *The Last Superpower Summits*, 474.

42. Matlock, *Autopsy on an Empire*, 676.

43. Putin remarks, State Duma, Moscow, Russia, 25 Apr. 2005, http://kremlin.ru/events/president/transcripts/22931.

44. Raleigh, *Russia's Sputnik Generation*, 5.

45. Bush and Scowcroft, *A World Transformed*, 499.

46. Putin, *Ot pervogo litsa*, 71–72.

47. Bush remarks, 31 May 1989, Mainz, West Germany, *Public Papers of the Presidents: George H. W. Bush, 1989*, 1:650–654.

48. Chris Miller, *Putinomics*, 5–6.

49. Freeland, *Sale of the Century*, 171–174.

50. Iazov, *Na strazhe mira i sotsializma*.

51. Abarinov, "Chechnia ne byla dlia menia Rubikonom," 9.

52. Shifrinson, "Deal or No Deal?," 8.

53. Goldgeier, *Not Whether but When*, 1.

54. Talbott, *Russia Hand*, 300.

55. Freeland, *Sale of the Century*, 169–171.

56. Yeltsin remarks, Moscow, Russia, 31 Dec. 1999, http://kremlin.ru/events/president/transcripts/24080.

57. Putin remarks, Moscow, Russia, 17 May 2000, http://kremlin.ru/events/president/transcripts/21440.

58. Hill and Gaddy, *Mr. Putin*, 114, 119.

59. Chris Miller, *Putinomics*, 9; Colton, *Yeltsin: A Life*, 278–279.

60. Walker, *Long Hangover*, 104.

61. Gunitsky and Tsygankov, "The Wilsonian Bias in the Study of Russian Foreign Policy," 385–386.

62. Putin, "Rossiia na rubezhe tysiacheletiĭ."

63. Putin remarks, Moscow, Russia, 5 May 2005, http://kremlin.ru/events/president/transcripts/22948.

64. Putin, *Ot pervogo litsa*, 72–73.

65. Krauthammer, "The Unipolar Moment," 23.

66. Putin remarks, Munich Conference on Security Policy, Munich, Germany, 10 Feb. 2007, http://kremlin.ru/events/president/transcripts/24034.

67. Putin remarks, State Duma, Moscow, Russia, 18 Mar. 2014, http://kremlin.ru/events/president/transcripts/20603.

BIBLIOGRAPHY

Archival Sources

Australia

National Archives of Australia, Canberra (NAA)
    Series A1838: Department of Foreign Affairs, Correspondence Files
    Series A2539: Department of Foreign Affairs, Master Set of Departmental Briefs
       and Briefing Notes

Canada

Library and Archives Canada, Ottawa, Ont. (LAC)
    Record Group 25: Department of External Affairs Fonds (RG 25)

Czech Republic

Archiv Bezpečnostních Složek, Prague (ABS)
    Zpravodajská Správa Generálního Štábu (ZSGŠ)
        Pomocný Materiál (PM)
Archiv Ministerstva Zahraničních Věcí, Prague (AMZV)
    Teritoriální Odbory–Tajné (TOT)
        1980–1989
            Německá Demokratická Republika (NDR)
            Německá Spolková Republika (NSR)
            Spojené Státy Americké (SSA)
            Svaz Sovětských Socialistických Republik (SSSR)
            Velká Británie (VB)
Národní Archiv České Republiky, Prague (NAČR)
    Fond 1261/0/7: Předsednictvo Ústředního Výboru Komunistické Strany
       Československa, 1976–1981
    Fond 1261/0/8: Předsednictvo Ústředního Výboru Komunistické Strany
       Československa, 1981–1986
    Fond 1261/0/44: Gustáv Husák

France

Archives Diplomatiques, La Courneuve (AD)
    91 QO: Direction d'Amérique, 1976–1981
    1929 INVA: Direction d'Europe, 1976–1981
    1930 INVA: Direction d'Europe, 1981–1985

202 BIBLIOGRAPHY

1935 INVA: Direction d'Europe, 1986–1990
1977 INVA: Direction des affaires économiques et financières, 1945–1991
Archives Nationales, Pierrefitte-sur-Seine (AN)
    5 AG 3: Papiers des chefs de l'État, Valéry Giscard d'Estaing, 1974–1981
    5 AG 4: Papiers des chefs de l'État, François Mitterrand, 1981–1995

Germany

Bundesarchiv, Koblenz (BA)
    B 122: Bundespräsidialamt
    B 136: Bundeskanzleramt
Bundesbeauftragte für die Unterlagen des Staatssicherheitsdienstes der Ehemaligen
    Deutschen Demokratischen Republik, Berlin (BStU)
    Abteilung 10: Internationale Verbindungen (Abt. 10)
    Abteilung 19: Sicherung der Auslandsbeziehungen der SED (Abt. 19)
    Allgemeine Sachablage (AS)
    Arbeitsgruppe des Ministers (AdM)
    Bezirksverwaltung Potsdam (BVP)
    Büro der Leitung / Dokumentaufbewahrung (BdL / Dok.)
    Dokumentenstelle (DSt.)
    Hauptabteilung 3: Funkaufklärung und Funkabwehr (HA 3)
    Juristischen Hochschule, Potsdam (JHS)
    Sekretariat des Ministers (SdM)
    Sozialistische Einheitspartei Deutschlands–Kreisleitung (SED–KL)
    Zentrale Auswertungs- und Informationsgruppe (ZAIG)
    Zentraler Operativstab (ZOS)
Militärarchiv, Freiburg im Breisgau (MA)
    DVW 1: Ministerium für Nationale Verteidigung
Politisches Archiv des Auswärtigen Amts, Berlin (PAdAA)
    B 150: Deklassifizierte Dokumente für die Edition der *Akten zur Auswärtigen
    Politik der Bundesrepublik Deutschland*
    M 1: Ministerium für Auswärtige Angelegenheiten
Stiftung Archiv der Parteien und Massenorganisationen der Deutschen De-
    mokratischen Republik, Berlin (SAPMO)
    DY 30: Sozialistische Einheitspartei Deutschlands

Russia

Arkhiv Gorbachev-Fonda, Moscow (AGF)
    Fond 1: Mikhail Sergeevich Gorbachev
    Fond 2: Anatoliĭ Sergeevich Cherniaev
    Fond 3: Vadim Valentinovich Zagladin
    Fond 5: Georgiĭ Khosroevich Shakhnazarov
Arkhiv Rossiĭskoĭ Akademii Nauk, Moscow (ARAN)
    Fond 2021: Institut SShA i Kanady Rossiĭskoĭ Akademii Nauk
Gosudarstvennyĭ Arkhiv Rossiĭskoĭ Federatsii, Moscow (GARF)
    Fond 10063: Aleksandr Nikolaevich Iakovlev
Rossiĭskiĭ Gosudarstvennyĭ Arkhiv Noveĭsheĭ Istorii, Moscow (RGANI)

BIBLIOGRAPHY 203

Fond 80: Leonid Il'ich Brezhnev
Fond 82: Iuriĭ Vladimirovich Andropov
Fond 83: Konstantin Ustinovich Chernenko
Fond 89: Kollektsiia kopiĭ dokumentov, rassekrechennykh pri vypolnenii
  tematicheskikh zaprosov v protsesse nauchno-issledovatel'skoĭ raboty

Ukraine

Haluzevyĭ Derzhavnyĭ Arkhiv Ministerstva Zakordonnykh Sprav, Kyiv (HDAMZS)
  Fond 1: Dokumenty z osnovnoï diial'nosti Spravi postiĭnoho zberihannia
Haluzevyĭ Derzhavnyĭ Arkhiv Sluzhby Bezpeky Ukraïny, Kyiv (HDASBU)
  Fond 16: Sekretariat Komitet derzhavnoï bezpeky Ukraïns'ka Radians'ka
  Sotsialistychna Respublika
Tsentral'nyĭ Derzhavnyĭ Arkhiv Hromads'kikh Ob'edan' Ukraïni, Kyiv (TsDAHO)
  Fond 1: Tsentral'nyĭ Komitet Kommunisticheskoĭ Partii Ukrainy

United Kingdom

British Library of Political and Economic Sciences, London School of Economics,
  London (BLPES)
  2RR: *The Second Russian Revolution*
Churchill Archives Centre, Cambridge University, Cambridge (CAC)
  MITN: Papers of Vasiliy Mitrokhin
  THCR: Papers of Margaret Thatcher
Liddell Hart Centre for Military Archives, King's College London, London (LHCMA)
  BOA: *1983: The Brink of Apocalypse*
  FOTW: *The Fall of the Wall*
  TNA: *The Nuclear Age*
National Archives of the United Kingdom, Kew (NAUK)
  AVIA 120: Department of Transport, International Aviation Division, 1983–1988
  FCO 7: Foreign and Commonwealth Office, Latin American Department,
  1967–1983
  FCO 9: Foreign and Commonwealth Office, Southern European Department,
  1967–1983
  FCO 28: Foreign and Commonwealth Office, East European and Soviet Depart-
  ment, 1968–1983
  FCO 82: Foreign and Commonwealth Office, North America Department,
  1971–1983
  FCO 105: Foreign and Commonwealth Office, Southern African Department,
  1979–1983
  HO 322: Home Office, Civil Defence, 1939–1990
  PREM 15: Prime Minister's Office, Correspondence and Papers, 1970–1974
  PREM 19: Prime Minister's Office, Correspondence and Papers, 1979–1997

United States

Bates College Archives, Lewiston, Maine (BCA)
  Edmund S. Muskie Papers (ESMP)
    US Secretary of State (SOS)

204   **BIBLIOGRAPHY**

David M. Rubenstein Rare Book and Manuscript Library, Duke University, Durham, N.C. (RRBML)
 Arthur F. Burns Papers (AFBP)
 Jack and Rebecca Matlock Papers (JRMP)
George H. W. Bush Presidential Library, College Station, Texas (GBPL)
 Presidential Records (PR)
  President's Foreign Intelligence Advisory Board (PFIAB)
   Subject Files (SF)
  Vice-Presidential Records (VPR)
   National Security Affairs (NSA)
    Donald P. Gregg Files (DPGF)
     Country Files (CF)
     Foreign Travel Files (FTF)
     Meetings with Foreigners Files (MFF)
Gerald R. Ford Presidential Library, Ann Arbor, Mich. (GFPL)
 Arthur F. Burns Papers (AFBP)
 National Security Advisor (NSA)
  Kissinger-Scowcroft West Wing Office Files (KSWWOF)
  National Security Council Meeting File (NSCFM)
  Presidential Agency File (PAF)
 President Ford Committee Records (PFCR)
 Rogers Morton Files (RMF)
 Ron Nessen Papers (RNP)
Hoover Institution Archives, Stanford, Calif. (HIA)
 Anatoliĭ L. Adamishin Papers (ALAP)
 Committee on the Present Danger Records (CPDR)
 Fred C. Iklé Papers (FCIP)
 Hoover Institution and Gorbachev Foundation Collection (HIGFC)
 Jim Mann Papers (JMP)
 Richard V. Allen Papers (RVAP)
 Ronald Reagan Subject Collection (RRSC)
 Teimuraz G. Stepanov-Mamaladze Papers (TGSMP)
 William J. Casey Papers (WJCP)
Jimmy Carter Presidential Library, Atlanta, Ga. (JCPL)
 Chief of Staff Files (CSF)
  George D. Moffett Subject Files (GDMSF)
  Hamilton Jordan 1980 Campaign Files (HJCF)
  Hamilton Jordan Subject Files (HJSF)
  Landon Butler Subject Files (LBSF)
 Jody L. Powell Papers (JLPP)
  Subject Files (SF)
 James C. Free Papers (JCFP)
  Subject File (SF)
 National Security Affairs (NSA)
  Country File (SF)
 Records of Susan Clough (RSC)

BIBLIOGRAPHY   205

Susan Clough 1980 Political Files (SCPF)
Remote Archives Capture (RAC)
Zbigniew Brzezinski Collection (ZBC)
Library of Congress, Manuscript Division, Washington, D.C. (LOC)
Alexander M. Haig Papers (AMHP)
Caspar W. Weinberger Papers (CWWP)
Dmitriĭ Antonovich Volkogonov Papers (DAVP)
Donald T. Regan Papers (DTRP)
Paul H. Nitze Papers (PHNP)
William E. Odom Papers (WEOP)
Minnesota Historical Society, St. Paul, Minn. (MNHS)
Max M. Kampelman Papers (MMKP)
Walter F. Mondale Papers (WFMP)
National Archives and Records Administration, Archives II, College Park, Md.
(NARA)
Central Intelligence Agency Records Search Tool (CREST)
Record Group 59: General Records of the Department of State (RG 59)
Subject Files of Edmund S. Muskie (SFESM)
Record Group 263: Records of the Central Intelligence Agency (RG 263)
Intelligence Reports on the USSR for Princeton University Conference
(PUC)
National Intelligence Estimates (NIE)
Records of Team A and Team B Estimates of the Soviet Offensive Threat
(SOT)
National Defense University Archives, Washington, D.C. (NDUA)
Papers of John W. Vessey (PJWV)
Ronald Reagan Presidential Library, Simi Valley, Calif. (RRPL)
1980 Campaign Papers (1980 CP)
Anne V. Higgins Files (AVHF)
Anthony R. Dolan Files (ARDF)
Crisis Management Center–National Security Council (CMC–NSC)
David S. Addington Files (DSAF)
Dennis C. Blair Files (DCBF)
Donald T. Regan Files (DTRF)
Edward P. Djerejian Files (EPDF)
European and Soviet Affairs Directorate–National Security Council
(ESAD–NSC)
Executive Secretariat–National Security Council (ES–NSC)
Country File (CF)
Head of State File (HSF)
Meeting File (MF)
National Security Planning Group File (NSPG)
National Security Study Directives (NSSD)
Subject File (SF)
Jack F. Matlock Files (JFMF)
John Lenczowski Files (JLF)
Linas J. Kojelis Files (LJKF)

206 BIBLIOGRAPHY

Linton F. Brooks Files (LFBF)
Paula J. Dobriansky Files (PJDF)
Peter W. Rodman Files (PWRF)
Richard E. Pipes Files (REPF)
Robert C. McFarlane Files (RCMF)
Robert E. Linhard Files (RELF)
Ronald F. Lehman Files (RFLF)
Sven F. Kraemer Files (SFKF)
William P. Clark Files (WPCF)
Seeley G. Mudd Manuscript Library, Princeton University, Princeton, N.J. (SMML)
Don Oberdorfer Papers (DOP)

Published Primary Sources

Abarinov, Vladimir. "Andreĭ Kozyrev: 'Chechnia ne byla dlia menia Rubikonom.'"
Segodnia, no. 200 (20 Oct. 1995): 9.
Adams, Bruce. Tiny Revolutions in Russia: Twentieth Century Soviet and Russian History
in Anecdotes and Jokes. New York: Routledge Curzon, 2005.
Afinov, V. V. "Razvitie v SShA vyzokotochnogo oruzhiia i perspektivy sozdaniia
razvedyvatel'no-udarnykh kompleksov." Voennaia mysl', no. 4 (1983): 63–71.
Akhromeev, Sergeĭ, and Georgiĭ Kornienko. Glazami marshala i diplomata: Kriticheskiĭ
vzgliad na vneshniuiu politiku SSSR do i posle 1985 goda. Moscow: Mezhdunarodnye Otnosheniia, 1992.
Aleksandrov, V. A. "O dolgosrochnoĭ voennoĭ programme NATO." Voennaia mysl',
no. 7 (1982): 79–80.
Aleksandrov-Agentov, Andreĭ. Ot Kollontai do Gorbacheva: Vospominaniia diplomata,
sovetnika Gromyko, i pomoshchnika Brezhneva, Andropova, Chernenko i Gor-
bacheva. Moscow: Mezhdunarodnye Otnosheniia, 1994.
Allen, Richard V. "Ronald Reagan: An Extraordinary Man in Extraordinary Times."
In The Fall of the Berlin Wall: Reasserting the Causes and Consequences of the End
of the Cold War, edited by Peter Schweizer, 49–60. Stanford, Calif.: Hoover
Institution Press, 2000.
Andreeva, Nina. "Ne mogu postupat'sia printsipami." Sovetskaia rossiia, no. 60
(13 Mar. 1988): 3.
Andropov, Iuriĭ V. Iu.V. Andropov: Izbrannye rechi i stat'i. 2nd ed. Moscow: Politizdat,
1983.
———. "Zaiavlenie Generalnogo sekretaria TsK KPSS Predsedatelia Presidiuma
Verkhovnogo Sovieta SSSR Iu.V. Andropov." Pravda, no. 272 (29 Sept. 1983): 1.
Arbatov, Georgiĭ. Zatianuvsheesia vyzdorovlenie, 1953–1985: Svidetel'stvo sovremennika.
Moscow: Mezhdunarodnye Otnosheniia, 1991.
Artizov, A. N., and N. G. Tomilina, Andropov: K 100-letiiu so dnia rozhdeniia. Moscow:
Kuchkogo Pole, 2014.
Ashlin, Karen Howard. Public Papers of the Presidents of the United States: George H. W.
Bush, 1992–1993. 2 vols. Washington, D.C.: US Government Printing Office, 1993.
Baltizer, Alfred, and Gerald Bonetto, eds. A Time for Choosing: The Speeches of Ronald
Reagan, 1961–1982. Chicago: Regnery Gateway, 1983.

BIBLIOGRAPHY   207

Banks, William K., ed. *Public Papers of the Presidents of the United States: George H. W. Bush, 1988.* 2 vols. Washington, D.C.: US Government Printing Office, 1990.

——, ed. *Public Papers of the Presidents of the United States: Ronald Reagan, 1985.* 2 vols. Washington, D.C.: US Government Printing Office, 1988.

Baturin, A. S. "Nauchno-tekhnicheskaia revoliutsiia i voennye prigotovleniia SShA." *Voennaia mysl'*, no. 2 (1981): 75–80.

Berkutov, S. N. "Iadernye sredstva NATO na Evropeĭskom teatre voĭny." *Voennaia mysl'*, no. 9 (1981): 53–60.

Bobkov, Filipp. *KGB i vlast'.* Moscow: Veteran MP, 1995.

Bondarenko, V. M. "XXVI s"ezd KPSS o nauchnom potentsiale razvitogo sotsializma: Vliianie nauchnogo potentsiala na povyshenie voennoĭ moshchi Sovetskogo gosudarstva." *Voennaia mysl'*, no. 12 (1981): 53–63.

Bothwell, Robert, and J. L. Granatstein. *Trudeau's World: Insiders Reflect on Foreign Policy, Trade, and Defence, 1968–84.* Vancouver: University of British Columbia Press, 2018.

Brezhnev, Leonid I. *Rabochie i dnevnikovye zapisi*, ed. Andreĭ Artizov. 3 vols. Moscow: IstLit, 2016.

Brinkley, Douglas, ed. *The Reagan Diaries.* 2 vols. New York: HarperCollins, 2009.

Brook-Shepherd, Gordon. *The Storm Birds: Soviet Post-War Defectors.* London: Weidenfeld and Nicolson, 1988.

Brutents, Karen. *Nesbyvsheesia: Neravnodushnye zametki o perestroĭke.* Moscow: Mezhdunarodnye Otnosheniia, 2005.

——. *Tridtsat' let na staroĭ ploshchadi.* Moscow: Mezhdunarodnye Otnosheniia, 1998.

Bush, George H. W. *All the Best: My Life in Letters and Other Writings.* New York: Simon and Schuster, 2013.

Bush, George H. W., and Brent Scowcroft. *A World Transformed.* New York: Alfred A. Knopf, 1998.

Caldicott, Helen Broinowski. *A Desperate Passion.* New York: W. W. Norton, 1996.

Chazov, Evgeniĭ. *Zdorov'e i vlast': Vospominaniia kremleskogo vracha.* Moscow: Tsentrpoligraf, 2015.

Cherkashin, Viktor. *Spy Handler: Memoirs of a KGB Officer.* With Gregory Feifer. New York: Basic Books, 2005.

Chernenko, Konstantin U. *Narod i partiia ediny: Izbrannye rechi i stat'i.* Moscow: Politizdat, 1984.

Cherniaev, Anatoliĭ. *Shest' let s Gorbachevym: Po dnevnikovym zapisiam.* Moscow: Kul'tura, 1993.

——. *Sovmestnyĭ iskhod: Dnevnik dvukh epokh, 1971–1991 gody.* Moscow: Rosspen, 2008.

——, ed. *V Politbiuro TsK KPSS: Po zapisiam Anatoliia Cherniaeva, Vadima Medvedeva, Georgiia Shakhnazarova, 1985–1991.* Moscow: Alpina, 2006.

Chervov, N. F. "Ravnestvo i odinakovaia bezopasnost'—osnova okranicheniia i sokrashcheniia iadernykh vooruzheniĭ." *Voennaia mysl'*, no. 5 (1983): 17–30.

Chojnacki, Piotr, ed. *PZPR a Solidarność, 1980–1981: Tajne dokumenty Biura Politycznego.* Warsaw: Instytut Pamięci Narodowej, 2013.

Church, George J. "Can Capitalism Survive?" *Time* 6, no. 2 (1975): 52–63.

——. "Men of the Year: Ronald Reagan and Yuri Andropov." *Time* 123, no. 1 (1984): 16–35.

208 **BIBLIOGRAPHY**

Department of Defense, *Soviet Military Power*. Washington, D.C.: US Government Printing Office, 1981.

Dobrynin, Anatoliĭ. *Sugubo doveritel'no: Posol v Vashingtone pri shesti prezidentakh SShA, 1962–1986 gg.* Moscow: Avtor, 1996.

Donohoe, Margaret M., Kenneth R. Payne, Wilma P. Greene, and Doris O'Keefe, eds. *Public Papers of the Presidents of the United States: Gerald R. Ford, 1975.* 2 vols. Washington, D.C.: US Government Printing Office, 1976.

Dvinina, L. I. "'Zvezdnye voĭny': Illiuzii i opasnosti." *Voennaia mysl'*, no. 9 (1985): 15–28.

Elson, John, and Henry Muller, "Some Practical and Realistic Advice: Eight Statesmen, American and Foreign, Suggest How to Reduce Tensions." *Time* 123, no. 1 (1984): 38–40.

Ermarth, Fritz W. "Observations on the 'War Scare' of 1983 from an Intelligence Perch." Parallel History Project on NATO and the Warsaw Pact. 6 Nov. 2003. http://www.php.isn.ethz.ch/lory1.ethz.ch/collections/colltopic320b.html?lng=en&id=17325&navinfo=15296.

Falin, Valentin. *Bez skidok na obstoiatel'stva.* Moscow: Izdatel'stvo Respublika, 1999.

Fitzpatrick, Sheila. *A Spy in the Archives: A Memoir of Cold War Russia.* London: I.B. Tauris, 2015.

Fitzwater, Marlin. *Call the Briefing! Reagan and Bush, Sam and Helen: A Decade with Presidents and the Press.* New York: Times Books, 1995.

Garton Ash, Timothy. *The File: A Personal History.* New York: Random House, 2007.

Geraghty, Timothy J. *Peacekeepers at War: Beirut 1983—the Marine Commander Tells His Story.* Washington, D.C.: Potomac Books, 2012.

Glitman, Maynard W. *The Last Battle of the Cold War: An Inside Account of Negotiating the Intermediate Range Nuclear Forces Treaty.* New York: Palgrave Macmillan, 2006.

Gorbachev, Mikhail S. *Naedine s soboĭ.* Moscow: Grin Strit, 2012.

——. *Sobranie sochineniĭ.* 27 vols. Moscow: Ves' Mir, 2008.

——. *Zhizn' i reformy.* 2 vols. Moscow: Novosti, 1995.

Gorbacheva, Rasia M. *Ia nadeius'.* Moscow: Novosti, 1991.

Gordievsky, Oleg. *Next Stop Execution.* London: Macmillan, 1995.

Gotlieb, Allan. *The Washington Diaries, 1981–1989.* Toronto, Ont.: McClelland and Stewart, 2007.

Grachev, Andreĭ S. *Gorbachev's Gamble: Soviet Foreign Policy and the End of the Cold War.* Cambridge: Polity, 2008.

——. *Kremlevskaia khronika.* Moscow: Eksmo, 1994.

Greene, Wilma P., and William K. Banks, eds. *Public Papers of the Presidents of the United States: Ronald Reagan, 1984.* 2 vols. Washington, D.C.: US Government Printing Office, 1986.

Greene, Wilma P., Katherine A. Mellody, and Kenneth R. Payne, eds. *Public Papers of the Presidents of the United States: Ronald Reagan, 1982.* 2 vols. Washington, D.C.: US Government Printing Office, 1983.

Greene, Wilma P., Katherine A. Mellody, Kenneth R. Payne, and William K. Banks, eds. *Public Papers of the Presidents of the United States: Ronald Reagan, 1981.* Washington, D.C.: US Government Printing Office, 1982.

Grinevskiĭ, Oleg. *Taĭny sovetskoĭ diplomatii.* Moscow: Vagrius, 2000.

BIBLIOGRAPHY   209

Grishin, Viktor. *Ot Khrushcheva do Gorbacheva: Politicheskie portreti piati gensekov i A.N. Kosygina*. Moscow: ASPOL, 1996.

Gurov, A.A. "Rost ekonomicheskogo potentsiala razvitogo sotsialisticheskogo obshchestva—reshaiushchiĭ faktor ukrepleniia oboronnoĭ moshchi Sovetskogo gosudarstva i ego Vooruzhennykh Sil." *Voennaia mysl'*, no. 11 (1981): 62–70.

Haig, Alexander M. *Caveat: Realism, Reagan, and Foreign Policy*. New York: Macmillan, 1984.

Hawke, Bob. *The Hawke Memoirs*. Melbourne: William Heinemann, 1994.

Head, Ivan L., and Pierre Elliott Trudeau. *The Canadian Way: Shaping Canada's Foreign Policy, 1964–1984*. Toronto, Ont.: McLellan and Stewart, 1995.

Hill, Maxine, and Thomas Kevan, eds. *Public Papers of the Presidents of the United States: Ronald Reagan, 1983*. 2 vols. Washington, D.C.: US Government Printing Office, 1984.

Hines, John E., Ellis M. Mishulovich, and John F. Shull, eds. *Soviet Intentions, 1965–1985*. 2 vols. *Soviet Post–Cold War Testimonial Evidence*. McLean, Va.: BDM Federal, 1995.

Holdren, John P., David Holloway, and Deborah Shapley. "Three Minutes to Midnight." *Bulletin of the Atomic Scientists* 40, no. 1 (1984): 2.

Howe, Geoffrey. *Conflict of Loyalty*. London: Macmillan, 1994.

Iakovlev, Aleksandr. "Protiv antiistorizma." *Literaturnaia gazeta*, no. 46 (15 Nov. 1972): 4–5.

——. *Sumerki*. Moscow: Materik, 2003.

Iazov, Dmitriĭ T. *Na strazhe mira i sotsializma*. Moscow: Voenizdat, 1987.

Ivashov, L. G. "Dostizhenie voenno-tekhnicheskogo prevoskhodstva nad fashistskoĭ Germanieĭ vazhneĭshiĭ faktor pobedy v Velikoĭ Otechestvennoĭ voĭne." *Voennaia mysl'*, no. 4 (1985): 42–48.

Jones, Nate, ed. *Able Archer 83: The Secret History of the NATO Exercise That Almost Triggered Nuclear War*. New York: New Press, 2016.

Kevorkov, Viacheslav. *Taĭnyĭ kanal*. Moscow: Geia, 1997.

Kissinger, Henry. *White House Years*. New York: Little, Brown, 1979.

Kohl, Helmut. *Erinnerungen*. 2 vols. Munich: Droemer, 2004.

Kornienko, Georgiĭ. *Kholodnaia voina: Svidetel'svo ee uchastnika*. Moscow: Olma, 2001.

Korochianskiĭ, I. F. "Narushenie voenno-strategicheskogo ravnovesiia—tsel' militaristskikh prigotovleniĭ SShA." *Voennaia mysl'*, no. 3 (1982): 15–22.

Kostenko, I. A. "O vnezapnosti v vooruzhennoĭ bor'b." *Voennaia mysl'*, no. 11 (1983): 70–74.

Kostikov, Mikhail. "Protiv iadernogo bezumiia." *Pravda*, no. 153 (2 June 1983): 5.

Kovalev, Sergeĭ. "Suverenitet i internatsional'nye obiazannosti sotsialisticheskikh stran." *Pravda*, no. 270 (26 Sept. 1968): 4.

Krauthammer, Charles. "The Unipolar Moment." *Foreign Affairs* 70, no. 1 (1990): 23–33.

Kruchinin, A. G. "Partnerstvo imperializma i pekinskovo gegemonizma—novaia ugroza miru." *Voennaia mysl'*, no. 5 (1981): 52–58.

Kudriashov, Sergeĭ. *General'nyĭ sekretar' L.I. Brezhnev, 1964–1982: Vestnik Arkhiva Prezidenta*. Moscow: Arkhiv Prezidenta Rossiĭskoĭ Federatsii, 2006.

Kurdiumov, Nikolaĭ. "Politika terrorizma." *Pravda*, no. 204 (22 July 1984): 5.

210   BIBLIOGRAPHY

Lehman, John. *Oceans Ventured: Winning the Cold War at Sea*. New York: W. W. Norton, 2018.

Leonov, Nikolaĭ S. *Likholet'e*. Moscow: Russkiĭ Dom, 1995.

Mashchenko, V. A., and Iu. V. Dmitriev. "Primenenie kosmicheskikh sistem gidrometeorologicheskoĭ razvedki SShA v voennykh tseliakh." *Voennaia mysl'*, no. 1 (1981): 76–80.

McFarlane, Robert C. *Special Trust*. With Zofia Smardz. New York: Cadell and Davies, 1994.

Medvedev, Vadim. *V komande Gorbacheva: Vzgliad iznutri*. Moscow: Bylina, 1994.

Medvedev, Vladimir. *Chelovek za spinoĭ*. Moscow: Russlit, 1994.

Mellody, Katherine A., Kenneth R. Payne, Brian L. Hermes, and Gwendolyn J. Henderson, eds. *Public Papers of the Presidents of the United States: Jimmy Carter, 1979*. 2 vols. Washington, D.C.: US Government Printing Office, 1980.

Meshcheriakov, V. I. "Strategicheskaia razvedka SShA—orudie imperialisticheskoĭ vneshneĭ politiki." *Voennaia mysl'*, no. 9 (1981): 15–27.

Nitze, Paul H. *From Hiroshima to Glasnost: At the Center of Decision*. With Ann M. Smith and Steven L. Rearden. New York: Weidenfeld, 1989.

——. "Reagan as Foreign Policy Strategist." In *Foreign Policy in the Reagan Presidency: Nine Intimate Perspectives*, edited by Kenneth W. Thompson, 145–157. Lanham, Md.: University Press of America,1993.

Ogarkov, Nikolaĭ V. "Zashchita sotsializma: Opyt istorii i sovremennost'." *Krasnaia zveszda*, no. 189 (9 May 1984): 2–3.

Palazhchenko, Pavel. *My Years with Gorbachev and Shevardnadze: The Memoir of a Soviet Interpreter*. University Park: Pennsylvania State University Press, 1997.

Pavlovskiĭ, R. I., and V. V. Kariakin. "Ob opyte primeneniia matematicheskikh modeleĭ." *Voennaia mysl'*, no. 3 (1982): 54–57.

Perry, John. "Please, Japan, Return the Favor: Occupy Us." *New York Times*, no. 44,877 (4 Mar. 1981): A1.

Petrov, N. F. "O iadernoĭ strategii SShA." *Voennaia mysl'*, no. 8 (1981): 14–25.

Pipes, Richard. *Vixi: Memoirs of a Non-Belonger*. New Haven, Conn.: Yale University Press, 2003.

Popov, K. M. "Sostoianie i perspektivy razvitiia v SShA kosmicheskoĭ sistemy nabliudeniia za zapuskami ballisticheskikh raket." *Voennaia mysl'*, no. 3 (1981): 68–73.

Pribytkov, Viktor. *Apparat: 390 dneĭ i vsia zhizn' Genseka Cherneko*. Moscow: Molodaia Gvardiia, 2002.

Putin, Vladimir V. *Ot pervogo litsa: Razgovory s Vladimirom Putinym*. Moscow: Vagrius, 2000.

——. "Rossiia na rubezhe tysiacheletiĭ." *Nezavisimaia gazeta*, 30 Dec. 1999, http://www.ng.ru/politics/1999-12-30/4_millenium.html.

Raleigh, Donald, ed. *Russia's Sputnik Generation: Soviet Boomers Talk about Their Lives*. Bloomington: Indiana University Press, 2006.

Reagan, Nancy. *My Turn*. With William Novak. New York: Random House, 1989.

Reagan, Ronald. *An American Life: The Autobiography*. New York: Simon and Schuster, 1990.

Reed, Thomas C. *At the Abyss: An Insider's History of the Cold War*. New York: Presidio Press, 2004.

BIBLIOGRAPHY   211

Regan, Donald T. *For the Record: From Wall Street to Washington.* San Diego, Calif.: Harcourt Brace Jovanovich, 1988.

Ryzhkov, Nikolaĭ. *Perestroĭka: Istoriia predatel'stv.* Moscow: Novosti, 1992.

Safire, William. "Intelligence Fiasco." *New York Times,* no. 48,218 (27 Apr. 1990): A35.

Sakharov, Andreĭ. *Vospominaniia.* 3 vols. Moscow: Vremia, 2006.

Savranskaya, Svetlana, and Thomas Blanton, eds. *The Last Superpower Summits: Conversations that Ended the Cold War.* Budapest: Central European University Press, 2016.

Shakhnazarov, Georgiĭ. *S vozhdiami i bez nikh.* Moscow: Vagrius, 2001.

——. *Tsena svobody: Reformatsiia Gorbacheva glazami ego pomoshchnika.* Moscow: Zevs, 1993.

Shevardnadze, Eduard A. *Moĭ vybor: V zashchitu demokratii i svobody.* Moscow: Novosti, 1991.

Shkadov, I. N. "Povyshat' otvetstvennost' i distsiplinu, sovrshenstvovat' stil' raboty rukovodiashchikh voennykh kadrov." *Voennaia mysl',* no. 12 (1980): 3–13.

Shultz, George P. *Turmoil and Triumph: Diplomacy, Power, and the Victory of the American Ideal.* New York: Charles Scribner's Sons, 1993.

Sidorenko, A. G., ed. *Andropov: V vospominaniiakh i otsenkakh soratnikov i soslyzhivtsev.* Moscow: Artstil'-Poligrafiia, 2011.

Skinner, Kiron, Annelise Anderson, and Martin Anderson, eds. *Reagan: A Life in Letters.* New York: Free Press, 2003.

Skinner, Kiron, Annelise Anderson, and Martin Anderson, eds. *Reagan: In His Own Hand; The Writings of Ronald Reagan That Reveal His Revolutionary Vision for America.* New York: Simon and Schuster, 2001.

Slavin, Boris. *Neokonchennaia istoriia: Tri tsveta vremeni.* Moscow: Mezhdunarodnye Otnosheniia, 2005.

Stalin, Iosif. *Sochineniia.* 13 vols. Moscow: Gosudarstvennoe Izdatel'stvo Politicheskoĭ Literatury, 1955.

Stearman, William L. *An American Adventure: From Early Aviation through Three Wars to the White House.* Annapolis, Md.: Naval Institute Press, 2012.

Talbott, Strobe. *The Russia Hand: A Memoir of Presidential Diplomacy.* New York: Random House, 2002.

Teller, Edward. *Memoirs: A Twentieth-Century Journey in Science and Politics.* With Judith L. Shoolery. Cambridge, Mass.: Perseus, 2001.

Thatcher, Margaret. *The Downing Street Years.* London: Harper Collins, 1993.

Turner, Stansfield. *Burn Before Reading: Presidents, CIA Directors, and Secret Intelligence.* New York: Hyperion, 2005.

Vance, Cyrus. *Hard Choices: Critical Years in America's Foreign Policy.* New York: Simon and Schuster, 1983.

Vasil'chenko, M. V. "Operativnaia podgotovka ob"edinennykh vooruzhennykh sil NATO v 1980 godu." *Voennaia mysl',* no. 4 (1980): 62–69.

Védrine, Hubert. *Les Mondes de François Mitterand: À l'Elysée, 1981–1985.* Paris: Fayard, 1996.

Volcker, Paul A. *Keeping at It: The Quest for Sound Money and Good Government.* With Christine Harper. New York: Public Affairs, 2018.

Vorotnikov, Vitaliĭ. *A bylo eto tak: Iz dnevnika chlena Politbiuro TsK KPSS.* Moscow: Kniga i biznes, 2003.

212   **BIBLIOGRAPHY**

Weinberger, Caspar. *Fighting for Peace: Seven Critical Years in the Pentagon*. New York: Warner Books, 1990.

Whelan, Eugene. *Whelan: The Man in the Green Stetson*. With Rick Archbold. Toronto, Ont.: Irwin, 1986.

Will, George F. "The Price of Power." *Newsweek* 102, no. 19 (1983): 142.

Wohlforth, William, ed. *Witnesses to the End of the Cold War*. Baltimore, Md.: Johns Hopkins University Press, 1996.

Wolf, Markus. *Man without a Face: The Autobiography of Communism's Greatest Spymaster*. With Anne McElvoy. London: Jonathan Cape, 1997.

Zaĭnullin, R. Kh. "Ideologicheskoe protivoborstvo dvukh sistem: Sushchnost', osnovnye tendentsii." *Voennaia mysl'*, no. 8 (1985): 63–73.

Zaslavskaia, Tat'iana. "The Novosibirsk Report." Translated by Teresa Cherfas. *Survey* 28, no. 1 (1984): 88–108.

Zhuravlev, E. A. "O povyshenii effektivnosti voenno-nauchnykh issledovani." *Voennaia mysl'*, no. 7 (1985): 43–44.

Secondary Sources

Abrams, Elliot. "Gingrich and Reagan." *National Review*, 25 Jan. 2012. https://www.nationalreview.com/2012/01/gingrich-and-reagan-elliott-abrams/.

Ambinder, Marc. *The Brink: President Reagan and the Nuclear War Scare of 1983*. New York: Simon and Schuster, 2018.

Andrew, Christopher, and Oleg Gordievsky. *Comrade Kryuchkov's Instructions: Top Secret Files on KGB Foreign Operations, 1975–1985*. Stanford, Calif.: Stanford University Press, 1993.

——. *KGB: The Inside Story of its Foreign Operations from Lenin to Gorbachev*. London: Hodder and Stoughton, 1990.

Arbel, David, and Ran Edelist. *Western Intelligence and the Collapse of the Soviet Union, 1980–1990: Ten Years That Did Not Shake the World*. London: Frank Cass, 2003.

Bacon, Edwin, and Mark Sandle, eds. *Brezhnev Reconsidered*. Houndmills: Palgrave Macmillan, 2002.

Bange, Oliver. "'Keeping Détente Alive': Inner-German Relations under Helmut Schmidt and Erich Honecker, 1974–1982." In *The Crisis of Détente in Europe: From Helsinki to Gorbachev, 1975–1985*, edited by Leopoldo Nuti, 230–243. London: Routledge, 2009.

Barrass, Gordon. "Able Archer 83: What Were the Soviets Thinking?" *Survival* 58, no. 6 (2016): 7–30.

——. *The Great Cold War: A Journey through the Hall of Mirrors*. Stanford, Calif.: Stanford University Press, 2009.

Bartel, Michael. "The Triumph of Broken Promises: Oil, Finance, and the End of the Cold War." Ph.D. diss., Cornell University, Ithaca, N.Y., 2017.

Békés, Csaba. "Why Was There No 'Second Cold War' in Europe? Hungary and the East-West Crisis Following the Soviet Invasion of Afghanistan." In *NATO and the Warsaw Pact: Intrabloc Conflicts*, edited by Mary Ann Heiss and S. Victor Papacosma, 219–232. Kent, Ohio: Kent State University Press, 2008.

Biven, W. Carl. *Jimmy Carter's Economy: Policy in an Age of Limits*. Chapel Hill: University of North Carolina Press, 2002.

BIBLIOGRAPHY   213

Blainey, Geoffrey. *The Causes of War*. 3rd ed. Baisingstoke: Macmillan, 1988.
Boldin, Valeriĭ. *Krushenie p'edestala: Shtrikhi k portretu M.S. Gorbacheva*. Moscow: Respublika, 1995.
Bonin, Hubert. "Business Interests versus Geopolitics: The Case of the Siberian Pipeline in the 1980s." *Business History* 49, no. 2 (2007): 235–254.
Bothwell, Robert. *Your Country, My Country: A Unified History of the United States and Canada*. Oxford: Oxford University Press, 2015.
Bothwell, Robert, and J. L. Granatstein. *Pirouette: Pierre Trudeau and Canadian Foreign Policy*. Toronto, Ont.: University of Toronto Press, 1990.
Brands, Hal. *Latin America's Cold War*. Cambridge, Mass.: Harvard University Press, 2010.
——. *Making the Unipolar Moment: US Foreign Policy and the Rise of the Post–Cold War Order*. Ithaca, N.Y.: Cornell University Press, 2016.
——. *What Good Is Grand Strategy? Power and Purpose in American Statecraft from Harry S. Truman to George W. Bush*. Ithaca, N.Y.: Cornell University Press, 2014.
Brauer, Carl M. *Presidential Transitions: Eisenhower through Reagan*. New York: Oxford University Press, 1986.
Brooks, Stephen G., and William C. Wohlforth. "Power, Globalization, and the End of the Cold War: Reevaluating a Landmark Case for Ideas." *International Security* 25, no. 3 (2000): 5–53.
Brown, Archie. *The Gorbachev Factor*. Oxford: Oxford University Press, 1996.
——. *Seven Years That Changed the World: Perestroika in Perspective*. Oxford: Oxford University Press, 2007.
Bullock, Alan. *Ernest Bevin: Foreign Secretary, 1945–1951*. London: Heinemann, 1983.
Burovskiĭ, Andreĭ. *Velikiĭ Andropov: Zheleznyĭ Gensek*. Moscow: Eksmo, 2014.
Cannon, Lou. *Governor Reagan: His Rise to Power*. New York: Public Affairs, 2003.
——. *President Reagan: The Role of a Lifetime*. New York: Simon and Schuster, 1991.
Caryl, Christian. *Strange Rebels: 1979 and the Birth of the 21st Century*. New York: Basic Books, 2014.
Chamberlin, Paul Thomas. *The Cold War's Killing Fields: Rethinking the Long Peace*. New York: Harper Collins, 2018.
Charles, Elizabeth C. "Gorbachev and the Decision to Decouple the Arms Control Package: How the Breakdown of the Reykjavik Summit Led to the Elimination of the Euromissiles." In *The Euromissile Crisis and the End of the Cold War*, edited by Leopoldo Nuti, Frédéric Bozo, Marie-Pierre Rey, and Bernd Rother, 66–84. Washington, D.C.: Woodrow Wilson Center Press, 2015.
Chen, Zhong Zhong. "Defying Moscow: East German–Chinese Relations during the Andropov- Chernenko Interregnum, 1982–1985." *Cold War History* 14, no. 2 (2014): 259–280.
Chiampan, Andrea. "'Those European Chicken Littles': Reagan, NATO, and the Polish Crisis, 1981–1982." *International History Review* 37, no. 4 (2015): 682–699.
Cimbala, Stephen J. "Revisiting the Nuclear 'War Scare' of 1983: Lessons Retro- and Prospectively." *Journal of Slavic Military Studies* 27, no. 2 (2014): 234–253.
Clark, William A. *Crime and Punishment in Soviet Officialdom: Combating Corruption in the Political Elite, 1965–1990*. Armonk, N.Y.: M.E. Sharpe, 1993.
Clausewitz, Carl. *On War*. Edited and translated by Michael Howard and Peter Paret. Princeton, N.J.: Princeton University Press, 1989.

BIBLIOGRAPHY

Cogan, Charles G. "Desert One and Its Disorders." *Journal of Military History* 67, no. 1 (2003): 201–216.

Colbourn, Susan. "'Cruising toward Nuclear Danger': Canadian Anti-Nuclear Activism, Pierre Trudeau's Peace Mission, and the Transatlantic Partnership." *Cold War History* 18, no. 1 (2018): 19–36.

——. "Defining Détente: NATO's Struggle for Identity, 1967–1984." Ph.D. diss., University of Toronto, Toronto, Ont., 2018.

——. "The Elephant in the Room: Rethinking Cruise Missile Testing and Pierre Trudeau's Peace Mission." In *Undiplomatic History: The New Study of Canada and the World*, edited by Asa McKercher and Philip van Huizen, 253–276. Montreal, Que. and Kingston, Ont.: McGill-Queen's University Press, 2019.

Colton, Timothy J. *Yeltsin: A Life*. New York: Basic Books, 2008.

Copeland, Dale C. *The Origins of Major War*. Ithaca, N.Y.: Cornell University Press, 2000.

Cowie, Jefferson. *Stayin' Alive: The 1970s and the Last Days of the Working Class*. New York: New Press, 2010.

Craig, Campbell, and Fredrik Logevall. *America's Cold War: The Politics of Insecurity*. Cambridge, Mass.: Belknap Press of Harvard University Press, 2010.

Davis, Vicky. *Myth Making in the Soviet Union and Modern Russia: Remembering World War II in Brezhnev's Hero City*. London: I.B. Tauris, 2018.

De Groot, Michael. "Disruption: Economic Globalization and the End of the Cold War Order in the 1970s." Ph.D. diss., University of Virginia, Charlottesville, Va., 2018.

DiCicco, Jonathan M. "Fear, Loathing, and Cracks in Reagan's Mirror Images: Able Archer 83 and an American First Step toward Rapprochement in the Cold War." *Foreign Policy Analysis* 7, no. 3 (2011): 253–274.

Downing, Taylor. *1983: Reagan, Andropov, and a World on the Brink*. New York: Da Capo, 2018.

Drozov, Iu., and V. Fartyshev. *Na puti k vozrozhdeniiu: Iurii Andropov i Vladimir Putin*. Moscow: Vympel, 2000.

Edelstein, David M. *Over the Horizon: Time, Uncertainty, and the Rise of Great Powers*. Ithaca, N.Y.: Cornell University Press, 2017.

Eichengreen, Barry. *The European Economy since 1945: Coordinated Capitalism and Beyond*. Princeton, N.J.: Princeton University Press, 2007.

Ekedahl, Carolyn McGiffert, and Melvin A. Goodman. *The Wars of Eduard Shevardnadze*. University Park: Pennsylvania State University Press, 1997.

Engel, Jeffrey A. *When the World Seemed New: George H. W. Bush and the End of the Cold War*. Boston, Mass.: Houghton Mifflin Harcourt, 2017.

English, John. *The Life of Pierre Elliott Trudeau*. Vol. 2, *Just Watch Me, 1968–2000*. Toronto, Ont.: Vintage, 2009.

English, Robert D. "Power, Ideas, and New Evidence on the Cold War's End: A Reply to Brooks and Wohlforth." *International Security* 26, no. 4 (2002): 70–92.

——. *Russia and the Idea of the West: Gorbachev, Intellectuals, and the End of the Cold War*. New York: Columbia University Press, 2000.

Evangelista, Matthew. *Unarmed Forces: The Transnational Movement to End the Cold War*. Ithaca, N.Y.: Cornell University Press, 1999.

Ezell, Edward Clinton, and Linda Neuman Ezell. *The Partnership: A History of the Apollo-Soyuz Test Project.* Washington, D.C.: National Aeronautics and Space Administration, 1978.

Fischer, Benjamin B. "Scolding Intelligence: The PFIAB Report of the Soviet War Scare." *International Journal of Intelligence and Counterintelligence* 31, no. 1 (2018): 102–115.

Fischer, Beth A. *The Myth of Triumphalism: Rethinking President Reagan's Cold War Legacy.* Lexington: University Press of Kentucky, 2019.

——. *The Reagan Reversal: Foreign Policy at the End of the Cold War.* Columbia: University of Missouri Press, 1997.

Foglesong, David S. *The American Mission and the "Evil Empire": The Crusade for a "Free Russia" since 1881.* New York: Cambridge University Press, 2007.

Franke, Ulrich, and Kaspar Schiltz. "'They Don't Really Care about Us!': On Political Worldviews in Popular Music." *International Studies Perspectives* 14, no. 1 (2013): 39–55.

Freeland, Chrystia. *Sale of the Century: Russia's Wild Ride from Communism to Capitalism.* New York: Crown Business, 2000.

Freeman, Stephanie. "Looking over the Horizon: Nuclear Abolitionism and the End of the Cold War, 1979–1989." Ph.D. diss., University of Virginia, Charlottesville, Va., 2017.

Gaddis, John Lewis. "The Long Peace: Elements of Stability in the Postwar International System." *International Security* 10, no. 4 (1986): 99–142.

——. *On Grand Strategy.* New York: Penguin Press, 2018.

——. "On Starting All Over Again: A Naïve Approach to the Study of the Cold War." In *The Cold War—Reassessments,* edited by Arthur L. Rosenbaum and Chae-Jin Lee, 1–26. Claremont, Calif.: Keck Center for International and Strategic Studies, 2000.

——. *Strategies of Containment: A Critical Appraisal of American National Security Policy during the Cold War.* 2nd ed. Oxford: Oxford University Press, 2005.

Gaidar, Yegor. *Collapse of an Empire: Lessons for Modern Russia.* Translated by Antonia W. Bouis. Washington, D.C.: Brookings Institution Press, 2007.

Gala, Marilena. "The Euromissile Crisis and the Centrality of the 'Zero Option.'" In *The Euromissile Crisis and the End of the Cold War,* edited by Leopoldo Nuti, Frédéric Bozo, Marie-Pierre Rey, and Bernd Rother, 158–175. Washington, D.C.: Woodrow Wilson Center Press, 2015.

Garthoff, Raymond L. *Détente and Confrontation: American-Soviet Relations from Nixon to Reagan.* 2nd ed. Washington, D.C.: Brookings Institution Press, 1994.

——. *The Great Transition: American-Soviet Relations and the End of the Cold War.* Washington, D.C.: Brookings Institution Press, 1994.

——. "Soviet Leaders, Soviet Intelligence, and Changing Views of the United States, 1965–91." In *The Image of the Enemy: Intelligence Analysis of Adversaries since 1945,* edited by Paul Maddrell, 28–67. Washington, D.C.: Georgetown University Press, 2015.

Gavin, Francis J. "Strategies of Inhibition: US Grand Strategy, the Nuclear Revolution, and Nonproliferation." *International Security* 40, no. 1 (2015): 9–46.

George, Alexander. *Forceful Persuasion: Coercive Diplomacy as an Alternative to War.* Washington, D.C.: United States Institute of Peace Press, 1991.

216   BIBLIOGRAPHY

Gilpin, Robert. *War and Change in World Politics*. Cambridge: Cambridge University Press, 1981.

Glaser, Charles L. *Rational Theory of International Politics: The Logic of Competition and Cooperation*. Princeton, N.J.: Princeton University Press, 2010.

Goldgeier, James M. *Leadership Style and Soviet Foreign Policy: Stalin, Khrushchev, Brezhnev, Gorbachev*. Baltimore, Md.: Johns Hopkins University Press, 1994.

——. *Not Whether but When: The US Decision to Enlarge NATO*. Washington, D.C.: Brookings Institution Press, 1999.

Gregory, Paul R. "Productivity, Slack, and Time Theft in the Soviet Economy." In *Politics, Work, and Daily Life in the USSR*, edited by James R. Millar, 241–275. Cambridge: Cambridge University Press, 1987.

Greiner, Bernd, "Angst im Kalten Krieg: Bilanz und Ausblick." In *Angst im Kalten Krieg*, edited by Bernd Greiner, Christian Müller, and Direkt Walter, 7–33. Hamburg: Hamburger Edition, 2009.

Gromyko, Anatoliĭ. *Andreĭ Gromyko: Polet ego strely*. Moscow: Nauchnaia Kniga, 2009.

Grosser, Pierre. "Serrer le jeu sans le fermer: l'Élysée et les relations franco-soviétiques de 1981 à 1984." In *François Mitterrand: Les années du changement, 1981–1984*, edited by Serge Berstein, Pierre Milza, and Jean-Louis Bianco, 253–281. Paris: Berrin, 2001.

Guasconi, Maria Eleonora. "Public Opinion and the Euromissile Crisis." In *The Euromissile Crisis and the End of the Cold War*, edited by Leopoldo Nuti, Frédéric Bozo, Marie-Pierre Rey, and Bernd Rother, 271–289. Washington, D.C.: Woodrow Wilson Center Press, 2015.

Gunitsky, Seva, and Andrei P. Tsygankov. "The Wilsonian Bias in the Study of Russian Foreign Policy." *Problems of Post-Communism* 65, no. 6 (2018): 385–393.

Halliday, Fred. *The Making of the Second Cold War*. 2nd ed. London: Verso, 1986.

Hänni, Adrian. "A Chance for a Propaganda Coup? The Reagan Administration and *The Day After*." *Historical Journal of Radio, Television, and Film* 36, no. 3 (2016): 415–435.

Hanson, Philip. *The Rise and Fall of the Soviet Economy: An Economic History of the USSR from 1945*. London: Longman, 2003.

Hart, Douglas M. "Soviet Approaches to Crisis Management: The Military Dimension." *Survival* 26, no. 5 (1984): 214–223.

Haslam, Jonathan. *Russia's Cold War: From the October Revolution to the Fall of the Wall*. New Haven, Conn.: Yale University Press, 2011.

Hayward, Steven F. *The Age of Reagan*. Vol. 2, *The Conservative Counterrevolution, 1980–1989*. New York: Crown Forum, 2009.

——. "Reagan Reclaimed: Against the Liberal Revised Standard Version of Our 40th President." *National Review* 63, no. 2 (2011): 34–36.

Heefner, Gretchen. *The Missile Next Door: The Minuteman in the American Heartland*. Cambridge, Mass.: Harvard University Press, 2012.

Heigerson, John. *Getting to Know the President: Intelligence Briefings of Presidential Candidates, 1952–2004*. 2nd ed. Washington, D.C.: US Government Printing Office, 2012.

Herz, John H. "Idealist Internationalism and the Security Dilemma." *World Politics* no. 2 (1950): 157–180.

BIBLIOGRAPHY 217

Hill, Fiona, and Clifford G. Gaddy. *Mr. Putin: Operative in the Kremlin*. 2nd ed. Washington, D.C.: Brookings Institution Press, 2015.

Hoffman, David E. *The Dead Hand: The Untold Story of the Cold War Arms Race and Its Dangerous Legacy*. New York: Anchor Books, 2009.

Ikenberry, G. John. *After Victory: Institutions, Strategic Restraint, and the Rebuilding of Order After Major Wars*. Princeton, N.J.: Princeton University Press, 2001.

Inboden, William. "Grand Strategy and Petty Squabbles: The Paradox and Lessons of the Reagan NSC." In *The Power of the Past: History and Statecraft*, edited by Hal Brands and Jeremi Suri, 151–180. Washington, D.C.: Brookings Institution Press, 2016.

Jacobs, Meg. *Panic at the Pump: The Energy Crisis and the Transformation of American Politics in the 1970s*. New York: Hill and Wang, 2016.

Jentleson, Bruce W. *The Peacemakers: Leadership Lessons from Twentieth-Century Statesmanship*. New York: W. W. Norton, 2018.

——. *Pipeline Politics: The Complex Political Economy of East-West Energy Trade*. Ithaca, N.Y.: Cornell University Press, 1986.

Jervis, Robert. *Perception and Misperception in International Politics*. Princeton, N.J.: Princeton University Press, 1976.

Kalinovsky, Artemy M. *A Long Goodbye: The Soviet Withdrawal from Afghanistan*. Cambridge, Mass.: Harvard University Press, 2011.

Keefer, Edward C. *Harold Brown: Offsetting the Soviet Military Challenge, 1977–1981*. Washington, D.C.: US Government Printing Office, 2017.

Kengor, Paul. *The Crusader: Ronald Reagan and the Fall of Communism*. New York: HarperCollins, 2006.

Kennedy, Paul. *The Rise and Fall of the Great Powers: Economic Change and Military Conflict from 1500 to 2000*. New York: Random House, 1987.

Khinshtein, Aleksandr. *Skazka o poteriannom vremeni: Pochemu Brezhnev ne smog stat' Putinym*. Moscow: Olma, 2018.

Khlobustov, Oleg. *Neizvestnyĭ Andropov*. Moscow: Eksmo, 2009.

Khristoforov, Vasiliĭ S. *Afganistan: Voenno-politicheskoe prisutstvie SSSR, 1979–1989 gg.* Moscow: Institut Rossiĭskoĭ Istorii RAN, 2016.

Kieninger, Stephan. *The Diplomacy of Détente: Cooperative Security Policies from Helmut Schmidt to George Shultz*. Abingdon: Routledge, 2018.

Kotkin, Stephen. *Armageddon Averted: The Soviet Collapse, 1970–2000*. Oxford: Oxford University Press, 2001.

——. *Magnetic Mountain: Stalinism as a Civilization*. Berkeley, University of California Press, 1995.

Kramer, Mark. "Die Nicht-Krise um 'Able Archer 1983': Fürchtete die sowjetische Führung tatsächlich einen atomaren Großangriff im Herbst 1983?" In *Wege zur Wiedervereinigung: Die beiden deutschen Staaten in ihren Bündnissen 1970 bis 1990*, edited by Oliver Bange and Bernd Lemke, 129–149. Munich: Oldenbourg, 2013.

Kunz, Diane B. *Butter and Guns: America's Cold War Economic Diplomacy*. New York: Free Press, 1997.

Kydd, Andrew H. *Trust and Mistrust in International Relations*. Princeton, N.J.: Princeton University Press, 2005.

218 BIBLIOGRAPHY

Leffler, Melvyn P. *For the Soul of Mankind: The United States, the Soviet Union, and the Cold War*. New York: Hill and Wang, 2007.

——. "Ronald Reagan and the Cold War: What Really Mattered." *Texas National Security Review* 1, no. 3 (2018): 77–89.

Lettow, Paul. *Ronald Reagan and His Quest to Abolish Nuclear Weapons*. New York: Random House, 2005.

Liakhovskiĭ, Aleksandr A. *Plamia Afgana*. Moscow: Vagrius, 1999.

——. *Tragediia i doblest' Afgana*. Moscow: Iskona, 1995.

Long, Austin, and Brendan Rittenhouse Green. "Stalking the Secure Second Strike: Intelligence, Counterforce, and Nuclear Strategy." *Journal of Strategic Studies* 38, nos. 1–2 (2015): 38–73.

Longley, Kyle, Jeremy D. Mayer, Michael Schaller, and John W. Sloan. *Deconstructing Reagan: Conservative Mythology and America's Fortieth President*. Armonk, N.Y.: M.E. Sharpe, 2007.

Macrakis, Stella. *Seduced by Secrets: Inside the Stasi's Spy-Tech World*. Cambridge: Cambridge University Press, 2008.

Maisurian, Aleksandr. *Drugoĭ Brezhnev*. Moscow: Vagrius, 2004.

Manchanda, Arnav. "When Truth Is Stranger Than Fiction: The Able Archer Incident." *Cold War History* 9, no. 1 (2009): 111–133.

Mann, James. *The Rebellion of Ronald Reagan: A History of the End of the Cold War*. New York: Viking, 2009.

Markusen, Ann, "Cold War Workers, Cold War Communities." In *Rethinking Cold War Culture*, edited by Peter J. Kuznick and James Gilbert, 35–60. Washington, D.C.: Smithsonian Institution Press, 2001.

Marlo, Francis H. *Planning Reagan's War: Conservative Strategists and America's Cold War Victory*. Washington, D.C.: Potomac Books, 2012.

Matlock, Jack F. *Autopsy on an Empire: The American Ambassador's Account of the Collapse of the Soviet Union*. New York: Random House, 1995.

——. *Reagan and Gorbachev: How the Cold War Ended*. New York: Random House, 2004.

——. *Superpower Illusions: How Myths and False Ideologies Led America Astray—And How to Return to Reality*. New Haven, Conn.: Yale University Press, 2011.

Maurer, John D. "Divided Counsels: Competing Approaches to SALT, 1969–1970." *Diplomatic History* 43, no. 2 (2019): 353–377.

McKevitt, Andrew C. *Consuming Japan: Popular Culture and the Globalizing of 1980s America*. Chapel Hill: University of North Carolina Press, 2017.

Medvedev, Roĭ. *Iuriĭ Andropov: Neizvestnoe ob izvestnom*. Moscow: Vremia, 2004.

Miles, Simon. "The Domestic Politics of Superpower Rapprochement: Foreign Policy and the 1984 Presidential Election." In *The Cold War at Home and Abroad: Domestic Politics and US Foreign Policy since 1945*, edited by Andrew L. Johns and Mitchell B. Lerner, 267–288. Lexington: University Press of Kentucky, 2018.

——. "Envisioning Détente: The Johnson Administration and the October 1964 Khrushchev Ouster." *Diplomatic History* 40, no. 4 (2016): 722–749.

——. "The War Scare That Wasn't: Able Archer 83 and the Myths of the Second Cold War." *Journal of Cold War Studies*, forthcoming.

Miller, Chris. *Putinomics: Power and Money in Resurgent Russia*. Chapel Hill: University of North Carolina Press, 2018.

BIBLIOGRAPHY 219

———. *The Struggle to Save the Soviet Economy: Mikhail Gorbachev and the Collapse of the USSR*. Chapel Hill: University of North Carolina Press, 2016.

Miller, Jennifer M. *Cold War Democracy: The United States and Japan*. Cambridge, Mass.: Harvard University Press, 2019.

Morgan, Michael Cotey. *The Final Act: The Helsinki Accords and the Transformation of the Cold War*. Princeton, N.J.: Princeton University Press, 2018.

Njølstad, Olav. "The Carter Legacy: Entering the Second Era of the Cold War." In *The Last Decade of the Cold War: From Conflict Escalation to Conflict Transformation*, edited by Olav Njølstad, 196–225. London: Frank Cass, 2004.

Oberdorfer, Don. *From the Cold War to a New Era: The United States and the Soviet Union, 1983–1991*. Baltimore, Md.: Johns Hopkins University Press, 1998.

Odom, William E. *The Collapse of the Soviet Military*. New Haven, Conn.: Yale University Press, 1998.

Organski, A. F. K., and Jacek Kugler. *The War Ledger*. Chicago: University of Chicago Press, 1980.

Ouimet, Matthew J. *The Rise and Fall of the Brezhnev Doctrine in Soviet Foreign Policy*. Chapel Hill: University of North Carolina Press, 2003.

Peacock, Margaret. "Samantha Smith in the Land of the Bolsheviks: Peace and the Politics of Childhood in the Late Cold War." *Diplomatic History* 43, no. 3 (2019): 418–444.

Pikhoia, Rudol'f. *Moskva, Kreml', vlast': Sorok let posle voĭny, 1945–1985*. Moscow: Rus'-Olymp, 2007.

———. *Sovetskiĭ soiuz: Istoriia vlasti, 1945–1991*. Novosibisrsk: Sibirskiĭ Khronograf, 2000.

Plokhy, Serhii. *Chernobyl: The History of a Nuclear Catastrophe*. New York: Basic Books, 2018.

Prados, John. *How the Cold War Ended: Debating and Doing History*. Washington, D.C.: Potomac Books, 2011.

Preble, Christopher A. "'Who Ever Believed in the Missile Gap?': John F. Kennedy and the Politics of National Security." *Presidential Studies Quarterly* 33, no. 4 (2003): 801–826.

Pringle, Robert W. "Putin: The New Andropov?" *International Journal of Intelligence and Counterintelligence* 14, no. 4 (2001): 545–558.

Prozorov, Boris. *Rassekrechennyĭ Andropov: Vzgliad izvne i iznutri*. Moscow: Gudok, 2004.

Prozumenščikov, Michail. "Die Entscheidung im Politbüro der KPdSU." In *Beiträge*, vol. 1 of *Prager Frühling: Das internationale Krisenjahr 1968*, edited by Stefan Karner, 205–241. Cologne: Böhlau, 2008.

Pry, Peter Vincent. *War Scare: Russia and America on the Nuclear Brink*. Westport, Conn.: Praeger, 1999.

Putnam, Robert D. "Diplomacy and Domestic Politics: The Logic of Two-Level Games." *International Organization* 42, no. 3 (1988): 427–460.

Radchenko, Sergey. *Two Suns in the Heavens: The Sino-Soviet Struggle for Supremacy, 1962–1967*. Washington, D.C.: Woodrow Wilson Center Press, 2009.

———. *Unwanted Visionaries: The Soviet Failure in Asia at the End of the Cold War*. Oxford: Oxford University Press, 2014.

Raines, Edgar F. *The Rucksack War: US Army Operational Logistics Grenada, 1983*. Washington, D.C.: US Army Center of Military History, 2010.

220 BIBLIOGRAPHY

Raleigh, Donald J. "'I Speak Frankly Because You Are My Friend': Leonid Ilich Brezhnev's Personal Relationship with Richard M. Nixon." *Soviet and Post-Soviet Review* 45, no. 2 (2018): 151–182.

——. "'Soviet' Man of Peace: Leonid Il'ich Brezhnev and His Diaries." *Kritika: Explorations in Russian and Eurasian History* 17, no. 4 (2016): 837–868.

Rossinow, Doug. "The Legend of Reagan the Peacemaker." *Raritan* 32, no. 3 (2013): 56–76.

——. *The Reagan Era: A History of the 1980s.* New York: Columbia University Press, 2015.

Ryan, Michael. "Life Expectancy and Mortality Data from the Soviet Union." *British Medical Journal* 296, no. 6635 (1988): 1513–1515.

Sayle, Timothy Andrews. *Enduring Alliance: A History of NATO and the Postwar Global Order.* Ithaca, N.Y.: Cornell University Press, 2019.

Salmin, Nikolaĭ. *Internatsionalizm v deĭstvii: Lokal'nye voĭny i vooruzhennye konflikty s uchastiem sovetskogo komponenta, 1959–1989.* Ekaterinburg: Izdatel'stvo Gumanitarnogo Universiteta, 2001.

Sargent, Daniel J. *A Superpower Transformed: The Remaking of American Foreign Relations in the 1970s.* Oxford: Oxford University Press, 2015.

Sarotte, Mary Elise. *Dealing with the Devil: East Germany, Détente, and Ostpolitik, 1969–1973.* Chapel Hill: University of North Carolina Press, 2001.

——. *1989: The Struggle to Create Post–Cold War Europe.* Princeton, N.J.: Princeton University Press, 2009.

Savel'yev, Aleksandr' G., and Nikolay N. Detinov. *The Big Five: Arms Control Decision-Making in the Soviet Union.* Edited by Gregory Varhall. Translated by Dmitriy Trenin. Westport, Conn.: Praeger, 1995.

Sayle, Timothy Andrews. "Andropov's Hungarian Complex." *Cold War History* 9, no. 3 (2009): 427–439.

Schrecker, Ellen, ed. *Cold War Triumphalism: The Misuse of History After the Fall of Communism.* New York: The New Press, 2006.

Schweizer, Peter. *Reagan's War: The Epic Story of His Forty-Year Struggle and Final Triumph over Communism.* New York: Doubleday, 2002.

——. *Victory: The Reagan Administration's Secret Strategy That Hastened the Collapse of the Soviet Union.* New York: Atlantic Monthly Press, 1994.

Schulz, Matthias, and Thomas A. Schwartz. "The Superpower and the Union in the Making: US-European Relations, 1969–1980." In *The Strained Alliance: US-European Relations from Nixon to Carter,* edited by Matthias Schulz and Thomas A. Schwartz, 355–374. Cambridge: Cambridge University Press, 2010.

Scott, Len. "Intelligence and the Risk of Nuclear War: Able Archer-83 Revisited." In *Intelligence in the Cold War: What Difference Did It Make?,* edited by Michael Herman and Gwilym Hughes, 5–23. London: Routledge, 2013.

Sell, Louis. *From Washington to Moscow: US-Soviet Relations and the Collapse of the USSR.* Durham, N.C.: Duke University Press, 2016.

Service, Robert. *The End of the Cold War, 1985–1991.* New York: Public Affairs, 2015.

——. *Trotsky: A Biography.* Cambridge, Mass.: Belknap Press of Harvard University Press, 2009.

Shifrinson, Joshua R. Itzkowitz. "Deal or No Deal? The End of the Cold War and the US Offer to Limit NATO Expansion." *International Security* 40, no. 4 (2016): 7–44.

BIBLIOGRAPHY 221

——. *Rising Titans, Falling Giants: How Great Powers Exploit Power Shifts.* Ithaca, N.Y.: Cornell University Press, 2018.

Shulgan, Christopher. *The Soviet Ambassador: The Making of the Radical Behind Perestroika.* Toronto, Ont.: McClelland and Stewart, 2008.

Smith, Tony. "New Bottles for New Wine: A Pericentric Framework for the Study of the Cold War." *Diplomatic History* 24, no. 4 (2000): 567–591.

Snyder, Sarah B. *Human Rights Activism and the End of the Cold War: A Transnational History of the Helsinki Network.* Cambridge: Cambridge University Press, 2011.

——. "'Jerry, Don't Go': Domestic Opposition to the 1975 Helsinki Final Act." *Journal of American Studies* 44, no. 1 (2010): 67–81.

——. "'No Crowing': Reagan, Trust, and Human Rights." In *Trust, but Verify: The Politics of Uncertainty and the Transformation of the Cold War Order, 1969–1991,* edited by Martin Klimke, Reinhild, Kreis, and Christian F. Ostermann, 42–62. Washington, D.C.: Woodrow Wilson Center Press, 2016.

Soldatov, Andrei, and Irina Borogan. *The New Nobility: The Restoration of Russia's Security State and the Enduring Legacy of the KGB.* New York: Public Affairs, 2010.

Sonne, Werner. *Leben mit der Bombe: Atomwaffen in Deutschland.* Wiesbaden: Springer, 2018.

Sparrow, Bartholomew. *The Strategist: Brent Scowcroft and the Call of National Security.* New York: Public Affairs, 2015.

Streusand, Douglas E., Norman A. Bailey, and Francis H. Marlo, eds. *The Grand Strategy That Won the Cold War: Architecture of Triumph.* Lanham, Md.: Lexington Books, 2016.

Suny, Ronald Grigor. *The Revenge of the Past: Nationalism, Revolution, and the Collapse of the Soviet Union.* Stanford, Calif.: Stanford University Press, 1993.

——. *The Soviet Experiment: Russia, the USSR, and the Successor States.* Oxford: Oxford University Press, 1998.

Suri, Jeremi. "Explaining the End of the Cold War: A New Historical Consensus?" *Journal of Cold War Studies* 4, no. 4 (Fall 2002): 60–92.

——. *Power and Protest: Global Revolution and the Rise of Détente.* Cambridge, Mass.: Harvard University Press, 2003.

Taubman, William. *Gorbachev: His Life and Times.* New York: W. W. Norton, 2017.

——. *Khrushchev: The Man and His Era.* New York: Free Press, 2003.

Tismaneanu, Vladimir. *Stalinism for All Seasons: A Political History of Romanian Communism.* Berkeley: University of California Press, 2003.

Trachtenberg, Marc. "Assessing Soviet Economic Performance during the Cold War: A Failure of Intelligence?" *Texas National Security Review* 1, no. 2 (2018): 77–101.

Trubowitz, Peter. *Defining the National Interest: Conflict and Change in American Foreign Policy.* Chicago: University of Chicago Press, 1998.

Ulam, Adam B. *Lenin and the Bolsheviks: The Intellectual and Political History of the Triumph of Communism in Russia.* London: Seckler and Warburg, 1966.

Umbach, Frank. *Das rote Bündnis: Entwicklung und Zerfall des Warschauer Paktes 1955 bis 1991.* Berlin: Christoph Links, 2005.

Van Evera, Stephen. *Causes of War: Power and the Roots of Conflict.* Ithaca, N.Y.: Cornell University Press, 1999.

222   BIBLIOGRAPHY

Villaume, Poul, and Odd Arne Westad. "The Secrets of European Détente." In *Perforating the Iron Curtain: European Détente, Transatlantic Relations, and the Cold War, 1965–1985*, edited by Poul Villaume and Odd Arne Westad, 7–17. Copenhagen: Museum Tusculanum, 2010.

Volkogonov, Dmitriĭ. *Sem' vozhdeĭ: Galereia liderov SSSR*. 2 vols. Moscow: Novosti, 1995.

Wacker, Grant. *America's Pastor: Billy Graham and the Shaping of a Nation*. Cambridge, Mass.: Belknap Press of Harvard University Press, 2014.

Walker, Shaun. *The Long Hangover: Putin's New Russia and the Ghosts of the Past*. Oxford: Oxford University Press, 2018.

Weinberg, Steve. *Armand Hammer: The Untold Story*. Boston, Mass.: Little, Brown, 1989.

Weiss, Gus W. "Duping the Soviets: The Farewell Dossier." *Studies in Intelligence* 39, no. 5 (1996): 121–126.

Wendt, Alexander E. "The Agent-Structure Problem in International Relations Theory." *International Organization* 41, no. 3 (1987): 335–370.

Wenkel, Christian. "Overcoming the Crisis of Détente, 1979–1983: Coordinating Eastern Policies between Paris, Bonn, and London." In *The Long Détente: Changing Concepts of Security and Cooperation in Europe, 1950s–1980s*, edited by Oliver Bange and Poul Villaume, 235–252. Budapest: Central European University Press, 2017.

Westad, Odd Arne. *Restless Empire: China and the World since 1750*. New York: Basic Books, 2012.

Wilson, James Graham. "How Grand Was Reagan's Strategy, 1976–1984?" *Diplomacy and Statecraft* 18, no. 4 (2007): 773–803.

——. *The Triumph of Improvisation: Gorbachev's Adaptability, Reagan's Engagement, and the End of the Cold War*. Ithaca, N.Y.: Cornell University Press, 2014.

Winik, Jay. *On the Brink: The Dramatic, Behind-the-Scenes Saga of the Reagan Era and the Men and Women Who Won the Cold War*. New York: Simon and Schuster, 1996.

Wittner, Lawrence S. *The Struggle against the Bomb*. Vol. 3, *Toward Nuclear Abolition: A History of the World Nuclear Disarmament Movement, 1971 to the Present*. Stanford, Calif.: Stanford University Press, 2003.

Wolford, Scott. "The Turnover Trap: New Leaders, Reputation, and International Conflict." *American Journal of Political Science* 51, no. 4 (2007): 772–788.

Yarhi-Milo, Keren. *Knowing the Adversary: Leaders, Intelligence, and Assessment of Intentions in International Relations*. Princeton, N.J.: Princeton University Press, 2014.

Yurchak, Alexei. *Everything Was Forever, Until It Was No More: The Last Soviet Generation*. Princeton, N.J.: Princeton University Press, 2006.

Zemtsov, Ilya. *Chernenko: Sovetskiĭ Soiuz v kanun perestroĭki*. London: Overseas Publications Interchange, 1989.

Zubok, Vladislav M. *A Failed Empire: The Soviet Union in the Cold War from Stalin to Gorbachev*. Chapel Hill: University of North Carolina Press, 2007.

——. *Zhivago's Children: The Last Russian Intelligentsia*. Cambridge, Mass.: Belknap Press of Harvard University Press, 2009.

Index

Able Archer 83, 80–81, 82
Abrasimov, Petr, 43–44
Adamishin, Anatoliĭ, 23, 26, 128
Afghanistan: invasion/occupation, 12, 13–14; regrets/withdrawal, 26, 109, 118–19, 194n141
AFL-CIO, 33
airspace incidents, 57–58, 71, 73–77, 99, 133
Akhromeev, Sergeĭ, 118, 134
Albright, Madeleine, 138
alcohol abuse and policy, 116, 192n111
Aleksandrov-Agentov, Andreĭ, 79–80, 124
Allen, Richard, 11, 19, 45
Andreeva, Nina, 134
Andropova, Tat'iana, 92, 181n94
Andropov, Iuriĭ: anticorruption and reforms, 59, 64, 90, 115–16; biography and personality, 21, 60, 63, 167n58, 167n60; career and rise, 21–22, 59–60, 108, 167n60; Cold War pessimism, 62–63; economic policy, 63–64, 113; foreign policy and engagement, 21, 52, 58, 60–63, 67, 75–77, 82–83, 84, 85, 86–88, 96, 117; funeral, 92, 93, 181n94; health, 59, 75, 82–83, 84, 89, 90, 110; KGB history/ activity, 7, 20, 21–22, 59, 62–63, 70, 92, 112; military and arms control policy, 67, 70–71, 88; peace policy, 30, 72, 75; on Reagan administration, 2, 24–25, 30, 61–62, 67; speeches, 62, 63; tenure, 4, 10, 21, 60, 89–90, 91
anti-nuclear stances and movements, 58, 68, 72–73, 79, 85, 88–89
Arbatov, Georgiĭ, 25, 55
archival materials: Cold War–related, 3, 4–5; Reagan-related, 143n63
Armacost, Michael, 121
arms control policy and negotiations: challenges and sticking points, 13, 15, 49, 95, 103, 118; global meetings, 56, 87–88, 102–3, 104, 120–27; public desires and opinion, 58, 68, 79, 85, 104; treaties, 14, 50–51, 86, 133–34; US methodology, 17, 47–48, 49–50, 101–2, 104–5, 120–22, 152n8; US-Soviet, 17, 43, 47–51, 56, 67, 68–69, 70, 79, 87–88, 95, 99–100, 101–5, 111–12, 120–23, 125–28
arms race: as Cold War component, 12–13, 31, 38–39, 70, 79, 101, 114; de-escalation wishes, 17, 50–51, 111, 120, 122, 123, 128; Soviet escalation, 22, 28; US escalation, 23, 25, 35, 37–38, 78–79, 104, 117–18; US history, 31. *See also* arms control policy and negotiations; military and defense policy
atomic bomb, 37–38, 177n2
Attali, Jacques, 98
Australia, 84, 94, 95–96
Axen, Hermann, 99
Azerbaijan, 141n13

Baker, James, 19
balance of power: Cold War's end, 85, 129, 130, 131–32, 139; economic systems, 5–6, 12, 25–26, 39, 66, 67–68, 91; military and defense, 35–36, 39, 70–71, 78, 79, 91–92, 101–3, 117–18; shifts, 3, 4, 5–6, 8, 10, 15, 64, 65–67, 77, 82, 107, 117, 120, 129, 131–32, 139; superpower relations, 4, 5–6, 10, 11–12, 22, 23, 24, 30, 44, 60–61, 65–66, 66–67, 70–71, 82–83, 85, 89, 93, 94, 99, 101, 103, 105, 117, 119, 120–23, 129. *See also* perception, reality, and optics
ballistic missiles: arms control negotiations, 15, 48–51; assumptions of US, 69, 71, 78, 81, 160n161; first- and second-strike capabilities, 69–70, 79, 125; Soviet development and arsenal, 12–13, 28, 48, 49, 50, 186n211; US development and arsenal, 15, 36, 37, 48, 49, 50, 67, 72–73, 78–79, 80–81. *See also* INF weapons
Beirut US Embassy attack (1983), 77

223

224 INDEX

Berlin, Germany: back-channel communications, 43, 44; Berlin Wall fall (1989), 115, 130, 135, 136–37
Bevin, Ernest, 145n41
Bishop, Maurice, 77–78
Brady, James, 33
Brezhneva, Galina, 22
Brezhnev Doctrine, 52–53, 115, 135
Brezhnev, Leonid: on American militarism, 35; arms control, 51; domestic policy, 6, 27–28, 63; drug addiction, 20; foreign policy, 6, 22, 23, 24, 26, 30, 31–32, 34, 46, 47, 52–53, 56, 92; health and passing, 20, 22, 30, 59–60; Reagan correspondence, 34, 41–42, 48, 51, 131; tenure, 4, 6, 10, 12, 20–21, 22, 30, 56, 59–60, 64
Buckley, James, 55
Burns, Arthur, 42–44, 46
Burt, Richard, 44, 99
Bush, George H. W.: intelligence briefings, 11; presidency, 130, 134, 135; Reagan administration communication, 19, 46; VP and foreign policy duties, 1, 18–19, 38, 60–61, 82, 92–93, 94, 112, 114

Callaghan, James, 85
Canada: ambassadors, 8, 54, 109, 110; intelligence, 55; US/Soviet foreign relations, 84, 88, 94–95, 109–10
capitalism. *See* economic systems
Carrington, Peter, 40, 41–42, 54
Carstens, Karl, 62, 155–56n62
Carter, Jimmy, and administration: campaign/election, 14–16, 22, 23–24; foreign policy: Iran, 13; foreign policy: Soviet Union, 8, 12, 13–14, 22–23, 31, 42, 53, 104; military policy, 8, 22–23, 36; opinions by Reagan and administration, 12, 14–16, 18, 31, 34, 40, 56, 145n38; opinions on Reagan, 14
Casey, William, 11
Ceaușescu, Nicolae, 27
Central Intelligence Agency (CIA): Bush and, 61; Cold War intelligence and briefings, 11, 12, 31; on Soviet leaders/succession, 21, 22, 60–61, 112, 121; Soviet projects, 55
Central/Latin America policy, 9, 12, 14, 61
Chebrikov, Viktor, 63–64, 75, 113
Chechnya, 137
Cherkashin, Viktor, 81, 176n258
Chernenko, Konstantin: arms control negotiations, 102–5; career and rise, 21,

90–91, 92; foreign policy, 92–93, 94, 95–96, 97–100, 102–5; health, 7, 59, 92, 93–94, 97–98, 100, 107–8, 111–12; jokes, 1; tenure, 4, 7, 10, 75, 85, 92–94, 100, 104, 107–8, 111–12
Cherniaev, Anatoliĭ, 100, 112, 115, 191n85, 192n111
Cheysson, Claude, 41
children, 72
China: economy, 117; Soviet relations, 38; US relations, 38, 86
Chornobyl' explosion (1986), 132–33
Clark, William: administration/staff relations, 45, 46, 82; Soviet policy and dialogue, 64–65, 74–75, 77
Clinton, Bill, 138
Cobb, Tyrus, 35
"coercive diplomacy," 47–48
Cold War, 5; balance of power, 4, 5–6, 8, 10, 11–12, 15, 23, 24, 30, 60–61, 64, 65–67, 70–71, 79, 82, 89, 91–92, 93, 117–18, 120, 129, 131–32, 139; dangerous events, 57–58, 73–77, 79, 103, 177n2; end of, and violence, 141n13; end of, timeline and study, 1–2, 3, 4–6, 7, 8–10, 115, 129, 130–39; fear and paranoia, 9, 71, 79–82, 84, 103, 121; impacts and legacy, 10, 136–39; optics, perception, and reality, 3, 5–6, 11–12, 44, 46, 56, 73, 107, 120, 124, 136; phases/eras, 2–3, 5–8, 9–10, 58, 61, 79–80, 84, 85, 96–97, 105, 108, 113–14, 128–29, 130–32, 139; US directives and plans, 65–66, 77, 93, 99, 131. *See also* arms control policy and negotiations; arms race; diplomacy; military and defense policy
Commonwealth nations, 78
communism: anticommunist ideology, 14, 16–17, 38, 65, 145n41, 145n45; Gorbachev commitment, 110–11, 114, 116, 121, 124; national ends, 135–36, 137; US-China relations and, 38
Communist Party Congresses, 29–30, 92, 132
Conference on Confidence- and Security-Building Measures and Disarmament in Europe (1984–1986), 87–88
Conference on Security and Cooperation in Europe (1981), 47, 63
cooperation: Cold War's end, 3, 20, 114; vs. confrontation, 20, 24, 105; vs. engagement, 5, 88; US demonstrations, 86–87; US skepticism, 46. *See also* diplomacy

INDEX

corruption: oligarchy, 137, 138; Soviet leaders, 90; Soviet reforms, 59, 64, 90, 121
coups, 134–35
covert engagement. *See* engagement
Crimea annexation, 139
Crowe, William J., 134
currency and exchange systems, 66, 68
Czechoslovakia: international relations/commentary, 24, 25, 74, 81, 91, 128; invasion (1968), 27, 51
Czech Republic, 137

Dam, Kenneth, 78
Danilevich, Andrian, 81
The Day After (TV movie), 80
Deaver, Michael, 19
defense policy. *See* arms race; military and defense policy
de Margerie, Emmanuel, 125
democracy and democracy-building: Eastern Europe, 4, 135–36, 137–38; organizations, 155n61; Western policy, 1–2, 39, 52, 155n61
Deng Xiaopeng, 95, 117
derzhavnost', 139
détente: Carter policy, 22–23; European policy, 3, 23; Reagan policy, 2–3, 12, 16–17, 25, 35, 92, 97, 128; shifts from, 2, 12, 16–17, 23, 97–98; Soviet policy: Andropov, 62–63; Soviet policy: Brezhnev, 30–31, 92, 94; Soviet policy: Chernenko, 10, 92, 94, 97, 98; Soviet policy: Gorbachev, 5, 128
diplomacy: agenda-setting, 65–66; "coercive," 47–48; engagement, 5, 30, 31–32, 40–44, 52, 75, 82–83, 85, 96, 97, 98–100, 105, 131–32; public diplomacy, 17–18, 40, 66, 86, 87, 88, 124–25, 127–28; "quiet," 3, 40, 46–47, 62–63, 64, 75, 82, 86, 89, 92, 93, 126, 131; Soviet Union/Andropov, 60–61, 62–63, 70–71, 74, 76–77, 79, 82–83, 84–85; Soviet Union/Brezhnev, 30–31, 41–42, 47, 55–56; Soviet Union/Chernenko, 92–95, 99–105; Soviet Union/Gorbachev, 120–29; summit meetings, desires and planning, 30, 42, 43, 55–56, 62, 65, 66, 67, 120–25, 127; summit meetings, historical, 9, 10, 67, 124–29, 132, 133; US allies, 41–42, 67, 84–85, 92–98, 105, 109–11; US/Reagan, 3, 5, 17–18, 19–20, 24, 31–32, 34, 39–49, 49–50, 54, 56, 60, 64–69, 73, 76–77, 81–82, 86, 89, 92–93, 98–105, 120–29, 131

disarmament. *See* arms control policy and negotiations
Dobrynin, Anatoliĭ: arms control dialogue, 102, 123; diplomacy and dialogue, 24, 25, 40–41, 42, 44–45, 46–47, 58, 61, 65, 74, 86, 88; Gorbachev administration, 119
domestic policy. *See* economic conditions; infrastructure; specific leaders
domestic production, Soviet Union, 28–29, 40, 53, 115–16
doomsday clock, 177n2
Dual-Track Decision (1979), 15, 50

Eagleburger, Lawrence, 74, 86, 94
early warning systems, 71–72
East Germany: economy, 27–28, 39; military/intelligence (Stasi), 59, 69, 72, 76, 80–81, 136–37; Soviet relations, 24–25, 27–28, 43, 44, 63–64, 70, 76, 135, 136–37, 139, 193n125; US diplomacy, 43, 80; West Germany and, 68, 135
East-West relations: Brezhnev policy, 24, 26, 31–32, 55–56; commercial ventures, 27, 53–55; Germanies, 68, 135; Gorbachev policy, 114–15, 117, 119–20, 129; international opinions and diplomacy, 24–25, 32, 35, 38, 41, 42, 45–46, 55, 56, 58, 72–73, 74, 76, 85, 88, 92–98, 102, 104, 105–6, 113–14, 127, 173–74n207; nuclear danger, 72–73, 79–80, 119; Reagan administration policy, 17–18, 18–20, 24–26, 31–32, 34–35, 39–47, 51, 60–62, 74–75, 81–83, 93, 97, 98–105, 114, 120–21, 122–23, 127, 129; Soviet diplomatic policy, 24, 25–26, 31–32, 40–41, 43–44, 46–47, 55–56, 60–62, 74, 75–77, 82–83, 92–93, 95–96, 97–98, 113–14, 119–20, 122–23. *See also* arms control policy and negotiations; arms race; diplomacy; peace initiatives
economic conditions: American/Soviet, and reversals, 5, 6, 7, 9, 91, 109–10, 131; Eastern Europe, 27–28, 68; market structures and, 5–6, 28–29, 116–17, 137; public diplomacy and, 17–18, 40; Soviet struggles, 22, 28–29, 40, 53, 63, 91, 110, 115–16, 132, 137; US improvements, 66; US struggles, 12, 13, 14, 18, 24–25, 28, 31, 33, 36–37; WWII, 147n71. *See also* economic systems
economic systems: anticommunist ideology, 16–17, 38, 65; Cold War balance of power, 5–6, 12, 25–26, 39, 66, 67–68, 91; currency systems and clout, 66, 68;

226   **INDEX**

economic systems (*continued*)
  Russian restructuring, 138; Soviet
  restructuring, 90, 110, 115–17, 133,
  134–35; state effects, 5–6, 28–29, 64, 68,
  91, 109–10, 110–11, 115–17, 135–36, 137.
  See also economic conditions; monetary
  policy
economists, 37, 43
Eisenhower, Dwight D., 31, 120, 152n8
elections. *See under* Carter, Jimmy, and
  administration; Mondale, Walter;
  Reagan, Ronald, and administration
El Salvador, 14
emigration policy, Soviet, 46–47, 63, 72, 107,
  124
end of the Cold War. *See* Cold War
energy industry. *See* petroleum industry
engagement: vs. cooperation, 5, 88, 105;
  Eastern bloc nations, 27; economic, shifts,
  55, 66; public vs. private, 42, 43, 44, 46,
  55–56, 62–63, 77, 88, 89, 93, 132;
  US-Soviet, 5–6, 30, 31–32, 34, 40–44, 52,
  58–59, 62–63, 64, 66–67, 75, 82–83, 85–87,
  93–94, 96–101, 105, 117, 129, 131–32
Esin, Viktor, 81
Europe, Eastern: American relations, 17, 69;
  British relations, 96–97; military
  installations, 49, 81; Soviet bloc and
  influence, 4–5, 15, 17, 26–28, 51–53, 60,
  67–68, 115, 135–36; Soviet crackdowns
  and violence, 141n13; US/USSR opinions,
  24–25, 69. *See also* Warsaw Pact states;
  specific nations
Europe, Western: Eastern European
  relations, 27, 28, 118; energy and trade,
  53–55; military/weapons installations, 15,
  48–50, 67, 72–73, 79, 80–81, 85; on Soviet
  leaders, 20–21; US/USSR opinions and
  diplomacy, 15, 23, 25, 32, 45–46, 74, 98,
  102, 105–6, 114, 125. *See also* North
  Atlantic Treaty Organization (NATO);
  specific nations
"evil empire" verbiage, 2, 68, 83, 84

Falklands War (1982), 38
first-strike capability: Europe missile
  positioning, 79; SDI, 69–70, 125
Fitzwater, Marlin, 130
food prices and rationing, 28, 40
Ford, Gerald, 16–17, 73, 145n45
foreign policy and relations. *See under*
  Andropov, Iurii; Brezhnev, Leonid; Carter,
  Jimmy, and administration; détente;

diplomacy; East-West relations;
  engagement; Gorbachev, Mikhail;
  politburo; Reagan, Ronald, and
  administration; Soviet Union; specific
  policies
France, 41, 94, 98
funerals, 1; Andropov, 92, 93, 181n94;
  Brezhnev, 59–60, 175n243; Chernenko,
  112, 113–14, 135

Gates, Robert, 59
Geneva Summit (1955), 120, 128–29
Geneva Summit (1985), 9, 10, 106–7, 120–27;
  expectations and goals, 121–23, 125;
  groundwork and planning, 104–5, 120–25,
  127; outcomes, 126–27
Genscher, Hans-Dietrich, 23, 41, 74, 76, 79,
  95, 102, 116
Georgia, 141n13
Germany. *See* East Germany; West
  Germany
Gingrich, Newt, 127, 198n227
glasnost', 90, 110, 134–35, 138
globalization, 66, 91
G7 meetings, 67
gold standard (currency), 66
Goldwater, Barry, 16
Gorbachev, Mikhail: biography and
  personality, 63, 108, 110–11, 113, 114,
  120–21, 123–24, 125; career, 63, 90, 100,
  108–9, 110, 111, 112–13, 121, 190n40;
  Cold War's end, 2, 3, 4, 5, 8, 10, 114–15,
  132–39; domestic and economic policy,
  90, 107, 110, 113, 115–16, 115–17, 122,
  128, 132–33, 134–35; foreign policy/
  techniques, 2, 3, 5, 7–8, 10, 75–76, 107,
  108–11, 114–15, 117–29, 132, 134; Geneva
  Summit, 9, 10, 106–7, 120–27; military
  policy, 28, 117–19, 120, 122, 126, 133–34,
  194n141, 199n21; on Soviet policy/
  history, 3–4, 6–7, 108, 109, 115; staff, 115,
  119, 124; tenure and influence, 3, 7–8, 10,
  91, 112–17, 131, 134–39
Gordievskiĭ, Oleg, 80
Gotlieb, Allan, 8, 54, 143n46
Graham, Billy, 9, 94
Grenada invasion (1983), 77–78
Grishin, Viktor, 113, 190n40, 191n72
Gromyko, Andreĭ: Andropov administration, 67, 68–69, 75–76, 88; Brezhnev
  administration, 22, 23, 35, 41–42; British
  meetings and relations, 42, 85, 97;
  Chernenko administration, 90, 91, 95–96,

97–98, 112–13; foreign policy opinions and control, 75, 76, 91, 97–98, 100; German meetings and relations, 95; Gorbachev administration, 112–13, 119, 120, 128, 135; US dialogue: arms control, 48, 49, 68–69, 70, 79, 95, 101, 104–5, 120; US dialogue challenges, 85, 95, 97, 100; US dialogue: Shultz, 46, 70, 76, 88, 104–5, 120; US meetings and relations, 41–42, 61, 76, 100–101, 104–5, 120, 128
ground-launched cruise missiles. *See* INF weapons
Die Grünen (German political party), 73
Grybkov, Anatoliĭ, 52–53
Guatemala, 14
Gypsy, Boris the, 22

Haig, Alexander, 19, 40–42, 44–45, 52, 61
Hammer, Armand, 94
Harriman, W. Averell, 70–71
Hartman, Arthur, 42, 59, 60, 71, 77, 78, 124
Hawke, Bob, 84, 95
Hayden, Bill, 95–96
Helsinki Accords (1975), 27
Henkel, Bill, 106
Hinckley, John, 33–34
Honecker, Erich, 27–28, 68, 80
Howe, Geoffrey, 97–98, 110
human rights issues: Carter administration, 8, 22; popular activism, 2; Reagan administration, 24, 46–47, 61–62, 63, 114, 119–20, 126; Soviet policy and messaging, 61–62, 114, 119–20
Hungary, 21, 96–97, 137, 167n60, 178n32

Iakolev, Aleksandr, 71, 78, 109, 110, 122, 189n35, 190n40
imperialism, American, 38, 39, 60, 71, 139
inaugural addresses, 31
industrial espionage, 55
inflation, 36–37, 137
infrastructure: Soviet housing, 137; Soviet transportation, 64, 115–16; US projects/jobs, 33
INF (Intermediate-Range Nuclear Forces) Treaty (1987), 133–34
INF weapons: arms control negotiations, 48–51, 102, 103, 133–34; NATO and, 15, 49, 50, 72–73, 78–79; US development and arsenal, 15, 36, 79, 85. *See also* arms control policy and negotiations; arms race; ballistic missiles; nuclear weapons

intelligence and intelligence services: Eastern European entities, 24–25, 70, 71–72, 80–81, 82, 113, 123, 124; Reagan administration, 11, 12, 31, 55, 61, 81–82, 111, 121; Soviet opinions of US, 76; US estimates and reports, 13, 21, 121, 145n45; US sources/operations, 55, 100, 111
intercontinental ballistic missiles (ICBMs). *See* ballistic missiles
intermediate-range ballistic missiles (IRBMs). *See* ballistic missiles
intermediate-range nuclear forces (INF). *See* INF weapons
International Civil Aviation Organization, 74, 76
interventionism, American, 9, 77–78
interventionism, Soviet: Afghanistan, 26–27; Poland, 51–53, 62; shifts from, 62, 115
Iran, and US foreign policy, 9, 12, 13

Japan, 14, 116–17
Jaruzelski, Wojciech, 53, 54
job creation, US, 18, 33
jokes, 1, 49–50

Kádár, János, 96, 97
Kamal, Babrak, 119
Kampelman, Max, 47
Keeble, Curtis, 40
Kennedy, John F., 31
KGB: under Andropov, 7, 20, 21–22, 61, 62–63, 63–64, 70, 112; counterintelligence, 55; diplomats, 47, 55, 62–63, 63–64, 100; Gorbachev support, 113; military intelligence, 72, 80–81; Putin background, 136–37, 138, 139; surveillance, 59, 136–37
Khomeini, Ruhollah, 9, 13
Khrushchev, Nikita, 22, 27, 108, 120
Kochemasov, Vyacheslav, 44
Kohl, Helmut: domestic conditions, 73; East-West German relations, 68; Soviet diplomacy, 67, 68, 85, 92–93, 95, 111, 114; US/UK dialogue, 67, 111, 114, 185n179
Koivisto, Mauno, 76, 173–74n207
Kondrashev, Sergeĭ, 47, 63
Kondratiev, Igor, 81
Korean Air Lines flight 007 (1983), 57–58, 73–77, 99
Kornienko, Georgiĭ, 28, 128
Kosovo, 138

228 INDEX

Kozyrev, Andreĭ, 137
Kriuchkov, Vladimir, 76
Kvitsinskiĭ, Iuliĭ, 50, 79
Kvorkov, Vyacheslav, 62–63

labor movements: Eastern Europe, 26–27, 51–52, 53; UK, 145n41; US, 33
Latin/Central America policy, 9, 12, 14, 61
Latvia, 141n13
Lázár, György, 96–97
Lebanon, 77
Lenczowski, John, 65, 86, 99
Lithuania, 141n13
Los Angeles Olympic Games (1984), 99

MacEachen, Allan, 88
Madrid CSCE Conference (1981), 47, 63
Mao Zedong, 38
Matlock, Jack, 66, 75, 77, 87, 91, 93, 100, 102, 106, 120–21, 136, 173n194
McFarlane, Bud, 82, 93, 102, 104, 107, 123, 126
medium-range missiles. See ballistic missiles
Meese, Ed, 11, 19, 77, 82
Mielke, Erich, conversations, 25, 64, 70, 76
military and defense policy: Cold War focus and outcomes, 5, 6, 7, 12–13, 47–49; Soviet anti-reconnaissance, 57–58, 73–74, 75–76; Soviet policy, 6, 7, 12–13, 13–14, 22, 36, 51–52, 67, 101, 118–19, 133–34, 194n141; Soviet spending, 12–13, 63, 118, 120, 122, 133–34; US/Carter, 8, 22–23, 36; US/Clinton, 138; US history, 31, 35, 37–38; US/Reagan, 5, 8, 9, 16–19, 23, 25, 35–36, 37–39, 47–49, 50–51, 69–70, 72–73, 77–79, 82, 86, 87, 101–2, 104, 111, 118, 119, 125–26, 133–34; US spending, 8, 18, 36–37, 38, 77–78, 87. See also arms control policy and negotiations; arms race; US Department of Defense
military intelligence, 70, 71–72, 80–81, 82, 91
military press, 101
military training, 69, 80–81
Milošević, Slobodan, 138
missiles. See ballistic missiles
missile silos, 37
Mitterand, François, 98
Mondale, Walter, 85, 88–89, 103–4
monetary policy, 37, 137
Moscow Olympic Games (1980), 14
mutually-assured destruction, 17, 104, 125

National Endowment for Democracy, 155n61
nationalism, in Soviet Union, 135
national security: Bush administration, 134; Reagan administration staff, 19, 45, 46, 64–65, 66–67, 75, 77, 82, 86, 102, 123, 124, 181n92; Reagan administration strategy, 36, 37, 65, 66–67, 69, 74–75, 78, 120, 131
National Security Council (US): meetings, 9, 31; policy/communication, 35, 39–40, 74–75, 120; staff, 66–67
Nicaragua, 14
Nitze, Paul, 50, 75
Nixon, Richard: administration staff, 19, 45–46; campaigns, 31; Regan policy and relations, 25, 42, 84, 146n56, 149n131; US-Soviet relations, 25, 34, 42, 46, 84, 149n131
North Atlantic Council, 127
North Atlantic Treaty Organization (NATO): antinuclear stances, 72–73; exercises: Able Archer and Autumn Forge, 80–81, 82; figures and diplomacy, 41–42, 46, 67, 92–97, 109–11, 114; membership and expansion, 10, 52, 137–38; military capabilities, 13, 15, 38, 39, 48, 49, 50, 52, 67, 70, 79, 80–81, 91, 138; Poland policy, 51–52; public relations and support, 40, 48; strife, 12
nuclear accidents, 132–33
Nuclear and Space Talks (1984), 102–4, 118
nuclear weapons: Carter policy, 23; and nuclear war, 9, 17, 70–71, 72–73, 79–82, 89, 95, 101, 104, 119, 123, 125, 177n2; public opinion and protest, 2, 58, 68, 72–73, 79, 85, 88–89; Reagan policy, 2, 17, 23, 36, 37–38, 47, 50–51, 68–70, 79, 82, 86, 88–89, 99, 125, 133–34, 152n8; Soviet policy/capabilities, 12–13, 17, 28, 36, 49, 70, 101; strategy, and Zero Option, 48–50. See also arms control policy and negotiations; arms race; ballistic missiles

Ogarkov, Nikolaĭ, 26, 101, 118
oil industry. See petroleum industry
oligarchy, 137, 138
Olympic Games (1980, 1984, 2014), 14, 99, 138
Operation Barbarossa (1941), 71
optics, of Cold War. See perception, reality, and optics
Organization of Petroleum Exporting Countries (OPEC), 13, 29
Osipovich, Gennadiĭ, 57–58, 73–74, 75–76

INDEX 229

Pahlavi, Reza Shah, 13
peace initiatives: Afghanistan invasion, 26; antinuclear movements, 2, 58, 68, 72–73, 79, 85, 88–89; leaders and peace "credit," 17, 30, 42, 58, 72, 74–75, 87, 92–95, 101, 122. *See also* arms control policy and negotiations
"peace through strength": critiques, 88–89; policy, 3, 8, 17, 18, 36, 46, 65, 68, 79, 89, 127, 131; Soviet explanations, 70
perception, reality, and optics: Cold War balance of power, 3, 5–6, 11–12, 23, 107, 120, 136; Cold War communication, 44, 46, 56, 73, 124; nature of Cold War, 5
perestroĭka, 90, 110, 133, 134–35
Pershing missiles. *See* INF weapons
petroleum industry: Cold War geopolitics, 12, 13, 29, 53–55, 94; natural gas pipelines, 53–54, 55; Soviet production and reserves, 29, 53, 68, 116, 133, 163n214
Pipes, Richard, 19, 45, 53, 59, 121
Poland: military junta, 53, 54; NATO membership, 137; Soviet influence and interventionism, 26–27, 51–52, 62, 115
politburo: corruption and reform, 59, 64, 90; discourse environments, 63, 90–91, 100, 115–16; foreign policy, 52–53, 62, 67, 75–76, 88, 92, 108–9, 119–20, 123, 128; Gorbachev opposition, 134–35; human rights policy, 61–62; internal strife, 3–4, 6–7, 20–21, 22; interventionism, 52–53, 62, 167n58; Party Congresses, 29–30, 92, 132–33; Soviet history and succession, 1, 4, 7, 20–22, 59–61, 62, 86, 89–91, 111–13, 190n40. *See also* specific individuals
Prague Spring (1968), 27
productivity, Soviet economy, 28–29, 40, 53, 115–16
Project RIaN, 71–72
Putin, Vladimir, 7, 136–37, 138–39

"quiet diplomacy": examples, 62–63, 93, 131; limitations, 75; Reagan on, 3, 40, 46, 82, 89, 92, 126; successes, 46–47, 64, 86

radio broadcast messaging, 59, 73, 92, 118, 124
Reagan, Nancy, 51, 56, 77, 89, 101, 106, 190n50
Reagan, Ronald, and administration: anticommunism, 3, 14, 16–17, 25, 38, 77, 145n45; assassination attempt, 33–34, 45; biography and personality, 8–9, 16, 19–20,

24, 58, 69, 106–7, 125; campaigns/ elections, 5, 11, 12, 14–16, 20, 22, 23–24, 25, 51, 85, 88–89, 103–4; Cold War optimism, 65–66, 79; Cold War pessimism, 5, 11–12, 18, 24, 31–32, 56, 61, 132; Cold War's end, 2–3, 5, 8–9, 10, 85, 130, 141n14; diary writings, 66–67, 87, 101, 106–7, 127, 185n179; economic policy, 9, 18, 25, 33, 36–37, 40, 146n56, 147n71; foreign policy/techniques, 4, 5–6, 8–9, 10, 14, 16–20, 34–35, 38, 39–56, 58, 60–62, 66–67, 82, 84–89, 92, 98–105, 114, 120–29, 131–32, 134; Geneva Summit, 9, 10, 106–7, 120–27; grand strategy, 2–3, 4, 19–20, 56, 83, 89, 127, 131; intelligence briefings, 11–12, 31, 81–82; legacy criticism, 9, 143n48, 143n63; likened to Adolf Hitler, 2, 128; military/defense policy, 2, 5, 6, 8, 9, 16–19, 23, 25, 35–36, 37–39, 47–49, 50–51, 72–73, 77–79, 82, 86, 87, 88–89, 101–2, 104, 111, 118, 119, 125–26, 133–34; peace policy and "credit," 17, 42, 58, 87, 92, 122; Soviet relations: rhetoric and quotations, 1–2, 8, 9, 17, 19–20, 24, 34, 39–40, 43, 44, 51, 58, 68–69, 74, 80, 83, 84, 89, 93, 103, 122; Soviet takes on policy, 2, 8, 22, 24–25, 30, 68–69, 88, 104, 114, 119, 122, 124, 128; speeches, 12, 31, 50–51, 68–69, 85–89, 92–93, 99, 102, 105, 155n61, 178n32; staff and personalities, 1, 8–9, 11, 18–19, 44–46, 64–65, 66–67, 75, 77, 82, 86, 158n124
reality vs. perception. *See* perception, reality, and optics
Regan, Donald, 121
religious organizations, 68
Republican Party: National Convention (1980), 12; Reagan political history, 16–17
research. *See* archival materials
Reykjavik Summit (1986), 133
Romania, 27
Romanov, Grigoriĭ, 190n40
Roosevelt, Theodore, 78
Rupp, Rainier, 81
Rusakov, Konstantin, 113
Russia, 137–39
Rust, Mathias, 133
Ryzhkov, Nikolaĭ, 63

Sakharov, Andreĭ, 26, 135
sanctions: Australian policy, 95; Carter administration policy, 13–14, 40; Reagan administration policy, 34, 40, 53–55; Siberian oil pipeline, 53–55

230 INDEX

Schabowski, Günter, 135
Schmidt, Helmut: Brezhnev/admin dialogue, 49; Reagan/admin dialogue, 51, 54, 55, 56, 147n71
Scowcroft, Brent, 134, 154n32
"Second Cold War," 2, 80
Serbia, 138
Shakhnazarov, Georgiĭ, 68, 78, 112
Shcherbyts'kyĭ, Volodymyr, 111–12
Shevardnadze, Eduard, 119, 123
Shevchenko, Arkadiĭ, 120–21
Shultz, George: career, 45–46, 158n124; Soviet policy and diplomacy, 42, 45–47, 60–61, 64–66, 74–75, 82, 86, 87–88, 89, 95, 96, 99, 100, 101, 103, 104–5, 114, 120, 123–24; US nuclear and arms control policy, 69, 70, 82, 102, 104–5, 120, 123, 126, 134
Siberian Seven, 46–47, 63, 86
Sinatra Doctrine, 135–36
Smirnoff, Vladen, 81
Smith, Samantha, 72
Sokolov, Iuriĭ, 64
Sokolov, Oleg, 74
Solarz, Stephen, 22–23
Solidarność (Poland), 26–27, 51, 52, 53
Solzhenitsyn, Aleksandr, 73
Soviet Air Force, 57–58, 73–74, 75–76, 81
Soviet Army, 13, 118–19, 133, 137, 199n21
Soviet Union: Asian relations, 38; Cold War confidence/optimism, 11–12, 24, 25–26, 30–31; Cold War grand strategy and policy, 4, 5–6, 7–8, 9–10, 22, 25–26, 30–31, 60–63, 75–76, 83, 92, 107; Eastern Bloc relations and influence, 4–5, 15, 26–28, 51–52, 60, 115; end, 7, 10, 18, 130–39; history, 3–4, 6–7, 10, 19, 91–92, 108, 117, 120–21, 138–39; state systems, 5–6, 28–30, 53, 115–16. See also economic conditions; KGB; politburo; specific leaders
space: exploration programs, 86–87, 138; weapons programs, 69–70, 95, 102–5, 111, 117–18, 123, 125–26, 128, 133
Spain, 52
Stalinism, 27, 59, 108
Stasi (DDR), 59, 72, 76, 81, 136–37
state visits, 27, 101, 110
Stearman, William, 52
Strategic Arms Limitation Talks/Treaties (SALT), 13–14, 51, 86
Strategic Arms Reduction Talks/Treaties (START), 50–51, 103
Strategic Defense Initiative (SDI): arms control, 95, 102–5, 117–18, 123, 125–26,

128, 133–34, 190n45; descriptions, 69–70, 104, 117–18, 125; disabling, 128; Reagan announcement and policy, 69; Soviet views, 69, 95, 102, 103, 111, 114, 117–18, 123, 125, 128, 186n211, 190n45
succession: Russia, 138; Soviet system and leaders, 1, 4, 7, 20–22, 59–61, 86, 89–91, 111–13, 190n40

Tarasenko, Sergeĭ, 42
Team B, 145n45
Thatcher, Margaret: Cold War policy, 15, 52, 54, 96–97; Falklands War, 38; quotations, 28, 39, 95, 96; Reagan/US and, 38, 39–40, 52, 54, 55, 60, 67, 75, 77, 78, 86, 97, 111, 124, 191n85; Soviet diplomacy, 92–93, 96, 97, 110–11, 114, 191n85
"Thaw generation," 108
Tikhonov, Nikolaĭ, 75, 90, 103
Time (periodical), 84
trade: Eastern Europe, 27, 68; sanctions, 13–14, 34, 40, 53–55, 95; Soviet economy, 53–54, 68, 116; US power, 66
trade unions: Europe, 26–27, 51; United States, 33
transportation infrastructure, 64, 115–16
"triumphalism," 2, 141n14
Trotskiĭ, Lev, 154n7
Trudeau, Pierre: Soviet relations, 92–93, 94–95, 109, 190n40; US relations, 84, 88
Turner, Stansfield, 11, 12

Ukraine: Chornobyl' disaster, 132–33; Soviet relations, 60; US relations, 22–23
Umbrella Talks (1984), 102–4, 118
United Kingdom: Cold War foreign policy, 14, 15, 41–42, 45–46, 52, 54, 67, 96–97; military conflicts and policy, 38, 78; Soviet diplomacy, 44, 92–93, 94, 96, 97–98, 110–11, 113–14, 191n85
United Nations: Commission on Human Rights, 61; disarmament sessions, 56; General Assembly meetings, 101, 102, 123, 133; ICAO, 74, 76
United States. See Carter, Jimmy, and administration; Cold War; economic conditions; Reagan, Ronald, and administration
US Air Force, 57
US Congress: defense policy, 14, 36, 85; elections, 16; foreign policy, 22–23; Gorbachev communication, 119–20, 127

INDEX 231

US Department of Defense: budgets and spending, 8, 18, 19, 36–37, 38, 77–78, 87; publications, 36; Soviet relations and arms control, 50, 82, 93, 123, 124, 125; surveillance, 72
US Department of State, 19, 46, 74, 93, 125. *See also* Albright, Madeleine; Haig, Alexander; Shultz, George
US dollar, 66
US Federal Reserve, 37, 43
Ustinov, Dmitriĭ, 21, 22, 51, 75, 76, 90, 91

Varennikov, Valentin, 26
Vessey, John, 35–36
Volcker, Paul, 37

Wałęsa, Lech, 26
war gaming and exercises, 71–72, 80–81, 82
Warsaw Pact states, 7; foreign policy and assumptions, 24–25, 78, 79; leaders' meetings, 22, 43, 91; military capabilities, 13, 15, 37–39, 70, 91, 133, 137; military exercises, 51–52; military intelligence, 70, 71–72, 80–81, 82, 91; nations, and Soviet influence/control, 26–28, 52–53, 67–68, 115, 135–36; NATO expansion, 10, 137–38

Weinberger, Caspar, 19, 36, 50, 69, 82, 93, 123, 124, 125
Western Europe. *See* Europe, Western
West Germany: East Germany and, 68, 135; military tensions, 71, 73, 79, 118; Soviet diplomacy, 49, 56, 58, 62–63, 68, 92–93, 94, 95, 114, 118; US diplomacy and relations, 42–43, 44, 46, 67, 95
Whelan, Eugene, 109, 110
Will, George, 75, 77–78
Wolf, Markus, 72
World War II: atomic warfare, 37–38; commemoration, 101; economic conditions, 147n71; Soviet memory and fear, 71, 99, 103, 108, 121, 185n179; technology, 91–92
World War III, 70–71, 72–73, 79–80

Yeltsin, Boris, 135, 137, 138, 139

Zagladin, Vadim, 26, 30, 35, 93, 103
"Zero Option" (arms control), 48–50
Ziuganov, Gennadiĭ, 138
Zorin, Valerian, 103